The Affordable Care Act

The Affordable Care Act

At the Nexus of Politics and Policy

James M. Brasfield

LYNNE
RIENNER
PUBLISHERS

BOULDER
LONDON

Published in the United States of America in 2022 by
Lynne Rienner Publishers, Inc.
1800 30th Street, Suite 314, Boulder, Colorado 80301
www.rienner.com

and in the United Kingdom by
Lynne Rienner Publishers, Inc.
Gray's Inn House, 127 Clerkenwell Road, London EC1 5DB

© 2022 by Lynne Rienner Publishers, Inc. All rights reserved

Library of Congress Cataloging-in-Publication Data
Names: Brasfield, James M., 1942– author.
Title: The Affordable Care Act : at the nexus of politics and policy /
  James M. Brasfield.
Description: Boulder, Colorado : Lynne Rienner Publishers, Inc., 2022. |
  Includes bibliographical references and index. | Summary: "An in-depth
  discussion of the politics and policy of the Affordable Care Act, its
  successes/failures in achieving its goals, and possible future
  scenarios"— Provided by publisher.
Identifiers: LCCN 2021047876 (print) | LCCN 2021047877 (ebook) | ISBN
  9781955055239 (hardcover) | ISBN 9781955055291 (ebook)
Subjects: LCSH: United States. Patient Protection and Affordable Care Act.
  | Health insurance—Law and legislation—United States. | Health care
  reform—United States.
Classification: LCC KF3605.A328201 B73 2022 (print) | LCC KF3605.A328201
  (ebook) | DDC 344.7302/2—dc23/eng/20220202
LC record available at https://lccn.loc.gov/2021047876
LC ebook record available at https://lccn.loc.gov/2021047877

British Cataloguing in Publication Data
A Cataloguing in Publication record for this book
is available from the British Library.

Printed and bound in the United States of America

∞ The paper used in this publication meets the requirements
of the American National Standard for Permanence of
Paper for Printed Library Materials Z39.48-1992.

5 4 3 2 1

To Judy
Her loving encouragement and support
was indispensable for the long task of completing this book.

To Maureen
My daughter has always been a champion of my endeavors
and never failed to be there for her mother through a long illness.
Her daily dedication as a health professional is a constant inspiration.

To Conner, Emma, Carson, and Haley
My college-age grandchildren will, as adults, live in a world
in which the Affordable Care Act shapes the finances of health care.
I hope that policymakers in the coming decade
will make wise choices about the future of the ACA
to enable their generation to avoid major financial burdens
when serious illness strikes.

Special thanks to Conner and Emma,
who each spent time in a summer assisting
with the research for this book.

Contents

List of Tables and Figures   ix

1   The Origins of the ACA: A Century of Debate   1
2   The Promised Land: Health Reform at Last   33
3   The Hard Work Begins: ACA Implementation   69
4   The Dog Caught the Car: Now What?   115
5   The Trump Administration's Sabotage Strategies   141
6   An Assessment: What Has Been Achieved?   169
7   The Verdict: Public Opinion, Legal Opinions   195
8   Cost Control: An Elusive Goal   221
9   The ACA Today . . . and Tomorrow   265

Bibliography   299
Index   307
About the Book   325

Tables and Figures

Tables
1.1	Health Policy Windows of Opportunity	27
2.1	Path to the Affordable Care Act	41
2.2	Summary of Basic Provisions of the Affordable Care Act of 2010	47
2.3	ACA Revenue and Expense Summary, 2010 Estimates	53
3.1	ACA Implementation Timeline	71
6.1	Individual Market Enrollment, 2015–2018	173
6.2	Average, High, and Low Premiums for Second-Lowest-Cost Silver Plan	174
6.3	Medicaid Expansion	185
7.1	Division of Partisan Opinion on the ACA	198
7.2	Major Cases Seeking to Invalidate the ACA	202
8.1	Health Expenditures and GDP Compared, 2011–2019	224
8.2	CPI and NHE per Capita Change	225
8.3	Increase in Sector Cost by Decade	226
8.4	Average Annual Premiums for Employment-Based Insurance	228
8.5	ACA Cost-Control Ideas	244

Figures
6.1	Number of Uninsured and Uninsured Rate, 2008–2019	170
6.2	Total Marketplace Enrollment, State and Federal, 2014–2021	172
7.1	Public Opinion on the ACA over the First Ten Years	196
8.1	Contributions to Total Health Expenditures by Individuals, 2016	227

1

The Origins of the ACA: A Century of Debate

Past is prologue.
—William Shakespeare

They gathered around a table at the Truman Library in Independence, Missouri, on July 30, 1965. President Lyndon Johnson was joined by former president Harry Truman, who twenty years earlier had proposed a national health insurance program. Seventy-two pens were used in the Medicare bill-signing ceremony. One was distributed to Wilbur Cohen, an intellectual father of the Medicare idea. Various members of Congress and the administration who contributed to the bill's passage also received a keepsake. In his remarks, the president said, "No longer will older Americans be denied the healing miracle of modern medicine. No longer will illness crush and destroy the savings that they have so carefully put away over a lifetime so that they might enjoy dignity in their later years."[1]

Many in the auditorium that afternoon were confident the new legislation was the first major step in the achievement of President Truman's goal of a universal public health insurance program as part of the Social Security System. Probably no one present could have imagined that the next signing ceremony for major legislation expanding health insurance coverage would take place forty-five years later, when President Barack Obama employed twenty-two pens to sign the Patient Protection and Affordable Care Act (ACA) on March 23, 2010. He commented before affixing his signature, "The bill I'm signing will set in motion reforms that generations of Americans have fought for and marched for and hungered to see. . . .Today we are affirming that essential truth, a truth every generation is called to rediscover for itself, that we are not a nation that scales back its aspirations."[2]

The bill signed by President Obama did not follow Medicare as its organizing concept. The late 1960s expectation of an expanded social insurance approach to universal health coverage was not the nucleus of the new legislation. Rather, it built on Medicaid, barely noticed initially and a long-underestimated part of the 1965 law. The ACA expanded Medicaid and used premium subsidies to make private health insurance more affordable for those not part of the employment-based system.

Medicare and the ACA are the bookends of almost fifty years of national health policy debate. The 2010 social and political context was starkly different from that of 1964. The science of medicine had become more intricate, the aggregate health cost to society exponentially greater, and the medical system institutionally more complex. National and state politics have been transformed as the two parties sorted more consistently along geographic and ideological lines. Perhaps most significantly, citizen views of government as a provider of services have become much more negative. In 1964 three in four Americans trusted the government most of the time. Fifteen years later only a quarter of the population expressed the same trust. By 2010 only one in five reported trusting the government.[3]

The 1965 aspiration of Medicare as a first step toward a universal public health insurance program appeared unattainable by 2009. Neither public opinion nor elite support appeared sufficient in the first decade of the twenty-first century to expand Medicare to cover the entire population. It was Medicaid, the welfare-based afterthought, that became the most significant link between the Affordable Care Act and Medicare. The common thread across half a century was the idea that government ought to be responsible for arranging a system to assure financial access to health care.

By 2009 Medicare had evolved but remained largely the same program in scope and approach that it was in 1966. The primary beneficiaries were those over age sixty-five. The only additions were beneficiaries in the Social Security disability program and individuals suffering from end-stage renal disease. Medicare Part A covered hospitalization and was financed through the payroll tax paid by current workers. Part B covered physician costs and was paid for by a beneficiary premium set at 25 percent of program costs. The balance of Part B financing was from federal government general revenue. Most beneficiaries purchased private supplemental insurance to cover significant deductibles and copayments. A private insurance prescription drug program had been recently added, which combined a modest premium with significant general revenue financing. Medicare had also been modified to allow private insurance companies to offer plans in competition with traditional Medicare. This is Medicare Advantage, and it included about 20 percent of the Medicare population at the time of ACA enactment.[4]

Medicaid, on the other hand, had grown from a modest program providing medical vendor payments for some of the poor covered by the existing welfare system into a vast and complex funding system covering many of the poor and near poor. This was a federal-state program, with the federal government paying approximately 60 percent of the total cost and states covering the remainder, although the funding formula differed depending on the wealth of the state. Within federal guidelines, each state program could have different federal contribution limits, services covered, and eligible populations.[5]

In Chapter 2 we will explore in more depth the reasons why Medicaid, rather than Medicare, was chosen to be a major vehicle for the public expansion part of the ACA law. In the following pages of this chapter, we will summarize what President Obama called the struggle by generations in our examination of both the politics and the policy ideas associated with health reform beginning in the early twentieth century.

Dawn of the Twentieth Century

The story of the ACA is a quest tale that spans a century of American history. The Holy Grail pursued by various Galahads was universal financial health care coverage. As the nineteenth century turned into the twentieth, Europe and America experienced a series of transformative changes. The Industrial Revolution exploded in the United States in the decade after the Civil War. In his magisterial study of major changes in the American economy, Robert Gordon traces the development of unprecedented American economic growth from 1870 to 1970 and identifies revolutionary developments such as electricity, the telephone, refrigeration, and the internal combustion engine.[6] These were all in place before 1920. They were transformative changes, especially in urban America. Change came slower to the rural parts of the country. As the third decade of the twentieth century began, daily living would have been almost unrecognizable to a visitor from the Civil War era just fifty years earlier.

Life expectancy increased from forty to sixty-four years in the half century after 1890. Infant mortality and fatal childhood disease declined, and life expectancy after the age of twenty increased. Gordon and others have observed that enhanced medical treatment was not the only factor.[7] There was an exponential growth of clean water and sewer systems, and food became safer. A study by David Cutler and Grant Miller concluded that clean-water technologies, such as filtration and chlorination, caused a substantial reduction in urban mortality and accounted for most of the infant and child mortality reduction.[8]

The development of anesthetics, X-rays, and antiseptic surgery transformed the practice of medicine by the turn of the twentieth century. Louis Pasteur's germ theory of disease began to dominate medical science by then. Atkul Gawande, in tracing the history of surgery, observes that between the mid-1880s and the 1920s, surgical advances accounted for half of all *New England Journal of Medicine* articles. "Surgery became a dominant force in medical advancement," he concluded about the early twentieth century.[9] The Flexner Report was a comprehensive study of medical education, which in 1910 called for massive changes in the way doctors were trained, with greater emphasis on science education.[10]

In the nineteenth century the dominant mode of health care delivery was a doctor seeing patients in the office. Rosemary Stevens notes, "Between 1870 and 1917 the American hospital was transformed from an asylum for the indigent into a modern scientific institution."[11] As physicians practiced more scientific medicine, their authority and professional autonomy increased.[12] Physician specialization among surgeons grew as the types of surgery increased. By the end of World War I (1918), the hospital was already becoming an essential part of the delivery of medical services, with more than 1,500 hospitals across the country as early as 1904.[13]

The last decade of the nineteenth century and first two decades of the twentieth were the most transformative in American and world history. Critical technologies revolutionized daily living. Breakthroughs in medical technology made it possible to routinely open the chest and successfully perform surgery for a variety of medical problems. The hospital was becoming the major locus of medical treatment rather than a warehouse where the ill poor went to die.

When serious illness and early death were no longer seen as a routine part of life, the average American sought access to the latest medical treatment. However, the cost of care rose rapidly as hospitals could no longer afford to be purely charitable institutions. Several policy ideas and approaches began to be discussed. A progressive group, the American Association of Labor Legislation (AALL), proposed in 1915 a model state bill for working-class health insurance that included payments for physicians and hospitals as well as sick pay. Under the plan, workers, employers, and the state would participate in financing the benefits.

Despite initial physician support, the American Medical Association (AMA) ultimately joined labor unions and employers in opposing the AALL health insurance approach. At this point both Germany and Britain had, with national legislation, created early-sickness fund health insurance systems for workers, with payments by workers, employers, and the government. These models encouraged reformers to believe the same ideas could be brought to America. AALL plan advocates were hopeful that California would be the first state to enact a health insurance plan, but the voters rejected it in

November 1918. A similar proposal in New York passed in the state's Senate but was never brought to the floor of the House for a vote.

The plans for government-sponsored health insurance did not emerge, but individual industrial sickness funds sponsored by businesses or labor unions did grow significantly in the first decades of the twentieth century. The extent of their coverage of industrial workers is disputed, but John E. Murray claims the number might have been as high as 30 percent.[14]

These were not health insurance plans as we know them today. They provided payments in lieu of wages for employees who were too ill to work. The employer plans were financed by worker-paid premiums and shared payments by employers. The union plan funds were more often taken out of general union dues. In both instances premium payments would have needed to be much higher to also cover doctor and hospital costs. Typical plans did not cover medical costs. According to Murray, workers were unwilling to pay the additional premium for such benefits.[15]

Why would urban workers not want to have coverage for physician and hospital costs? A century ago office visits were usually in the neighborhood and probably relatively inexpensive. Surgery and extended hospital stays were still rare and likely not in the foreseeable future for a healthy worker. Public hospitals were also becoming more prevalent. In 1904, 15 percent of all hospitals were public hospitals, and 25 percent of all admissions were to public hospitals. Income from paying patients covered less than 10 percent of all costs.[16] The average urban worker might well have calculated that the local public hospital would be available in time of need for little or no cost and that the quality of care there was equivalent to that in a private facility.

Two Decades Between World Wars

No one reading this section will have a personal memory of the 1920s. Our collective sense of the decade is shaped by movies and popular culture. It was the era of flappers, Prohibition, speakeasies, and a booming stock market. Less well understood are the critical changes in the delivery and financing of health care that had been accumulating and became evident in the 1920s.

Cutler and Miller state, "Mortality rates in the US fell more rapidly during the late 19th and early 20th Centuries than any other period in American history."[17] They further argue that nearly all of the decline can be attributed to infectious disease decline due largely to the widespread introduction of clean water and sewer systems in urban areas.[18]

At the same time radical medical school reforms produced by the Flexner Report began to change the medical profession in several ways. New physicians were better educated and emerged from a revised system of supervised training that generated higher standards. Hospitals began to limit privileges, and surgery specialization quickly emerged. World War I and the flu epidemic of 1918–1919 also contributed to the emerging central role of the hospital in the provision of medical services. Many doctors returning from field hospital experience during the war had gained a lifetime's worth of surgical experience in a year.

For the average middle-class person living in a city in the 1920s, routine surgeries were becoming more commonplace and expensive. Private hospitals had semiprivate rooms rather than wards, in addition to other amenities. But they also charged a daily room rate as well as fees for lab tests and other necessities. Physicians, especially surgeons, had incurred higher medical education costs, and with more regulated entry into the profession, they enjoyed more of a monopoly position. Market prices for medical services rose.

The creation of the Committee on the Cost of Medical Care (CCMC) was symbolic of the emerging concern with the impact of rising medical care costs for the average middle-class person. This group, organized by academic medicine leaders and funded by major foundations, instituted dozens of studies between 1927 and 1932, which constituted the first systematic review of medical costs. They identified hospital costs in 1929 as 13 percent of a family's total health costs—double the proportion of a decade earlier. They also identified a large variation among families reflecting extent of treatment with some spending much more because of serious illness.

The CCMC offered a series of recommendations that included delivery of services by organizations of physicians in group practice or community medical centers, rather than solo practitioners, and financing of medical costs on a group basis by insurance, taxation, or both. However, they did not endorse the idea of compulsory health insurance.[19]

During the Great Depression of the early 1930s, the work of the CCMC contributed to revamping the political and economic environment. Voluntary health insurance on a large scale appeared out of reach, and the possibility of a public compulsory insurance program again appeared to be politically feasible to Franklin Roosevelt's New Deal administration. By the mid-1930s the Roosevelt administration was planning a major social insurance program to include retirement benefits, unemployment compensation, old-age benefits, grants to the states for dependent children, and state grants for maternal and child welfare.[20] These policy ideas would ultimately become the Social Security Act of 1935.

The biggest controversy surrounding the development of the bill within the Roosevelt administration was whether or not to include health insurance as one of the elements of the program. The overall plan was developed by the administration's Committee on Economic Security. Was a health insurance component to be focused on income replacement for the sick, as with earlier proposals, or would this be an insurance plan to cover physician and hospital costs? The final recommendation was the creation of state health insurance programs financed by a tax on employers for the middle class and general revenue for the poor.[21] The AMA opposed these ideas, and Roosevelt did not include them in the final legislative package sent to Congress, although the final law did include a provision for the new Social Security Board to study innovative ways to provide health insurance.[22]

This did not completely remove health insurance from the administration's long-range agenda. Roosevelt had essentially put off consideration of health insurance until after the 1936 election. In 1937 a technical committee was created that ultimately recommended a program that "included expansion of the maternal and child health program, federal grants for hospital construction, grants to the states to pay for medical care for the 'medically indigent' (those too poor to pay for medical bills), a voluntary program of grants to the states that wanted to set up statewide health insurance programs for the general public, and a disability program."[23]

Senator Robert Wagner introduced a bill with those provisions, but the absence of presidential backing and the outbreak of war in Europe, as well as AMA opposition, doomed the effort. Thus, the first attempt to create a publicly sponsored health insurance program failed to generate either broad public interest or political support. The basic policy idea was for the federal government to provide grants to states to organize health insurance programs and to pay for medical care for the medically indigent. From today's perspective this looks more like Medicaid than Medicare.

As the Roosevelt administration dipped its toe in the public health insurance water and found it too cold for a plunge, work-based private insurance was experiencing rapid growth. In the early twentieth century, a number of industries (railroads, coal, steel) organized hospital associations with prepaid care arrangements for company facilities. There were also industry and labor health insurance plans, which provided replacement income for sick or injured workers. The initiation of hospital insurance as we know it today began in Dallas in 1929. Local schoolteachers and the Baylor University Hospital entered into an arrangement in which a monthly fee entitled them to three weeks of hospital care. This quickly expanded to other hospitals in the area, and the concept spread to major cities across the country. These local arrangements were linked under a single insignia, a blue cross. The Blue Cross associations were closely aligned with the American Hospital Association.[24]

Commercial insurance companies were still reluctant to offer health insurance that covered hospitalization and physician services, and this left the market open for Blue Cross during most of the 1930s. The AMA had endorsed the idea of private health insurance as a better alternative to a public plan. State medical societies by the late 1930s had begun to form prepayment associations for physician payments that were eventually called

Blue Shield and marketed with Blue Cross, although they remained organizationally distinct.

By the end of the 1930s, 1.5 million individuals were covered by Blue Cross plans and 300,000 by commercial insurance companies that were beginning to find a market for this product.[25] Work-based private health insurance was expanding rapidly by 1940 and, perhaps as a consequence, moderating demand for a public program.

World War II and the Postwar Era

Little occurred during the 1940s that was not influenced by World War II. War production stimulated the economy and created a demand for factory labor. The wartime wage and price controls limited employers' ability to compete for workers by offering higher wages. However, offering health insurance benefits was not ruled to be in violation of wage controls. This incentive contributed to the rapid growth of work-based health insurance. By 1950, 140 million people were enrolled in private health plans, which was seven times more than in 1940.[26]

By the late 1940s labor unions had solidified their position as significant participants in most major manufacturing industries. In the postwar period, the unions sought expanded health insurance benefits as a key part of their contract negotiations. In the mid-1950s the Internal Revenue Service proposed to tax employer-sponsored health insurance as worker income, but congressional legislation upheld the tax-exempt status of the benefit.[27] In the decades ahead, the scope of work-based private health insurance benefits would expand, and by 1960 employment-based private health insurance with dependent coverage had become the norm for most American families.

Shortly before his death, President Roosevelt again initiated a discussion of public compulsory health insurance but did not advocate a plan. The Wagner-Murray-Dingell bill of 1943 shifted its approach from the earlier version, which proposed state insurance plans financed by employer taxes and federal grants. The advocates of public health insurance came to believe the states did not have the capacity to administer such programs. From this point forward, the series of proposals, including the one by President Truman in 1948, presumed a federal program financed by taxes, which would be placed in a trust fund. Opposition from Republicans and conservative Democrats in Congress, as well as from interest groups such as the AMA and the private insurance industry, rendered legislative passage impossible.[28]

Republican senator Robert Taft introduced alternative legislation that provided grants to the states to help the poor purchase insurance, and others advocated a similar private insurance approach rather than a public program.[29] The outlines of the coming decades of struggle were clear in 1948. In May of that year, Helen Fuller wrote in the *New Republic*, "But clearly it will take more years and much more energy, on the part of the administration as well as of public minded lobbies, to force the passage of the Wagner-Murray-Dingell Bill, the first step in an adequate program of protection."[30] The advocates of compulsory public insurance had staked out the basic elements of their policy ideas. Opponents responded by arguing the emerging predominantly employment-based private health insurance system was a better approach. The basic philosophic debates would engage the opposing sides for decades to come.

In 1951 Oscar Ewing was a director of the Federal Security Administration, responsible for the administration of the Social Security program. He was one of the architects of the social insurance system created in 1935 and an advocate of universal health insurance. However, he and other colleagues were pessimistic that the legislation proposed by President Truman could pass Congress in the near future. Instead they suggested a narrower focus that concentrated on hospitalization insurance for the elderly. In the spring of 1952 House and Senate Democrats introduced the legislation that came to be called Medicare.[31]

During the eight years of the Dwight Eisenhower administration, liberal Democrats in Congress continued to advocate for the Medicare bill. By the late 1950s the Medicare bill sponsored by Representative Aime Forand was a top priority for many Democrats. Despite a Democratic congressional majority, a coalition of conservative Southern Democrats and Republicans managed to block consideration of Medicare. They were supported by interest groups, such as the AMA, which strongly resisted any public health insurance program. Since the elderly were largely excluded from the emerging system of work-based insurance, public support for a Medicare approach grew.

National Health Insurance for the Elderly: Medicare

Medicare advocacy was a major campaign issue during the 1960 presidential election. Representative Wilbur Mills and Senator Robert Kerr, both Conservative Democrats, pushed legislation through Congress in June 1960 that created an alternative approach to assist the elderly with medical bills. The Kerr-Mills bill provided matching grants to the states to assist low-income elderly with medical costs.

This did not deter liberal Democrats from continuing to champion Medicare. Senator John F. Kennedy of Massachusetts became the party nominee and was elected president in November 1960. Medicare was at the top of his list of policy priorities. Despite controlling the White House, liberal Democrats still had to find a way to break the conservative coalition in

Congress. Over the next three years, the Kennedy administration worked to move the bill forward and gained important interest group support after a compromise with the American Hospital Association. Unlike a decade earlier with the Truman proposal, labor unions were key supporters of Medicare, but the AMA remained adamantly opposed.

After President Kennedy's assassination, President Johnson was unsuccessful in attempting to pass Medicare before the election.[32] His 1964 election campaign featured strong Medicare advocacy. The landslide victory over Barry Goldwater not only assured the Democrats of four more years in the White House but caused a seismic shift in their congressional majority. Liberal Democrats now had a working majority in the House and Senate. In January 1965 it was clear Medicare had the votes to pass in both the House and the Senate. President Johnson was a masterful legislative strategist who provided executive leadership in the building of a legislative majority coalition for Medicare. What followed in the next few months remains one of the most outstanding instances of legislative strategy and tactics in American history.

The King-Anderson bill, which became the vehicle for Medicare, proposed funding hospitalization insurance for the elderly through an expansion of the existing Social Security payroll tax and the creation of a separate Medicare Trust Fund. It was to be administered by the Social Security Administration. This was the policy idea Democrats had advocated for a decade. It was a scaled-down version of the Truman national health insurance proposal. Beneficiaries were limited to the elderly, and only hospitalization, not physician fees, was covered. The exclusion of physician fees was an attempt to mitigate some of the AMA opposition.[33]

The AMA had been the most vociferous opponent of any federal government role in the financing of health care. It had been joined by insurance companies, the US Chamber of Commerce, and other Republican-oriented interest groups. The labor unions were the strongest Medicare supporters.[34]

Congressional Republicans, sensing a political tide in support of King-Anderson, countered with a bill from Representative John Byrnes, which featured a voluntary insurance program covering both hospital and physician fees. It was to be financed by premiums and federal government general revenue. The AMA pushed Elder Care, which was a bill to expand Kerr-Mills as a state-federal grant program for the poor elderly. Both had broader benefits than King-Anderson. Separately, the Johnson administration was proposing the Child Health and Medical Assistance Act to expand Kerr-Mills medical benefits to include children on welfare.[35]

The House Ways and Means Committee became the key pivotal setting for moving Medicare through the legislative process. The support of Chairman Wilbur Mills was crucial. He had been an opponent but recognized that the November Democratic landslide had changed the majority political coalition in the House and the committee. Two pro-Medicare Democrats had been added to the Ways and Means Committee. A new procedure for the powerful Rules Committee enabled the majority to force a bill from the committee after twenty-one days of inaction. These changes appeared to make House passage of Medicare inevitable with or without Mills's support. Recognizing this new reality, Mills moved from opponent to champion of Medicare.[36]

When Johnson administration officials appeared before the House Ways and Means Committee on March 2, 1965, to testify on the bill, Chairman Mills shocked them by not only supporting the bill but advocating a second element to cover physician payments based on the Byrne bill. In addition, he proposed the creation of a new matching grant program of medical vendor payments for those covered by the existing welfare system, which was a major expansion of the Kerr-Mills program.[37]

For decades it was assumed that President Johnson and those in his administration were taken completely by surprise by the Mills proposal.[38] We now know that for several months Johnson had been engaged in negotiation with Mills over a significant expansion of the Medicare bill to include physician fees and broadening of Kerr-Mills to include the poor of all ages covered under the existing welfare programs.[39] Before November, neither would have known the extent of the growth of the Democratic majority, especially in the House. The discussed expansion included "adding a Part B to Medicare based in part on a Republican proposal that would provide payments for physician fees expanding the Kerr-Mills program to include money for medical payments for the welfare poor."

Probably an important feature of the deal was Johnson's promise to let Mills take the credit for the idea. Mills had the ambition to be Speaker of the House. With the liberals now in a solid majority within the Democratic House caucus, his authorship of an expanded version of Medicare was perhaps a ticket to the speakership.[40]

Despite the size and scope of the new Medicare proposal, it moved quickly through the legislative process. After a March 29 Ways and Means Committee recommendation, it was taken up by the whole House of Representatives on April 8 and ultimately passed the House by a three-to-one margin, but a preliminary vote to recommit was much closer.[41] The Senate Finance Committee held hearings and deliberated until the end of June. The Senate version was more generous with benefits and also passed by a two-to-one margin. The Conference Committee quickly resolved a number of differences. Most of the issues in dispute reflected difference in the duration and type of benefit and were resolved by compromise. The most contentious question was whether hospital specialists, such as radiologists, would be paid under Part A or Part B. Mills successfully insisted on Part B payments.

On cost grounds the administration had not supported some Senate provisions, such as covering outpatient prescription drugs and catastrophic costs. David Blumenthal and James Morone note the Johnson administration was concerned about future costs but tended to downplay this element to help secure passage. If Congressional Budget Office economic analysis of proposals had existed in 1965, they speculate, Medicare may not have passed because of the projected costs.[42] By the end of July both Houses had passed the revised bill, and it was signed by President Johnson on July 30.[43]

While the hospitalization piece had been under discussion for a decade, the three-part version had only been part of the public discussion for four months when the bill was signed. What Mills called "the three-layer cake" consisted of the original Medicare hospitalization plan (Part A), the Republican version modified to focus on physician fees (Part B), and the expansion of the Kerr-Mills program to include the welfare poor (Medicaid). Despite the addition of significant new elements to the original Medicare policy idea, it was a quick legislative process, especially compared to the fifteen-month gestation of the Affordable Care Act.

The new Parts A and B were added as Title 18 of the original Social Security Act of 1935. Title 19 was the expansion of Kerr-Mills and labeled Grants to the States for Medical Assistance, not Medicaid, the name later applied. In the press coverage surrounding the passage, Medicare far exceeded the expansion of Kerr-Mills in number of mentions.[44]

The major participants recognized that Title 19 represented a major step forward in providing medical vendor payments on behalf of the welfare poor—namely, the poor who were beneficiaries of one of the federal-state welfare programs. The expanded Kerr-Mills program also created a new eligibility category, the medically indigent, composed of individuals who became poor as a result of high medical expenses.[45]

It seems unlikely that any of them realized how Medicaid's scope would expand in the decades to follow. Ultimately it became one of the centerpieces of the Affordable Care Act. In 1966 the Medicare supporters viewed it as the first step toward universal health insurance, and Medicaid was perceived as a temporary measure, until the goal of a single national program resembling Medicare could be enacted.[46]

At the bill signing, President Johnson turned to his aides and told them to make certain when the program went into effect eleven months later that any eligible person could walk into a hospital or doctor's office and be covered by Medicare. There were some rough edges in the early implementation of the program, but Johnson's demand was met.[47] On July 1, 1966, eligible beneficiaries across the country were effectively covered by Medicare.

The administration of Medicaid by the states developed much more haphazardly. The federal government had a cadre of capable and experienced administrators in the Social Security Administration. This was missing in most states, and it would be years before Medicaid had achieved an effective administrative apparatus.[48]

Universal Coverage on the Agenda

With the passage and quick implementation of Medicare in the mid-1960s, the basic structure of the current system of health financing was largely in place. A majority of working-age individuals and their families were covered by employment-based insurance, with the employer selecting a single insurance program for all employees. Over the decades the scope of coverage expanded, and greater cost sharing by employees has been the norm, but employers typically pay more than half the cost.

Those over sixty-five and retired are covered by Medicare, which is financed by a payroll tax, a premium, and general revenue. The introduction of private plans and a prescription drug program has modified Medicare but left the essential features in place. Medicaid covers the welfare poor with federal and state funding. Eligibility for Medicaid has broadened over the years, and states have frequently expanded coverage. Working-age families left out of the employer-based system were either uninsured or had to obtain coverage in the expensive individual market.

This description of coverage in 1970 continued to be fundamentally the same in 2009 when discussion of the Affordable Care Act began. However, between 1970 and 2009, there was an intermittent series of attempts to significantly change the system of financing health care. The leaders of the Medicare campaign always had universal social insurance as the ultimate goal. For them Medicare was an interim step in the journey toward universal coverage.

The first impediment toward quickly moving Medicare to universal coverage was the Vietnam War, which was rapidly draining resources that might have been used for additional social programs, such as expanded health care. Trust in government and confidence in the Johnson administration also declined as support for the war plummeted. A privately funded effort stimulated the next round of endeavors to achieve universal coverage.

Under the leadership of Walter Ruether of the United Auto Workers, the Committee of 100 was formed in 1969 to examine paths to universal coverage. It returned to an updated version of the Truman-era plan to achieve universal coverage with social insurance in a system resembling Social Security. Medicare, Medicaid, and work-based insurance would all be folded into a single federal government system that would provide coverage for all without copayments. The British system was a coverage model for this program without a move toward public ownership of facilities.

A key member of the committee was Senator Edward Kennedy of Massachusetts. Not only had Kennedy taken health care as a policy area of special interest, but he was regarded at the time as the Democratic Party's most likely presidential nominee in 1972. His ability to generate media attention rivaled that of President Richard Nixon. Kennedy introduced legislation to achieve universal health coverage and launched a series of public hearings to highlight the problems with the current system, especially for those with serious illness and inadequate insurance.[49] This moved the issue to a high place on the congressional agenda.

President Nixon responded with a plan of his own, which required employment-based insurance, retained Medicare, and expanded government-provided insurance for the poor and those not part of a work-based system. Thus, his plan preserved private insurance covered by employers for about half the population.[50] At this point work-based insurance had been in place on a large scale for three decades, and most American families were satisfied with their coverage.

In 1973 Kennedy joined with Representative Wilbur Mills in a compromise with an employer mandate and expanded Medicare with a public program for the rest of the population. Patient cost sharing was more extensive than under the earlier Kennedy bill, and employers/employees would pay a payroll tax.[51] This bridged some of the critical differences between the original Kennedy plan and the Nixon plan. It appeared to set the stage for a grand compromise leading to a national health insurance program, but the emerging Watergate scandal drove most policy issues off the legislative agenda.[52]

In August 1974 President Nixon resigned and was succeeded by Vice President Gerald Ford. By the end of the year Mills was involved in a personal scandal and was no longer the political deal maker he had been a decade earlier with Medicare. The Democrats won a substantial congressional victory in November 1974 and were confident of recapturing the White House in 1976. Kennedy and other leading Democrats returned to advocating for universal and comprehensive national health insurance legislation. They did not wish to compromise when total victory seemed to be at hand.

As anticipated, a Democrat, Jimmy Carter, was elected president in November 1976. During the campaign he had advocated for national health insurance. However, other issues had a higher place on the White House agenda during his first year in office. He faced problems of high inflation, a growing federal deficit, an oil crisis, and escalating health expenditures.

The Carter administration was reluctant to support the Kennedy-backed social insurance approach without first attacking health costs. After a systematic review of options over several months, the administration initially recommended a limited plan for a phased move toward universal coverage that first included all low-income children and catastrophic Medicare coverage. Only later would others be included without a phase-in timetable.[53]

This was not acceptable to Kennedy, and he countered with a plan to require all employers to provide insurance to full-time workers and dependents, with premiums paid to a private insurance company, a health management organization (HMO), or a quasi-public corporation. In response Carter proposed requiring employers to pay for catastrophic coverage, expanded Medicaid for the low income, and provided a subsidy for small businesses to purchase insurance for employees.[54]

Despite a solid congressional majority, the Democrats were divided on the best approach to expanding health care coverage. Senator Kennedy challenged President Carter in the 1980 presidential primaries but failed to win the nomination. The Iran hostage crisis, not health insurance, dominated the 1980 election. In November, Governor Ronald Reagan defeated President Carter, and Republicans gained control of the Senate and picked up seats in the House. This effectively ended the decade-long effort by Democrats to enact a national health insurance program.[55]

This 1970s campaign for universal health coverage ended with the 1980 election. No one knows if a compromise along the lines of the Nixon or Carter plans would have succeeded. It is doubtful that the Kennedy national health insurance plan ever had a majority of votes in Congress. The debate did, however, manage to define two distinctive approaches to achieving a significant expansion of health insurance coverage.

The Kennedy/United Auto Workers plan embodied the social insurance ideal articulated by advisors forty years earlier in the Roosevelt administration and advocated by President Truman in his 1948 message to Congress. This strategy envisioned a universal public insurance program in which everyone participated on an equal basis with the same benefit structure. Unlike in the British system, the government would neither own hospitals nor employ physicians. Rather, it would be similar to the Medicare system, and the public entity would collect a payroll tax from current workers and also use general revenues to pay health care providers. The benefit structure would be comprehensive, with little cost sharing at the point of service. Medicare would be folded into the new plan, and benefits would be more comprehensive. The Medicare benefit structure resembled a standard 1964 Blue Cross plan. By the late 1970s, a typical employment-based insurance plan included a wider range of benefits and fewer limits on catastrophic illness coverage.

The strategy envisioned by the Nixon or Carter proposals retained the existing employer-based coverage, maintained a key role for private insurance companies, and replaced Medicaid with an expanded public program for the poor. Medicare would be retained, and thus the distinction between insurance for the aged and for the rest of the population would be maintained.

Many reformers today would be happy to have a version of the Nixon or Carter plans. Was this an example of a missed opportunity? President Carter's reelection defeat in 1980 ended the first major push for health finance reform legislation. The Carter administration never placed a top priority on health reform. The Democratic congressional majority remained divided between those who sought a single universal plan and supporters of more modest change that retained work-based insurance at the center of the system. There was never a real legislative test of whether a universal coverage plan could pass the House and the Senate.

The Reagan Years: Health Reform in the Wilderness

The 1980 election of Ronald Reagan began a twelve-year hiatus in the long quest for universal coverage. Supporters understood that health reform legislation required presidential support, and that was not forthcoming under Republican presidents Ronald Reagan and George H. W. Bush. During the 1980s Democrats did succeed in expanding Medicaid coverage for children and pregnant women and passed a Medicare Catastrophic Coverage Act in 1988, only to see it repealed a year later.[56]

The most significant health reform development of the 1980s was the broad acceptance among reformers of new ideas about how to obtain the universal coverage goal. Kennedy's flirtation with a compromise approach and the retrospective assessment that expansion of Medicare to the entire population was going to be politically very difficult in a more conservative political environment caused reformers to explore alternative approaches.

Three related developments in the 1980s shaped the next round of health reform legislation in 1993 and 1994. During the Reagan and Bush administrations Medicare policy emphasis was on cost control, not expansion. Two significant Medicare reimbursement reforms were enacted into law. A shift to hospital prospective payments based on diagnosis-related groups contributed to a reduction in the rate of growth of Medicare hospital spending. This was followed by legislation that shifted the basis for physician payments to a fee schedule derived from a resource-based relative value scale. Together these and subsequent modifications allowed the federal government to temper the rate of growth of overall Medicare costs. Eventually many insurance companies began to use similar payment mechanisms but with generally higher rates of payment.

The single attempt to expand Medicare benefits during the Reagan administration was the Medicare Catastrophic Coverage Act of 1988. The administration proposed a Medicare catastrophic coverage limit on out-of-pocket costs to be paid for with an additional small premium. Democrats in Congress expanded the scope of the bill to also include prescription drugs and limited additional long-term-care benefits. The broadened bill was passed in June 1988. By summer 1989 strong opposition had developed because of the significant premium increases required. A movement to repeal most of the act succeeded with the repeal of most of the provisions in November 1989.[57]

As health care costs became a larger total share of gross domestic product in the 1980s, business leaders became alarmed by increasing health insurance premiums. Many companies instituted utilization review and other forms of managed care. Some saw HMOs and other types of limited networks as panaceas for escalating expenditures. The more aggressive stance of businesses toward employee health insurance costs led them to conclude that broader government intervention was unnecessary.[58]

In the world of health policy academics and think tanks, the view was emerging that neither government nor businesses were capable of controlling costs without significant structural change in the organizations delivering health care. The fascination with HMOs as a model for system change began in the 1970s and continued in the next decade, which featured a growth of HMOs seeking to both control costs and improve quality by creating an integrated delivery system with a fixed, prepaid yearly fee for providers.[59] In the dominant fee-for-service system, each provider action was billed. By the 1980s dissatisfaction grew with the fee-for-service payment model that dominated public and private payment systems and was seen as responsible for escalating costs. *Managed care* became an umbrella term for both traditional HMOs and the emerging practice of corporate health insurance plans to control cost growth by use of limited provider networks and prior approval for costly procedures. In the 1990s consumer dissatisfaction with some excessive managed-care practices led to modifications in but not elimination of the approach.[60]

Despite the inability of congressional Democrats to overcome the Reagan administration's opposition to expansion of health insurance using Medicare or other approaches to federal subsidy, the 1980s saw an incremental growth of Medicaid coverage, especially for women and children. Led by Representative Henry Waxman, chair of the House Health Subcommittee, Democrats used the annual reconciliation act to incrementally expand Medicaid availability for pregnant women and children in poor families. These so-called Waxman amendments separated Medicaid from the welfare system by first offering states options and later turning them into mandates.

Since they were part of the budget reconciliation, they were not subject to filibuster in the Senate, and many were not immediately effective, reducing the short-term budget impact. Several southern governors, led by Governor Richard Riley of South Carolina, advocated for these changes as part of their campaign to reduce infant mortality in their states. These changes were transformative for Medicaid enlargement to cover the poor, even those not eligible for existing welfare programs.[61]

The steady rise in premiums and out-of-pocket costs for the average American led, by the end of the 1980s, to putting health reform back on the policy agenda. In 1990 an underdog Democratic candidate for the Senate in

Pennsylvania won after he made health reform a major issue. As Democrats began the process of selecting their next presidential candidate, each of the contenders advocated health reform ideas and promised to make the issue a legislative priority. As the 1992 election approached, Democrats held a 12-vote advantage in the Senate and a 100-vote margin in the House. Health reform supporters believed that the election of a Democrat as president would make health reform a reality.

However, this was not the early 1970s, when most reformers agreed on a strategy built around a universal national health insurance proposal. Among policy analysts who favored health reform, there were clear divisions of opinion on how to best achieve the common goal. This was also true within the solid Democratic majority in Congress.

Some continued to support a universal national health insurance program similar to what Senator Kennedy had proposed in the early 1970s. Others sought to build on the entrenched employment-based system by mandating that all employers provide health insurance and expanding public programs to cover others. This resembled what President Nixon had proposed.

Those who believed the existing work-based system had significant defects advocated individual choice of insurance companies for families, with premiums subsidized by employers and tax credits for insurance purchase for those not part of the existing system.

Each of these sets of policy ideas had a common goal, which was universal or near-universal coverage with affordable payments by consumers. For reform to succeed in the early 1990s, a legislative majority would need to coalesce around a single policy idea.

Democrats Regain the White House: The Clinton Years

Conservative Republicans had occupied the White House for twelve years when Bill Clinton was elected president in 1992. For much of the time Democrats had controlled Congress, but health reform seemed out of reach without presidential support. During the campaign Clinton advocated a managed-care approach but did not provide detail about his plan. Soon after the election, he appointed a task force headed by Hillary Clinton to develop a plan.

The evolution of the policy ideas that ultimately became the Clinton health plan began in the late 1970s and were debated and refined during the health reform legislation hiatus of the Reagan years. During the debate of the 1970s, the central issue was whether or not to move toward a social insurance system with the government in the central role. The alternative was seen as a retention and expansion of the existing employment-based system, with the government responsible for those not covered by their employer.[62] The preferred policy for many reformers was universal social insurance.

As the 1992 presidential contest began, several other ideas were receiving attention in the health policy community. The Heritage Foundation, a conservative think tank, proposed a consumer-choice plan that would replace the tax exclusion for employer-sponsored insurance with a universal tax credit to be used to purchase insurance in the marketplace, regardless of work status. Everyone would be mandated to have at least catastrophic coverage, with a right to renew at a reasonable premium irrespective of health status.[63]

Alain Enthoven, a Stanford business professor, articulated what he called a "managed-competition" approach. Employers would be required to offer employees a choice among several health insurance plans and pay a fixed part of the cost. Competition among health plans, including HMOs, would restrain costs. In each state a public sponsor would offer a choice of insurance plans for those outside work-based insurance systems.[64] A group of insurance executives, Republican members of Congress, and academics with a similar perspective met in Jackson Hole, Wyoming, and fashioned a proposal based on Enthoven's managed-competition ideas.

Conservative Democrats, led by Representative Jim Cooper of Tennessee, proposed a variation of Enthoven's managed-competition idea. Their proposal left employers the option of providing health insurance and thus did not envision universal coverage.[65]

On the liberal side, two sets of policy ideas were gaining support among health policy experts and political leaders. Some still supported the universal social insurance approach advocated by Kennedy and organized labor in the 1970s.[66] A subset of this group pointed to the more decentralized example of universal coverage that had developed in Canada, with each province assuming responsibility and the national government setting general rules and paying a share of the costs.[67]

Some Democrats had concluded that moving away from the employment-based system was politically unwise because of the large tax increase it would require and the general satisfaction people had with their own health insurance coverage. They supported a "play-or-pay" approach. This combined an employer mandate with a public program financed by taxes and premiums for those outside the work-based system. Employers could "play" (provide insurance) or "pay" taxes to support their employees in the public program.[68]

During the campaign Clinton vacillated between the advice of two sets of health policy experts. At first, he seemed to endorse the "play-or-pay" approach but then began to move in the direction of a liberal version of the "managed-competition" approach. The plan developed by California insurance commissioner John Garamendi seemed to combine elements of managed competition with a social insurance approach seeking universal coverage and regulation of participating private insurance plans.[69] Clinton campaign advisors, such as Paul Starr and Ira Magaziner, convinced the candidate to support managed competition rather than play-or-pay as his basic health policy position.

Early in the first year of the Clinton presidency, a task force was formed to develop a health reform plan. It was chaired by Hillary Clinton, with Ira Magaziner as the key staff person. The Garamendi plan was modified. A detailed proposal and accompanying bill were sent to Congress in September 1993 after a national address by the president.

Key elements of the bill were as follows:[70]

- All residents would be covered with a standard benefit package.
- States would create regional health alliances (health purchasing cooperatives) to collect premiums and arrange insurance plans to sponsor coverage. Alliances could be nonprofits or state agencies.
- Large employers (over 5,000 employees) could be their own alliance.
- Health plans might be fee-for-service, preferred provider, or health management organizations and would be paid by alliances on a risk-adjusted basis; health plans would set their prices and offer different levels of cost sharing.
- Premiums would be based on community rating, with employers paying 80 percent of the average premium.
- Low-income individuals would receive assistance with premiums and cost sharing.
- Medicaid recipients' premiums would be paid by federal and state governments.
- Medicare would remain the same, except for the addition of a prescription drug program.
- A home-based long-term-care program would be added for the disabled.

The Clinton plan was comprehensive in its approach to universal coverage. It retained a role for insurance companies, although they would exist in a more tightly regulated environment. Like the original managed-competition idea developed by Alain Enthoven, it envisioned an expanding role for closed-panel HMOs. Enthoven, a Stanford professor, was familiar with the Kaiser-Permanente system and believed this type of structure was the best way to achieve quality care at a reasonable price.[71] The plan retained a major role for large corporations but limited their ability to trim expenses by increasing worker cost sharing. Private insurance plans continued to have a part in the system, but it limited their ability to sweeten their risk pools by not accepting poor risks. Overall, the Clinton plan represented a major shift in the financing of health care, but it was not as radical in its strategy as the social insurance approach.

When Congress received the Clinton plan in the fall of 1993, there were serious roadblocks to building a supporting majority coalition. The Democrats enjoyed a fifty-seven to forty-three majority in the Senate but lacked the sixty votes to break a filibuster. In the House there were eighty-two more Democrats than Republicans, which meant they could lose support from thirty-eight of their members and still have a majority for passage.

However, legislation must come to the floor from a committee. There were multiple committees of jurisdiction and sharp divisions of opinion within the Democratic majority. Committee work did not begin until March 1994. The House Energy and Commerce Committee could not produce a bill, despite the presence of Representatives John Dingell and Henry Waxman, who were health policy leaders in the chamber. The committee members best represented a cross-section of Democrats in the House.

In 1994 the Education and Labor Committee reported both a benefit-expanded version of the Clinton plan and a universal social insurance bill in June. This reflected the liberal orientation of the committee, but its bills clearly did not have the support of a majority of House Democrats.

A subcommittee of the Ways and Means Committee reported a bill in March with the key element being an expansion of Medicare for those not covered by work-based insurance. It also dropped several key elements of the Clinton plan, such as the alliances. Full committee chairman Sam Gibbons reworked the bill to respond to some business concerns and provide a larger role for private insurance. It was reported out in late June.

On the Senate side, the Education and Labor Committee was led by Senator Kennedy, who attempted to gather Republican support by weakening some key features of the Clinton plan, such as making the alliances voluntary. The effort to build bipartisan support was unsuccessful as only one Republican voted for the bill in committee.

Senate Finance Committee chairman Patrick Moynihan was not committed to health reform. At the last minute the committee reported a bill that did not have an employer mandate or a goal of universal coverage.[72]

As the congressional committees were struggling to find a health reform approach acceptable to a legislative majority coalition, interest groups were vocally supporting or opposing the Clinton health reform effort. Initially, it appeared as if a wide spectrum of groups were supportive. AARP, organized labor, the AMA, and the Chamber of Commerce expressed support for reforming health insurance coverage. From the beginning opponents included the National Federation of Independent Business, the insurance industry, and the Christian Coalition. Additionally, congressional Republican leaders were determined to oppose the effort with no willingness to compromise in the legislative process, and conservative groups followed this approach in their denunciation of the reform plan with very strident language.

By the summer of 1994 some of the key groups began to peel away or became less than fully supportive of the Clinton plan with organizational resources. Labor was fighting the North American Free Trade Agreement, and AARP was cautious, recalling that it had been burned by support for the Medicare catastrophic bill four years earlier. Both AMA and Chamber of Commerce national leaders were challenged by local branches because of their support. As Congress struggled to find a majority for health reform, the enthusiasm of key groups withered.[73]

The House leadership selected the Ways and Means Committee's Medicare-oriented bill to bring to the floor, even though it appeared to lack majority support. In the Senate, the Finance Committee bill was the leadership vehicle, although it did not appear to have enough votes to overcome a filibuster threat. By September 1994, one year after the dramatic presidential speech announcing a health reform plan, the White House and congressional leaders recognized Congress was near adjournment prior to that year's midterm elections, and in neither the House nor the Senate did any of the committee-recommended bills appear to have the support of a majority coalition. They announced the end of the effort to secure passage of a bill in that legislative session.[74]

Two months later Republicans would sweep to a stunning congressional victory that ousted the Democratic majorities in both the House and the Senate. Democrats would not regain majority status in Congress for another twelve years.

Much has been written about why the Clinton effort was unsuccessful.[75] Was it just a partisan political defeat of a sound plan? Or did the central policy idea itself not resonate with key legislators in both parties? There is a variety of opinion among those who have studied in detail the 1993–1994 saga of the Clinton health plan.

Theda Skocpol argues that among Democrats there was never a majority coalition prepared to support the central idea of the Clinton plan: managed competition with a budget. She contends that no other set of policy ideas could have garnered a majority either. While some Republicans initially expressed support for the concept of reform, there was an explicit effort by their leadership to present a solid front of opposition. As public support declined, the opposition solidified.[76]

Polls taken between the fall 1993 rollout of the plan and the following spring confirm a significant drop in public support. This reflected both greater awareness of some plan details and the partisan critique that accelerated in the spring.[77] Lawrence Jacobs argues that negative polls were perhaps the result, not the cause, of shifts in position among policymakers, who arrived at negative views based on their ideology and policy preferences, then used the polls as an excuse.[78] Their opposition caused further decline in the polls. The average citizen, who supported the concept of health reform in the abstract, became less sympathetic if reform threatened their existing health service arrangements or resulted in higher taxes.

Generic poll questions found support for reform centered on coverage for everyone and moderated costs increases.

Sven Steinmo and Jon Watts contended that the fundamental problem with health reform in the early 1990s, and previously, was the structural nature of the American government. The decentralized power structure in Congress allowed for interest group pressures to maintain the status quo over any proposed changes.[79]

Jacob Hacker critiqued the Clinton team for a policy development strategy utilizing a policy analysis approach to finding common ground rather than more traditional political compromise. This led them to see the managed-competition idea as a middle ground, when in fact scores of members of Congress perceived it as a radical reform. In retrospect he also did not see any of the other major alternatives as having sufficient congressional support to pass in 1994.[80]

James Morone asserted that the central policy idea, managed competition with a budget, represented a significant new strategy with little initial public understanding of its implications. He contrasts this with the Medicare concept adopted thirty years earlier, which had been the subject of debate for several years before enactment. He concluded that a "Medicare for All" approach would have been more understandable to the public.[81]

Allen Schick criticized the Democratic congressional leadership for failing to better manage the legislative process. He lamented the lack of a bipartisan approach but did recognize that the Republicans in Congress sought greater unity with outright opposition, not compromise.[82]

In the end, the Clinton plan never had enough votes in either the House or the Senate. For a decade Democrats had been divided over the best approach to health reform. When health reform was not on the agenda, the differences were debating points that did not matter. The Clinton administration attempted to use a new policy idea that it perceived as a compromise among the various positions but was never able to convince congressional Democrats to rally around a single plan. Republicans concluded that opposing all reform, rather than seeking common ground, was the better political position for them. It does not appear that a different policy idea or better leadership would have ever produced the three or four Republican votes in the Senate necessary to overcome a filibuster.

The 1994 congressional elections ended any attempt at comprehensive health reform for the rest of the Clinton presidency. Subsequent Republican congressional attempts failed to shift Medicare to a voucher system or transform Medicaid into a block grant.

A significant incremental reform, the State Children's Health Insurance Program (SCHIP), was adopted in 1997 as a result of bipartisan compromise between Senators Ted Kennedy and Orrin Hatch. This effectively expanded coverage for children of the working poor through either state expansion of Medicaid or a separate state insurance program. It was still a federal-state program, but the federal share was larger than under traditional Medicaid.[83] The SCHIP program was part of the Balanced Budget Act of 1997. This was not a new idea.[84] For more than a decade, advocates for children had argued for coverage expansion for uninsured kids. At the heart of their argument were two main points: the cost of health coverage for children is cheap relative to that for adults, and finding and treating problems early can lead to a healthier life for decades.

Several key policy issues separated the bipartisan supporters of better coverage for children, especially for working-poor families. Should this be an expansion of Medicaid eligibility or a subsidy for private health insurance? How broad should the scope of benefits be? How should the costs be apportioned between the state and federal governments? Should coverage funding be structured as an entitlement or a block grant?[85]

The SCHIP legislation reflected a series of bipartisan compromises on these issues. It was a block grant approach in which the federal government paid a higher share than the existing Medicaid formula. States could choose to fold the new program into Medicaid, create a separate program, or devise a hybrid. It was authorized for only ten years, not an open-ended entitlement like Medicare and Medicaid. States had to at least provide benefits comparable to Medicaid. The beneficiaries would be children in working-poor families—namely, those with incomes a little above the Medicaid cut off.[86]

As the decade ended and the process for selection of a new president began, both Democrats and Republicans advocated ideas for expanding Medicare to cover what was found to be a major coverage gap: prescription drugs. The idea of expanding Medicare to include prescription drugs first appeared in a report to the president in 1967, one year after the start of the program. This was also part of the Clinton health plan. President Clinton had proposed expanding Medicare to include a voluntary prescription drug benefit plan in his final year in office. In the 2000 election campaign, both Governor George W. Bush and Vice President Al Gore offered different Medicare prescription drug plans.[87]

In 2003 Congress passed a Medicare Prescription Drug Plan (Part D), which provided significant subsidies for Medicare beneficiaries to purchase a private plan that covered most, but not all, of the costs for consumers. One of the major issues of contention was the original Bush administration proposal that conditioned prescription drug eligibility on beneficiaries selecting a Medicare-subsidized private plan rather than traditional Medicare. This was rejected by Congress. Part D employed competitive insurance plans offering drug-only insurance, which was heavily subsidized by public funds in addition to a modest premium for beneficiaries.[88]

An enduring controversial provision of the Part D legislation was the "doughnut hole." In order to both meet a low administration budget constraint and avoid a high deductible for all participants, the bill provided for a deductible for individuals after a certain level of spending, which continued until a higher plateau was reached. At that point most of the cost was again covered. Thus, the term *doughnut hole* referred to a spending level in the middle, which was the responsibility of the beneficiary.[89] This was a political construct, not a logical approach to insurance. The ACA incrementally eliminated the doughnut hole.

For the first six years of the new decade, Republicans held both the White House and slim congressional majorities. But reformers continued to discuss ways of expanding affordable health insurance coverage. This included both the liberal and conservative perspectives. In 2001 the Economic and Social Research Institute published the first of a three-volume document titled *Covering America: Real Remedies for the Uninsured*.[90] In the series academic policy experts offered plans for health reform from a wide variety of intellectual perspectives. There was anticipation that the next round of reform would be on the political agenda before the end of the decade.

Conclusion

After the 2006 midterm election, the Democrats gained control of both the House and the Senate for the first time in more than a decade. President George W. Bush was leaving office in two years and had a low approval rating. Thus, Democrats were very optimistic about achieving the political trifecta of control of Congress and the White House in 2009. There was optimism within the health policy community that the century-long quest for universal health insurance was at hand.

We will take up the quest story again in Chapter 2 with an in-depth look at the politics and policy issues involved in the creation of the Affordable Care Act in 2009 and 2010, the first two years of the Obama presidency.

John Kingdon's policy-streams conceptual framework provides an approach to understanding the complex policymaking process. He suggests *issues* appear high on the legislative agenda when situations are perceived as problems, especially when the president signals a high priority. Over time *policy ideas* are discussed and refined by experts in academia, think tanks, and interest groups, which constitute *advocacy coalitions*, whose members share a similar intellectual perspective on problems and solutions.

In the *political arena*, building majority legislative coalitions is the key endeavor. Elections, interest groups, and public perceptions shape and reshape possible coalitions. A window of legislative opportunity is created when issues are high on the agenda, a set of policy ideas appears to be a viable solution to the problem at hand, and there exists the possibility of a majority coalition in the legislature to support the proposed idea.

Windows of opportunity usually only remain open for a brief period. If action is not taken, the window closes, and another might not open for years or decades. Throughout the rest of the book, this conceptual framework will help organize the explanation of what happened with the Affordable Care Act and why events unfolded as they did.[91]

In our brief jaunt through a century-long quest for health financing reform, Kingdon's framework enables us to understand and explain what happened. Several times health reform achieved a place on the agenda because the conditions related to health care were perceived as problems to be addressed. Under the presidencies of Truman, Kennedy/Johnson, Nixon, Carter, and Clinton, health reform had an elevated place on the agenda. In each instance the placement of health reform on the presidential agenda was the consequence of unique circumstances. Truman, shortly after ascending to the presidency, proposed universal health care as an expansion of Roosevelt's New Deal. Kennedy and Johnson pursued health insurance for the elderly after the idea had been advocated by liberal Democrats for several years.

Presidents Nixon and Carter appeared more reactive than committed to reform. Nixon's health reform proposal was a response to a push for universal coverage by congressional Democrats, and thus the issue was really placed on the agenda by Congress, with the president responding with a plan of his own. During the primary season, Carter responded to pressure from liberal Democrats for health reform by making it a central part of his campaign rhetoric, but once he was in office it seemed to be a low priority.

It was congressional Democrats with a proposal of their own who pushed Carter to advocate a plan, but divisions within the party prevented passage of a bill. In the lead-up to the 1992 nomination, Clinton and all of the other Democratic candidates promised to push for health reform, and he did make this one of his major priorities in his first year in office.

The issue was off the agenda in the 1980s not because the problem had essentially changed but because it was not a priority for Presidents Ronald Reagan and George H. W. Bush. After two years President Clinton faced Republican majorities in Congress and removed health reform from his priorities. In 2000 President George W. Bush did not place a high priority on health reform despite early Republican congressional majorities, but he did push for Medicare drug coverage.

Beginning in the early 1970s there was continuing and active discussion of health reform policy ideas. As time progressed a multitude of diverse policy ideas floated around within diverse advocacy coalitions. Debates among individuals in the broad health policy community continued year after year irrespective of how high the issue might be on the agenda. The analysis of a wide range of ideas contributed to a set of distinctive policy options during the policy windows that occurred in 1978 and 1992.

Policy entrepreneurs are individuals who seek to build a majority coalition by combining ideas into a package that can gain broad support. Big policy ideas have multiple components. Entrepreneurs will attempt to build a plan to solve a problem by combining pieces from different ideas. In both 1978–1979 and 1992–1993, entrepreneurs were unable to fashion a package of ideas capable of drawing the support of a majority coalition.

Table 1.1 illustrates a series of health reform open windows and whether a policy was enacted.

As we reflect on this century of effort, several policy ideas have been central to the debate over health reform. The most persistent concept has been universal public insurance. Under this idea all citizens or residents would be eligible for the same set of health benefits, with taxation the major method of financing.

Table 1.1 Health Policy Windows of Opportunity

Time/Window	President	Central Policy Idea	Competing Idea	Outcome
1935	F. D. Roosevelt	Health insurance as part of Social Security		Never proposed by administration
1948	H. Truman	Comprehensive national health insurance program	Expansion of private work-based insurance	President proposed; Congress never acted
1961–1965	J. Kennedy and L. Johnson	National health insurance for the elderly	Private insurance	Medicare/Medicaid enacted
1971–1975	R. Nixon and G. Ford	Universal national health insurance	Work-based insurance and public program for others	Democrats waited for 1976 elections
1978–1980	J. Carter	Employer mandate for catastrophic coverage; subsidized premiums for small business, and public program for unemployed	Universal national health insurance	Democrats were divided and did not act
1993–1994	B. Clinton	Managed-competition plan with budget	Universal national health insurance Pay-or-play employer mandate	No majority for single idea by Democrats; no floor vote
1997	B. Clinton	Block grant to states for children's coverage for working poor		Bipartisan support; legislation passed
2003	G. W. Bush	Medicare prescription drug coverage using private plans	Prescription drug coverage as part of basic Medicare	Enacted with close vote

The second idea is provision of private health insurance by employers. For decades nearly two of three nonelderly have received their health coverage in this fashion. Since the enactment of Medicare/Medicaid, the employment-based system has existed beside public programs to cover the elderly and many, but not all, of the poor. In recent decades a related idea is to require that all employers provide coverage and at the same time to expand public programs to cover those not employed.

A third idea that has gained credence among conservative policy analysts is to replace employment-based insurance with a tax credit that can be used to subsidize premiums. They have also proposed a voucher system to replace Medicare and Medicaid. Eligible individuals would receive a voucher to cover most, but not all, of the cost of a private insurance policy as a substitute for a public financed plan.

In the policy stream, variations of these three basic policy ideas have been proposed, analyzed, and modified since the late 1970s. In our examination of the Affordable Care Act, we will see that it is a product of combining parts of each of these broad ideas to create a plan capable of sustaining majority coalition support in the legislative arena.

Notes

1. John D. Morris, "President Signs Medicare Bill; Praises Truman," *New York Times*, July 31, 1965, 1.

2. Sheryl Gay Stolberg and Robert Pear, "Obama Signs Health Care Overhaul Bill, with a Flourish," *New York Times*, March 23, 2010, A19.

3. Pew Research Center, "Public Trust in Government: 1958–2014," Pew Research Center, November 13, 2014, www.people-press.org/2014/11/13/public-trust-in-government.

4. For an excellent history of Medicare's first four decades, see Jonathan Oberlander, *The Political Life of Medicare* (Chicago: University of Chicago Press, 2003).

5. To further explore the history of Medicaid, see David G. Smith and Judith D. Moore, *Medicaid Politics and Policy*, 2nd ed. (New York: Routledge, 2017); Laura Karz Olson, *The Politics of Medicaid* (New York: Columbia University Press, 2010). A recent assessment of both is Alan B. Cohen et al., eds., *Medicare and Medicaid at 50: America's Entitlement Programs in the Age of Affordable Care* (New York: Oxford University Press, 2015).

6. Robert J. Gordon, *The Rise and Fall of American Growth: The U.S. Standard of Living Since the Civil War* (Princeton, NJ: Princeton University Press, 2016).

7. Paul Starr, *The Social Transformation of American Medicine: The Rise of a Sovereign Profession and the Making of a Vast Industry* (New York: Basic Books, 1982).

8. David Cutler and Grant Miller, "The Role of Public Health Improvements in Health Advances: The 20th Century United States," NBER Working Paper No. 10511, National Bureau of Economic Research, February 2004, www.nber.org/papers/w10511.

9. Atkul Gawande, "Two Hundred Years of Surgery," *New England Journal of Medicine* 366, no. 18 (May 3, 2012): 1716–1723.

10. Thomas P. Duffy, "The Flexner Report—100 Years Later," *Yale Journal of Biological Medicine* 84, no. 3 (September 2011): 269–276.
11. Rosemary Stevens, *In Sickness and in Wealth: American Hospitals in the Twentieth Century* (New York: Basic Books, 1989), 17.
12. Starr, *The Social Transformation of American Medicine*, 144.
13. Rosemary Stevens, *American Medicine and the Public Interest* (New York: Yale University Press, 1971).
14. John E. Murray, *Origins of American Health Insurance: A History of Industrial Sickness Funds* (New Haven, CT: Yale University Press, 2007), 91.
15. Ibid., 92.
16. Stevens, *In Sickness and in Wealth*, 24.
17. Cutler and Miller, "The Role of Public Health Improvements in Health Advances," 3–4.
18. Ibid.
19. Joseph S. Ross, "The Committee on the Costs of Medical Care and the History of Health Insurance in the United States," *Einstein Quarterly Journal of Biological Medicine* 19 (2002): 129–134, www.einstein.yu.edu/uploadedFiles/EJBM/19Ross129.pdf.
20. "Legislative History: Social Security Act of 1935," Social Security Administration, www.ssa.gov/history/35act.html.
21. David Blumenthal and James A. Morone, *The Heart of Power: Health and Politics in the Oval Office* (Berkeley: University of California Press, 2009), 37.
22. Ibid., 38.
23. Ibid., 44.
24. Louis Reed, "Private Health Insurance in the United States: An Overview," *Social Security Bulletin* (December 1965): 4–5, www.ssa.gov/policy/docs/ssb/v28n12/v28n12p3.pdf.
25. Ibid.; Sylvia A. Law, *Blue Cross: What Went Wrong?*, 2nd ed. (New Haven, CT: Yale University Press, 1976), 11.
26. David Blumenthal, "Employer-Sponsored Health Insurance in the United States—Origins and Implications," *New England Journal of Medicine* 355 (July 6, 2006): 83.
27. Thomas C. Buchmueller and Alan C. Monheit, "Employer-Sponsored Health Insurance and the Promise of Health Insurance Reform," *Inquiry* 46 (summer 2009): 188.
28. Jill Quadagno, *One Nation Uninsured: Why the U.S. Has No National Health Insurance* (New York: Oxford University Press, 2005), 34–43.
29. Blumenthal and Morone, *The Heart of Power*, chap. 2; Rick Mayes, *Universal Coverage: The Elusive Quest for National Health Insurance* (Ann Arbor: University of Michigan Press, 2004), 36–39.
30. Helen Fuller, "Playing Politics with the Health Issue," *New Republic*, May 3, 1948, https://newrepublic.com/article/122399/playing-politics-health-issue.
31. Blumenthal and Morone, *The Heart of Power*, 94–95.
32. Julian E. Zelizer, "How Medicare Was Made," *New Yorker*, February 15, 2018, www.newyorker.com/news/news-desk/medicare-made.
33. Theodore R. Marmor, *The Politics of Medicare*, 2nd ed. (New York: Aldine De Gruyter Publishing, 2000), 17–21.
34. Ibid.
35. Edward Berkowitz, "Medicare and Medicaid: The Past as Prologue," *Health Care Financing Review* 27, no. 2 (winter 2005–2006): 18.
36. Zelizer, "How Medicare Was Made."

37. Wilbur Cohen, "Reflections on the Enactment of Medicare and Medicaid," *Health Care Financing Review* (Suppl.) (1985): 6–7.

38. Marmor, *The Politics of Medicare*, 62–70; Mayes, *Universal Coverage*, 68–69; Oberlander, *The Political Life of Medicare*, 30–31.

39. Blumenthal and Morone, *The Heart of Power*, 178–180; Shanna Rose, *Financing Medicaid: Federalism and the Growth of America's Health Care Safety Net* (Ann Arbor: University of Michigan Press, 2013), chap. 1.

40. Ibid., 178–181.

41. Ibid., 192.

42. Ibid.

43. Marmor, *The Politics of Medicare*, 47–58; Cohen, "Reflections on the Enactment of Medicare and Medicaid," 7.

44. Olson, *The Politics of Medicaid*, 25–26.

45. Aid to the Blind, Aid to the Permanently and Totally Disabled, Aid to Families with Dependent Children; for a detailed discussion of the provisions, see Smith and Moore, *Medicaid Politics and Policy*, chap. 2.

46. Jonathan Oberlander and Theodore R. Marmor, "The Road Not Taken: What Happened to Medicare for All," in *Medicare and Medicaid at 50: America's Entitlement Programs in the Age of Affordable Care*, ed. Alan B. Cohen et al. (New York: Oxford University Press, 2015), 55–74.

47. Judith Feder, "Medicare Implementation and the Policy Process," *Journal of Health Politics, Policy and Law* 2, no. 2 (summer 1977): 173–189.

48. For an early history of Medicaid problems, see Robert Stevens and Rosemary Stevens, *Welfare Medicine in America* (New Brunswick, NJ: Transaction Publishers, 2003); Frank Thompson, *Health Policy and the Bureaucracy: Politics and Implementation* (Cambridge, MA: MIT Press, 1983), chap. 4.

49. Richard Lyons, "National Health Insurance Proposed by 15 Senators," *New York Times*, August 28, 1970, 1; Quadagno, *One Nation Uninsured*, 113. The full transcripts of the 1971 hearing scan be found at "1971 Public Hearings on the Health Care Crisis in America," Healthcare-NOW, www.healthcare-now.org/legislation/1971-public-hearings-on-the-health-care-crisis-in-america. That same year both the Senate Finance Committee and the House Ways and Means Committee held extensive hearings on national health insurance.

50. Karen Davis, *National Health Insurance: Benefits, Costs, and Consequences* (Washington, DC: Brookings Institution, 1975), 89–97.

51. Ibid., 105–109.

52. "Health Insurance: No Action in 1974," *CQ Almanac*, 1974, https://library.cqpress.com/cqalmanac/document.php?id=cqal74-1225149; Blumenthal and Morone, *The Heart of Power*, 242–282.

53. Quadagno, *One Nation Uninsured*, 129–132.

54. Ibid.; Blumenthal and Morone, *The Heart of Power*, 271–278.

55. A comprehensive analysis of the failure of the Carter proposal can be found in Robert Finbow, "Presidential Leadership or Structural Constraints? The Failure of President Carter's Health Insurance Proposals," *Presidential Studies Quarterly* 28, no. 1 (winter 1998): 169–189.

56. Rose, *Financing Medicaid*, 110–118; Frank J. Thompson, "Medicaid Rising: The Perils and Potential of Federalism," in *Medicare and Medicaid at 50: America's Entitlement Programs in the Age of Affordable Care*, ed. Alan B. Cohen et al. (New York: Oxford University Press, 2015), 194–196; Colleen Grogan and Eric Patashnik, "Between Welfare Medicine and Mainstream Entitlement: Medicaid at the Political Crossroads," *Journal of Health Politics, Policy and Law* 28, no. 5 (October

2003): 829–836; Marilyn Moon, *Medicare Now and in the Future*, 2nd ed. (Washington, DC: Urban Institute Press, 1995), chap. 5.

57. Ibid.; Mark A. Peterson, "Reversing Course on Obamacare: Why Not Another Medicare Catastrophic?" *Journal of Health Politics, Policy and Law* 43, no. 4 (August 2008): 605–650.

58. Cathie Jo Martin, "Together Again: Business, Government, and the Quest for Cost Control," *Journal of Health Politics, Policy and Law* 18, no. 2 (summer 1993): 359–393.

59. Lynn R. Gruber, Maureen Shadle, and Cynthia L. Polich, "From Movement to Industry: The Growth of HMOs," *Health Affairs* 7, no. 3 (summer 1988): 197–208.

60. Jonathan P. Weiner and Gregory de Lissovoy, "Razing a Tower of Babel: A Taxonomy for Managed Care and Health Insurance Plans," *Journal of Health Politics, Policy and Law* 18, no. 1 (spring 1993): 75–103; Jacob Hacker and Theodore R. Marmor, "The Misleading Language of Managed Care," *Journal of Health Politics, Policy and Law* 24, no. 5 (October 1999): 1033–1043. The latter article is part of an excellent special issue on managed care.

61. Grogan and Patashnik, "Between Welfare Medicine and Mainstream Entitlement," esp. 832–833, for an excellent summary of the reconciliation measures; Smith and Moore, *Medicaid Politics and Policy*, 169–183, for detailed discussion of the amendments; Rose, *Financing Medicaid*, chap. 4; Michael S. Sparer, "Medicaid at 50: Remarkable Growth Fueled by Unexpected Politics," *Health Affairs* 34, no. 7 (July 2015): 1084–1091.

62. For a contemporary assessment of the various perspectives, see Davis, *National Health Insurance*.

63. Stuart Butler, "Assuring Affordable Health Care for All Americans," Heritage Lectures 218, October 2, 1989, http://thf_media.s3.amazonaws.com/1989/pdf/hl218.pdf; Robert Moffit, "Consumer Choice in Health: Learning from the Federal Employee Health Benefits Program," Heritage Foundation, February 6, 1992, https://www.heritage.org/social-security/report/consumer-choice-health-learning-the-federal-employeehealth-benefits-program.

64. Alain Enthoven and Richard Kronick, "A Consumer Choice Health Plan for the 1990s," parts I and II, *New England Journal of Medicine* 320, no. 5 and 320, no. 12 (January 1989): 29–37 and 94–101; Alain Enthoven, "The History and Principles of Managed Competition," *Health Affairs* 12 (Suppl. 1) (1993): 24–48.

65. Jacob Hacker, *The Road to Nowhere: The Genesis of President Clinton's Plan for Health Security* (Princeton, NJ: Princeton University Press, 1997), 131–132.

66. David Himmelstein and Steffie Woolhandler, "A National Health Program for the United States: A Physicians' Proposal," *New England Journal of Medicine* 320 (1989): 102–108.

67. Theodore Marmor, "Canada's Health Insurance and Ours: The Real Lessons, the Big Choices," *American Prospect*, December 5, 2000, http://prospect.org/article/canadas-health-insurance-and-ours-real-lessons-big-choices.

68. Sheila R. Zedlewski, Gregory P. Acs, and Colin W. Winterbottom, "Play-or-Pay Employer Mandates: Potential Effects," *Health Affairs* 11, no. 1 (spring 1992): 60–83.

69. Thomas R. Oliver and Emery B. Dowell, "Interest Groups and Health Reform: Lessons from California," *Health Affairs* 13, no. 2 (spring II 1994): 123–141; Walter Zelman, "The Rationale Behind the Clinton Health Reform Plan," *Health Affairs* 13, no. 1 (spring I 1994); Susan Moffat, "Insurance Chief Offers Universal Health Care Plan," *Los Angeles Times*, February 13, 1992, http://articles.latimes.com/1992-02-13/business/fi-3139_1_universal-health-care.

70. Zelman, "The Rationale Behind the Clinton Health Reform Plan"; Paul Starr and Walter Zelman, "Bridge to Compromise: Competition Under a Budget," *Health Affairs* 12 (Suppl.) (1993): 7–23.

71. Enthoven, "The History and Principles of Managed Competition," 25–48.

72. Excellent sources for the legislative process are Julie Rovner, "Congress and Health Reform," in *Intensive Care: How Congress Shapes Health Policy*, ed. Thomas Mann and Norman J. Ornstein (Washington, DC: American Enterprise Institute and Brookings Institution, 1995), 179–225; Allen Schick, "How a Bill Did Not Become a Law," in Mann and Ornstein, *Intensive Care*, 227–272.

73. Theda Skocpol, *Boomerang: Health Care Reform and the Turn Against Government* (New York: W. W. Norton, 1996), chap. 5.

74. Rovner, "Congress and Health Reform"; Schick, "How a Bill Did Not Become a Law."

75. Hacker, *The Road to Nowhere*; Skocpol, *Boomerang*.

76. Skocpol, *Boomerang*, chap. 5.

77. Ibid.

78. Lawrence R. Jacobs and Robert Y. Shapiro, "Don't Blame the Public for Failed Health Care Reform," *Journal of Health Politics, Policy and Law* 20, no. 2 (summer 1995): 411–424.

79. Sven Steinmo and Jon Watts, "It's the Institutions, Stupid! Why Comprehensive National Health Insurance Always Fails in America," *Journal of Health Politics, Policy and Law* 20, no. 2 (summer 1995): 329–372.

80. Hacker, *The Road to Nowhere*, 179.

81. James A. Morone, "Nativism, Hollow Corporations, and Managed Competition: Why the Clinton Health Care Reform Failed," *Journal of Health Politics, Policy and Law* 20, no. 2 (summer 1995): 391–398.

82. Schick, "How a Bill Did Not Become a Law," 265–272.

83. Alice Sardell, *Insuring Children's Health: Contentious Politics and Public Policy* (Boulder, CO: Lynne Rienner Publishers, 2014).

84. Alice Sardell and Kay Johnson, "The Politics of EPSTD in the 1990s: Policy Entrepreneurs, Political Streams, and Children's Health Benefits," *Milbank Quarterly* 76, no. 2 (1998): 175–205.

85. Kenneth E. Thorpe, "Incremental Approaches to Covering Uninsured Children: Design and Policy Issues," *Health Affairs* 16, no. 4 (July/August 1997): 64–78.

86. Sara Rosenbaum et al., "The Children's Hour: The State Children's Health Insurance Program," *Health Affairs* 17, no. 1 (January/February 1998): 75–89; Frank J. Thompson, *Medicaid Politics: Federalism, Policy Durability, and Health Reform* (Washington, DC: Georgetown University Press, 2012), chap. 3.

87. Thomas R. Oliver, Philip R. Lee, and Helene L. Lipton, "A Political History of Medicare and Prescription Drug Coverage," *Milbank Quarterly* 82, no. 2 (2004): 283–354.

88. Ibid.

89. Ibid.

90. This three-volume work is no longer readily available online but may be accessed through Google Books or in selective libraries. Jack A. Meyer and Elliot Wicks, eds., *Covering America: Real Remedies for the Uninsured* (Reston, VA: Economic and Social Research Institute, 2001), www.google.com/books/edition/_/WDv7QgAACAAJ.

91. John Kingdon, *Agendas, Alternatives, and Public Policies*, 2nd ed. (New York: Harper Collins, 1995).

2

The Promised Land: Health Reform at Last

Believe me, the reward is not so great without the struggle.

—Wilma Rudolph

Nearly 300 people attended the White House bill-signing celebration in March 2010. President Barack Obama characterized the new health reform law as expressing "the core principle that everybody should have some basic security when it comes to their health care."[1] The event was forty-five years removed from Lyndon Johnson's signature ceremony in Independence, Missouri, to celebrate the legislative enactment of the Medicare/Medicaid law. The Affordable Care Act (ACA) was the most comprehensive health policy enactment since 1965.

This chapter offers a brief conceptual overview of the interplay between politics and policy ideas inherent in the legislative process before providing a detailed case study of the legislative process and conceptual ideas that produced the Affordable Care Act.

Early in the twentieth century, reformers sought to enact legislation to help citizens to pay for the rising cost of health care. Decades would pass before Congress finally approved the Medicare/Medicaid legislation to achieve part of the original goal. In the following half century, several attempts were made to expand government health financing to ease the burden of health costs for the whole population. Those in the room with President Obama in March 2010 assumed they were witness to another major step forward in the long quest for universal health coverage. As we will see in subsequent chapters, success was to be limited and opposition strident in the years ahead.

We begin this chapter with a brief overview of how events played out during the first months of the Obama administration. Democratic political leaders characterized the rising cost of health care and access problems as justifying a very high place for health reform on the policy agenda. Developing and maintaining a legislative majority coalition capable of enacting health reform was critical. Over the years since Medicare and Medicaid was enacted, many ideas for expanding coverage had been debated. Even with a potential legislative majority coalition available, division of opinion over the best reform idea had rendered moving legislation to completion difficult. As at the beginning of the Bill Clinton administration, there was a window of opportunity to pass health reform legislation, but that effort had failed. Would this quest finally end with success? Or would the failure of 1993–1994 repeat?

Intersection of Politics and Policy Ideas

A common theme in the chapters to follow is the nexus of politics and policy ideas in the legislative process.[2] A window of legislative opportunity opens when an issue has reached a high place on the agenda, a majority coalition is available to support it, and a policy idea, or set of ideas, to address the problem is perceived as offering a workable solution.

By the time a problem garners a dominant place on the agenda, one or more policy ideas have likely emerged as a potential basis for new legislation. These ideas will begin to crystalize and gain support from within a majority coalition as the process unfolds.

Why do some ideas receive in-depth consideration and others quickly fall by the wayside? This results from a combination of the politics of coalition support and the dynamics of idea development. There is an intersection of coalition building and transforming ideas into legislative language. Congress does not wholly adopt a single organized system of policy ideas for addressing a problem. Rather various policy ideas are placed on the table by factions within a potential majority coalition. The crafting of legislation involves blending various policy ideas in a process of bargaining and compromise.

Policy entrepreneurs are at the center of the process of building a majority coalition. They take the lead in modifying ideas to bring more people into the supporting coalition. If they are successful, a law will pass. The ultimate product is likely a set of policy ideas resembling the initial formulation but different in many respects from the initial set.

The politics of coalition building is perhaps the easiest to understand. The legislative process consists of a series of majority votes. Failure to muster a majority at any point in the process may doom the effort. This includes both committee actions and votes of the entire body on the floor. Partisan division is the most common and powerful determinant of majority coalitions. In recent decades, votes on significant issues tend to find Republicans on one side and Democrats on the other.

However, local constituent interests or philosophic differences within the parties do lead some to vote contrary to the majority of their partisan colleagues. Interest groups either reinforce partisan division or seek to persuade legislators to support or reject proposals because of the impact on constituents for whom the group speaks. These swing-vote legislators often determine the outcome. Otherwise every legislative decision would be the automatic result of a unified party vote with outcomes determined by the party balance in each chamber.

Those aligned with each party commonly hold clusters of ideas, or *policy paradigm*. These ideas constitute a *belief system,* which guides the evaluation of specific policy proposals. If proposed legislation appears to fall within the policy paradigm of the party, it becomes easier to build a majority coalition. A policy paradigm can be a powerful interpretative filter that rejects new ideas. The policy paradigms within each party are sufficiently distinct that most policies fall within one or the other. Swing legislative votes emerge when either the policy overlaps paradigms or constituents exert pressure on the legislator to abandon the party majority.

Why do some ideas emerge from the policy paradigm and others not? Within and sometimes across the parties, there are policy communities. These comprise individuals from government, academia, interest groups, and other institutions who are policy experts in a specialized field, and subgroups among them develop belief systems. These individuals and sets of institutions analyze policy ideas even when the relevant problem is not high on the agenda. As we move into the legislative case study of the Affordable Care Act, the following questions will be addressed. We will return to these questions at the end of the case study:

- Why was health reform given a high place on the Obama agenda?
- What core policy ideas were embedded in the ACA?
- How difficult was assembling the majority coalition necessary to enact the ACA?

The following section presents a case study of the legislative process, and an examination of several key issues will illustrate how ideas and politics intersected to produce the final policy design in the law.

Politics, 2007–2008

The November 2006 elections were a triumph for Democrats. They recaptured the House and Senate. In the final two years of his presidency, George W. Bush's popularity was in decline, and Democrats were optimistic about regaining the White House in the 2008 election. The new Democratic majorities in Congress were eager to move on health policy but understood that control of the White House in the next election was essential to enact real reform.

Health policy emerged as a critical issue in the 2008 presidential election according to a 2007 Kaiser Foundation poll.[3] Cost and coverage were pivotal health policy concerns. The issue was especially salient among Democrats as they began the process of picking their nominee for the 2008 election.

Unlike in 1992, Democrats began to coalesce around a single set of policy ideas. In 2006 Massachusetts enacted major health reform legislation. It included an individual mandate, an employer mandate for companies with more than eleven employees, a purchasing pool for individuals and small businesses, sliding scale subsidies for the purchase of insurance, and expansion of the Medicaid program.[4] As the 2008 election approached, the Massachusetts reform plan was being implemented.[5]

As the presidential primary election process began, each of the major candidates touted the Massachusetts plan as an emerging success and a likely model for a national plan after the 2008 election. The three major Democratic candidates shared a health policy advisor, Massachusetts Institute of Technology professor Jonathan Gruber, who was one of the intellectual architects of the Massachusetts plan. The Massachusetts legislation was developed in a bipartisan fashion by Republican governor Mitt Romney and the Democratic legislature, which enhanced its attractiveness as a model that might be applied nationally.[6] Unlike the debates on a wide range of ideas in 1992, the 2008 health care discussion among Democratic candidates focused on variations of the Massachusetts model that might be applied to the entire country, with very few differences among the major candidates. Health care policy was a highly salient issue among Democrats, and the recession had contributed to new concerns about the cost and availability of health insurance for the average American.

Policy Ideas

In the months before the 1992 presidential election, several divergent health reform ideas were actively debated. The Democratic candidates each championed a distinctive approach. It was no surprise when the Clinton health reform proposal did not enjoy universal support among congressional Democrats. After the 1994 failure of President Clinton's proposal, various ideas continued to be discussed and analyzed. Some individuals and groups supported single-payer or Medicare for All plans, others advocated approaches built around an employer mandate, and some proposed more market-oriented ideas. When President George W. Bush won the closely contested 2000 presidential election, it seemed clear that major health reform legislation would not be pursued in the near future.

The health reform discussion continued in a variety of forums. Perhaps the most comprehensive was a series of papers published by the now defunct Economic and Social Research Institute beginning in 2001 under the title *Covering America: Real Remedies for the Uninsured*.[7] In this and other forums, health policy scholars analyzed a wide range of approaches for reducing the number of uninsured Americans. In 2007 a subsequent set of proposals by various health policy scholars in the Brookings Institution's Hamilton Project updated and refined some of the same policy ideas.[8]

Many policy scholars deemed the Medicare for All idea, the oldest, as the best approach. However, it was most transformative and often labeled politically unachievable. This approach in its purest form would eliminate all private insurance and cover everyone with a public program. Over the years, first England and later Canada became the model for comprehensive reform. The unfortunate label "single payer" became the shorthand way of referring to comprehensive coverage for all with a public program. James Morone, in his contribution to the *Covering America* document, advocated Medicare for All.[9] His 2002 proposal featured an expanded Medicare to cover all legal residents and would be funded with a new federal value-added tax. This and similar ideas remained the ultimate goal of many liberal reformers.

As the 2008 election approached, political scientist Jacob Hacker proposed a public insurance option for the individual market. Many liberal reformer activists saw this as a Trojan horse approach to move toward universal coverage without a sudden massive shift from private insurance to a public plan.[10] While the public option did not become law, it was a major element in many of the draft versions of the Affordable Care Act.

Since a majority of Americans receive health insurance through the workplace, another reform strategy was to require all employers to provide health insurance, perhaps combined with an expansion of Medicaid to cover all those not working. Since the 1980s many health reform proposals had sought to build on the breadth and popularity of employment-based coverage with a coverage mandate for all company employees.[11] In 2007 the Commonwealth Fund staff produced papers analyzing various approaches and assessing the proposals of the major candidates as well as current bills in Congress. They termed one featured approach *mixed private-public group insurance with shared responsibility*.[12] The critical features of this approach included employer and individual mandates, exchanges for the purchase of insurance by individuals and small businesses with premium assistance, and expansion of Medicaid for all low-income individuals.

The employer mandate was sometimes proposed as a play-or-pay system in which employers could either pay for employee insurance or pay a tax equivalent that would be used to finance employee participation in a public plan.[13] The major Democratic candidates in 2008 each advocated a version of the mixed public-private approach.

Conservatives favored a more market-based system that would utilize tax credits to encourage the purchase of private insurance as an alternative to public programs and employment-based insurance. The cost of employer-sponsored insurance (ESI) is not treated as taxable income for workers, which encourages the practice. The tax-credit approaches would incentivize employers to end insurance purchase for employees and allow those individuals to purchase their own health insurance with the tax credit. Low-income individuals would receive additional subsidies to help defer the cost.

Stuart Butler's proposal in *Covering America* and later as part of the Hamilton Project was a good example of this approach to replacing government and employment-based programs with vouchers or tax credits for individuals to purchase health insurance in the marketplace.[14]

The participants in the debate over health reform proposed permutations of all of these basic approaches. Without the move by Massachusetts, the Democrats might have once again gone into the primary election campaign with all of the candidates proclaiming health reform as a critical objective but differing sharply on the approach.

In the 2008 general election campaign, Senator John McCain advocated a market-based reform that ended the favorable tax treatment for employer-sponsored insurance and instead granted a $5,000-a-year tax credit per family to use for the purchase of insurance. Senator Obama argued for a nationalized version of the Massachusetts plan with Medicaid expansion and tax credits for purchase of insurance on an exchange, although not a broad individual mandate.[15] The Obama victory set the stage for the next phase of the health reform saga.

For more than a decade, a vigorous discussion had ensued among health reform analysts despite the obvious lack of congressional and presidential support. During this period policy ideas were refined and adjusted. As the 2008 election neared, there was a sense of anticipation. A window of opportunity might open a decade and half after the last one slammed shut.

Affordable Care Act Legislative Process: A Case Study

An old and widely quoted aphorism says that one does not want to observe either sausage or laws being made. Sausage making is not an edifying process. The legislative process is often criticized for its lack of grace. In this case study of the ACA legislative process, we will examine the pathway toward its eventual enactment.[16]

Both public perceptions of a problem with the health financing system and the emphasis placed on it by Democrats in the campaign assured that health reform would have a high place on the agenda as the new administration and Congress took office in January 2009. Because the county was still mired in the economic aftermath of the 2007–2008 recession, it was not immediately clear if this issue was at the very top of the agenda or only near the top.

A policy idea consensus among Democrats that emerged in the campaign was to use the Massachusetts model as the basis for the reform legislation. Due to vetting of the basic idea by both policy experts and elected politicians, this approach came to be the preferred reform design.[17] The Democratic majorities in the House and Senate appeared to confirm the assessment that potential coalitions existed to pass a health reform law. The window of opportunity for health reform was open for the first time in fifteen years. Was the quest finally almost over?

The sausage process emerges when coalition building intersects with the refining of the basic policy idea, especially when key individual legislators begin to tinker with bill language. A policy idea begins life as a general concept and along the way gets converted into the detailed language of the bill. The case study that follows will first describe the coalition-building process that began in January 2009 and concluded with the bill signing in March 2010. Then it explores the critical design elements within the bill that shaped the policy as passed and implemented. The intersection of politics and policy in the process occurs when critical policy ideas shaping the content of a bill become points of dispute within a potential majority coalition.

Those outside the potential coalition are expected to dispute the key policy ideas in the proposal. Their opposition is part of the calculus. What drives the final content and coalition availability is how internal divisions determine whether a majority coalition is obtained or the window of opportunity closes without success, as occurred in 1994.

Administrative Initiative

By September 2008 Senator Obama believed he would win the election, and he began to turn his attention to legislative priorities for the first months of the new administration. On the fall campaign trail, he emphasized health reform more than he had during the primaries.[18] As the new administration took office in January 2009, an internal debate occurred over whether or not to push immediately for health reform. The fiscal crisis demanded immediate attention and legislation. On that point members of the new administration agreed. Chief of Staff Rahm Emanuel opposed a major push for comprehensive health reform and argued for a more incremental approach.[19] He had been in the Clinton White House and had firsthand experience with the difficulty of achieving health legislation, even when most Democrats saw this as a pressing problem.

President Obama rejected the calls for caution and pushed ahead with health legislation. However, the tactic employed represented a sharp departure from the Clinton White House. The Obama White House did not dispatch a detailed plan to Congress. Taking advantage of the broad consensus among congressional Democrats in favor of developing a proposal based on the ideas in the Massachusetts law, the Obama administration sent Congress a general outline of health reform goals and depended on the relevant committees to draft the bill.

The move toward consensus within the Democratic Party had begun months earlier. Senator Edward Kennedy met during the summer campaign with Senator Max Baucus, the Democratic chair of the Senate Finance Committee, to map a postelection legislative strategy. Kennedy, perhaps the most liberal member of the Senate, had long championed a national health insurance approach. Baucus, from Montana, was among the more conservative Democrats in the Senate. But they agreed on an approach along the lines of the Massachusetts plan. In the months leading up to the election and inauguration, Kennedy and his staff also held sessions with various key health lobby groups. The message was to take part in shaping the health legislation or potentially be left at a disadvantage. These meetings came to be called the "workhorse sessions."[20]

Baucus and his staff proceeded to develop a white paper outlining the major elements of a plan based on the Massachusetts law concepts.[21] It included an individual mandate. During the campaign, Senator Obama had only advocated an individual mandate for children, but many of the participants in the discussions had come to believe that without a requirement that everyone have insurance, millions would remain uninsured and premiums would escalate.[22] In the months ahead staff members of the various congressional committees would shape sections of the law, but the Baucus white paper would remain a key blueprint. The Senate Finance Committee bill ultimately became the primary vehicle for the law.

The public kickoff of the effort to pass health reform was a March 5, 2009, White House summit on health care. Invitees included bipartisan legislative leaders as well as reform advocates and industry representatives. The Obama administration had already submitted its first budget and earmarked over $600 billion for health reform for the coming decade. Obama administration officials would continue to play a major role in both shaping some of the key elements of the legislation and contributing to the process of coalition building in the year ahead, but the center of action shifted to Congress for the rest of 2009.

Congressional Process Part I, 2009

In grade school civics, we learn the process by which a bill becomes a law. A member of the legislative body submits a draft bill. The bill is assigned to a committee. Hearings are then held, and a committee markup session results in content changes. The leadership determines when the bill comes to the floor, at which time amendments may be proposed and either accepted or rejected by the whole body. This clears the way for a final vote to determine passage or rejection.

The actual path from bill to law is not as clear and formalized as our civics class diagram. This was true for the Affordable Care Act. Table 2.1, showing the major events in the yearlong path to creation of the ACA,

Table 2.1 Path to the Affordable Care Act (day in parentheses)

Date	House	Senate	Administration
2/2009			Reform money budgeted (26)
3/2009	Tri-Com staff begin drafting (31)		White House holds Health Forum, a public meeting on reform (5)
4/2009		Sen. Spector switches to Democratic party, providing 60 votes (28)	
5/2009			
6/2009	Discussion draft released (19) Hearings by Tri-Com		
7/2009	Tri-Com reports HB 3200 (14) Tri-Com marks up HB 3200 (15–30)	HELP Committee reports SB 1679 HELP markup (15)	
8/2009			
9/2009			Obama addresses Congress (9)
10/2009	HB 3692 replaces HB 3200 (29)	Finance Committee reports SB 1796 (13)	
11/2009	Stupak Amendment approved; House passes HB 3962 (7)	Reid proposes combined bill (18)	White House lobbies reluctant Democratic senators
12/2009		Lieberman opposition causes Medicare buy-in and public option to be dropped (12) Senate passes SB 3590 (24)	
1/2010			
2/2010			Obama takes rescue lead; offers compromise plan (22)
3/2010	House passes Senate version as HB 3590 (21) House passes reconciliation bill HB 4872 (25)	Senate passes reconciliation bill HB 4872 (25)	Obama signs bill (26)

provides a snapshot of the significant steps toward final passage. This overview for the reader provides context for the details of House and Senate passage that follow.

The House and Senate are distinct legislative bodies, with their own rules, traditions, and responses to constituencies. During 2009 each had a significant role in the development of the ACA. Since the House version passed first, we will initially take up the path of the ACA through the House and then consider the Senate. Table 2.1 helps the reader envision the timeline crosswalk. With the ACA, as is often the case, the early stages in the House and Senate processes were fairly independent, with the administration taking responsibility for some elements of coordination.

House Passage

Despite opting not to submit a formal White House plan in bill form, by March 2009 the Obama administration was publicly committed to health reform. The first Obama budget sent to Congress in February included over $600 billion earmarked for health reform. The chairmen of the three House committees of jurisdiction mobilized their staffs to begin drafting a common bill.[23] This working group came to be called Tri-Com. Each committee held hearings, and then the three chairmen and Speaker Nancy Pelosi developed a Tri-Com "discussion draft," which was unveiled June 19, 2009.[24] Each committee again held hearings focused on the draft legislation (HB 3200). On July 14 it was formally introduced by the committee chairs.

The House bill proposed Medicaid expansion for those with incomes under 150 percent of the federal poverty level (FPL), nationally operated insurance exchanges with robust powers, employer and individual mandates, a high-income surtax, and a public option with rates determined by provider negotiation.[25] Another round of hearings followed with HB 3200 as the focus. The committee leadership avoided the traditional public markup sessions but opted for negotiated modifications. By July 17 the Ways and Means and the Education and Labor Committees reported their versions of HB 3200 to the House floor.

The Energy and Commerce Committee took until the end of the month as conservative Democratic members threatened to withhold their votes without changes to the bill reducing the cost and modifying the public-option plan. The moderate Democratic members on the committee were adamant about changes like allowing provider rate negotiations in the public option and greater assistance for small businesses.[26] HB 3200 remained on the House calendar until mid-October, as the House was reluctant to proceed until the direction in the Senate was clear. The bill was further modified after negotiation among various elements of the Democratic caucus.

The new version, HB 3962, was brought to the floor on November 7, 2009. The House Rules Committee had exercised its traditional role by providing a special rule for consideration of the bill, which limited debate and provided for only two amendments. One was the Republican health proposal, and the other critical amendment was that of Democratic representative Bart Stupak, which prohibited federal funding of abortion under the proposed law.[27]

The vote on the Stupak Amendment was the make-or-break vote in the House on HB 3962. The Democratic pro-life bloc was unwilling to support the bill without the antiabortion provision. They represented a critical part of the majority coalition, and without their support the bill could not pass. Many adamantly pro-choice Democrats were refusing to give ground on abortion. Speaker Pelosi met with those vehemently opposed to the Stupak Amendment and convinced them that the future of health reform hinged on accepting it.[28]

The Democratic House leadership worked diligently to secure the final votes one by one. After successfully jumping over various procedural hurdles, HB 3962 passed by a vote of 220–215 on November 7, 2009, with one Republican voting in support and thirty-nine Democrats voting nay. The no votes tended to be from freshmen representatives who had won in districts that voted for Senator McCain in the 2008 election, with more than half from southern states. For some, the abortion provision was a major issue. Others were fiscal conservatives opposed to the level of new expenditures. By 2015 only a handful of the opponents remained in Congress.[29]

The House had passed health reform legislation not as liberal in its provisions as some wished and with reservations from more conservative members. It contained a public option, but one not as strong as liberals sought. It created a single national health insurance exchange. Despite the modifications for Blue Dog Democrats, the final version was similar to the initial HB 3200 bill introduced in June in most critical features.[30]

Senate Passage

By 2009 Senator Kennedy was too ill from brain cancer to continue active engagement in the development of health reform legislation, but as he was chair of the Committee on Health, Education, Labor, and Pensions (HELP), his staff continued to pursue his decades-long quest for health reform legislation. With Kennedy's encouragement, Finance Committee chair Max Baucus had developed a proposal and by summer was pursuing a bipartisan approach based on his ideas.

The House tri-committee effort resulted in a consensus around a single proposal by July 2009, but significant differences remained between the two Senate committees. Both followed the basic consensus emerging within the Democratic Party on Medicaid expansion, subsidies for the low-income uninsured to purchase insurance through an electronic marketplace, guaranteed issue regulations, and an individual mandate. On a number of critical details related to financing, level of subsidy, and the public option, the Senate HELP and Finance Committees followed their own paths during the summer of 2009.

With his 2008 white paper, Baucus had started early and made an extended, but ultimately futile, effort to create a bipartisan bill. He instituted a conversation involving three Democrats and three Republicans on the Finance Committee. Not until early fall was it clear that the effort was not successful. In September Baucus first introduced a chairman's mark, which is a first draft of a bill to be considered by a committee. He subsequently modified it after criticism even from supporters.[31] The full Finance Committee took up the bill and made revisions over several days of consideration. By the first week of October, the committee had completed its work. This became SB 1796.

In the HELP Committee, the chairman's mark had been developed by Kennedy's staff and adjusted during June, especially after the Congressional Budget Office (CBO) scored the initial version as very expensive. The committee markup, though completed by mid-July, was not actually reported to the Senate until mid-September. It became SB 1679.

After both bills were reported to the Senate, Majority Leader Harry Reid, with other Democratic leaders and White House staff, began the arduous task of combing the two bills into a single version for the Senate vote. Senator Reid introduced the combined bill in mid-November.[32] The basic elements were similar to those of the House bill but were less expensive and covered fewer uninsured individuals. Insurance regulations were similar. The exchanges were to be established by the states with a federal fallback. Instead of an employer mandate, the bill imposed a fine on employers who failed to provide coverage. It did contain a public option, which had not been in the Finance Committee version, but states could opt out.[33]

There were sixty Democrats in the Senate. With sixty votes required to break a filibuster and no Republican support, every Senate Democrat had to support the bill. This led to negotiations between mid-November and the Christmas Eve final vote in which individual senators obtained amendments, which came to be labeled the "Cornhusker Kickback" and the "Louisiana Purchase." The public-option plan was removed at the insistence of Senator Joe Lieberman.[34]

The new Senate vehicle for Reid's bill was HB 3590, a nonrelated bill on the Senate calendar, which had been stripped of its earlier content and amended to contain that of the Reid bill. A series of closure votes were taken as the Senate laboriously waded through the several procedural steps necessary before a final vote could be taken. Barbara Sinclair described it as a marathon beginning on November 30 and continuing throughout December.[35] Majority Leader Reid finally secured the last Democrat holdout, Senator Ben Nelson of Nebraska, on December 19.[36] Still Republicans sought to erect roadblocks, hoping to delay a final vote until after the Christmas break.[37]

Finally, with a snowstorm in progress and all senators wishing to be home for Christmas, the Republican leadership agreed to have a vote at 8 a.m. on December 24.[38] The final vote on what had been renamed the Patient Protection and Affordable Care Act was 60–39.

Congressional Process Part II, 2010

For health reform champions, the 2010 New Year's celebration was enhanced by the late-2009 House and Senate votes passing slightly different versions of the Affordable Care Act. They were similar in their basic approach to reform with differences in details that appeared resolvable through the traditional conference committee approach, despite the nearly unanimous opposition of Republicans. Then, Republican Scott Brown unexpectedly won the Massachusetts special election to fill the Senate seat vacated with the death of Senator Kennedy.

This left the Democratic majority in the Senate one vote shy of the sixty needed to break a filibuster. Suddenly, health reform appeared to be just out of reach. A conference committee compromise would be subject to a filibuster in the Senate. A sense of gloom descended on the health reform community.

Before the final count was tallied in Massachusetts, President Obama met with Speaker Pelosi and Majority Leader Reid. The options seemed limited at the January 19 meeting. The House could accept the already-passed Senate version, or the administration could seek to scale down the bill to include only provisions that could garner some bipartisan support. Pelosi asserted that she could never assemble a Democratic majority in the House for the Senate bill as it stood. Neither Obama nor the congressional leadership wanted to pass a watered-down bill that did not represent significant reform and expansion of coverage.[39]

In the weeks that followed, Pelosi continued attempting to build a majority in the House Democratic caucus. President Obama reached out to Republicans in two meetings covered by live television without success in gathering support from across the aisle. The preparations had been made months earlier to potentially include health reform legislation as part of the reconciliation bill for the congressional session. But, under Senate rules, only provisions with a fiscal impact could be included. The Democrats had initially hoped for some bipartisan support for health reform and wanted to avoid reconciliation as a mechanism to circumvent a Senate filibuster.[40]

The legislative strategy envisioned would have the House accept the Senate bill as passed and sent to the president for signature. Step two would be the crafting of a reconciliation bill in the House that included changes in the Senate bill, as agreed to by the leadership of both houses. This measure would then be sent to the Senate, which could pass it with a simple majority. Thus, it would not be subject to a filibuster under Senate rules.[41] The reconciliation bill was referred to as a "sidecar."

This was a difficult step for many members of the House. They needed to vote for provisions they opposed in the Senate version and then trust that a majority of their Democratic colleagues in the Senate would in fact pass the reconciliation bill modifying the Senate version.

In early March President Obama announced the move forward to complete health reform passage with the agreed compromises.[42] These included modification of the so-called Cadillac tax on high-cost health plans and extension of its effective date. The House Democrats had opposed the tax idea. The public option and the single national online marketplace for insurance purchase, which the House favored, were not included.

Once again, the abortion provision in the Senate version nearly caused the intricate house of cards to crumble. The pro-life faction among House Democrats would not accept what they considered the weaker provision in the Senate version. Because it was not budget related, a modification of the abortion provision in the Senate bill could not be a subject in the reconciliation bill. President Obama promised to issue an executive order that accomplished what the pro-life Democrats sought, thus creating a 219–212 voter majority for the ACA in the House. Thirty-four Democrats and all Republicans in the House voted nay. The Senate approved the reconciliation bill 56–43, and the Affordable Care Act became law after the president's signature.[43]

Major Provisions

The Affordable Care Act of 2010 was a large and complex piece of legislation with many elements. Table 2.2 summarizes the major features of the law. It attempted, with three new initiatives, to provide affordable coverage for a significant number of Americans who were uninsured at the time of its enactment.[44]

First, the individual insurance market would be enhanced. Insurance exchanges would offer insurance plans with a set of minimum benefits. Individuals who were not part of an employment-based or public insurance program could purchase these plans. If their income was between 100 and 400 percent of the federal poverty level, they would be eligible for tax-credit subsidies for premium and cost sharing on a sliding scale.

Second, new insurance rules would preclude excessive premiums or denial of coverage because of preexisting conditions, and renewal would be guaranteed. They prohibited extended waiting periods for coverage, offered preventive coverage without cost sharing, eliminated yearly and lifetime dollar limits on essential benefits, capped out-of-pocket costs, required

Table 2.2 Summary of Basic Provisions of the Affordable Care Act of 2010

Sections	Provisions	Brief Description
Individual insurance market	Individual mandate	Mandate that all residents must have insurance or face a tax penalty Include several categories of exemption, such as financial hardship, religious objection, and insurance cost equaling more than 8 percent of income
	Premium credits	Provide premium credits for individuals between 100 and 400 percent of FPL for purchasing insurance through the exchanges
	Cost-sharing subsidies	Provide cost-sharing subsidies for those between 100 and 400 percent of FPL
	Insurance exchanges	Allow states to opt to create exchanges for the individual purchase of health insurance or to use a federally created exchange Allow states to create exchanges for small businesses (up to 100 employees) for insurance purchase
	Rating rules	Require guaranteed issue and renewability with rating variation limited to 3:1 ratio based on age, rating area, and family composition Prohibit placing lifetime limits on coverage and rescinding coverage Limit deductibles to $4,000 per family; prohibit denial of coverage for preexisting conditions
Public programs	Medicaid expansion	Expand Medicaid coverage to all individuals under sixty-five with incomes below 133 percent of FPL Provide federal funding of 100 percent for three years, scaled back to 90 percent by 2020 Reduce disproportionate share hospital (DSH) payments
	Children's Health Insurance Program (CHIP)	Require state maintenance of effort for CHIP program with 23 percent increase in CHIP match rate beginning in 2015
Employer requirements	Play-or-pay	Impose a fee of $2,000 per employee for employers with more than fifty FT employees that do not offer coverage and one employee receives subsidy in exchange Impose fee of $3,000 per employee for employers with more than fifty FT employees that do not offer coverage and one employee receives subsidy in exchange
	Automatic enrollment	Require large employers (220 FT employees) to automatically enroll employees in health plan unless they opt out
Insurance plans	Essential benefits (including ESI)	Require all plans to cover essential benefits, cap out-of-pocket costs, eliminate preexisting conditions, insure kids until age twenty-six, and impose no lifetime limits
	Loss ratio and rate increases	Require plans to spend at least 80 percent of premium dollars on services and states to review premium increases
	Reinsurance	Collect payments from plans for reinsurance to compensate for covering high-risk individuals
Tax changes	Income/payroll	Increase Medicare Part A tax for those over $200,000 Impose a 3.8 percent additional tax on unearned income for high-income taxpayers
	Industry taxes	Tax insurers and medical device and pharmaceutical manufacturers
	Cadillac tax	From 2018 implement tax on employers for high-cost health insurance plans

Source: "Summary of Coverage Provisions in the Patient Protection and Affordable Care Act," Kaiser Family Foundation; McDonough, *Inside National Health Reform*, pt. 2.

maternity coverage, and allowed children to remain on parents' insurance until age twenty-six. These rules applied to employer-sponsored insurance as well as marketplace plans.

Third, the Medicaid program would be expanded to cover all individuals below 133 percent of FPL regardless of family situation. To encourage states to accept this expansion, the federal government would pay 100 percent of the additional cost for three years for the newly covered Medicaid population, with a scaling down of federal payments for this group to 90 percent by 2020. This represented a significant increase in the federal share of Medicaid costs.

Employers with more than fifty full-time (FT) employees who did not provide health insurance would be required to pay a fee of $2,000 per employee, if any of their employees accepted tax credits in the exchanges. If an employer did provide insurance but any of its employees accepted tax credits, it would also be assessed a fee. This provision was intended to provide employers with an incentive to continue providing employee health insurance.

Since insurance plans were to be required to accept customers and retain them regardless of health status with a standard premium, two provisions sought to maintain fiscal health for the insurance companies. First, all citizens would be required to purchase health insurance (individual mandate), thus expanding the individual market. Second, insurance plans would contribute to a fund to compensate firms in a market that incurred higher-than-average costs in their customer pool because of higher risk factors.

Critical Policy Design Decisions

The Affordable Care Act has ten titles, or sections, containing hundreds of provisions. Not all are equal in importance; nor were all the subject of controversy and debate. The critical design elements were those fundamental to the major goals of the bill. We will first examine the key provisions and then briefly assess the policy idea design elements at the center of controversies within the Democratic Party coalition. These key design features were at the center of the majority deliberation.

Basic Elements of the Bill

Three fundamental elements constitute the core of the ACA policy idea: Medicaid expansion, insurance market reform, including tax credits to purchase insurance in the exchanges along with regulation of underwriting practice, and the individual mandate. We will assess each of them. All were part of the Massachusetts plan that became the policy idea model for the ACA.

Medicaid expansion. Medicaid began as an almost unnoticed add-on to the Medicare legislation in 1965. Reformers regarded it as a transition program to provide care for some of the very poor, until Medicare could be expanded into a comprehensive national health insurance program. It was insurance coverage for the poor, who were part of the welfare system. Over forty years later, as health reform emerged as a critical policy agenda item, Medicaid had become almost the equal of Medicare as a linchpin of the public health insurance system.

The fundamental idea of Medicaid expansion was to increase the eligible population to include low-income individuals who were not part of the existing welfare public programs. All individuals below an income cutoff would be eligible regardless of family situation. Policy scholars who argued for a mixed public-private system under reform saw Medicaid expansion to cover all the poor as the best way to reduce the number of very low-income uninsured.[45]

States had long experience with Medicaid. Medicaid expansion was seen as a low-cost and efficient way of providing coverage for the very poor.[46] The additional financial burden on states would be mitigated by the federal government's initially assuming 100 percent of the costs for the expansion population and then permanently taking responsibility for 90 percent.

From the beginning Republicans opposed Medicaid expansion, usually claiming the program was poorly run and dysfunctional. John McDonough quotes four Republican senators making this claim during the ACA floor debate.[47] As Frank Thompson demonstrates, Republican ideological opposition to Medicaid dates at least to the Ronald Reagan era and has been a defining characteristic of Republicans for forty years.[48] A closer look within the Republican Party finds internal GOP differences, with business and health interests viewing Medicaid more positively than conservative ideological activists with their strident opposition.[49] Republicans have sought to either devolve more responsibility and funding to the states by converting Medicaid from an entitlement to a block grant or providing Medicaid recipients with vouchers for purchase of private insurance. In either approach the fiscal and administrative role of the federal government would be reduced. This was the policy goal.[50]

Among Democrats the only dispute was the level of eligibility. Would it extend only up to 100 percent of FPL or as high as 150 percent? The House version favored the latter; the Senate settled on 133 percent of FPL. Since the alternative to Medicaid expansion was providing tax credits in the exchange for the very poor, the higher the level of eligibility, the lower the total program cost. It was cheaper to cover an individual under Medicaid than to pay the insurance policy subsidy in the exchange for that individual.[51]

Both Senate and House versions sought to ease financial burdens for states with 100 percent federal payment for expansion in the first three years and 90 percent thereafter. This is a much greater federal government share than under traditional Medicaid. For those favoring a single national plan, Medicaid expansion was a second-best approach to the preferred idea of a comprehensive public program.

Tax credits in the exchange and insurance market regulation. The second major element of the ACA was to provide financial assistance to lower-middle-income people who were outside the employment-based system and to use regulations to protect consumers in both the individual market and the employment-based system.

For some time conservatives had argued that the use of tax credits was a superior way of subsidizing the real cost of health insurance for the average person. Conservative health economist Mark Pauly was a notable advocate for this policy idea.[52] Pauly promoted use of tax credits to replace work-based insurance. The architects of the Massachusetts plan took a more limited approach to the idea. They retained and expanded work-based coverage but used the tax-credit idea to strengthen the individual market. Gruber and others then proposed that the Massachusetts model be applied nationally.[53] Thus, the use of tax credits to strengthen the individual market became an essential part of the ACA policy idea.

Most Democrats did not embrace the tax-credit idea as a universal approach. But expanding Medicaid to include those up to 400 percent of FPL seemed politically unattainable. Unlike with earlier reform efforts, Democrats across the spectrum united in their acceptance of the Massachusetts model of Medicaid expansion for the very poor and tax credits to purchase insurance for lower-middle-income people outside the employment-based insurance system. To further assist in making health insurance affordable for this group, cost-sharing subsidies were also included for those under 200 percent FPL.

The companion piece to tax credits was new insurance market regulations that required insurance companies to offer basic health benefits, limit the premium range, prohibit declining issuance based on preexisting conditions, and prohibit yearly and lifetime benefits. Since states had primary authority for insurance regulation, this was a rich source of ideas for national application.[54] Standard industry practices in the individual market, such as denial of coverage or very high premiums for preexisting conditions and annual or lifetime benefit caps, had been highlighted in press coverage of the issue. There was little controversy about the inclusion of new individual market regulations in the ACA; nor was there concerted opposition to the application of the new rules to employer-sponsored insurance.

In 2009 insurance companies were not popular institutions. Practices such as denying coverage for preexisting conditions and setting annual benefit limits were viewed as insurance companies seeking profits over helping the sick. Few elected officials wished to defend some of these common insurance practices.[55] Why was there no massive insurance company lobbying assault on the new rules? The individual mandate is the answer.

Individual mandate. For insurance companies the quid pro quo for acceptance of new market regulations was the opportunity provided by the individual mandate. This was an essential component of the Massachusetts model and offered insurance companies the prospect of new customers, many of whom would be younger people paying more in premiums than they generated in costs. The companies wagered the requirement that all individuals purchase insurance would offset the additional cost generated by the new regulations.

The individual-mandate idea originated in the Republican response to the Clinton plan. The conservative Heritage Foundation in 1989 and Republican senator John Chaffee in 1993 offered this idea as a market-based alternative.[56] In subsequent years there was a bipartisan exploration of this idea as a critical piece of health reform proposals. It became part of the ACA because it was a familiar concept and offered a carrot to insurance companies to offset the stick of additional regulation. Opposition to the individual mandate only emerged later. At the time of enactment there was modest disagreement over the size of the penalty.

The drama of ACA enactment did not pivot around the core provisions of the bill. Despite some quibbling on subsidy levels and how far to take Medicaid expansion, most Democrats in Congress accepted the foundational ideas of the ACA. These were Medicaid expansion for the poor, insurance market regulation and use of an electronic exchange with tax and cost-sharing credits for the purchase of insurance in the individual market, and an individual mandate to enhance coverage with a diverse risk pool.

The most significant marketplace difference between the House and Senate versions was the nature of the exchanges. The House opted for a single national exchange with modest regulatory authority over insurance plans, and the Senate version called for state exchanges with a backup of federal exchanges in the states.[57]

Financing

Money tends to be at the root of most political disputes. In the yearlong legislative debate over the ACA, differences over the financial structure design tended to be one of the dominant disagreements among Democrats as well as between the parties. Hovering over every financial issue was the Congressional Budget Office score. Since the late 1970s, the CBO has analyzed major legislation for its budgetary impact. The score process involves the application of a complex set of rules and precedents since the agency strives for consistency and objectivity. Today legislative language is often crafted with an eye to the best possible CBO score.[58]

The CBO, in its evaluation of the ACA, projected the impact of several elements of the legislation. President Obama's budget had assumed a ten-year program cost of $940 billion. Thus, lawmakers attempted to achieve a projection of costs and revenue that would not exceed that target.

The component pieces of the macroeconomic projection included the new revenue generated, the projected savings from current programs, the number of individuals using tax credits to purchase insurance in the exchanges, the cost-sharing subsidies, and the federal share of the Medicaid expansion. As the legislative committees and the leadership crafted and reworked the component pieces of the bill, they felt constrained to tinker with the language of each element to maintain an overall budget constraint within the CBO score.

John McDonough offers the example that as the bill proceeded, the cost of the subsidies in the exchanges declined from $723 billion to $602 billion to $449 billion as the start date was modified and the generosity of the benefit was modified. The original HELP Committee bill had a 2012 start date. The final Senate version had 2014 for the program commencement.[59] This shaved two years of expenditures from the ten-year window for CBO calculation, which began with the 2010 enactment.

We don't typically fight wars with a budget constraint; nor has Congress normally enacted new taxes earmarked to pay for military expeditions. The ACA approach was different. The administration and Congress sought to expand insurance coverage through the ACA by creating new revenue streams from within the health system rather than taking the money from existing general revenue. Conservative Democrats in the Senate insisted on this approach. The House leadership sought additional taxes on the wealthy as a primary method of generating new revenue. In the end a combination of both was employed.[60]

A critical design feature in any bill is the source of money to pay for the new program. When Congress in 2003 passed the Medicare prescription drug bill, general revenue was to pay for about 70 percent of the total cost, with beneficiary premiums absorbing the rest.[61] With the ACA the design decision was made to utilize new revenue to pay for the costs.

Columnist George Will once observed that cutting taxes was as easy for Congress as inviting the kids in his neighborhood to go out for free pizza and ice cream. To extend the analogy, legislating new taxes is perhaps like getting the kids to eat their vegetables. The strategy of the legislative architects was to look for new revenue in two places.

Medicare changes represented a major source of the necessary revenue. The Medicare cuts constituted reductions in Medicare Advantage payments to providers and in rates of growth for hospital payments, as well as elimination of the disproportionate share program, which provides special payments to hospitals that serve high numbers of poor patients. The Medicare payroll tax was increased for high-income individuals.

Provider groups were seen as secondary beneficiaries of the ACA. Insurance companies would have new clients, device makers would sell more products, hospitals would have fewer patients unable to pay their bills, and pharmaceutical companies were expected to have a larger market for their products. Early in the legislative process, Senate leaders, such as

Senators Kennedy and Baucus, began to press these provider groups to be willing to negotiate their fair-share contribution to offsetting the total ACA expenditures.[62] On the other hand the House committees believed that additional taxes on wealthy individuals should be a prime source of new revenue to finance expansion.

It is easy to become lost in a maze of CBO budget spreadsheets in looking at the financial design of the ACA. This is not our purpose. Table 2.3 summarizes the financial design choices by illustrating the anticipated expenditures and revenues according to the CBO and other estimates. In the interest of big picture clarity, there is considerable rounding of numbers and omission of many small items on both the revenue and the expenditure sides.

The CBO projected the House bill would incur over $600 billion in exchange subsidies over the ten-year period and slightly higher Medicaid costs. On the revenue side, the House bill envisioned a surtax on wealthy individuals to pay for about half the total cost of the program. The House provided for greater payments by employers who did not provide insurance to employees.[63] The Senate bill became the vehicle for the final legislation

Table 2.3 ACA Revenue and Expense Summary, 2010 Estimates (billions $)

Total Expenditures		Total Revenue and Offsets	
Exchange subsidies	$464	Medicare Advantage reductions	$136
Medicaid	$434	Medicare Fee for Service (FFS) payment update reductions	$196
Small-employer tax credits	$40	Medicare/Medicaid DSH elimination	$36
		Other Medicare/Medicaid changes	$87
		Mandate penalties	$69
		Cadillac tax penalties	$32
		Tax on insurers	$60
		Tax on drug and device companies	$47
		Medicare tax increase for high-income individuals	$210
		Other revenue provisions	$82
Total	$938		$1,008

Source: John E. McDonough, *Inside National Health Reform* (Berkeley: University of California Press, 2011), chap. 13; Douglas W. Elmendorf, letter to the Honorable Nancy Pelosi estimating the spending and revenue effects of HR 4872, Congressional Budget Office, March 20, 2010, www.cbo.gov/sites/default/files/hr4872_0.pdf; "Estimated Revenue Effects of the Amendment in the Nature of a Substitute to H.R. 4872, the Reconciliation Act of 2010, as Amended, in Combination with the Revenue Effects of H.R. 3590, the Patient Protection and Affordable Care Act ('PPACA'), as Passed by the Senate, and Scheduled for Consideration by the House Committee on Rules on March 20, 2010," Joint Committee on Taxation, March 20, 2010, https://www.jct.gov/publications/2010/jcx-17-10.

without the benefit of a conference committee, and thus the Senate approach to the overall revenue and expenditure projection was the basis for the final fiscal estimate.[64]

The CBO projected that the ACA, as modified by the reconciliation bill, was going to cost $938 billion over the ten-year period from enactment to 2019. Of the total, 50 percent would be incurred by the exchange subsidies and related items; 46 percent would cover the federal share of Medicaid expansion, with the remaining 4 percent used for small-employer tax credits.[65]

The offsetting revenue, as estimated by the CBO and the congressional Joint Committee on Taxation, was a more complicated mix that totaled $1.08 trillion.[66] The $143 billion difference was targeted for deficit reduction. Medicare modifications of over $600 billion accounted for more than half the total. Two-third of this was in the form of payment reductions to Medicare Advantage plans and providers. The increased Medicare tax for high-income individuals generated the balance of Medicare-related revenue.[67]

Because the Senate version became the final statute without a normal conference process, the key financial differences between House and Senate were not a point of major contention. Within each body there was a Democratic Party tug-of-war between liberals who wished to see a more generous set of subsidies and conservatives who sought less total spending. Major constraints were President Obama's upper budget number and the CBO score of various provisions to reach a final set of revenue and expenditure projections over ten years. The result was a tinkering with several provisions to produce a CBO score within the budget constraint. While the fiscal shape might have been marginally different with a traditional House and Senate conference, the overall fiscal picture would not likely have been much different.

Cost Containment

One of the potent forces driving reform to the public agenda was dissatisfaction with the escalating cost of health care. Soon after ACA passage, key Obama administrative officials, Peter Orszag and Ezekiel Emanuel, conceded, "Many commentators have claimed that the bill focuses mostly on coverage and contains little in the way of cost control."[68] They and other ACA defenders cite several elements as contributing to future cost control.[69] These include the tax on high-priced health plans (Cadillac tax), establishment of an Independent Payment Advisory Board (IPAB), creation of accountable care organizations and other provider incentives and alternative payment strategies, cost savings through insurance market reforms, payment reductions to Medicare Advantage, and efforts to reduce waste and fraud.

Jonathan Oberlander expressed a skeptical view: "Is there, then, reason to believe that the ACA will decisively rein in US medical care spending? Alas, probably not. The enthusiasm for the cost-containment provisions in health reform is striking precisely because so many of those provisions are tepid. Put simply, the Affordable Care Act lacks systemwide, reliable cost control."[70]

The estimated federal budget savings from the two most prominent cost-control innovations (Cadillac tax and IPAB) are greater than nine other innovations combined.[71] Cost control was a frequently invoked goal, and the law contains a wide variety of proposals that had been circulating in the policy stream. Each was seen as marginally contributing, if effectively implemented, to a slowdown in the rate of growth of health costs. It is not hard to join Oberlander in concluding that significant price-control strategies would have destabilized the fragile coalition that had been assembled to pass the ACA, which included many provider interests for whom more significant cost controls were unacceptable.

Apprehension about the escalating cost of health care was a major talking point as reform began to take shape before the 2008 election. The ACA champions argued that ultimately the law would "bend the cost curve."[72] In the design of the law, the policy ideas and cost-containment provisions were not the subject of debate and division, probably because few saw them as capable of instituting major change in the financing system.[73]

Public Option
Few new policy ideas were embedded in the ACA, but until the end one fresh concept was integral to the discussion: the public option. It was a simple concept. A publicly sponsored insurance entity was to be created and compete with private plans in the individual and small-group market. Political scientist Jacob Hacker proposed in 2008 that a public insurance company be created and available in the health exchanges to compete with private insurance.[74] First John Edwards and later Hillary Clinton and Obama included this idea in their primary election policy proposals. In part this was a policy gesture to the liberal wing of the primary electorate, which perceived the public option as a first step toward a universal public plan.

Hacker argued that the public option would be a benchmark and leverage in the marketplace when competing with private plans. The idea began to receive serious consideration when it was included in the Baucus white paper in late 2008.[75] Conservative and industry opposition began to develop.

The House tri-committee draft included a public option, as did the Senate HELP Committee version, although there were differences in the design details. Only the Senate Finance Committee version did not include the public option. Finance chairman Baucus had replaced it with a "co-op" model alternative during the committee markup. In his subsequent merger of the HELP and Finance Committee bills, Majority Leader Reid included a public option in the initial version brought to the Senate floor. But with the Democrats needing sixty votes to break a filibuster, Senator Lieberman of Connecticut had a key point of leverage. He demanded the removal of the public-option provision as a stipulation for his vote. Congressional leaders and the administration were not willing to see the bill fail over the public-option provision.[76]

Analytic assessments by the CBO, Lewin Group, and others varied on the projection of the ultimate size of the public option. These details were not the deal breaker. The existence of the idea as part of the health reform policy package became a symbol for the continuing debate over the proper role of government in the financing of health care. Critics called it a Trojan horse for a single-payer plan. They were correct. This was the ultimate goal of many proponents, although the Trojans may never have been able to leave the horse if private insurance plans were successful in the exchanges.[77]

Cadillac Tax

The Cadillac tax provides for a 40 percent excise tax on insurers and self-insured employers when employer-sponsored insurance exceeds set values. The effective date of the tax was postponed until 2018 to provide an opportunity for employers to adjust their insurance plans to avoid the tax. The tax is formally paid by insurers but the cost would probably be passed on to employers and ultimately employees.

The initial target of the tax appeared to be "gold-plated" health plans for corporate executives, thus the label "Cadillac tax." Soon it became evident that many health plans with above-average costs were in union-negotiated contracts.[78] Projected revenue from this provision was helpful in obtaining a favorable score from the Congressional Budget Office.

The origins of this policy idea can be traced back to 1954 legislation that excluded as taxable income health insurance premiums paid by employers. Beginning in the 1970s economists argued that the exclusion created an incentive for excessive insurance.[79] The Reagan administration attempted to limit the exclusion, but opposition from both business and labor killed the effort.[80] Advocacy for limitations on the exclusion continued over the years, with ACA proponent Jonathan Gruber among those endorsing the idea.[81]

A tax-exclusion limit, a provision in the Baucus white paper, became part of the Senate Finance Committee bill but was not in any of the other versions. By early October the House was moving toward resolving the internal differences in its version, but the tax treatment was not an issue. It was off the table as far as the House leadership was concerned.[82]

The administration endorsed the exclusion idea, and it was contained in the Senate combined bill. As it became evident that the Senate bill with its Cadillac tax provision was going to be the main vehicle for the legislation, the intellectual case against it, as well as the political argument, was made more forcefully.[83] However, some liberal policy organizations, such as the Center on Budget and Policy Priorities, issued papers supporting the Cadillac tax plan in the bill.[84]

During the negotiations leading to the reconciliation approach to amending the Senate bill, the Cadillac tax became a critical issue. The White House compromised with labor unions and House leaders to postpone the effective date until 2018 as well as to create additional exemptions. This compromise allowed the ACA to go forward with a tax-exclusion-limit provision but postponed the ultimate implementation to a distant future.[85] Opponents wanted health reform to move forward but knew they would have future opportunities to crush the Cadillac tax.

Abortion

The 1973 *Roe v. Wade* Supreme Court decision set in motion political battles that have persisted for nearly half a century between those who champion a woman's right to an abortion and those who believe this procedure should not be legal. In 1978 the antiabortion advocates succeeded in passing the Hyde Amendment, which prohibits the use of federal funds for abortion except in a limited set of circumstances.[86] This includes Medicaid, but states may use their own funds for this purpose.

This intensely contentious issue became a flashpoint in the development of the ACA. There was no attempt to reverse the Hyde Amendment provisions. The original House version provided that insurance in the exchanges could be used for abortion coverage, but insurance companies had to use funds other than federal subsidies for this purpose. The Senate version allowed abortion coverage in exchange policies but required the payment of a separate small premium for this purpose, thus segregating the payments from federal subsidies.

A coalition of antiabortion Democrats in the House succeeded in adding the Stupak Amendment to the final House bill, thereby prohibiting plans in the exchanges from offering abortion coverage for customers who received federal subsidies. The issue became a point of dispute between the two versions. The reconciliation process rules did not allow inclusion of a nonbudgetary provision in the bill, which was to be the vehicle for adjusting the Senate version. Stupak and his allies were unwilling to accept the Senate's abortion provision because they regarded it as circumventing the Hyde Amendment principle.

When this threatened to derail the House acceptance of the Senate version, as modified by the reconciliation bill, President Obama, in a compromise move, offered an executive order stipulating that the Hyde Amendment provisions applied to insurance policies purchased in the exchanges. With this administrative clarification, Stupak and enough of his allies supported the bill to ensure passage of the Senate version in the House.[87]

The abortion issue elicited intense emotional and ideological reactions for many of the participants. Even several years later, it was difficult to ascertain the real impact the final ACA language had on service coverage.[88] All of the versions envisioned a financial limitation on use of federal funds to provide abortion coverage for policies offered in the exchange. Both sets of Democrats emerged unhappy with the final arrangement, but compromise was possible because the total impact of the ACA was in reality more important to both sides than this single issue.[89]

Employer Approach

Since the early 1970s one health reform strategy built on, rather than eliminated, employer-sponsored insurance. A mandate for all employers to offer health insurance represented an approach to universal coverage for the working population without increasing public expenditures. It was an incremental approach in that it expanded the largest coverage system, which included more than half the population.[90]

Richard Nixon's, Jimmy Carter's, and Bill Clinton's plans all featured an employer mandate. This policy idea often featured "play-or-pay," which required either purchase of insurance for employees or payment of a tax, with the proceeds used to finance public coverage. Since not all the uninsured were employed, this policy idea would not by itself achieve universal coverage. It was perceived as a key tool for achieving universal coverage by those who sought to do so with a mixed private-public system. The Massachusetts plan included a business contribution for each uninsured employee.[91]

The House ACA version included a play-or-pay percentage of payroll for employee health insurance, with payment of the amount to the federal government as the alternative. The Senate Finance Committee bill was less onerous. It required a small payment for each employee who received a tax credit in the exchange. The reconciliation sidecar kept the Senate approach but significantly increased the amount. The inclusion of this provision also contributed significant revenue in the CBO scoring of the bill.[92]

Existing employer-sponsored insurance also had to abide by new rules, such as no limits on essential health benefits, free preventive care, children remaining on parents' plan until age twenty-six, and coverage of pre-existing conditions.

Exchanges and Federalism

The idea of purchasing pools to both broaden risk and ease consumer choice in the individual market had been discussed since the 1980s. This was an essential feature of Alain Enthoven's consumer-choice model and a key component of the Clinton health plan. The Massachusetts Connector, an electronic health insurance marketplace, was a pivotal part of their state reform. The idea combined conservative market principles with insurance regulatory concepts favored by liberals.[93] There was little debate about the idea of a purchasing pool feature within the ACA.

House and Senate differences in the exchange design reflected different approaches to federalism and the ACA. The House version was a single national exchange capable of active regulation of coverage and rates. The public option was to be part of the exchange. States were allowed to form their own exchanges, but under federal rules. The Senate rejected this approach, and its version featured state exchanges with federal operation of the exchange if a state failed to create one. Under the Senate approach, the exchange had a more passive role without authority over rate increases.[94]

In the January 2010 negotiations over changes to be included in the reconciliation adjustments, it was determined the structure of the exchanges had no budgetary impact and was not eligible for inclusion. The Senate's state-based version with federal backup became the ACA basis for exchange organization.

This was one example of federalism shaping major features of the ACA. In the evolution among reformers of policy ideas that became the ACA, there was a tendency for liberals to favor a national approach, and moderates wished to have states play a central role. This has been a policy debate on many issues over the years. In this instance, the Senate, especially moderate Democrats in the Senate, preferred a significant role for states in the health reform legislation. Michael Sparer points to a long history of federal health legislation over the past century reflecting a major role for states. Both political culture and interest group politics sustain a national health reform approach in which acceptable policy ideas are embedded in principles of federalism.[95]

Intersection of Politics and Ideas

Once an issue reaches a high place on the agenda, a window of opportunity emerges. Legislation is unlikely without viable and acceptable policy ideas for addressing the issue. Majority coalitions must be built and sustained at the various stages of the process. It is in the coalition building that we find the intersection of politics and ideas. Legislation consists of policy ideas woven into legislative language. At each critical juncture in the process, support for a particular set of ideas is essential.

At the beginning of the chapter, we asked three questions about the placement of health reform on President Obama's agenda, the core ACA ideas, and the difficulties assembling a majority coalition. In the legislative case study, we saw the president place health reform high on the agenda, despite the misgivings of some White House advisors. The congressional leadership agreed. There was a Democratic Party consensus around a set of core policy ideas, which included Medicaid expansion, tax credits to be used in electronic health exchanges, insurance regulation, and an individual mandate. This basic set of policy ideas constituted the nucleus of all the versions of the ACA that emerged from the House and Senate committees. Nevertheless, the process of assembling the various majority coalitions in the legislative process was arduous and nearly collapsed at several stages because of disagreements over individual provisions and concerns over the fiscal scope of the bill. Unlike in the Clinton reform effort, the disagreements were over details, not the fundamental set of policy ideas. None of the Democratic lawmakers were seeking to exclude Medicaid expansion or substitute Medicare for All in place of tax credits in the marketplaces.

Political scientist Jacob Hacker, who both developed ideas and was engaged in the legislative process, compared the successful ACA effort with the failed Clinton attempt. He identified several factors associated with the ACA success. The economic crisis highlighted weaknesses in the insurance system and propelled health reform to a higher place on the agenda.

Democrats were able to coalesce around a set of policy ideas in the Massachusetts plan. There was a health reform opportunity in the first two years for both Presidents Clinton and Obama. Both made the issue a major priority and had solid Democratic majorities in the House and Senate. For President Obama there was a consensus on a single broad set of health reform policy ideas. This was missing with President Clinton's effort. Interest group support, or lack of strong opposition, is a critical element of legislative coalition building. Key interest groups were willing to support, or at least not oppose, the ACA because they perceived doing so to be to their benefit.[96]

The White House and congressional Democrats exhibited the willingness to both engage and bargain with interest groups on key issues. Health care providers, drug companies, and the insurance industry were all part of a two-year process of engagement and compromise, which both shaped some provisions within the ACA and helped secure legislative majorities at various stages of the process.[97]

As the process evolved, division among Democrats on key issues, such as the public option and abortion, required compromise to sustain the coalition. The Senate filibuster rule and other institutional constraints, such as the CBO score, forced reform advocates to abandon some provisions they believed important.

In 2010, health reform champions had succeeded where others had failed for decades. This was a cause for celebration, even when many of them wished for something more. They took advantage of a window of opportunity and did not fully appreciate at the time of the bill signing that the coming November election defeat meant there would not have been a second chance if they had failed in early 2010.

The passage of legislation is only the first step in policy success. In the next chapter we will examine the long and difficult process of transforming a signed bill into a set of policies with a real impact on people's lives.

Notes

1. Sheryl Gay Stolberg and Robert Pear, "Obama Signs Health Care Overhaul Bill, with a Flourish," *New York Times*, March 23, 2010, 4, www.nytimes.com/2010/03/24/health/policy/24health.html.

2. John Kingdon, *Agendas, Alternatives, and Public Policies*, 2nd ed. (New York: Harper Collins, 1995). This framework is mostly derived from the work of John Kingdon, but also see Paul A. Sabatier and Hank C. Jenkins-Smith, eds., *Policy Change and Learning: An Advocacy Coalition Approach* (Boulder, CO: Westview Press, 1993); Christopher M. Weible and Paul A. Sabatier, eds., *Theories of the Policy Process* (Boulder, CO: Westview Press, 2018).

3. "Kaiser Health Tracking Poll: Election 2008—Issue 4," Kaiser Family Foundation, October 2007, www.kff.org/other/poll-finding/kaiser-health-tracking-poll-election-2008-october-2.

4. John E. McDonough et al., "The Third Wave of Massachusetts Health Care Access Reform," *Health Affairs* 25, no. 6 (September 14, 2006): 420–431, www.healthaffairs.org/doi/pdf/10.1377/hlthaff.25.w420; "Massachusetts Health Care Reform Plan: An Update," Kaiser Commission on Medicaid and the Uninsured, June 2007, https://kaiserfamilyfoundation.files.wordpress.com/2013/01/7494-02.pdf.

5. John E. McDonough et al., "Massachusetts Health Reform Implementation: Major Progress and Future Challenges," *Health Affairs* 27, no. 64 (July–August 2008): 285–297, www.healthaffairs.org/doi/10.1377/hlthaff.27.4.w285.

6. Jonathan Gruber, "Taking Massachusetts National: An Incremental Approach to Universal Health Insurance," Brookings Institution, July 2008, www.brookings.edu/wp-content/uploads/2016/06/07_healthcare_gruber.pdf.

7. "Covering America Project Develops Proposals to Increase Health Insurance, but Finds Federal Money Tight," Robert Wood Johnson Foundation, November 1, 2006, www.rwjf.org/content/dam/farm/reports/program_results_reports/2006/rwjf16859.

8. Jason Furman, ed., *Who Has the Cure? Hamilton Project Ideas on Health Care* (Washington, DC: Brookings Institution, 2009).

9. James Morone, "Medicare for All," in *Covering America: Real Remedies for the Uninsured*, ed. Jack A. Meyer and Elliot Wicks (Reston, VA: Economic and Social Research Institute, 2002), 2:63–74.

10. James Brasfield, "The Politics of Ideas: Where Did the Public Option Come From and Where Is It Going?," *Journal of Health Politics, Policy and Law* 36, no. 3 (June 2011): 455–460.

11. Sheila R. Zedlewski, "Expanding the Employer-Provided Health Insurance System: Effects on Workers and Their Employers," Urban Institute, Report 91-3, 1991.

12. Sara R. Collins et al., "A Roadmap to Health Insurance for All: Principles for Reform," Commonwealth Fund, October 2007, https://www.commonwealthfund.org/publications/fund-reports/2007/oct/roadmap-health-insurance-all-principles-reform.

13. Shelia R. Zedlewski, Gregory P. Acs, and Colin W. Winterbottom, "Play-or-Pay Employer Mandates: Potential Effects," *Health Affairs* 11, no. 1 (spring 1992): 62–83.

14. Stuart M. Buter, "Evolving Beyond Traditional Employer-Sponsored Health Insurance," Hamilton Project, May 2007, www.hamiltonproject.org/assets/legacy

/files/downloads_and_links/Evolving_Beyond_Traditional_Employer-Sponsored_Health_Insurance.pdf.

15. "2008 Presidential Candidates: Health Care Issues Side-by-Side," Kaiser Family Foundation, September 29, 2008, www.kff.org/health-reform/2008-presidential-candidates-health-care-issues-side.

16. Much has been written about the ACA legislative process. Major comprehensive sources for this case study are Stuart Altman and David Shactman, *Power, Politics, and Universal Health Care: The Inside Story of a Century-Long Battle* (New York: Prometheus Books, 2011), pt. 4; John Cannan, "A Legislative History of the Affordable Care Act: How Legislative Procedure Shapes Legislative History," *Law Library Journal* 105, no. 2 (2013): 131–173; Jonathan Cohn, "How They Did It: The Inside Account of Health Reform's Triumph," *New Republic*, June 10, 2010, https://newrepublic.com/article/75077/how-they-did-it; Staff of the Washington Post, ed., *Landmark: The Inside Story of America's New Health-Care Law and What It Means for Us All* (New York: Public Affairs, Perseus Book Group, 2010); Lawrence Jacobs and Theda Skocpol, *Health Care Reform and American Politics: What Everyone Needs to Know*, 3rd. ed. (New York: Oxford University Press, 2016); John E. McDonough, *Inside National Health Reform* (Berkeley: University of California Press, 2011); Barbara Sinclair, *Unorthodox Lawmaking*, 5th ed. (Thousand Oaks, CA: Sage Publications, 2017), chap. 7.

17. Gruber, "Taking Massachusetts National."

18. Jonathan Alter, *The Promise: President Obama, Year One* (New York: Simon & Schuster, 2010), chap. 3.

19. Dana Milbank, "Why Obama Needs Rahm at the Top," *Washington Post*, February 21, 2010, A13.

20. Cohn, "How They Did It."

21. Cohn, "How They Did It"; Max Baucus, *Call to Action: Health Reform 2009*, Senate Finance Committee, November 12, 2008, www.finance.senate.gov/imo/media/doc/finalwhitepaper1.pdf.

22. Sherry A. Glied, Jacob Hartz, and Genessa Giorgi, "Consider It Done? The Likely Efficacy of Mandates for Health Insurance," *Health Affairs* 26, no. 6 (November–December 2007): 1612–1621.

23. Ways and Means Committee (Charles Rangel, chair), Education and Labor Committee (George Miller, chair), and Energy and Commerce Committee (Henry Waxman, chair); Robert Pear, "Democrats Agree on a Health Plan; Now Comes the Hard Part," *New York Times*, March 31, 2009, www.nytimes.com/2009/04/01/us/politics/01health.html.

24. Cannan, "A Legislative History of the Affordable Care Act," 137.

25. Timothy Jost, "The Public Option and Insurance Exchange in the House Bill," *Health Affairs Blog*, October 30, 2009, www.healthaffairs.org/do/10.1377/hblog20091030.002668/full; Robert Pear and David M. Herszenhorn, "House Health Plan Outlines Higher Taxes on Rich," *New York Times*, July 15, 2009, www.nytimes.com/2009/07/15/health/policy/15health.html.

26. Patrick O'Connor and Carrie Budoff Brown, "Breakthrough on House Health Bill," *Politico*, July 29, 2009, www.politico.com/story/2009/07/breakthrough-on-house-health-bill-025570.

27. Cannan, "A Legislative History of the Affordable Care Act," 141–142.

28. David M. Herszenhorn and Jackie Calmes, "Abortion Was at the Heart of Wrangling," *New York Times*, November 7, 2009, www.nytimes.com/2009/11/08/health/policy/08scene.html.

29. McDonough, *Inside National Health Reform*, 88; for a detailed description of their characteristics, see "House Democrats Who Voted Against the Health Care

Bill," *New York Times*, November 8, 2009, https://archive.nytimes.com/www.nytimes.com/interactive/2009/11/08/us/politics/1108-health-care-vote.html; by 2015, only a handful remained in Congress: Jonathan Allen, "Only 3 of 45 House Democrats Who Voted 'No' on Obamacare Are Still There," *Vox*, September 1, 2015, www.vox.com/2015/9/1/9239511/obamacare-no-votes-democrats (the forty-five voted against the ACA in final passage in March 2010; thirty-nine had voted against it in the initial House approval in November 2009).

30. A Blue Dog Democrat is a member of Congress who is moderate or more conservative in their voting record and political philosophy than other, more liberal Democrats in the House and Senate. For a short history of the group, see Paul Kane, "Blue Dog Democrats Celebrate a Milestone but Stand Alone on a Core Issue—Fiscal Restraint," *Washington Post*, February 19, 2020, www.washingtonpost.com/powerpost/blue-dog-democrats-celebrate-a-milestone-but-stand-alone-on-a-core-issue—fiscal-restraint/2020/02/19/456b6310-533d-11ea-9e47-59804be1dcfb_story.html. Timothy Jost, "HR 3962 (The Affordable Health Care for Americans Act)," *Health Affairs Blog*, October 30, 2009, www.healthaffairs.org/do/10.1377/hblog20091030.002649/full.

31. Draft bill introduced by the chairman that had not been previously introduced on the floor.

32. Robert Pear, "Senate Health Care Bill Faces Crucial First Vote," *New York Times*, November 20, 2009, www.nytimes.com/2009/11/20/health/policy/20health.html.

33. Timothy Jost, "The Senate Health Reform Bill: A First Look," *Health Affairs Blog*, November 20, 2009, www.healthaffairs.org/do/10.1377/hblog20091120.002940/full.

34. Jane Norman and John Reichard, "Senate Democrats Drop the Public Option to Woo Lieberman, and Liberals Howl," Commonwealth Fund, December 15, 2009, www.commonwealthfund.org/publications/newsletter-article/senate-democrats-drop-public-option-woo-lieberman-and-liberals-howl.

35. Sinclair, *Unorthodox Lawmaking*, 186.

36. Robert Pear, David M. Herszenhorn, and Carl Hulse, "Democrats Clinch a Deal on Health Bill," *New York Times*, December 21, 2009, www.nytimes.com/2009/12/20/health/policy/20health.html.

37. David M. Herszenhorn and Carl Hulse, "Hopes Dim, G.O.P. Still Vows to Fight Health Bill," *New York Times*, December 21, 2009, www.nytimes.com/2009/12/21/health/policy/21health.html.

38. Sinclair, *Unorthodox Lawmaking*, 194; Cannan, "A Legislative History of the Affordable Care Act," 158.

39. Ceci Connolly, "The Rescue: Obama's Last Chance," in *Landmark: The Inside Story of America's New Health-Care Law and What It Means for Us All*, ed. Staff of the Washington Post (New York: Public Affairs Press, 2010), chap. 4.

40. "Created by the Congressional Budget Act of 1974, reconciliation allows for expedited consideration of certain tax, spending, and debt limit legislation. In the Senate, reconciliation bills aren't subject to filibuster and the scope of amendments is limited, giving this process real advantages for enacting controversial budget and tax measures." Since the Reagan administration reconciliation has been used twenty-one times to pass major legislation with budget impact, including for parts of the ACA. For more details about reconciliation, see David Reich and Richard Kogan, "Introduction to Budget 'Reconciliation,'" Center on Budget and Policy Priorities, January 22, 2021, www.cbpp.org/sites/default/files/atoms/files/1-22-15bud.pdf.

41. Sheryl Gay Stolberg and David M. Herszenhorn, "Obama's Plan for Health Bill Largely Follows Senate Version," *New York Times*, February 23, 2010, www.nytimes.com/2010/02/23/health/policy/23health.html.

42. Sheryl Gay Stolberg, "Obama Calls for 'Up-or-Down' Vote on Health Care Bill," *New York Times*, March 3, 2010, www.nytimes.com/2010/03/04/health/policy/04health.html.

43. Jacobs and Skocpol, *Health Care Reform and American Politics*, 112–119; David M. Herszenhorn and Robert Pear, "Final Votes in Congress Cap Battle on Health Bill," *New York Times*, March 25, 2010, www.nytimes.com/2010/03/26/health/policy/26health.html.

44. "Summary of Coverage Provisions in the Patient Protection and Affordable Care Act," Kaiser Family Foundation, April 25, 2013, www.kff.org/health-reform/fact-sheet/summary-of-the-affordable-care-act.

45. Lawrence D. Brown and Michael S. Sparer, "Poor Program's Progress: The Unanticipated Politics of Medicaid Policy," *Health Affairs* 22, no. 1 (January–February 2003): 31–44; Colleen Grogan and Eric Patashnik, "Between Welfare Medicine and Mainstream Entitlement: Medicaid at the Political Crossroads," *Journal of Health Politics, Policy and Law* 28, no. 5 (October 2003): 821–858.

46. John Holahan, "Alternatives for Financing Medicaid Expansions in Health Reform," Kaiser Commission on Medicaid and the Uninsured, December 2009, www.kff.org/wp-content/uploads/2013/01/8029.pdf; Edwin Park, "Expanding Medicaid a Less Costly Way to Cover More Low-Income Uninsured Than Expanding Private Insurance," Center on Budget and Policy Priorities, June 26, 2008, www.cbpp.org/research/expanding-medicaid-a-less-costly-way-to-cover-more-low-income-uninsured-than-expanding.

47. McDonough, *Inside National Health Reform*, 140; the Senators were Richard Burr, Bob Corker, Tom Coburn, and John Cornyn.

48. Frank J. Thompson, *Medicaid Politics: Federalism, Policy Durability, and Health Reform* (Washington, DC: Georgetown University Press, 2012).

49. Alexander Hertel-Fernandez, Theda Skocpol, and Daniel Lynch, "Business Associations, Conservative Networks, and the Ongoing Republican War over Medicaid Expansion," *Journal of Health Politics, Policy and Law* 41, no. 2 (April 2016): 239–286; Ronald Brownstein, "How GOP Voters Are Getting in the Way of a Medicaid Rollback," *The Atlantic*, April 30, 2017, www.theatlantic.com/politics/archive/2017/04/medicaid-expansion-obamacare-repeal/522798.

50. Joshua Zeitz, "How the GOP Turned Against Medicaid," *Politico*, June 27, 2017, www.politico.com/magazine/story/2017/06/27/medicaid-obamacare-repeal-gop-215314; Eric M. Patashnik and Jonathan Oberlander, "After Defeat: Conservative Postenactment Opposition to the ACA in Historical-Institutional Perspective," *Journal of Health Politics, Policy and Law* 43, no. 4 (August 2018): 651–682.

51. McDonough, *Inside National Health Reform*, 148–152.

52. Mark Pauly and Bradley Herring, "Expanding Coverage via Tax Credits: Trade-offs and Outcomes," *Health Affairs* 20, no. 1 (January–February 2001): 9–26; Mark V. Pauly and John Goodman, "Tax Credits for Health Insurance and Medical Savings Accounts," *Health Affairs* 14, no. 1 (spring 1995): 125–139.

53. Jonathan Gruber, "Taking Massachusetts National: Incremental Universalism for the United States," in *Who Has the Cure? Hamilton Project Ideas on Health Care*, ed. Jason Furman (Washington, DC: Brookings Institution Press, 2008), 121–142; McDonough et al., "The Third Wave of Massachusetts Health Care Access Reform," 420–431.

54. "Insurance Regulation: Background, Overview, and Legislation in the 114th Congress," Congressional Research Service, December 30, 2016, www.everycrsreport.com/files/20161230_R44046_2dfabc18334d8621da4c6de712e7df9159bb6c94.pdf; Mila Kofman and Karen Pollitz, "Health Insurance Regulation by States and the Federal Government: A Review of Current Approaches and Proposals for Change,"

Georgetown University Health Policy Institute, April 2006, www.everycrsreport.com/files/20161230_R44046_2dfabc18334d8621da4c6de712e7df9159bb6c94.pdf.

55. Steven T. Dennis, "House Rules Chairwoman Takes Aim at Health Insurers," *Roll Call*, August 12, 2009, www.rollcall.com/2009/08/12/house-rules-chairwoman-takes-aim-at-health-insurers.

56. Ezra Klein, "Unpopular Mandate," *New Yorker*, June 25, 2012, www.newyorker.com/magazine/2012/06/25/unpopular-mandate.

57. McDonough, *Inside National Health Reform*, 127–129.

58. Sinclair, *Unorthodox Lawmaking*, 200.

59. McDonough, *Inside National Health Reform*, 126.

60. Ibid., 250.

61. "An Overview of the Medicare Part D Prescription Drug Benefit," Kaiser Family Foundation, October 12, 2018, www.kff.org/medicare/fact-sheet/an-overview-of-the-medicare-part-d-prescription-drug-benefit.

62. Cohn, "How They Did It."

63. "Cost Estimate of the Patient Protection and Affordable Care Act," Congressional Budget Office, November 20, 2009, www.cbo.gov/doc.cfm?index=10741.

64. "Cost Estimate of the Patient Protection and Affordable Care Act," Congressional Budget Office, December 19, 2009, www.cbo.gov/doc.cfm?index=10868.

65. Douglas W. Elmendorf, letter to the Honorable Nancy Pelosi estimating the spending and revenue effects of HR 4872, Congressional Budget Office, March 20, 2010, www.cbo.gov/sites/default/files/hr4872_0.pdf.

66. The Joint Committee on Taxation is a nonpartisan committee of the US Congress, originally established under the Revenue Act of 1926. It operates with an experienced professional staff of economists, attorneys, and accountants who assist members of the majority and minority parties in both houses of Congress on tax legislation. "Overview," Joint Committee on Taxation, www.jct.gov/about-us/overview.

67. Sara R. Collins, Karen Davis, Rachel Nuzum, Sheila D. Rustgi, Stephanie Mika, and Jennifer L. Nicholson, "The Comprehensive Congressional Health Reform Bills of 2009: A Look at Health Insurance, Delivery System, and Financing Provisions," The Commonwealth Fund, October 2009 (updated January 7, 2010), https://collections.nlm.nih.gov/catalog/nlm:nlmuid-101529520-pdf; Douglas W. Elmendorf, letter to the Honorable Nancy Pelosi estimating the spending and revenue effects of HR 4872, Congressional Budget Office, March 20, 2010, www.cbo.gov/sites/default/files/hr4872_0.pdf; "Estimated Revenue Effects of the Amendment in the Nature of a Substitute to H.R. 4872, the Reconciliation Act of 2010, as Amended, in Combination with the Revenue Effects of H.R. 3590, the Patient Protection and Affordable Care Act ('PPACA'), as Passed by the Senate, and Scheduled for Consideration by the House Committee on Rules on March 20, 2010," Joint Committee on Taxation, March 20, 2010, https://www.jct.gov/publications/2010/jcx-17-10.

68. Peter Orszag and Ezekiel Emanuel, "Health Care Reform and Cost Control," *New England Journal of Medicine* 363, no. 7 (August 12, 2010): 601–603.

69. David Cutler, Karen Davis, and Kristof Stremikis, "The Impact of Health Reform on Health System Spending," Issue Brief, Commonwealth Fund, May 2010, www.commonwealthfund.org/sites/default/files/documents/___media_files_publications_issue_brief_2010_may_1405_cutler_impact_hlt_reform_on_hlt_sys_spending_ib_v4.pdf; David Cutler, Karen Davis, and Kristof Stremikis, "Why Health Reform Will Bend the Cost Curve," Issue Brief, Commonwealth Fund, December 2009, www.commonwealthfund.org/publications/issue-briefs/2009/dec/why-health-reform-will-bend-cost-curve; Stephen Zuckerman, "What Are the Provisions in the New Law for Containing Costs and How Effective Will They Be?,"

Urban Institute, August 2010, www.urban.org/research/publication/what-are-provisions-new-law-containing-costs-and-how-effective-will-they-be.

70. Jonathan Oberlander, "Throwing Darts, Americans' Elusive Search for Health Cost Control," *Journal of Health Politics, Policy and Law* 36, no. 3 (June 2011): 478.

71. McDonough, *Inside National Health Reform*, 177.

72. David Cutler, "How Health Care Reform Must Bend the Cost Curve," *Health Affairs* 29, no. 6 (June 2010): 1131–1135.

73. See Chapter 8 for a more detailed discussion of cost containment.

74. Jacob Hacker, "The Case for Public Plan Choice in National Health Reform: Key to Cost Control and Quality Coverage," Berkeley Law, December 17, 2008, www.law.berkeley.edu/files/Hacker_final_to_post.pdf.

75. Baucus, *Call to Action*, 27.

76. Norman and Reichard, "Senate Democrats Drop the Public Option to Woo Lieberman."

77. Brasfield, "The Politics of Ideas."

78. Jacobs and Skocpol, *Health Care Reform and American Politics*, 79.

79. Paul Ginsberg, "Altering the Tax Treatment of Employment-Based Health Plans," *Milbank Memorial Fund Quarterly: Health and Society* 59, no. 2 (spring 1981): 224–255.

80. Jonathan Fuerbringer, "Bill Would Keep Benefits Tax-Free," *New York Times*, September 30, 1983, www.nytimes.com/1983/08/09/business/president-said-to-back-away-from-tax-on-fringe-benefits.html.

81. Jonathan Gruber and James Poterba, "Tax Subsidies to Employer-Provided Health Insurance," Working Paper 5147, National Bureau of Economic Research, June 1995, www.nber.org/papers/w5147; Jonathan Gruber, "A Win-Win Approach to Financing Health Care Reform," *New England Journal of Medicine* 361, no. 1 (July 2, 2009): 4–5.

82. David Herszenhorn and Robert Pear, "Congress Is Split on Effort to Tax Costly Health Plans," *New York Times*, October 12, 2009, www.nytimes.com/2009/10/13/health/policy/13plans.html.

83. Joseph White and Timothy Jost, "Cadillacs or Ambulances? The Senate Tax on 'Excessive' Benefits," *Health Affairs Blog*, December 3, 2009, http://healthaffairs.org/blog/2009/12/03/cadillacs-or-ambulances-the-senate-tax-on-excessive-benefits.

84. Paul Van de Water, "Excise Tax on Very High-Cost Health Plans Is a Sound Element of Health Reform," Center on Budget and Policy Priorities, November 10, 2009, www.cbpp.org/research/excise-tax-on-very-high-cost-health-plans-is-a-sound-element-of-health-reform.

85. James M. Brasfield, "The Cadillac Tax: The Affordable Care Act's Significant Brawl Among Friends" (paper presented at the American Political Science Association annual meeting, Philadelphia, Pennsylvania, September 2, 2016); Robert Pear and Steven Greenhouse, "Accord Reached on Insurance Tax for Costly Plans," *New York Times*, January 15, 2010, www.nytimes.com/2010/01/15/health/policy/15health.html.

86. Jon O. Shimabukuro, "Abortion: Judicial History and Legislative Response," Congressional Research Service, March 24, 2014, 15, https://fas.org/sgp/crs/misc/RL33467.pdf.

87. Cannan, "A Legislative History of the Affordable Care Act," 167–168.

88. Alina Salganicoff and Laurie Sobel, "Abortion Coverage in Marketplace Plans, 2015," Issue Brief, Kaiser Family Foundation, January 2015, https://files.kff.org/attachment/issue-brief-abortion-coverage-in-marketplace-plans-2015.

89. Staff of the Washington Post, *Landmark*, chap. 14.

90. Altman and Shactman, *Power, Politics, and Universal Health Care*, 69–70.
91. Jill Quadagno, "Right-Wing Conspiracy? Socialist Plot? The Origins of the Patient Protection and Affordable Care Act," *Journal of Health Politics, Policy and Law* 39, no. 1 (February 2014): 35–56.
92. McDonough, *Inside National Health Reform*, 131–133.
93. David K. Jones, Katharine W. V. Bradley, and Jonathan Oberlander, "Pascal's Wager: Health Insurance Exchanges, Obamacare, and the Republican Dilemma," *Journal of Health Politics, Policy and Law* 39, no. 1 (February 2014): 97–137.
94. Jost, "The Public Option and Insurance Exchange in the House Bill."
95. Michael Sparer, "Federalism and the Patient Protection and Affordable Care Act of 2010: The Founding Fathers Would Not Be Surprised," *Journal of Health Politics, Policy and Law* 36, no. 3 (June 2011): 461–468.
96. Jacob Hacker, "The Road to Somewhere: Why Health Reform Happened: Or, Why Political Scientists Who Write About Public Policy Shouldn't Assume They Know How to Shape It," *Perspectives on Politics* 8, no. 3 (September 2010): 861–876.
97. Jacobs and Skocpol, *Health Care Reform and American Politics*, 70–75; Cohn, "How They Did It."

3

The Hard Work Begins: ACA Implementation

Ideas are easy. Implementation is hard.

—Guy Kawasaki

Eleven months after President Lyndon Johnson signed the Medicare legislation, beneficiaries began to arrive at hospitals and physician offices for treatments covered by the new law. At the signing ceremony the president told aides he wanted every eligible beneficiary to be able to have necessary procedures covered by Medicare the day the law went into effect. Judith Feder's comprehensive study of Medicare implementation illustrated the various problems addressed to put the program in place.[1]

It would be nearly four years after the Affordable Care Act (ACA) was signed before most beneficiaries received coverage under Medicaid and the insurance exchanges. Forty-five years earlier Medicare implementation had not been simple, but it was accomplished in one year before widespread computerization. The rest of this chapter will assess the problems, successes, and implementation failures of the ACA.

Implementation Theory
In recent decades public policy scholars have sought to better understand the dynamics associated with the implementation of policies enacted by Congress. Jeffrey Pressman and Aaron Wildavsky emphasized the critical importance of implementation for ultimate success. They highlighted the difficulty of putting into place national legislation in a decentralized federal system.[2]

Daniel Mazmanian and Paul Sabatier argued that implementation looks different from the perspectives of the central authority, the bureaucrats on the ground, and the program beneficiaries.[3] Richard Matlan suggested that the best implementation strategy should be fashioned based on a classification of policy ambiguity and conflict.[4]

Each of these approaches offers useful perspectives on assessing policy implementation either prescriptively or retrospectively. As we attempt to understand the implementation of the Affordable Care Act, the conceptual framework suggested by Peter May will be offered as a lens for viewing the complex events surrounding the path from enactment to application.[5]

May's intellectual framework begins with *policy regimes*, which he defines as "governing arrangements for addressing policy problems."[6] He breaks regimes down into three key elements: institutional arrangements, interest alignments, and shared ideas.[7] Complex regimes are said to be "boundary spanning," which requires coordination across various subsystems. *Institutional arrangements* include the structures and authority relationships among those responsible for implementation. *Interest alignments* display the extent of continued support and opposition during and after policy enactment. *Shared ideas* represent the basic understanding of the core purpose of the policy.

As we examine the implementation of the ACA from its 2010 enactment until the end of 2016, we will employ these core concepts as a conceptual framework to understand what occurred and why.

May argues that stronger policy regimes foster greater policy legitimacy, durability, and coherence.[8] Legitimacy leads to acceptance of the ideas and institutional arrangements. Durability flows from sustained political commitments over time. Coherence renders a common sense of purpose that encourages cooperation.

As we explore the decade after the enactment of the ACA, we will ask these questions:

- Were the *institutional arrangements* integral to the policy regime appropriately designed?
- Did the *critical interests* sustain their support? Did opponents shift or mitigate their hostility?
- Were the core ideas coherent during the implementation?

This will guide our ultimate assessment of ACA implementation success.

The Affordable Care Act was a large and complex piece of legislation. Under the best of circumstances implementation was likely to be slow and fraught with difficulty. This chapter will discuss the most significant issues and problems associated with putting the statute into practice during the Barack Obama administration. Table 3.1 takes a first step in explaining the

Table 3.1 ACA Implementation Timeline

Year	Implementation	Major Events
2010	Implement the following: Dependent coverage until age twenty-six Tax credits for small-business insurance No preexisting conditions under nineteen Preventive services at no cost in all plans Temporary high-risk pool No lifetime limits on policies Review of plan premium increases	Several state attorneys general file suit against ACA Tea Party opposition to ACA intensifies GOP gains control of House in midterm election
2011	Start long-term care program Begin Part D coverage-gap discounts Restructure Medicare Advantage payments Impose new annual fees on drug manufacturing	Health and Human Services (HHS) begins to write ACA regulations CLASS Act part of ACA is dropped Appeals court rulings on attorney general suits are mixed HHS allows states to define essential benefits
2012	Reduce Medicare payments readmissions Quality Medicare Advantage bonuses	March: Supreme Court hears oral arguments June: Supreme Court decision is announced Fall: various ACA regulations are promulgated Obama wins reelection; Democrats retain Senate control
2013	Begin marketplace open enrollment Increase Medicaid primary care reimbursements Increase Medicare Part A tax Begin medical device excise tax Create co-op program Begin limit on Part D coverage gap	First state exchanges are approved More state exchanges are approved Final rules are issued on key topics Employer mandate is delayed a year Suit is filed challenging tax credits in federal exchange October: exchange website experiences significant issues Many beneficiaries receive letters canceling coverage Additional year is granted for grandfathered policies Supreme Court hears contraception mandate case Small Business Health Options Program exchanges are delayed a year
2014	Create small-business exchanges Prohibit preexisting conditions Guarantee issue and renewability Essential health benefit package Put risk adjustment programs into effect Begin tax credits in exchanges Begin Medicaid expansion Impose new fees on health insurance sector Begin individual mandate Establish Independent Payment Advisory Board	First enrollment period ends Additional Medicaid expansions occur Hobby Lobby case is decided Supreme Court hears *King v. Burwell* GOP gains Senate majority
2015	Begin employer mandate (more than 100 workers) ACA appeal bill is vetoed	Supreme Court decides *King v. Burwell* Additional states accept Medicaid expansion Appropriation bill deal delays some ACA taxes
2016	Begin penalty for employers (more than fifty employees) offering no insurance	
2018	Begin Cadillac tax	

labyrinth by providing a simple chronology, listing the major milestones as mandated in the law and summarizing the major events during the period.

2010: First Implementation Steps

The participants in the yearlong struggle for health reform barely had time to heal their wounds when it became evident the legislative fight to enact the ACA would be just the first of many battles. The ink was hardly dry on the president's signature when several state attorneys general filed lawsuits challenging the law.[9] The lawsuits contended the commerce clause did not extend federal authority to require a citizen to purchase insurance, making the individual mandate unconstitutional. They also argued the Medicaid expansion created an undue burden on states. While several district judges upheld the ACA, in December Judge Henry Hudson in Virginia found the individual mandate unconstitutional, although fourteen other federal judges had dismissed suits.[10] By the end of 2010, it was clear the legal battle would likely end in the Supreme Court.

The full implementation of the ACA was years in the future, but some popular provisions came into effect immediately in 2010. These included dependent coverage for adult children until age twenty-six, coverage without cost sharing for preventative services, health insurance tax credits for small businesses, state coverage of childless adults under Medicaid, a rebate for Medicare beneficiaries in the Part D coverage gap, a halt to rescissions, elimination of preexisting conditions for children, and a temporary high-risk pool for those with preexisting conditions.[11]

Nevertheless, as the fall 2010 congressional elections approached, public opinion on the ACA was sharply divided. For Democrats the fall election was devastating. Sixty-three House seats were lost, as were six Senate seats. The House of Representatives in the 112th Congress would have a Republican majority in 2011, with forty-nine more seats than the Democrats. In the 111th Congress, Democrats had held forty-eight House seats in districts won by John McCain in the 2008 election. Only twelve of those remained. One political science study concluded Democrats lost their majority because of health reform votes.[12] The partisan shift was also evident in the states where the number with unified Republican control of both the legislature and the governorship increased from eight to eighteen.[13]

The conservative groups opposed to the ACA launched a strong campaign to criticize the law with the intent to use it as a wedge in future elections and ultimately repeal it. At the forefront of this effort was the Heritage Foundation, a conservative think tank. In July 2010 it published a report arguing the ACA would be a huge fiscal burden for states and urging states to adopt a posture of noncooperation.[14] This became the blueprint for resistance in Republican-dominated states.

The Obama administration had immediately begun to organize itself to produce the dozens of regulations required by the ACA statute. This process was complicated by the need to involve the Department of Health and Human Services (HHS), the Internal Revenue Service (IRS), and the Labor Department in issuing interim and final regulations related to several provisions of the ACA, as well as various regulatory guidance documents. In late December Timothy Jost summarized these efforts and characterized 2010 as a "banner year" for rule making. Interim final regulations in several areas included coverage for adult children, elimination of preexisting conditions for children, and prohibition of unreasonable premium increases. Regulatory guidance notices, which are not legally binding, were also issued for several parts of the ACA.[15] Taken together these were important first steps in the implementation process.

2011: Life for the ACA Under Divided Government Begins

The new Republican majority in the House began to dominate the legislative agenda in early 2011. The ACA was still in its infancy, not yet a year old, and vulnerable to legislatively induced ailments. Very quickly implementation became even more difficult. Led by Speaker Paul Ryan, Republicans immediately attempted to pass legislation to repeal the ACA. A short repeal-only bill passed the House in early January by a 245–189 vote, with three Democrats joining all Republicans.[16] They also set in motion a process for committees to develop an alternative plan. In early February, Senate Republicans attempted to pass the House repeal, but Democrats defeated the motion 47–51.[17]

House leaders promised to use spending control to undercut full implementation in 2011 by ending appropriations for various elements of the ACA.[18] Later in 2011 they attempted to pass legislation reducing access to ACA abortion coverage.[19] They recognized these efforts were futile as long as Democrats still had a Senate majority and a president ready to wield a veto pen, but the action and rhetoric were part of the concerted effort to make opposition to the ACA a central part of the 2012 presidential election as the Republican nomination competition began.

Legal Challenges

The Republican endeavors to repeal the ACA in 2011 were symbolic, but the advancing constitutional challenges were a mortal threat to the law's survival. Multiple lawsuits with similar legal arguments had been filed in 2010 seeking to have the ACA declared unconstitutional. By early 2011 judicial decisions were emerging from the district courts, with the losing sides taking their arguments to the courts of appeals.[20]

The individual mandate was the major issue in most of the cases. In late June the Sixth Circuit Court of Appeals (Ohio) upheld a district court finding that the mandate was constitutional.[21] On August 12, in two Eleventh Circuit decisions emanating from Florida cases, a three-judge panel found the individual mandate unconstitutional but upheld Medicaid expansion.[22] On September 8, the Fourth Circuit (Virginia) upheld the ACA statute, citing the plaintiff's lack of standing.[23] In early November the District of Columbia Court of Appeals upheld the individual mandate.[24]

Thus, by late November ten district courts had ruled on cases challenging the constitutionality of the ACA. Seven had upheld the law, and three had not. Other cases had been dismissed for lack of standing. The appeals courts had ruled on eight of the cases with only one finding the individual mandate unconstitutional.[25]

Given the significance of the question and the split nature of the appeals courts decisions, it was no surprise the Supreme Court announced in mid-November that it would consider the legal challenge to the ACA and hear oral arguments in March 2012.[26] A decision was expected before the 2012 election.

State Resistance

The election had also changed the 2011 landscape in several states. Republicans gained six governorships and expanded their control of state legislatures. The American Legislative Exchange Council (ALEC) continued its efforts to encourage Republican-dominated state legislatures to pass its model bill "Freedom of Choice in Healthcare Act." Eight states had done so in 2010, and more followed in 2011. The primary focus of this action was the individual mandate, but ALEC proposed other strategies in its 2011 *State Legislators Guide*, such as rejecting grants and refusing to enforce consumer protections.[27] ALEC had for several years been a vehicle for introducing conservative policy ideas to state legislatures.[28] It became a major advocate for state action to hamper implementation of and repeal the ACA.

ALEC was urging Republican state legislators to push for nonbinding resolutions, statutes, or constitutional amendments seeking to nullify all or part of the ACA, with the individual mandate a special target. This effort began in 2010 and continued into 2011 and beyond.[29] These were also largely symbolic actions because states had no constitutional authority to take them.

For many states the critical focus of legislative and executive action in 2011 was their position on establishing health insurance exchanges. The law presumed each state would act to create its own exchange or default to a federal exchange. Most states initially applied for federal grants to defray the cost of setting up exchanges. As ALEC and other conservative voices advocated a resistance posture, some returned the grants and refused to move toward creating exchanges.[30] But partisanship was not the only factor.

Even some Democrat-dominated states decided exchange creation was administratively too difficult and opted to allow the federal exchange to function in their states. Other states were waiting for the Supreme Court to determine the constitutionality of the ACA, but by the end of 2011 most had determined whether or not to create their own exchanges.[31]

For the Obama administration this created additional pressure to establish the system of federal exchanges using state-generated data to have an electronic marketplace available for purchasing health insurance.[32] At the end of 2011 the marketplace rollout was still nearly two years in the future, but much work remained, and state cooperation was uneven.

Rule Making

Despite the legislative threats from Republicans in Congress, state resistance, and multiple legal challenges, in 2011 the Obama administration aggressively moved forward with the regulatory steps essential for ACA implementation. In today's world it is typical for Congress to leave many critical details to the administrative rule-making process. A statute as sprawling as the ACA required extensive regulations to guide federal and state officials, as well as nongovernmental institutions involved in implementation.

The rule-making process involved coordination among multiple federal agencies in drafting proposed rules with appropriate supporting evidence, evaluating public comment, and writing the revisions to create the final rules. In addition to final rules, in 2011 the Obama administration continued to issue interim rules and guidance notices, which did not have the force of law but offered guidelines for state and nongovernmental administrators. All of these tasks were not completed in 2011, but the Obama administration was deeply engaged in this process throughout the year as the starting point for an implementation to be finally achieved in 2014.

A comprehensive accounting of the ACA rule-making process in 2011 is not attempted here. In February the administration granted temporary waivers to four states allowing existing and noncompliant insurance plans to remain in place, but by May it had stopped taking these waiver applications.[33] Despite opposition from some church groups, rules requiring insurance plans to cover contraception were announced in August.[34] Rules covering employer responsibilities, "plain English" plan language, insurance company spending ratios, premium increase reviews, and accountable care organizations were issued during the year.[35]

In the face of opposition, the 1099 business reporting provision was repealed by statute modification.[36] By late in the year the administration determined the financial structure of the Community Living Assistance Services and Supports (CLASS) Act was unsustainable, and the program was dropped before it ever began.[37]

Two sets of 2011 rule-making endeavors are worth discussing in more detail. These relate to ACA essential health benefits requirements and health exchanges.

Essential Health Benefits

One of the key elements of the ACA is the requirement that insurance plans offer essential health benefits. The statute listed ten categories of services but left the precise definition of what constituted essential benefits to be defined by regulation. Since there was no previous legal definition of benefits to be covered by the thousands of insurance plans across the fifty states, this was potentially a very disruptive issue. Early in 2011 HHS asked the Institute of Medicine (IOM) to convene an expert panel to recommend a definition of essential health benefits.

The IOM report in October recommended a set of national standards.[38] However, the Obama administration chose a different course of action. In December it issued a "bulletin," not a formal rule, allowing states to determine their essential benefits list based on a benchmark plan selected from a menu of options with a default to the largest small-group plan in the state.[39]

Observers later noted that an expanded and rich set of benefits would increase the cost of insurance in the individual and small-business market. Narrow benefit lists would likely result in a contraction of benefits in those insurance markets within states with a broader set of benefits. Thus, the compromise was to defer to the states on the issue. The final rule was not issued until 2013 but closely followed the original bulletin.[40]

The health exchanges were both a critical element of the ACA and a large, complex new government organization. The ACA, as enacted, envisioned state-based exchanges with a default to the federal government operating an exchange within states. State refusal to initiate an exchange was not a path to excluding the ACA. In July 2011 HHS released proposed rules for establishing state exchanges.[41] The approach followed the Medicaid/Children's Health Insurance Program (CHIP) tradition of allowing a great deal of state flexibility. The July proposed rules also included the guidelines for reinsurance, risk corridors, and risk-adjustment features within the insurance market under the ACA. These mechanisms mitigate risk for insurance companies. The final rules would ultimately be released in March 2012.[42]

As 2011 ended, less than two years remained before the major elements of the ACA were to be operational. Implementation progress was substantial, but serious questions remained.

- Would the Supreme Court strike down parts of the ACA?
- Would most states opt to create their own exchanges or default to the federal exchange?

- Most importantly, would voters express dissatisfaction with the ACA in November 2012 by making Barack Obama a one-term President?

2012: The Supreme Court Decides and a President Is Reelected

An election year with an incumbent president tends to act as a huge magnet that pulls attention away from everything else in the political environment. Ezra Klein of the *Washington Post* contended shortly before the election, "A vote for Obama is a vote for the law to take effect and for 30 million Americans to get health insurance they won't get otherwise. A vote for Romney is a vote for the law—and its spending and its taxes—to be repealed. There are few elections in which the stakes are so clear."[43]

An analysis of polls taken during 2012 found health care was the second most important issue for voters. Voter views on the ACA were split evenly between those approving and those disapproving. Health as an issue was more important for Democrats than Republicans.[44] In November President Obama won a decisive victory with a 332–206 margin in the Electoral College, and the Democrats added to their Senate majority by two seats. The election sustained the life of the ACA for its full implementation in 2014.

ACA Court Victory

Earlier in 2012 the ACA survived an existential legal threat. As described above, in 2011 the constitutional challenges received divided opinions in the courts of appeals, and the Supreme Court accepted the question for resolution. The parties in the case began to file briefs in January, and by February dozens of amicus briefs had been filed on both sides. The Court devoted an extraordinary three days to hearings at the end of March. Of the four legal issues raised in the suits, the constitutionality of the individual mandate and the penalty on states for refusing to expand Medicaid were the critical issues at the hearings.[45] Both sides had reason for optimism, and it seemed likely the decision might be the product of a narrow majority.

On June 28 the Court announced its 5–4 decision in *National Federation of Independent Business (NFIB) v. Sebelius*. Chief Justice John Roberts, speaking for the majority, found the individual-mandate penalty for not purchasing an insurance plan was a tax and therefore within the power of Congress to enact. ACA supporters had feared this key provision would be found unconstitutional and was perhaps so integral to the whole law that the entire statutory edifice would come down. The second part of the decision was less favorable. By a 7–2 margin the Court found the ACA's Medicaid expansion mandate was too coercive and therefore allowed states to opt out if they did not agree to go forward.[46]

For most of the ACA architects, the individual mandate was an essential component. A RAND study estimated elimination of the mandate would significantly reduce insurance purchase, especially among young adults, and thus increase premiums in the individual market.[47] We will see in the next chapter that the mandate was effectively repealed in 2017. This did cause some coverage decline, but probably less than anticipated.[48]

State Actions
Many states, especially those with Republican control, had been waiting for the Supreme Court decision before committing to a state exchange and/or Medicaid expansion.[49] The decision created a flurry of activity in the states for the rest of 2012 as they understood the legal ground rules for the future.

Even before the Court decision, Republican governors in New Jersey and New Mexico vetoed legislation to create state exchanges, but Governor Andrew Cuomo in New York moved to establish a state exchange by executive order, when the legislature failed to pass the necessary legislation.[50] By the end of May, however, most states were still not ready to move forward with establishing their own exchanges.[51]

Soon after the Court decision, Republican governors Rick Perry in Texas and Rick Scott in Florida made high-profile decisions not to expand Medicaid or create exchanges in their states. Governors in South Carolina and Louisiana also announced they would not establish state exchanges.[52] In the wake of the June decision, some states moved forward with a process to establish exchanges while others decided to wait for the outcome of the November election, even though the Obama administration expected state decisions before the end of the year.[53]

States did move forward in the important but less visible area of defining essential health benefits. By November over forty states were in the process of establishing their own benchmarks rather than defaulting to the HHS standard. This action was distinct from establishing their own exchanges and much less politically visible.[54]

By the December deadline, only eighteen states had indicated they planned to move forward with their own exchanges. The federal government would be responsible for organizing and running the exchanges in the rest of the states.[55] Despite high-profile state decisions against expansion, many states were still not taking a public position. HHS indicated in a December 2012 guidance there was no deadline for a state to opt for Medicaid expansion and no link between expansion and whether or not the state created its own exchange.[56]

New Regulations
Meanwhile the Obama administration had continued preparations for the fall 2013 rollout of regulations to guide and constrain state actions during

the 2013–2014 full implementation of the ACA. In February HHS released a frequently asked questions guidance on essential health benefits as a follow-up to the December 2011 bulletin. This further defined the state flexibility and responsibility for defining essential health benefits in the state insurance market.[57]

In early March HHS published the final rule governing state health insurance exchanges. By this time, it was evident many states would opt out of creating their own exchanges, but the rule focused on the governance and operation of state exchanges. The door was left open for states to create their own exchanges in the future.[58] The next immediate step was the release of the final rules for reinsurance, risk adjustment, and risk corridors.[59]

A few days later a final rule governing Medicaid expansion was released. It addressed income definition, coordination with premium tax credits, and the procedures for processing applications.[60] In late April a technical guidance was issued with principles to be used in calculating medical loss ratios for insurance plans.[61]

After a summer lull, the end of 2012 saw a new round of rules and guidance documents issued.[62] In November an additional rule on essential health benefits further clarified this critical ACA element based on comments received earlier in the year.[63] In December a frequently asked questions document on Medicaid expansion addressed whether states could expand Medicaid with an income ceiling lower than 133 percent of the federal poverty level (FPL) and still receive full federal funding. The answer was no.[64] At the end of December, there was a notice of proposed rule making for the employer mandate.[65]

As 2012 ended, the ACA had survived two existential threats. The Supreme Court had affirmed the constitutionality of the individual mandate, and the voters had given President Obama another four years in office. A partisan divide in the states showed no signs of disappearing. Republican-led states were hardening their opposition to state exchanges and Medicaid expansion. In the next two years the insurance coverage expansion of the ACA with premium tax credits in the exchanges and Medicaid expansion in willing states promised to achieve the fundamental ACA goal to reduce the number of individuals and families living without health insurance coverage.

2013: Implementation and the Computer System Crashes

Full implementation of the ACA began in January 2014, but the success of the effort was shaped by events unfolding in 2013 as preparations and decisions were made in advance of the formal start for the insurance exchanges and Medicaid expansion. As we have seen, the ACA escaped the perils of 2012 and now faced additional hazards on the path to full implementation in January 2014.

Timothy Jost wrote of a "burst of regulatory activity" in early 2013. This included HHS rules for risk adjustment, reinsurance, risk corridors, cost-sharing reductions (CSRs), federal exchanges, and medical-loss ratios.[66] The IRS and Department of Labor also issued regulations in areas such as insurer rules and multiple-employer welfare arrangements.[67] Changes were proposed in the earlier final rule for the Small Business Health Options Program (SHOP) exchanges. The changes delayed employee choice in the SHOP exchanges for at least a year.[68] The final rule on exceptions for the individual mandate was issued at the end of June, with the final rule on implementing the individual mandate published in August by the IRS.[69]

Also in June a final rule was issued addressing contraceptive coverage and religious accommodation. This area was already the subject of lawsuits by religious and other organizations.[70] An early-July announcement from the Treasury Department indicated there would be a one-year moratorium on the employer shared-responsibility provision.[71] Doubts were expressed about the legal authority for the delay, but it seemed unlikely anyone would have standing to sue, and most employers with more than fifty employees already offered insurance.[72] Early July also saw the publication of a final set of rules defining the crucial coordination between Medicaid/CHIP and the exchanges.[73]

The ACA had been signed into to law three years earlier. Why the delay and sudden rush to finish regulations months before the January 2014 start for the exchanges? An inspector general's report identifies the slow pace of regulation writing as a contributing factor in October rollout problems.[74] The scope and complexity of the regulations were a factor, especially with multiple federal agencies responsible for crafting rules. Some of the more controversial elements of the rules were probably delayed until after the 2012 presidential election to avoid their becoming an issue.

Medicaid Expansion and State Actions

Despite the 2012 Supreme Court ruling, Medicaid remained the second critical piece to achieve the ACA goal of reducing the uninsured. Most states with Democratic governors and legislative majorities had already agreed to expand. But many states with mixed or Republican control waited to see if the ACA survived the Supreme Court and who won the 2012 election. Early February 2013 found a number of holdout states beginning to approve Medicaid expansion.[75] Republican governor Chris Christie in New Jersey stated he would accept federal funds for Medicaid expansion.[76] In August Republicans in Michigan accepted expansion.[77] Arkansas received authorization from HHS to expand Medicaid by purchasing private insurance for the poor.[78] Ohio's Republican governor did an end run around the legislature to establish expansion in the state.[79]

Pennsylvania's Republican governor was seeking a variation of the Arkansas approach as a basis for that state's expansion.[80] However, Governors Scott Walker of Wisconsin and Rick Perry of Texas had rejected expansion in their states.[81] In Florida, despite Governor Scott's support, the state Senate rejected Medicaid expansion in March.[82]

By the end of 2013 twenty-six states and the District of Columbia had accepted Medicaid expansion. Another five states were considering it, but nineteen continued to resist. The Obama administration hoped reluctant states would embrace expansion in the near future, when the benefits became clear to the voters and political leadership.

Court Actions

The *NFIB v. Sebelius* decision affirmed the individual mandate against constitutional claims and thus allowed the ACA to proceed toward full implementation. Other legal challenges continued to move through the lower courts in 2013. The most prominent surrounded what Timothy Jost called "the most controversial single issue in the Affordable Care Act": the regulatory requirement for group health plans to provide contraceptive coverage. The objections of religious organizations led to rule-making accommodation in which the insurance company or third-party administrator must pay for the service without charge to the organization. In June HHS published the final rule.[83]

The HHS rule only applied to nonprofit organizations, such as hospitals and schools. Hobby Lobby, a privately held business, argued the rule infringed on its religious freedom. The Hobby Lobby case was one of more than thirty cases filed by corporations asserting a religious objection to required contraceptive insurance coverage. Mixed rulings from appellate courts in 2013 almost guaranteed Supreme Court acceptance of a case.[84] By the end of November, the Supreme Court had accepted two for review. While not a direct threat to the core of the ACA, these cases raised First Amendment religious freedom issues as well as plaintiff contention concerning violation of the Religious Freedom Restoration Act of 1993 (RFRA). The government argued both applied to individuals, not corporations.[85] Thus, the ACA would return to the Supreme Court in 2014.

Exchange Rollout

The House version of the ACA envisioned a single national exchange in which eligible citizens would select a health insurance plan and receive a tax credit to offset most of the premium. However, it was the Senate version that was adopted in 2010, which provided for state exchanges with a federally operated exchange in the state as the default. As 2013 began, a majority of states opted to default to the federal exchange. In some cases, this was a sign of political opposition; others deemed the task of building an effective state exchange too daunting.

The schedule was for both state and federal exchanges to open on October 1, 2013, and individuals would have until December 14 to select a plan effective January 1, 2014. The open enrollment period continued until March for later plan effective dates. It was anticipated that several million people would sign up for a plan during the enrollment period. ACA champions hoped purchasing an insurance plan on the exchange would be as easy as buying a book on Amazon. Reality literally came crashing down on this hope.

Despite early warnings about technical problems, the healthcare.gov site opened to fanfare on October 1. The federal exchange was initially overwhelmed and kept crashing. Only a handful of individuals actually managed to purchase a plan on the first day and following days. The scope of the failure dismayed the Obama administration.[86] As millions of individuals visited the site, they were met with blank screens, information was incorrectly handled, and they were unable to actually purchase a policy.[87]

In late October the site crashed twice in one week. Both Marilyn Tavenner, head of the Centers for Medicare and Medicaid Services (CMS), and HHS secretary Kathleen Sebelius faced hard questions from House Republicans at hearings on the rollout.[88] The second crash occurred as Sebelius was testifying. In an attempt to save what was becoming a disaster threatening the whole ACA edifice, the Obama administration brought in assistance from tech companies, such as Google and Oracle, at the end of October in a belated effort to fix the technical problems.

At the same time, a four-year-old presidential promise was causing a political problem for the ACA. President Obama had famously said, "If you like your current coverage, you can keep it." This was a simplification, not a precise prediction. Under the ACA rules, many existing insurance plans did not meet the new standards. As the January 1, 2014, ACA effective date approached, insurance companies began to send out cancellation letters for legacy and noncompliant insurance policies.

Complaints escalated when people receiving cancellation letters realized they would often pay more for a new plan in 2014. Those eligible for tax credits in the exchanges would pay less for a better insurance plan. But those in the individual market and not eligible for tax credits would experience premium increases. Republicans and some Democrats in Congress sought to pass legislation "grandfathering" existing plans.

In mid-November, the Obama administration announced a one-year moratorium for legacy insurance plans if the policyholders wanted to retain them.[89] A subsequent Urban Institute study estimated there were 2.6 million cancellations of 2014 policies in 2013 but only about 500,000 such actions in 2014 for the 2015 policy year.[90]

The first announcement of exchange enrollment in mid-November was a discouraging 106,000, although 850,000 had registered but not yet selected a plan. By late November the concerted effort with the influx of outside expertise began to bring technical stability to the website. The deadline for an insurance policy to begin January was moved to just before Christmas. As expected, there was a last-minute surge, and total enrollment through the federal website grew to slightly over 1 million at the end of the first enrollment phase. Another million had signed up through the state exchanges.[91]

Some of the state exchanges had encountered similar technical problems. Hawaii, Maryland, and Oregon, among others, had technical problems with their websites and had to delay the start of enrollment.[92] Other states, such as California, New York, Kentucky, and Connecticut, had more trouble-free rollouts than the federal site.[93]

What went wrong? Why did healthcare.gov, after three years of lead time, fail so badly on the October 2013 rollout? There were several inquiries into the causes. The most comprehensive was the report of the HHS inspector general released in February 2016. The report identified several major factors contributing to the October breakdown. It characterized the fundamental problem as the absence of clear leadership. Examples of this leadership failure included

- decisionmaking delays;
- lack of project task clarity;
- inability to recognize the magnitude of problems as they emerged.

Additionally, HHS and CMS did not move quickly enough in the policy-setting phase and thus delayed the start of website development, made poor technical judgments, and did not appropriately manage contractors.[94] The problems with state exchanges led to resignations of managers in Hawaii, Minnesota, Oregon, and Maryland.[95] These states experienced many of the same types of problems as the federal exchange, but by year's end most had fixed the technical issues.

Once again, the ACA experienced a significant threat. Medicaid enrollment in states accepting expansion did not experience the problems initially faced by many of the exchanges. The troubled rollout provided fodder for ACA critics in and out of Congress. Democrats were worried as they looked forward to the 2014 midterm elections. But the technical problems were largely resolved by year's end. Two million had signed up for insurance plans in the exchanges, and more than 4 million were new Medicaid recipients. By Christmas the future of the ACA looked more promising for the year ahead than it had in October.

2014: Coverage Begins

Four years after enactment, 2014 was the decisive year for assessment of the Affordable Care Act. The major coverage provisions began on January 1.

By the end of 2013, the federal and state exchanges had mostly addressed critical technology problems to accommodate the rush to purchase plans for coverage to begin on the first of the year. Many states had not agreed to Medicaid expansion, but for the others enrollment was expected to be brisk. Without a Medicaid acceptance deadline, additional states might decide to expand in 2014. Legal challenges continued to progress through the federal court system. The midterm elections loomed as a voter assessment of the Obama administration's most visible domestic policy.

Key Measure: Reducing the Uninsured
After all the initial technical problems with both the federal and state exchange websites, how successful did the ACA look by early 2014? As the initial numbers were compiled, there was an audible sigh of relief within the Obama administration.[96] The enrollment report through January 31 showed 3.3 million people purchasing plans in the federal (1.9 million) and state (1.4 million) exchanges. The Congressional Budget Office (CBO) had originally projected a 2014 enrollment of 8 million but downgraded it to 6 million in early 2014.[97]

As the enrollment period continued into March, the exchange numbers improved. By the end of April, the final 2014 exchange enrollment had climbed to 8 million (5.4 million federal, 2.6 million state).[98] By June Medicaid enrollment in expansion states had grown 15.3 percent compared to 3.3 percent in states not expanding, compared to the 2013 baseline. Even this did not capture all Medicaid expansion since some states had waivers to begin earlier, and individual applications were often still pending.[99] Together the strategies for reducing the number of uninsured were clearly succeeding. By midyear there were 9.5 million fewer uninsured adults, which was a reduction from 20 percent to 15 percent.[100] On April 1 the individual mandate became effective, which was one incentive for the rush of new insurance plan purchases in February and March.

Rules and Administrative Actions Including Small Businesses
By 2014 most of the critical rule making to implement the ACA had been issued, but both the IRS and HHS had a few key pieces to complete. In February the IRS issued final rules for the employer-responsibility provision, whose effective date had been delayed until 2015. Large employers (over fifty full-time employees) were required offer insurance coverage or face a penalty. Since most already did, this provision was primarily intended to discourage employers from dropping coverage.[101] In March HHS promulgated the final rule on noncompliant policies by allowing states to permit renewal of grandfathered policies until October 2016. This extension was not expected to involve large numbers of existing policyholders.[102] Throughout the year both rules and other guidance documents continued to be issued, but most dealt with minor or technical issues.

As the enrollment period ended, the expected resignation of Kathleen Sebelius as secretary of HHS occurred. She was replaced by Sylvia Burwell, who had been head of the Office of Management and Budget and came to the position with a reputation as a strong manager.[103] The Obama administration hoped to trigger a new start for the ACA with new leadership at HHS.

Although payments in the risk-corridor programs for insurance plan participants were not due until 2015, the question of whether the program would be budget neutral arose in early 2014. If the fees collected in 2014 were not sufficient to fund obligations in 2015, this might cause some insurance companies to abandon future participation in the marketplaces, but the ACA did not specifically appropriate additional funds for this purpose.[104] The risk corridor provisions were similar to the successful approach with implementing Medicare Part D a decade earlier, but in 2014 it was not clear whether sufficient fees would be collected to fund the obligations to insurance companies.[105] It was a warning sign of a potential problem.

State Actions

Most state governments enthusiastic about Medicaid expansion had moved to establish it in 2013 or earlier. In 2014 Republican governors in Pennsylvania and Indiana led efforts to expand with conditions such as premiums or copayments or purchase of private insurance through Medicaid. New Hampshire took a similar path with a Democratic governor.[106] Maine's Democratic legislature passed expansion, but the bill was vetoed by the Independent governor.[107] Democratic governors in Virginia, Tennessee, and Missouri were unable to convince their Republican-dominated legislatures to enact expansion.[108] After the election Arkansas state government became more Republican and retreated from its initial expansion with private insurance.[109]

Several states with their own exchanges moved in 2014 to improve the technology to better serve the coming second enrollment period.[110] Others, such as Oregon and Nevada, opted to use the federal exchange for the 2015 enrollment period.[111] The pending midterm election cast a shadow on potential ACA moves in many states. Governors and legislators were waiting to see how voter sentiment was reflected in the midterm election, which mostly left the ACA status quo in place for many states.

The Courts

The highest-profile ACA legal issue in 2014 focused on the objections of some organizations to the mandate requiring employee group insurance to provide preventive women's health services, including contraception, as a covered benefit with no cost sharing. The HHS definition of the scope of services was based on recommendations sought from the Institute of Medicine. The Obama administration attempted to accommodate religious-based organizations, including universities and hospitals, which claimed the requirement violated their religious principles and therefore religious freedom.

In late 2013 the Supreme Court had agreed to hear the ACA cases arising from the requirement that all organizations with employer-sponsored insurance offer contraceptive coverage. Accommodations were offered for religious-owned institutions but not for for-profit corporations. The lead case was *Burwell v. Hobby Lobby Stores, Inc.*, in which the plaintiff contended that for-profit companies can make a religious-freedom claim against a provision of a law that owners believe violates their beliefs. The Court heard oral arguments in March. The claim was not constitutionally based but cited the 1993 Religious Freedom and Restoration Act.

At the end of June 2014, in a 5–4 decision, the Supreme Court upheld Hobby Lobby's claim. Justice Samuel Alito's majority opinion did not reject the right of Congress to enact the statutory mandate but upheld Hobby Lobby's claim of entitlement to an accommodation based on the RFRA. The decision appeared to have a narrow application to closely held corporations in which owners assert religious convictions.[112]

A few days later a 6–3 Court majority supported Wheaton College's argument in *Wheaton College v. Burwell* that the administration's accommodation for the religious college was still an undue burden. The college had to submit a form to its insurer confirming its eligibility for a waiver, and the insurance plan had to then pay for the services with no charge to the college or the employees. The college contended the accommodation still required it to participate in arranging for payment of contraceptive services.[113]

By August the Obama administration had issued new rules in response to both the *Hobby Lobby* and *Wheaton* decisions. With an interim final rule, it was proposed to have the organization only inform HHS of its religious objection. The government would then notify the insurer of its obligation to pay for the contraceptive services. In a proposed rule in response to the *Hobby Lobby* decision, there was an attempt to define a closely held corporation and apply an approach similar to the procedure for a religious organization to have the insurer pay for the services and deduct the cost from the fee the company owed to the insurance exchange.[114]

The *Hobby Lobby* and *Wheaton* decisions threatened access to contraceptive services for some women, but the scope of the decisions was limited and based on a statutory claim, not a constitutional argument. Another emerging case was also based on statutory interpretation but constituted a more existential threat to the ACA.

King v. Burwell: *The Next Substantial Legal Threat*

In the section of the ACA dealing with tax credits for the purchase of insurance, the Senate version authorized the credits in "exchanges established by states." This phrase apparently reflected the early Senate approach, which featured only state exchanges. Along the path to enactment the phrase was never modified, despite the understanding of the participants and other sections of the law, which established the federal exchange as an alternative for states.[115]

Opponents seized on this wording to challenge the IRS rule that authorized the payment of premium tax credits in both federal and state exchanges. The Sixth Circuit upheld the IRS rule, but a three-judge panel of the DC Circuit did not. In August the plaintiffs requested a Supreme Court review.[116] The full DC circuit court subsequently overturned the panel and upheld the IRS rule, but in early November, the Supreme Court granted certiorari on the *King v. Burwell* case, which made a 2015 decision on the issue likely.[117] If premium tax credits could only be issued in state exchanges, a major element of the ACA would be decimated, as insurance in the federal exchanges would become unaffordable for most, and several other provisions would be rendered meaningless.[118]

The 2014 Election
The 2010 midterm elections returned the Republican majority in the House of Representatives. Their uncompromising opposition made ACA legislative adjustments impossible. The Obama victory in 2012 was a four-year ACA reprieve from legislative repeal. But, once again, in 2014 the midterm elections were a setback for Democrats, as Republicans gained nine seats in the Senate to retake the majority and thirteen seats in the House to add to their majority. The presidential veto would prevent a legislative dismantling of the ACA, but its existence was still precarious in 2015 because Republicans might use their congressional dominance to threaten various ACA-related appropriations.

James Capretta, resident fellow at the American Enterprise Institute, anticipated that congressional Republicans would vote on ACA repeal in 2015 but that the effort would be unsuccessful. He observed there had been no GOP agreement on an alternative and suggested some ACA provisions might be repealed with support from Democrats.[119] David Blumenthal of the Commonwealth Fund agreed that repeal efforts would not succeed, but budget attacks from Congress could be expected.[120] The ACA succeeded in significantly reducing the number of uninsured in 2014 but still faced wide opposition at the beginning of 2015.

2015: President Obama Versus a Republican Congress with Supreme Court Referee

Among ACA supporters, cautious optimism permeated as 2015 began. After the tech problems in late 2013, the marketplaces rebounded for a solid first-year enrollment, and second-year sign-ups for 2015 continued to be robust. A few more states were expected to accept Medicaid expansion. The storm cloud of another critical Supreme Court case threatened, but legal scholars were betting the ACA would once again escape a ruinous decision. As long as President Obama held a veto pen, the Republican majorities in the House and Senate could not likely repeal the ACA.

Courts

Most lower courts had rejected the plaintiff's arguments in *King v. Burwell*, but the Supreme Court accepted jurisdiction in late 2014. Oral arguments were heard in late March with a decision expected by midsummer. This was a statutory interpretation case centering on four words in the ACA. In one section, amending the IRS code to authorize premium tax credits in the exchanges, it referenced exchanges "established by the state."[121] The plaintiffs argued a literal interpretation of the language meant these credits could only be offered in state-based exchanges, not in those that were federally facilitated.

ACA defenders contended those words were accidentally left in the statute from an earlier draft when the Senate Finance Committee staff believed all exchanges would be operated by the states. Various participants in the drafting of the ACA asserted all the evidence pointed to an assumption throughout the legislative process that tax credits would be available in both state and federal exchanges.[122]

The draconian consequences of an adverse Supreme Court decision were elaborated in various analytic studies, which concluded several million people would lose their tax credits and insurance plans.[123] The Obama administration indicated it had no plan B if the Court ruled against tax credits in federal exchanges, emphasizing to the Court the loss of insurance coverage if the ruling favored the plaintiffs. Some Republican legislators proposed stopgap measures, but none seemed likely to replace the tax credits permanently.[124]

In late June the Supreme Court, in a 6–3 decision, affirmed the legality of tax credits in federal as well as state exchanges in *King v. Burwell*. Speaking for the majority, Chief Justice Roberts, in upholding the IRS rule allowing tax credits in federally facilitated exchanges, stated the Court should "construe statutes, not isolated provisions."[125]

Legal scholar Rachel Sachs pointed out a significant feature of the legal reasoning in the majority opinion. The Court had long held the Chevron doctrine, which deferred to an administrative interpretation of ambiguous statute language. Rather, the majority opinion was based on an interpretation of the law itself, not an IRS judgment of an ambiguous phrase in the statute. For the ACA this meant a future administration could not come to an alternative interpretation.[126] The ACA had once again escaped an existential threat. The millions of citizens who had purchased insurance plans in federal exchanges with a tax credit were not in danger of finding their premiums unaffordable.

The ACA contraceptive coverage mandate was in 2015 again the subject of court cases reaching all the way to the Supreme Court. Contraceptive services were included in the required preventive services mandated by the ACA. Houses of worship and religious employers, such as hospitals and schools, were granted accommodations in regulations. The *Hobby Lobby* case expanded the type of organizations able to claim accommodations under the Religious Freedom Restoration Act.

Further legal challenges contended the accommodations were inadequate because the organization had to both inform the government and provide the name of its insurance plan, which would then be responsible for paying for the services. In June the Supreme Court issued an order blocking the rule until the issues raised could be further argued.[127]

By September cases in several appeals court circuits had rejected the plaintiff's argument of insufficient accommodations.[128] But the Eighth Circuit in late September ruled for the plaintiffs. With conflicting rulings from appeals courts, the Supreme Court unsurprisingly agreed in November to a hearing with a decision likely in 2016.[129]

States
In 2015 Medicaid expansion was again the most significant ACA decision facing some states. Indiana, Pennsylvania, and Alaska joined the ranks of states expanding Medicaid. Pennsylvania had in 2014 accepted expansion with a waiver under the Republican governor, but the newly elected Democratic governor, Tom Wolf, immediately moved for expansion without the previous conditions.[130] Indiana's conservative Republican governor, Mike Pence, negotiated a Medicaid Section 1115 waiver with HHS as a condition for the state's expansion. The waiver allowed the state to collect premiums up to 2 percent of income for those above the poverty line. Earlier Iowa and Michigan had been allowed similar exceptions for their expansion population.[131] Alaska's governor was a former Republican who ran as an Independent. When the legislature refused to enact his proposed Medicaid expansion legislation, he asserted his authority under state law to accept expansion.[132]

Kentucky's Democratic governor, Steve Beshar, had been a champion of Medicaid expansion and received national attention. In the November 2015 election he was succeeded by Republican Matt Bevin, who had campaigned against Medicaid expansion and was expected to at least impose significant restrictions, if not outright repeal expansion.[133] In Arkansas a Republican governor, Ira Hutchinson, replaced Democrat Mike Beebe. Hutchinson faced a battle with legislators who wished to scrap the entire expansion, which featured the purchase of private insurance for Medicaid recipients. Instead he sought to modify the program with a premium similar to that of the Indiana approach.[134]

Florida governor Scott and the legislature continued their three-way scrum over Medicaid expansion. The governor had been for and against expansion at various times over the previous year. The Senate endorsed expansion, but the House rejected it. Despite nearly a quarter of the state's population being uninsured, the plan to use expansion dollars to purchase insurance was not acceptable to the House majority.[135]

Vermont represented dissatisfaction with the ACA from the opposite perspective. The state had a liberal Medicaid program and in 2011 had set in motion plans for a future waiver to create a single-payer plan with universal coverage. But problems with the financial projections and administrative issues with the marketplace website led the governor to conclude that the proposed plan to substitute a government-run insurance system for the exchange was too expensive.[136]

As 2015 ended, a Medicaid expansion pattern had emerged reflecting partisan differences. Democratic states had eagerly accepted expansion. Republican-dominated states, especially in the South and West, had legislatively rejected it, but some governors had pushed for expansion with constraints, such as insurance-purchase or partial-premium-payment conditions. Republican governors in competitive states were often open to expansion. Rapid movement toward expansion in all remaining states did not appear imminent. Even within the Republican Party, differences between the governors responsible for providing services, and perhaps to be held accountable, and the GOP senators and representatives were becoming more pronounced.[137]

By late 2015 thirty states and the District of Columbia had expanded Medicaid. The Obama administration was working with others to find a path for expansion, perhaps with the assistance of a waiver for specific accommodations.

Congress and the President

January 2015 was the first time since 2006 that Republicans had both a Senate and a House majority. Republican legislators had been calling for repeal of the ACA. They now had a working majority in both chambers. Would the ACA survive?

The Republican leaders moved on two tracks. First, they continued to hold largely symbolic votes to repeal, now in the Senate as well as the House. Second, they would use the budget and appropriations process to weaken, if not eliminate, the ACA. President Obama would veto any bill repealing the ACA, and they did not have the votes to override a veto. But would the president avoid another government shutdown by agreeing to either repeal of or major changes in the ACA?

Early in the session, House Republicans voted to repeal the ACA, and direct House committees worked to develop an alternative.[138] In early February Senators Orrin Hatch and Richard Burr with Representative Fred

Upton announced a "blueprint" for an ACA alternative, which included treatment of expensive health plans as taxable income, repeal of mandates, smaller tax credits for purchasing insurance, and a capped allocation of Medicaid to the states.[139]

In March the House approved a budget plan including ACA repeal. The adopted Senate plan also included ACA repeal but differed in critical details.[140] House and Senate leaders then worked for months to reconcile the differences and develop spending bills ultimately acceptable to the White House as well. The Senate's attempt to follow the House in repeal of major parts of the ACA were stymied by a parliamentarian ruling that parts of the House approach could not be part of a reconciliation bill.[141]

After protracted negotiations and compromise, the Republican leaders in Congress and the Obama administration reached a series of compromises on the annual appropriations that did not seriously weaken the ACA.[142] There were delays and suspensions of some ACA-related taxes as part of the budget deal. The Cadillac tax was delayed until 2020, the medical device tax suspended until 2017, and the tax on health insurance plans suspended for one year.[143] Senator Marco Rubio continued his efforts to halt risk-corridor payments to insurers. As originally envisioned, money collected from insurance plans would garner more premium dollars than spent on claims, compensating companies that lost money. But losses exceeded money collected, thus payments needed to draw on federal funds. Rubio's provision blocked payment from federal funds for the risk corridors.[144]

In 2014 the House of Representatives voted to initiate a lawsuit against the Obama administration, contending the payment of cost-sharing reductions was made without appropriations. The CSRs were payments made to reduce deductibles and coinsurance for low-income beneficiaries who had purchased insurance in the marketplaces. House Republicans contended the reimbursements to insurance companies for these payments required appropriations. The administration disagreed. In September 2015 the district court judge ordered the case to trial, rejecting the administration's argument for dismissal.[145] The case would wind its way through the court system before a final settlement was reached in 2018.

Administrative Actions

In 2015 HHS issued a final major rule covering benefits and payment parameters. The November 2014 proposed rule was partially modified after the comment period. The rule addressed a number of topics related to essential health benefits, including prescription drug benefits and network adequacy.[146]

By March the 2015 regular enrollment period had ended, and HHS reported an uninsured rate drop of 35 percent since the 2013 beginning of open enrollment. The decline occurred in both expansion and nonexpansion states, with a greater decline in expansion states.[147] Final 2015 enrollment data in June showed 9.9 million enrolled in the marketplaces, with 7.2 million in federal exchanges and 2.7 million in the states. This exceeded the target enrollment of 9.1 million. Eighty-four percent of enrollees received tax credits to cover part of the premium.

A dark cloud in the 2015 marketplace was cooperatives' struggle to survive. This alternative to the public option was included in the Senate bill, and some hoped they would provide a nonprofit alternative insurance option in at least some markets. A federal audit found most were losing money, and their survival prospects were not good.[148]

In late 2015 *New York Times* columnist Paul Krugman concluded, "Obamacare is an imperfect system, but it's workable—and it is working."[149] This is an apt synopsis of the state of the Affordable Care Act at the beginning of the final year of the Obama presidency. Medicaid expansion grew, but many states still resisted. The marketplaces were working, with enrollment up, but concerns about stability and insurance company future participation had not disappeared. Gaps and anomalies existed and were difficult to adjust because of congressional resistance to any positive modifications. As the 2016 election approached, the fate of the ACA probably rested with the voters once again.

2016: The ACA's Last Year in the Obama Administration

The ACA was the signature legislative accomplishment of the Obama presidency, but in the eighth year of his term, it was still a work in progress. Legal challenges to its existence had been repelled, but the barrage of lawsuits continued. Additional Medicaid expansion was slow and incomplete. Marketplace technical problems had been overcome, but enrollment still did not achieve initial projections.

Our look at 2016 can be understood as summarizing developments in the sixth year since passage or, more realistically, in the third year of full implementation. As the Obama administration raced to administratively bolster weak points and routinize the coverage expansion, the November election cast a huge shadow. A victory for Democrats with continued control of Congress in the hands of Republicans would assure continuation of the ACA but render legislative modifications difficult. A new Republican president would probably be a death knell for the health law.

Courts

The "Groundhog Day" ACA legal issue was the contraceptive coverage requirement as it applied to religious organizations. The earlier ruling on the legality of the accommodations did not satisfy the Little Sisters of the Poor, which in *Zubik v. Burwell* sought further limits on the requirement to provide the service. The Supreme Court held oral arguments in late March.[150] This was unexpectedly followed by a request for supplemental briefs aimed at trying to find a common-ground compromise.[151] The May supplemental briefs offered encouragement that a remedy not involving notice to the government could be found. The Supreme Court referred the cases back to the lower courts to pursue the effort.[152] In July the Obama administration requested information from interested parties on possible alternative approaches to accommodation.[153]

In *House v. Burwell* the federal district court ruled against the administration in the cost-sharing reduction case. House Republicans contended in the suit that CSR payments had never been appropriated, and therefore money could not be spent for this purpose. The administration argued the ACA requires reimbursement to insurance companies for the funds spent to reduce cost sharing for eligible low-income individuals, and the statute treated these payments the same as premium tax credits.[154] As expected the administration appealed to the court of appeals. After the election the House sought to delay further consideration of the question until February 2017 in anticipation that the new administration might take a different approach.[155]

States
In January 2016, the new Democratic governor of Louisiana, John Bell Edwards, established Medicaid expansion by executive order. Once the expansion was in effect by midyear, more than 400,000 were enrolled.[156] Montana coverage authorized in 2015 became effective. Legislative attempts in Maine failed because of Governor Paul LePage's veto. Kentucky, with a new Republican governor, moved to close its state exchange and defer to the federal exchange but did not attempt to withdraw from Medicaid expansion, despite earlier campaign rhetoric.[157] Liberal advocates in Colorado pursued a ballot initiative to create a universal health insurance system, but voters rejected the proposal.[158] Alaska insurers were threatened with significant losses, and the state government responded by creating a reinsurance plan to preserve the marketplace.[159] By the end of 2016, several states, including Hawaii, Alaska, and Minnesota, had begun to explore using Section 1332 waivers to improve implementation of the ACA.[160] Beginning in 2017 these waivers could be utilized to institute significant changes to the ACA in the state, if approved by HHS.

Administrative Actions
As 2016 opened, one element of "Obamacare" was certain. This was the final year of the Obama administration. A new administration was about to assume responsibility for President Obama's signature program. The management structure of the program had moved beyond the early marketplace stumbles. This complex program required extensive regulations and guidance

documents. A few were still pending; others required modifications based on experience or adjustment to court decisions. In February HHS issued the annual benefits and payment parameters rule for 2017. In addition to topics such as risk corridors, rate review, and essential health benefits, this omnibus rule also included modifications of previous rules.[161] In April SHOP rules were modified.[162]

Marketplace enrollment had been maintained in 2015, the second year, and all indications were that 2016 would be similar. Nevertheless, there was legitimate concern about the stability of the exchanges because of risk pool uncertainty and the potential for insurance companies to respond by market withdrawal. At the beginning of the year, the CBO lowered its projection of the number of people purchasing insurance in the marketplace from 21 million to 13 million. The former figure was probably never realistic, but the revised projection pointed to continuing market problems.[163]

An Urban Institute survey published in May examined the marketplace from the consumer perspective and found enrollment growth slowing, with more enrollees seeing their plan as having less value because of increased cost sharing and unexpected bills.[164] From the insurance company perspective, many markets were too small, with too few healthy participants, to offset the cost of sicker individuals. As a result, several major companies began to withdraw from many local markets, leaving less competition and thus contributing to rising prices.[165]

In early June the administration announced a set of regulatory actions and guidance designed to stabilize the marketplaces. Major features included the following:[166]

- Further restrictions on short-term policies to prevent substitution for ACA-compliant policies[167]
- Clarification on noncompliant coverage, such as expected benefits coverage, including travel insurance, indemnity plans, and specific disease policies, which do not satisfy the individual mandate
- Improvements in the risk-adjustment program
- Better transitioning of marketplace consumers to Medicare at age sixty-five, thus removing higher-risk individuals from the pool
- Tightening restrictions on access outside the regular enrollment period to limit gaming the system by not purchasing insurance until it is necessary
- Upgrading the data-matching program to avoid loss of customers because of missing documents

The proposed rules on expected benefit plans and limited-duration policies were finalized in October, but some of the other issues were further postponed. Under the new rule, limited short-term policies could not exceed three months' coverage.[168] At year's end, another set of rules issued by HHS covered several employer issues.[169]

Despite the implementation challenges presented by a divided government and a Congress hostile to the ACA, the Obama administration continued to seek improvements to the law by expanding and modifying regulations governing both customers and insurance companies to strengthen the marketplaces for consumers and stabilize the marketplaces.

Congress and President
The Republican Congress in 2016 continued attempting repeal of the ACA, despite unlikely prospects for success. Using the reconciliation process the House and then the Senate passed partial repeals in late 2015, but with different language. The House approved the Senate version in early January 2016. But President Obama vetoed the bill two days later, and the veto override failed in February.[170]

Democrats had challenged Republican leaders in Congress to produce an alternative plan if they intended to continue ACA repeal efforts. In June House speaker Paul Ryan introduced an ACA alternative plan. It embodied many of the ideas discussed by conservative health policy advocates for several years. The plan included major changes to Medicare and Medicaid and repealed or modified many of the ACA provisions.[171] With President Obama still in the White House, there was zero chance the plan could become law in 2016; it was as much a campaign document as a legislative draft. The Ryan ACA alternative plan only began to be taken seriously after the 2016 election.

Presidential Election
Elections have consequences. Nate Silver, the FiveThirtyEight election oracle, projected Hillary Clinton to have a 71 percent chance of winning the 2016 election.[172] Donald Trump's probability of winning was about the same as that of an NFL kicker missing a thirty-five-yard field goal. Every fan will remember their favorite team missing such a kick. The narrow but clear Trump victory immediately changed the perception of the future of the ACA.

Senator Clinton proposed expanding and strengthening the ACA by adding a public option, paying 100 percent of Medicaid expansion for those below 138 percent of FPL, giving a tax credit for high out-of-pocket costs, and fixing the family glitch, which kept some moderate income families from receiving tax credits.[173] Donald Trump advocated repeal of the ACA combined with allowing individuals to deduct health insurance premiums from tax returns, turning Medicaid into a block grant, and allowing the sale of insurance across state lines.[174] The sharply different approaches to the ACA, together with continued Republican control of both houses of Congress, cast serious doubt on the future of the ACA in late 2016.

Immediately after the election, Republican congressional leaders promised swift action on a conservative agenda, with ACA repeal near the top of the list.[175] There were some mixed messages as President-elect Trump indicated parts of the ACA might be retained.[176] "Repeal and replace" began to morph into a "repeal and delay" strategy in which formal legislative repeal would take place, but implementation would be delayed during a transitional period.[177]

This sudden advent of caution about ACA repeal was likely the result of an abrupt realization that "repeal Obamacare" was no longer merely a campaign slogan. With Trump's election it was now a real possibility with the potential for negative consequences for both millions of Americans dependent on the ACA for health insurance and future election of the instigators of the repeal effort. The 115th Congress, beginning in January 2017, posed both an opportunity and a threat for ACA opponents.

Implementation, 2010–2016: Midterm Grade

Every student understands a midterm grade is a preview of the final course mark. This chapter has traced the path of the Affordable Care Act from its signing ceremony to the end of the Obama administration. Perhaps six years should be enough time to give a final grade, but for the most critical ACA elements, only three years had passed since these pieces were put in place. Since the assessment is incomplete, this conclusion is a midterm grade.

The ACA is a complex law with many disparate parts, but the fundamental goals were to expand the number of citizens with a health insurance plan that was affordable and comprehensive in its coverage and to reduce undue financial burdens on families because of insurance limits or failures to provide essential benefits.

The ACA employed three strategies to achieve these goals. One was the creation of health insurance exchanges to improve the efficacy of the nongroup market by offering a choice of plans that were affordable because of tax credits and covered standard benefits. The second was to regulate health insurance to eliminate common practices, such as limits on preexisting conditions and annual expenditures. The third policy idea was the expansion of Medicaid to include individuals whose income was below 138 percent of FPL.

In the statute there were various other provisions, such as attempts to reduce the rate of growth of health expenditures, strengthen employment-based insurance, especially for small employers, and mitigate high prescription drug cost sharing for some Medicare recipients. For our midterm grade we will assess only the main goals of expanded insurance coverage by use of the insurance exchanges with tax credits, insurance market regulation, and Medicaid expansion.

The Obama Self-Grade

In August 2016 President Obama wrote a special communication in the *Journal of the American Medical Association* providing his assessment of the ACA to date.[178] In it he argued 20 million more people had health insurance coverage, with the uninsured rate down from 16 percent in 2010 to 9 percent in 2015. He cited studies demonstrating improved access to care and enhanced financial security for the newly covered.

President Obama's essay did not offer a grade, but let's call it a B+, since he did note incomplete work to be done, such as further Medicaid expansion in the remaining nineteen states, the absence of competition among multiple plans in many markets, and the continued inability of some families to afford insurance.

The Critics' Grade

Critics from conservative-leaning think tanks were unconvinced that the ACA was successful on the sixth anniversary. James Capretta and Joseph Antos from the American Enterprise Institute argued that "poorly conceived regulations" had made the exchanges unstable and predicted collapse.[179] Robert Moffitt of the Heritage Foundation contended the ACA caused rising prices for both premiums and cost sharing because of broader coverage requirements and overly complex subsidy rules. Less insurance plan market competition contributed to narrower networks and fewer choices for consumers. He conceded that Medicaid expansion successfully brought coverage to millions but insisted the quality of care was substandard.[180]

It appears that conservative health policy analysts assigned a midterm grade of D or D– to the ACA. They wished to see it replaced with a system relying more on markets with minimal government regulation of insurance practices.

The Scholarly Grade

In August 2016 Jonathan Oberlander, a health policy scholar from the University of North Carolina, referred to the ACA as "transformative incrementalism." Taken as a whole, the ACA sought to both expand coverage and transform many elements of the health system, but the approach to coverage expansion in the short run was incremental and built on an existing fragmented system. Many depending on the existing individual market were not eligible for significant subsidies or Medicaid expansion. He suggested a significant number of individuals in fact eligible for subsidized marketplace or Medicaid coverage had not signed up, indicating a lack of sufficient outreach in many places.

Partisan division over the ACA rendered legislative adjustments impossible. Perhaps Oberlander might have been tempted to give an incomplete grade, but based on his analysis we will say his midterm was a B or B–, with additional work to be done. He concluded by arguing the future of the ACA was heavily dependent on the outcome of the 2016 election.[181]

Timothy Jost, a prominent health policy legal scholar, assessing the ACA in December 2016, identified the drastically reduced number and percentage of individuals lacking health insurance as the major achievement of the ACA. He also pointed to the availability of insurance for those with pre-existing conditions and the requirement to provide preventive tests without cost sharing as significant achievements. Jost seemed to award a midterm grade of B+ to A–, but we should also note this came in the shadow of the 2016 Republican victory with a concern of repeal in 2017.[182]

Adele Shartzer, Sharon Long, and Nathaniel Anderson, writing in *Health Affairs* in January 2016, reported a systematic study finding improvements in access and affordability between 2013 and 2015, but gaps remained especially for low-income adults.[183] Their study did not extend to 2016. We will not assume they assigned a midterm grade.

Exchange Politics by David Jones examines the response of several states to the choices around creating their own marketplaces or deferring to the federal exchange.[184] States were more reluctant than expected to create their own exchanges, especially after the *King* decision allowed the use of the federal marketplace. The technical challenges, especially for small states, were also a deterrent. Jones did not foresee a movement toward more state-based exchanges after 2016.

Daniel Beland, Philip Rocco, and Alex Waddan's 2016 book *Obamacare Wars* examines the frequently contentious relationship between states and the federal government over ACA implementation.[185] The authors observed less conflict over creation of exchanges than over Medicaid expansion, especially after the legal viability of the federal exchanges was confirmed. They expected the prospect of significant federal Medicaid funds to be a lure for accepting expansion in the future, especially when championed by Republican governors, even over skeptical state legislatures. Both books highlight the significance of federalism for the early implementation of the ACA and demonstrate the past and future importance of state political coalitions in its future success.

In late 2016 an Urban Institute study attributed significant reductions in the uninsured to the ACA. Of the 20 million additional people covered, the study attributed 18 million to the ACA and the rest to improved economic conditions. Reductions were substantial in both expansion (45 percent) and nonexpansion (29 percent) states.[186] An analysis by the Center on Budget and Policy Priorities found insurance gains across demographic groups and all states.[187] A Commonwealth Fund study concluded that about 76 percent of the decline in uninsured in the first enrollment period was attributable to the ACA.[188] These late-2016 studies credit the ACA with significant success in achieving the central goal of coverage expansion.

Why was the ACA still unpopular in 2016? Shortly before the election, Robert Blendon reviewed an aggregate of public opinion polls on health policy. He found health care to be a second-tier issue for voters, who were generally satisfied with the health care they received but concerned about the cost. A slight majority of the population was dissatisfied with the ACA, and 50 percent reported it had no direct effect on them.

However, a deeper dive into the basis for these views revealed a stark partisan divide. Democrats were overwhelmingly supportive and Republicans negative about the ACA. At the heart of the division was a philosophical disagreement over the proper role of government. Republicans seek a lesser role for government, and Democrats believe government should be more engaged. In 2016 public opinion on health care seemed to be shaped by the partisan divide, not a distinct view of health policy details. Even with the negative view of the ACA, only about one-third want a complete repeal without a replacement.[189]

As President Obama prepared to leave office, the midterm grade for his signature health legislation was probably a B for work completed but an incomplete because some of the critical goals of 2010 were as yet unrealized. The number of people gaining insurance through the marketplaces was significant but not as great as expected. Medicaid expansion was successful in those states adopting it, but many still had not. The ACA had survived serious legal challenges, but more remained. The expected boost in popularity once it was fully operational had not materialized, and public opinion appeared to be driven by a partisan lens in a country with a growing divide.

The new occupant of the White House in 2017 had campaigned against the ACA and had Republican majorities in the House and Senate, which had already voted multiple times for ACA repeal. At the end of 2016 it appeared possible there would never be a final grade for the ACA because it would end before one could be issued.

In the beginning of this section, we identified three questions derived from Peter May's conceptual framework for understanding program implementation:[190]

- Were the *institutional arrangements* integral to the policy regime appropriately designed?
- Did the *critical interests* sustain their support? Did opponents shift or mitigate their hostility?
- Were the core ideas coherent during the implementation?

The basic *institutional arrangements* were the marketplace exchanges, the federalism-based complex Medicaid system, and the statutory authority of the federal bureaucracy to issue governing rules applicable to states and insurance companies. The complex set of institutions rendered implementation administration more difficult. This provided an opportunity for resistance and legal challenges threatening the implementation. The Supreme Court decision to render Medicaid expansion optional made implementation of this critical element much more problematic than anticipated.

The *critical interests*, such as insurance plans and providers, remained supportive of the ACA during the initial rollout. However, partisan hostility in both Congress and many states hampered implementation and stimulated persistent negative citizen perception. The expanded access to health insurance coverage did not significantly increase public support for the law and thus encouraged continued opposition, including repeal attempts.

The ACA *core ideas* remained coherent, with tax credits serving to expand coverage, Medicaid providing coverage to a new group of poor beneficiaries, and insurance regulation increasing protections for consumers in both the individual and group markets. These policy ideas continued to be the basic building blocks for ACA accomplishments, but success was more limited than the aspirational goals of 2010.

Implementation is hard. The Obama administration's implementation of the ACA faced multiple obstacles. Some of the problems were self-inflicted, such as inadequate initial attention given to the technical aspects of the rollout. Others were caused by the unrelenting legal and political Republican opposition. But the ACA had survived and been reasonably successful in achieving basic goals by January 2017 as the Trump administration prepared to occupy the White House with a unified government denied President Obama since 2011.

The following chapter takes up the story of the ACA during the Trump administration.

Notes

1. Judith Feder, "Medicare Implementation and the Policy Process," *Journal of Health Politics, Policy and Law* 2, no. 2 (summer 1977): 173–189.

2. Jeffrey L. Pressman and Aaron B. Wildavsky, *Implementation: How Great Expectations in Washington Are Dashed in Oakland* (Berkeley: University of California Press, 1973).

3. Daniel Mazmanian and Paul Sabatier, *Implementation and Public Policy* (Glendale, IL: Scott, Foresman Publications, 1983); Kevin B. Smith and Christopher W. Larimer, *The Public Policy Theory Primer*, 3rd ed. (Boulder, CO: Westview Press, 2017).

4. Richard Matlan, "Synthesizing the Implementation Literature: The Ambiguity-Conflict Model of Policy Implementation," *Journal of Public Administration Research and Theory* 5 (1995): 145–174.

5. Peter J. May and Ashley E. Jochim, "Policy Regime Perspectives: Policies, Politics, and Governing," *Policy Studies Journal* 41, no. 3 (2013): 426–452.

6. Peter J. May, "Implementation Failures Revisited: Policy Regime Perspectives," *Public Policy and Administration* 30, no. 3–4 (2015): 280.

7. Ibid.
8. May and Jochim, "Policy Regime Perspectives," 430–434.
9. Kevin Sack, "Florida Suit Poses a Challenge to Health Care Law," *New York Times*, May 10, 2010, www.nytimes.com/2010/05/11/health/policy/11lawsuit.html; N. C. Aizenman, "Health-Care Overhaul Is Up Against Long Campaign Across U.S.," *Washington Post*, May 12, 2010, www.washingtonpost.com/wp-dyn/content/article/2010/05/11/AR2010051104719.html.
10. Timothy Jost, "Examining Judge Hudson's Decision on the Individual Mandate," *Health Affairs Blog*, December 14, 2010, www.healthaffairs.org/do/10.1377/hblog20101214.008304/full.
11. Amanda Cassidy, "Near Term Changes in Health Insurance," *Health Affairs Blog*, April 30, 2010, www.healthaffairs.org/do/10.1377/hpb20100430.189148/full.
12. Brendan Nyhan et al., "One Vote Out of Step? The Effects of Salient Roll Call Votes in the 2010 Election," *American Politics Research* 40, no. 5 (September 2012): 844–879.
13. Daniel Beland, Philip Rocco, and Alex Waddan, *Obamacare Wars: Federalism, State Politics, and the Affordable Care Act* (Lawrence: University of Kansas Press, 2016), 57.
14. Edmund F. Haislmaier and Brian C. Blasé, "Obamacare: Impact on States," Backgrounder No. 2433, Heritage Foundation, July 1, 2010, http://thf_media.s3.amazonaws.com/2010/pdf/bg2433.pdf; two earlier reports argued a negative impact on the economy and taxpayers. Karen A. Campbell, Guinevere Nell, and Paul L. Winfree, "Obamacare: Impact on the Economy," WebMemo No. 3022, Heritage Foundation, April 14, 2010, http://thf_media.s3.amazonaws.com/2010/pdf/wm3022.pdf; Curtis S. Dubay, "Obamacare: Impact on Taxpayers," Backgrounder 2402, Heritage Foundation, April 14, 2010, http://s3.amazonaws.com/thf_media/2010/pdf/bg_2402.pdf.
15. Timothy Jost, "Implementing Health Reform: Little-Noticed but Important Guidances," *Health Affairs Blog*, December 30, 2010, www.healthaffairs.org/do/10.1377/hblog20101230.008440/full.
16. David Herszenhorn, "House Votes for Repeal of Health Law in Symbolic Act," *New York Times*, January 18, 2011, www.nytimes.com/2011/01/20/health/policy/20cong.html; Robert Pear, "House Republicans Plan Their Own Health Bills," *New York Times*, January 20, 2011, www.nytimes.com/2011/01/21/health/policy/21health.html.
17. David Herszenhorn, "Senate Rejects Repeal of Healthcare Law," *New York Times*, February 3, 2011, www.nytimes.com/2011/02/03/health/policy/03congress.html.
18. Robert Pear, "GOP to Fight Health Law with Purse Strings," *New York Times*, November 6, 2010, www.nytimes.com/2010/11/07/health/policy/07health.html; Congress and the Affordable Care Act, Health Policy Brief, *Health Affairs*, February 25, 2011, www.healthaffairs.org/do/10.1377/hpb20110225.325684/full.
19. Jennifer Steinhauer, "House Passes Another Bill to Reduce Access to Abortions," *New York Times*, October 13, 2011, https://thecaucus.blogs.nytimes.com/2011/10/13/house-debates-bill-restricting-abortions.
20. Timothy Jost, "Health Reform: The Legal Fight Moves to the Next Level," *Health Affairs Blog*, May 10, 2011, www.healthaffairs.org/do/10.1377/hblog20110510.010820/full.
21. Timothy Jost, "In First Appellate Decision, a Significant Victory for the Affordable Care Act," *Health Affairs Blog*, June 30, 2011, www.healthaffairs.org/do/10.1377/hblog20110630.012115/full.
22. William M. Sage, "The Legal Battle over Health Reform: Analyzing the 11th Circuit Opinions," *Health Affairs Blog*, August 16, 2011, www.healthaffairs.org/do

/10.1377/hblog20110816.013092/full; Timothy Jost, "Appellate Court: Individual Mandate Falls but Rest of Affordable Care Act Survives," *Health Affairs Blog*, August 15, 2011, www.healthaffairs.org/do/10.1377/hblog20110815.013062/full.

23. William M. Sage, "Health Reform in the Fourth Circuit: The Politics Strike Back," *Health Affairs Blog*, September 9, 2011, www.healthaffairs.org/do/10.1377/hblog20110909.013539/full.

24. John Schwartz, "Health Law Survives Test in Court of Appeals," *New York Times*, November 8, 2011, www.nytimes.com/2011/11/09/health/policy/appeals-court-upholds-health-care-law.html.

25. "Legal Challenges to Health Reform," Health Policy Brief, *Health Affairs*, October 31, 2011, www.healthaffairs.org/do/10.1377/hpb20111031.546762.

26. Adam Liptak, "Justices to Hear Health Care Case as Race Heats Up," *New York Times*, November 14, 2011, www.nytimes.com/2011/11/15/us/supreme-court-to-hear-case-challenging-health-law.html; Adam Liptak, "Supreme Court to Hear Health Care Case in Late March," *New York Times*, December 19, 2011, www.nytimes.com/2011/11/15/us/supreme-court-to-hear-case-challenging-health-law.html.

27. Christie Herrera, "State Legislative Guide to Repealing Obamacare," American Legislative Exchange Council, November 2011, www.alec.org/publication/the-state-legislators-guide-to-repealing-obamacare.

28. Nancy Scola, "Exposing ALEC: How Conservative-Backed State Laws Are All Connected," *The Atlantic*, April 14, 2012, www.theatlantic.com/politics/archive/2012/04/exposing-alec-how-conservative-backed-state-laws-are-all-connected/255869.

29. Richard Cauchi, "State Laws and Actions Challenging Certain Health Reforms," National Conference of State Legislatures, December 17, 2018, www.ncsl.org/research/health/state-laws-and-actions-challenging-ppaca.aspx.

30. David K. Jones, Katharine W. V. Bradley, and Jonathan Oberlander, "Pascal's Wager: Health Insurance, Exchanges, Obamacare, and the Republican Dilemma," *Journal of Health Politics, Policy and Law* 39, no. 1 (February 2014): 97–137.

31. David K. Jones, *Exchange Politics: Opposing Obamacare in Battleground States* (New York: Oxford University Press, 2013), 8–12; Simon Haeder and David Weimer, "You Can't Make Me Do It: State Implementation of Insurance Exchanges Under the Affordable Care Act," in "The Health Care Crucible Post-Reform: Challenges for Public Administration," ed. Frank J. Thompson, special issue of *Public Administration Review* 73, no. S1 (September–October 2013): S24–S33.

32. Julie Appleby, "Feds Face Challenges in Launching U.S. Health Exchange," *Kaiser Health News*, December 19, 2011, https://khn.org/news/federal-health-insurance-exchanges-2014.

33. Robert Pear, "Health Law Waivers Draw Kudos, and Criticism," *New York Times*, March 19, 2011, www.nytimes.com/2011/03/20/health/policy/20health.html; Robert Pear, "Program Offering Waivers for Health Law Is Ending," *New York Times*, June 17, 2011, www.nytimes.com/2011/06/18/health/policy/18health.html.

34. Robert Pear, "Insurance Coverage for Contraception Is Required," *New York Times*, August 1, 2011, www.nytimes.com/2011/08/02/health/policy/02health.html.

35. Bruce Japsen, "Labor Department Seeks Tougher Rules on 'Multiple-Employer' Plans," *New York Times*, December 5, 2011, https://prescriptions.blogs.nytimes.com/2011/12/05/labor-department-seeks-tougher-rules-on-multiple-employer-plans; Robert Pear, "Proposal Would Aid Deciphering of Benefits," *New York Times*, August 17, 2011, www.nytimes.com/2011/08/18/us/18insure.html; Bruce Japsen, "Final Rules Set for Insurers on Spending Ratios," *New York Times*, December 12, 2011, https://prescriptions.blogs.nytimes.com/2011/12/12/final-rules-set-for-insurers-on-spending-ratios; Timothy Jost, "Health Reform Implementation:

Premium Increase Final Rule," *Health Affairs Blog*, May 20, 2011, www.healthaffairs.org/do/10.1377/hblog20110520.011071/full; Reed Abelson, "New Regulations Proposed for Accountable Care Organizations," *New York Times*, March 31, 2011, https://prescriptions.blogs.nytimes.com/2011/03/31/new-regulations-proposed-for-accountable-care-organizations.

36. Robb Mandelbaum, "1099 Repeal Passes Senate, Heads to White House," *New York Times*, April 5, 2011, https://boss.blogs.nytimes.com/2011/04/05/1099-repeal-passes-senate-heads-to-white-house.

37. Robert Pear, "Health Law to Be Revised by Ending a Program," *New York Times*, October 14, 2011, www.nytimes.com/2011/10/15/health/policy/15health.html.

38. Institute of Medicine, *Essential Health Benefits: Balancing Coverage and Cost* (Washington DC: National Academies Press, 2012), www.nap.edu/resource/13234/essentialhealthbenefitsreportbrief.pdf.

39. Nicholas Bagley and Helen Levy, "Essential Health Benefits and the Affordable Care Act: Law and Process," *Journal of Health Politics, Policy and Law* 39, no. 2 (April 2014): 445–449; Robert Pear, "Health Care Law Will Let States Tailor Benefits," *New York Times*, December 16, 2011, www.nytimes.com/2011/12/17/health/policy/health-care-law-to-allow-states-to-pick-benefits.html.

40. Bagley and Levy, "Essential Health Benefits and the Affordable Care Act," 447–449; Timothy Jost, "Implementing Health Reform: The Essential Health Benefits Final Rule," *Health Affairs Blog*, February 21, 2013, www.healthaffairs.org/do/10.1377/hblog20130221.028453/full.

41. Timothy Jost, "Implementing Health Reform: Health Insurance Exchanges," *Health Affairs Blog*, Parts 1, 2, 3, July 12 and 13, 2011, www.healthaffairs.org/do/10.1377/hblog20110712.012318/full/, www.healthaffairs.org/do/10.1377/hblog20110712.012332/full/, www.healthaffairs.org/do/10.1377/hblog20110713.012351/full/.

42. Timothy Jost, "Implementing Health Reform: A Final Rule on Health Insurance Exchanges," *Health Affairs Blog*, March 13, 2012, www.healthaffairs.org/do/10.1377/hblog20120313.017612/full.

43. Ezra Klein, "The Most Important Issue of This Election: Obamacare," *Washington Post*, October 26, 2012, www.washingtonpost.com/news/wonk/wp/2012/10/26/the-most-important-issue-of-this-election-health-reform.

44. Robert J. Blendon, John M. Benson, and Amanda Brulé, "Understanding Health Care in the 2012 Election," *New England Journal of Medicine* 367, no. 17 (October 25, 2012): 1658–1661.

45. Lincoln Caplan and Philip M. Boffey, "A Moment of Truth for Health Care Reform," *New York Times*, March 24, 2012, www.nytimes.com/2012/03/25/opinion/sunday/a-moment-of-truth-for-health-care-reform.html.

46. Adam Liptak, "Supreme Court Upholds Health Care Law, 5–4, in Victory for Obama," *New York Times*, June 28, 2012, www.nytimes.com/2012/06/29/us/supreme-court-lets-health-law-largely-stand.html; Timothy Jost, "The Affordable Care Act Largely Survives the Supreme Court's Scrutiny—but Barely," *Health Affairs* 31, no. 8 (August 2012): 1659–1662.

47. Christine Eibner and Evan Saltzman, "How Does the ACA Individual Mandate Affect Enrollment and Premiums in the Individual Insurance Market?," RAND Corporation, 2015, www.rand.org/pubs/research_briefs/RB9812z4.html.

48. Matthew Fiedler, "The ACA's Individual Mandate in Retrospect: What Did It Do and Where Do We Go from Here?," *Health Affairs* 39, no. 3 (March 2020): 429–435.

49. Robert Pear, "Many States Take a Wait-and-See Approach on New Insurance Exchanges," *New York Times*, February 27, 2012, www.nytimes.com/2012/02/27/health/policy/a-wait-and-see-approach-for-states-on-insurance-exchanges.html.

50. Kate Zernike, "Christie Vetoes Health Insurance Exchange," *New York Times*, May 10, 2012, www.nytimes.com/2012/05/11/nyregion/christie-vetoes-health-insurance-exchange-for-new-jersey.html.

51. Jason Millman and J. Lester Feder, "Few States Set for Health Exchanges," *Politico*, May 21, 2012, www.politico.com/story/2012/05/few-states-set-for-health-exchanges-076596.

52. Robert Pear, "Republican Governor of Florida Says State Won't Expand Medicaid," *New York Times*, July 2, 2012, www.nytimes.com/2012/07/03/us/politics/republican-governor-of-florida-says-state-wont-expand-medicaid.html; Manny Fernandez, "Perry Declares Texas' Rejection of Health Care Law 'Intrusions,'" *New York Times*, July 9, 2012, www.nytimes.com/2012/07/10/us/politics/perry-says-texas-rejects-health-law-intrusions.html.

53. Dylan Scott, "After Court Ruling, States Turn to Health Exchanges," *Governing*, June 28, 2012, www.governing.com/archive/gov-supreme-court-ruling-states-turn-to-health-exchanges.html.

54. Sonya Schwartz, "States Take a First Step on the Path to Essential Health Benefits," *Health Affairs Blog*, October 3, 2012, www.healthaffairs.org/do/10.1377/hblog20121003.023780/full.

55. Phil Galewitz, "Facing Deadline, Most States Say no to Running Their Own Insurance Exchanges," *Kaiser Health News*, December 14, 2012, https://khn.org/news/facing-deadline-most-states-say-no-to-running-their-own-insurance-exchanges; Robert Pear and Abby Goodnough, "States Decline to Set Up Exchanges for Insurance," *New York Times*, November 16, 2012, www.nytimes.com/2012/11/17/us/states-decline-to-set-up-exchanges-for-insurance.html.

56. "Frequently Asked Questions on Exchanges, Market Reforms, and Medicaid," Centers for Medicare and Medicaid Service, December 10, 2012, www.cms.gov/CCIIO/Resources/Files/Downloads/exchanges-faqs-12-10-2012.pdf.

57. Timothy Jost, "Implementing Health Reform: Essential Health Benefits and Medical Loss Ratios," *Health Affairs Blog*, February 18, 2012, www.healthaffairs.org/do/10.1377/hblog20120218.017083/full.

58. Timothy Jost, "Implementing Health Reform: Final Rule on Health Insurance Exchanges," *Health Affairs Blog*, March 13, 2012, www.healthaffairs.org/do/10.1377/hblog20120313.017612/full.

59. Timothy Jost, "Implementing Health Reform: The Reinsurance, Risk Adjustment, and Risk Corridor Final Rule," *Health Affairs Blog*, March 17, 2012, www.healthaffairs.org/do/10.1377/hblog20120317.017746/full.

60. Timothy Jost, "Implementing Health Reform: A Final Rule on Medicaid Eligibility," *Health Affairs Blog*, March 18, 2012, www.healthaffairs.org/do/10.1377/hblog20120318.017783/full.

61. Timothy Jost, "Implementing Health Reform: Amid Turbulence Federal Work Goes On," *Health Affairs Blog*, April 27, 2012, www.healthaffairs.org/do/10.1377/hblog20120427.019033/full.

62. Timothy Jost, "Implementing Health Reform: The Dam Bursts," *Health Affairs Blog*, November 21, 2012, www.healthaffairs.org/do/10.1377/hblog20121121.025539/full.

63. Timothy Jost, "Implementing Health Reform: Essential Health Benefits, Actuarial Value, and Accreditation," *Health Affairs Blog*, November 21, 2012, www.healthaffairs.org/do/10.1377/hblog20121121.025577/full.

64. Sarah Rosenbaum and Timothy Westmoreland, "The Administration's Decision on Partial Medicaid Implementation: True to the Law," *Health Affairs Blog*, December 19, 2012, www.healthaffairs.org/do/10.1377/hblog20121219.026372/full;

Timothy Jost, "Implementing Health Reform: No Partial Medicaid Expansion with 100 Percent Federal Match and Other Answers," *Health Affairs Blog*, December 11, 2012, www.healthaffairs.org/do/10.1377/hblog20121211.026154/full.

65. Timothy Jost, "Implementing Health Reform: The Employer Mandate," *Health Affairs Blog*, December 29, 2012, www.healthaffairs.org/do/10.1377/hblog20121229.026707/full.

66. See Cynthia Cox et al., "Explaining Health Care Reform: Risk Adjustment, Reinsurance, and Risk Corridors," Kaiser Family Foundation, August 17, 2016, www.kff.org/health-reform/issue-brief/explaining-health-care-reform-risk-adjustment-reinsurance-and-risk-corridors; Sarah Goodell, "Risk Corridors: Health Policy Brief," *Health Affairs*, June 26, 2014, www.healthaffairs.org/do/10.1377/hpb20140626.480933/full/healthpolicybrief_118.pdf. *Risk adjustment*: redistribution of funds from plans with lower-risk enrollees to those with higher risks to protect against adverse selection (permanent program); *reinsurance*: payments to plans enrolling higher-cost individuals to limit premium increases (temporary provision); *risk corridors*: limitation of losses and gains beyond a range to stabilize premiums in first years (temporary provision).

See "Explaining Health Care Reform: Medical Loss Ratio (MLR)," Kaiser Family Foundation, February 29, 2012, www.kff.org/health-reform/fact-sheet/explaining-health-care-reform-medical-loss-ratio-mlr. Limits the share of premium dollars insurers may spend on administration, marketing, and profits. Those failing to meet the standard must pay rebates to customers.

67. Timothy Jost, "Implementing Health Reform: A Burst of Regulatory Activity," *Health Affairs Blog*, March 1, 2013, www.healthaffairs.org/do/10.1377/hblog20130301.028787/full.

68. Timothy Jost, "Implementing Health Reform: Small Business Health Insurance Marketplace," *Health Affairs Blog*, May 31, 2013, www.healthaffairs.org/do/10.1377/hblog20130531.031721/full.

69. Timothy Jost, "Implementing Health Reform: Exemptions from the Individual Mandate," *Health Affairs Blog*, June 27, 2013, www.healthaffairs.org/do/10.1377/hblog20130627.032474/full; Timothy Jost, "Implementing Health Reform: Final IRS Individual Mandate Regulations," *Health Affairs Blog*, August 28, 2013, www.healthaffairs.org/do/10.1377/hblog20130828.033922/full.

70. Timothy Jost, "Implementing Health Reform: Contraceptive Coverage Final Regulations," *Health Affairs Blog*, June 29, 2013, www.healthaffairs.org/do/10.1377/hblog20130629.032622/full.

71. For an excellent summary of the employer responsibility provision, see "Employer Responsibility Under the Affordable Care Act," Kaiser Family Foundation, July 2, 2019, www.kff.org/infographic/employer-responsibility-under-the-affordable-care-act.

72. Timothy Jost, "Implementing Health Reform: A One-Year Employer Mandate Delay," *Health Affairs Blog*, July 3, 2013, www.healthaffairs.org/do/10.1377/hblog20130703.032734/full.

73. Timothy Jost, "Implementing Health Reform: Final Rule on Premium Tax Credit, Medicaid, and CHIP Eligibility Determinations (Part 1)," *Health Affairs Blog*, July 7, 2013, www.healthaffairs.org/do/10.1377/hblog20130707.032799/full.

74. "CMS Management of the Federal Marketplace," OEI-06-14-00350, Office of the Inspector General, Department of Health and Human Services, February 2016, https://oig.hhs.gov/oei/reports/oei-06-14-00350.pdf.

75. Abby Goodnough and Robert Pear, "Governors Fall Away in G.O.P. Opposition to More Medicaid," *New York Times*, February 21, 2013, www.nytimes.com/2013/02/22/us/politics/gop-governors-providing-a-lift-for-health-law.html.

76. Kate Zernike, "Christie Says He'll Take U.S. Money to Expand Medicaid," *New York Times*, February 26, 2013, www.nytimes.com/2013/02/27/nyregion/christie-backs-medicaid-help-from-federal-government.html.

77. Monica Davey, "Medicaid Expansion Battle in Michigan Ends in Passage," *New York Times*, August 27, 2013, www.nytimes.com/2013/08/28/us/medicaid-expansion-battle-in-michigan-ends-in-passage.html.

78. Robert Pear, "One State's Way to Bolster Health Coverage for the Poor," *New York Times*, September 27, 2013, www.nytimes.com/news/affordable-care-act/2013/09/27/one-states-way-to-boost-health-coverage-for-poor.

79. Trip Gabriel, "Medicaid Expansion Is Set for Ohioans," *New York Times*, October 21, 2013, www.nytimes.com/2013/10/22/us/medicaid-expansion-is-set-for-ohioans.html.

80. Abby Goodnough, "Pennsylvania Wants to Use Federal Funds to Cover Poor," *New York Times*, December 6, 2013, www.nytimes.com/2013/12/07/us/pennsylvania-wants-to-use-federal-funds-to-cover-poor.html.

81. Jonathan Martin, "Health Law Is Dividing Republican Governors," *New York Times*, November 21, 2013, www.nytimes.com/2013/11/22/us/politics/health-law-is-dividing-republican-governors.html.

82. Lizette Alvarez, "Medicaid Expansion Is Rejected in Florida," *New York Times*, March 11, 2013, www.nytimes.com/2013/03/12/us/politics/florida-senate-committee-rejects-medicaid-expansion.html.

83. Jost, "Implementing Health Reform: Contraceptive Coverage Final Regulations."

84. Timothy Jost, "Implementing Health Reform: Contraceptive Coverage Litigation Moves Toward the Supreme Court," *Health Affairs Blog*, July 29, 2013, www.healthaffairs.org/do/10.1377/hblog20130729.033399/full.

85. Marcia Boumil and Gregory D. Curfman, "The Contraceptive Mandate: Public Health Versus Religious Freedom," *Health Affairs Blog*, December 27, 2013, www.healthaffairs.org/do/10.1377/hblog20131227.036086/full.

86. Robert Pear, Sharon LaFraniere, and Ian Austen, "From Start, Signs of Trouble at Health Portal," *New York Times*, October 12, 2013, www.nytimes.com/2013/10/13/us/politics/from-the-start-signs-of-trouble-at-health-portal.html.

87. Nick Bilton, "In Debut, Affordable Care Site Gets Off to a Rocky Start," *New York Times*, October 1, 2013, www.nytimes.com/news/affordable-care-act/2013/10/01/in-debut-affordable-care-web-site-baffles-many-users.

88. Sheryl Gay Stolberg, "Health Site Puts Agency and Leader in Hot Seat," *New York Times*, October 2013, www.nytimes.com/2013/10/29/us/politics/health-site-puts-agency-and-leader-in-hot-seat.html.

89. Timothy Jost, "Implementing Health Reform: An 'Administrative Fix' for Policy Cancellations," *Health Affairs Blog*, November 15, 2013, www.healthaffairs.org/do/10.1377/hblog20131115.035374/full.

90. Lisa Clemans-Cope and Nathaniel Anderson, "QuickTake: Health Insurance Policy Cancellations Were Uncommon in 2014," Urban Institute, March 12, 2015, http://hrms.urban.org/quicktakes/Health-Insurance-Policy-Cancellations-Were-Uncommon-in-2014.html.

91. Sheryl Gay Stolberg and Susanne Craig, "Only 106,000 Pick Health Insurance Plans in First Month," *New York Times*, November 13, 2013, www.nytimes.com/2013/11/14/us/health-law-enrollment-figures-far-lower-than-initial-estimates.html.

92. "Healthcare.gov Website Rollout," Ballotpedia, https://ballotpedia.org/Healthcare.gov_website_rollout.

93. Robert Pear and Abby Goodnough, "Uninsured Find More Success via Health Exchanges Run by States," *New York Times*, October 8, 2013, www.nytimes

.com/2013/10/09/us/politics/uninsured-find-more-success-via-health-exchanges-run-by-states.html; Paul Krugman, "California, Here We Come," *New York Times*, November 24, 2013, www.nytimes.com/2013/11/25/opinion/krugman-california-here-we-come.html.

94. "CMS Management of the Federal Marketplace," Office of the Inspector General.

95. Ian Lovett, "Head of Hawaii Insurance Exchange Steps Down," *New York Times*, November 22, 2013, www.nytimes.com/news/affordable-care-act/2013/11/22/head-of-hawaii-insurance-exchange-steps-down; Steven Yaccino, "Minnesota Becomes Fourth State to Lose Chief of Exchange," *New York Times*, December 18, 2013, www.nytimes.com/2013/12/19/us/fourth-state-abruptly-loses-chief-of-exchange.html.

96. Michael D. Shear and Reed Abelson, "Over 1 Million Added to Rolls of Health Plan," *New York Times*, February 12, 2014, www.nytimes.com/2014/02/13/us/over-1-million-added-to-rolls-of-health-plan.html.

97. Timothy Jost, "Implementing Health Reform: A January Exchange Enrollment Report," *Health Affairs Blog*, February 13, 2014, www.healthaffairs.org/do/10.1377/hblog20140213.037208/full.

98. Timothy Jost, "Implementing Health Reform: A Summary Health Insurance Marketplace Enrollment Report," *Health Affairs Blog*, May 1, 2014, www.healthaffairs.org/do/10.1377/hblog20140501.038822/full; "Health Insurance Marketplace: Summary Enrollment Report for the Initial Annual Open Enrollment Period," Office of the Assistant Secretary for Planning and Evaluation, May 1, 2014, www.healthaffairs.org/do/10.1377/hblog20140501.038822/full.

99. Timothy Jost, "Implementing Health Reform: Medicaid and CHIP Enrollment; Data Verification (Updated)," *Health Affairs Blog*, June 5, 2014, www.healthaffairs.org/do/10.1377/hblog20140605.039412/full.

100. Sara R. Collins, Petra W. Rasmussen, and Michelle M. Doty, "Gaining Ground: Americans' Health Insurance Coverage and Access to Care After the Affordable Care Act's First Open Enrollment Period," Commonwealth Fund, July 10, 2014, www.commonwealthfund.org/publications/issue-briefs/2014/jul/gaining-ground-americans-health-insurance-coverage-and-access.

101. Timothy Jost, "Implementing Health Reform: The Employer Responsibility Final Rule (Part 1)," *Health Affairs Blog*, February 11, 2014, www.healthaffairs.org/do/10.1377/hblog20140211.037118/full.

102. Timothy Jost, "Implementing Health Reform: Allowing Noncompliant Policies; Benefits and Payment Parameters Rule (Part 1)," *Health Affairs Blog*, March 7, 2014, www.healthaffairs.org/do/10.1377/hblog20140307.037663/full.

103. Michael D. Shear, "Sebelius Resigns After Troubles over Health Site," *New York Times*, April 10, 2014, www.nytimes.com/2014/04/11/us/politics/sebelius-resigning-as-health-secretary.html.

104. Scott Harrington, "Risk Corridors and Budget Neutrality," *Health Affairs Blog*, May 14, 2014, www.healthaffairs.org/do/10.1377/hblog20140514.038975/full; Timothy Jost, "Implementing Health Reform: Employer Orientation Periods; Risk Corridor Payments," *Health Affairs Blog*, June 21, 2014, www.healthaffairs.org/do/10.1377/hblog20140621.039733/full.

105. For a concise summary of the risk corridor programs, see "Risk Corridors: The ACA's Premium Stabilization Programs Encourage Insurers to Participate in Exchanges by Eliminating Unpredictability Around New Enrollees," Policy Brief, *Health Affairs*, June 26, 2014, www.healthaffairs.org/do/10.1377/hpb20140626.480933/full/healthpolicybrief_118.pdf.

106. Abby Goodnough, "Pennsylvania to Purchase Private Care for Its Poor," *New York Times*, August 28, 2014, www.nytimes.com/2014/08/29/us/pennsylvania

-to-purchase-private-care-for-its-poor.html; Abby Goodnough, "Indiana Seeks More Coverage for Poor, but Many Would Pay," *New York Times*, May 15, 2014, www.nytimes.com/2014/05/16/us/indiana-seeks-more-coverage-for-poor-but-many-would-pay.html; Jess Bidgood, "New Hampshire Senate Votes to Expand Health Insurance Coverage," *New York Times*, March 6, 2014, www.nytimes.com/2014/03/07/us/new-hampshire-senate-votes-to-expand-health-insurance-coverage.html.

107. Josh Barro and Margot Sanger-Katz, "Election Will Leave Medicaid Policies Largely Unchanged," *New York Times*, November 4, 2014, www.nytimes.com/2014/11/05/upshot/election-results-2014-the-effect-on-medicaid-expansion.html.

108. Trip Gabriel, "After First Plan Is Blocked, Virginia Governor Reduces Medicaid Expansion Goals," *New York Times*, September 8, 2014, www.nytimes.com/2014/09/09/us/after-first-plan-is-blocked-virginia-governor-terry-mcauliffe-reduces-medicaid-expansion-goals.html; Abby Goodnough, "With Hospitals Under Stress, Tennessee's Governor Pursues Medicaid Expansion," *New York Times*, December 15, 2014, www.nytimes.com/2014/12/16/us/with-hospitals-under-stress-tennessees-governor-pursues-medicaid-expansion.html.

109. Margot Sanger-Katz, "Election Results Endanger Innovative Arkansas Medicaid Plan," *New York Times*, November 6, 2014, www.nytimes.com/2014/11/07/upshot/elections-put-future-of-innovative-arkansas-medicaid-plan-in-doubt.html.

110. Abby Goodnough, "States Race to Improve Health Insurance Exchanges," *New York Times*, November 11, 2014, www.nytimes.com/2014/11/12/us/obamacare-states-exchanges-for-health-insurance-facing-a-new-enrollment-period-try-to-fix-flaws.html.

111. Robert Pear and Kirk Johnson, "Oregon Panel Recommends Switch to Federal Health Exchange," *New York Times*, April 24, 2010, www.nytimes.com/2014/04/25/us/politics/oregon-considers-handing-troubled-insurance-exchange-to-us.html.

112. John Kraemer, "The Supreme Court and the Contraception Mandate: A Temporary Setback for Contraception Coverage," *Health Affairs Blog*, July 1, 2014, www.healthaffairs.org/do/10.1377/hblog20140701.039859/full; Timothy Jost, "Implementing Health Reform: The Supreme Court Rules on Contraception Coverage (Updated)," *Health Affairs Blog*, June 30, 2014, www.healthaffairs.org/do/10.1377/hblog20140630.039846/full.

113. Robert Pear, "A Two-Page Form Spawns a Contraceptive Showdown," *New York Times*, July 12, 2014, www.nytimes.com/2014/07/13/us/a-two-page-form-spawns-a-contraceptive-showdown.html.

114. Timothy Jost, "Implementing Health Reform: New Accommodations for Employers on Contraceptive Coverage," *Health Affairs Blog*, August 22, 2014, www.healthaffairs.org/do/10.1377/hblog20140822.040980/full; Michael D. Shear, "Administration Proposes New Health Rules Addressing Religious Objections," *New York Times*, August 22, 2014, www.nytimes.com/2014/08/23/us/politics/administration-to-propose-new-health-rules-addressing-religious-objections.html.

115. Timothy Jost, "Implementing Health Reform: Appellate Decisions Split on Tax Credits in ACA Federal Exchange," *Health Affairs Blog*, July 23, 2014, www.healthaffairs.org/do/10.1377/hblog20140723.040310/full.

116. Timothy Jost, "Implementing Health Reform: King Plaintiffs Ask for Supreme Court Review," *Health Affairs Blog*, August 1, 2014, www.healthaffairs.org/do/10.1377/hblog20140801.040540/full.

117. Timothy Jost, "Implementing Health Reform: Supreme Court Will Review Tax Credits in Federal Exchanges," *Health Affairs Blog*, November 7, 2014, www.healthaffairs.org/do/10.1377/hblog20141107.042577/full.

118. David Blumenthal and Sara R. Collins, "The Supreme Court Decides to Hear King vs. Burwell: What Are the Implications?," *Commonwealth Fund Blog*, Novem-

ber 7, 2014, www.commonwealthfund.org/blog/2014/supreme-court-decides-hear-king-v-burwell-what-are-implications.

119. James C. Capretta, "Health Care Policy After the Mid-Term Elections," *Health Affairs Blog*, November 7, 2014, www.healthaffairs.org/do/10.1377/hblog20141107.042560/full.

120. David Blumenthal and David Squires, "2014: The Health Care Year in Review," *Commonwealth Fund Blog*, December 23, 2014, www.commonwealthfund.org/blog/2014/2014-health-care-year-review.

121. William M. Sage, "Four Words or 17 Syllables: Predicting King v. Burwell in Haiku," *Health Affairs Blog*, March 5, 2015, www.healthaffairs.org/do/10.1377/hblog20150305.045277/full.

122. Robert Pear, "Four Words That Imperil Health Care Law Were All a Mistake, Writers Now Say," *New York Times*, May 25, 2015, www.nytimes.com/2015/05/26/us/politics/contested-words-in-affordable-care-act-may-have-been-left-by-mistake.html.

123. Evan Saltzman and Christine Eibner, "The Effect of Eliminating the Affordable Care Act's Tax Credits in Federally Facilitated Marketplaces," RR-980-RC, RAND Corporation, 2015, www.rand.org/pubs/research_reports/RR980.html; Linda J. Blumberg, Matthew Buettgens, and John Holahan, "The Implications of a Supreme Court Finding for the Plaintiff in King vs. Burwell: 8.2 Million More Uninsured and 35% Higher Premiums," Urban Institute, January 2015, www.urban.org/sites/default/files/publication/49246/2000062-The-Implications-King-vs-Burwell.pdf.

124. Timothy Jost, "Implementing Health Reform: As King Decision Looms, GOP Senators Introduce Transition Plans," *Health Affairs Blog*, April 23, 2015, www.healthaffairs.org/do/10.1377/hblog20150423.047237/full.

125. Timothy Jost, "Implementing Health Reform: The Supreme Court Upholds Tax Credits in the Federal Exchange," *Health Affairs Blog*, June 25, 2015, www.healthaffairs.org/do/10.1377/hblog20150625.048888/full.

126. Rachel Sachs, "The ACA Survives—but with a Note of Caution for the Future?," *Health Affairs Blog*, June 30, 2015, www.healthaffairs.org/do/10.1377/hblog20150630.049009/full.

127. Robert Pear, "Court Lets Some Charities Avoid Rules on Birth Control Coverage," *New York Times*, June 29, 2015, www.nytimes.com/2015/06/30/us/court-lets-some-charities-avoid-rules-on-birth-control-coverage.html; Timothy Jost, "Implementing Health Reform: Contraceptive Coverage Religious Accommodations, House v. Burwell, and More," *Health Affairs Blog*, June 30, 2015, www.healthaffairs.org/do/10.1377/hblog20150630.048994/full.

128. Timothy Jost, "Implementing Health Reform: Plaintiffs Win Contraceptive Coverage Round; New Census Data; GAO on State IT Systems (Updated)," *Health Affairs Blog*, September 18, 2015, www.healthaffairs.org/do/10.1377/hblog20150918.050624/full.

129. Adam Liptak, "Supreme Court to Hear New Case on Contraception and Religion," *New York Times*, November 6, 2015, www.nytimes.com/2015/11/07/us/politics/supreme-court-health-care-contraception-coverage.html.

130. "Medicaid Expansion in Pennsylvania: Transition from Waiver to Traditional Coverage," Kaiser Family Foundation, August 3, 2015, www.kff.org/medicaid/fact-sheet/medicaid-expansion-in-pennsylvania.

131. Abby Goodnough, "Indiana Will Allow Entry to Medicaid for a Price," *New York Times*, January 27, 2015, www.nytimes.com/2015/01/28/us/politics/indiana-will-allow-entry-to-medicaid-for-a-price.html.

132. Abby Goodnough, "Over Objections of Legislature, Alaska's Governor Says He Will Expand Medicaid," *New York Times*, July 16, 2015, www.nytimes.com/2015

/07/17/us/over-objections-of-legislature-alaska-governor-bill-walker-says-he-will-expand-medicaid.html.

133. Abby Goodnough, "Kentucky, Beacon for Health Law, Now a Lab for Its Retreat," *New York Times*, November 27, 2015, www.nytimes.com/2015/11/28/us/kentucky-beacon-for-health-law-now-a-lab-for-its-retreat.html.

134. Abby Goodnough, "Arkansas Governor Wants to Keep Medicaid Expansion, but with Changes," *New York Times*, August 19, 2015, www.nytimes.com/2015/08/20/us/arkansas-governor-wants-to-keep-medicaid-expansion-but-with-changes.html.

135. Nick Madigan, "Health Care Expansion Is Rejected in Florida," *New York Times*, June 5, 2015, www.nytimes.com/2015/06/06/us/health-care-expansion-is-rejected-in-florida.html.

136. Abby Goodnough, "In Vermont, Frustrations Mount over Affordable Care Act," *New York Times*, June 4, 2015, www.nytimes.com/2015/06/05/us/in-vermont-frustrations-mount-over-affordable-care-act.html.

137. Robert Pear, "State-Level Brawls over Medicaid Reflect Divide in G.O.P.," *New York Times*, December 27, 2015, www.nytimes.com/2015/12/28/us/politics/state-level-brawls-over-medicaid-reflect-wider-war-in-gop.html.

138. Robert Pear, "House G.O.P. Again Votes to Repeal Health Care Law," *New York Times*, February 3, 2015, www.nytimes.com/2015/02/04/us/politics/house-gop-again-votes-to-repeal-health-care-law.html.

139. Robert Pear, "G.O.P. Lawmakers Propose Alternative to Obamacare," *New York Times*, February 4, 2015, www.nytimes.com/2015/02/05/us/politics/gop-lawmakers-propose-alternative-to-obamacare.html.

140. Jonathan Weisman, "House Republican Budget Overhauls Medicare and Repeals the Health Law," *New York Times*, March 16, 2015, www.nytimes.com/2015/03/17/us/politics/house-republican-budget-overhauls-medicare-and-repeals-the-health-law.html; Jonathan Weisman, "Senate Republicans Rebuff House Colleagues with Their Budget Plan," *New York Times*, March 18, 2015, www.nytimes.com/2015/03/19/us/senate-budget-rejects-house-bid-to-skirt-military-spending-caps.html.

141. Robert Pear, "Senate Rules Entangle Bid to Repeal Health Care Law," *New York Times*, November 12, 2015, www.nytimes.com/2015/11/13/us/senate-rules-entangle-bid-to-repeal-health-care-law.html.

142. Nicholas Fandos, "Paul Ryan Defends Compromise in Passing Spending Deal," *New York Times*, December 20, 2015, www.nytimes.com/2015/12/21/us/politics/paul-ryan-defends-compromise-in-passing-spending-deal.html.

143. Robert Pear, "In Likely Spending Plan, Congress Readies Blows to Obama's Health Care Law," *New York Times*, December 16, 2015, www.nytimes.com/2015/12/17/us/politics/in-likely-spending-plan-congress-readies-blows-to-obamas-health-care-law.html.

144. Robert Pear, "Marco Rubio Quietly Undermines Affordable Care Act," *New York Times*, December 9, 2015, www.nytimes.com/2015/12/10/us/politics/marco-rubio-obamacare-affordable-care-act.html.

145. Carl Hulse, "Judge Rules House Can Sue Obama Administration on Health Care Spending," *New York Times*, September 9, 2015, www.nytimes.com/2015/09/10/us/politics/judge-rules-house-can-sue-obama-administration-on-health-care-spending.html.

146. Timothy Jost, "Implementing Health Reform: 2016 Benefit and Payment Final Rule, Consumer and Provider Provisions," *Health Affairs Blog*, February 22, 2015, www.healthaffairs.org/do/10.1377/hblog20150222.044917/full.

147. "Health Insurance Coverage and the Affordable Care Act," Department of Health and Human Services, May 5, 2015, https://aspe.hhs.gov/system/files/pdf/139211/ib_uninsured_change.pdf.

148. Robert Pear, "Most Health Insurance Co-ops Are Losing Money," *New York Times*, August 14, 2015, www.nytimes.com/2015/08/15/us/most-health-insurance-co-ops-are-losing-money-federal-audit-finds.html.

149. Paul Krugman, "Health Reform Lives!," *New York Times*, November 23, 2015, www.nytimes.com/2015/11/23/opinion/health-reform-lives.html.

150. Timothy Jost, "Zubik v. Burwell Oral Arguments: Under Contraceptive Coverage Accommodation, Conscientious Objectors or Collaborators? (Update)," *Health Affairs Blog*, March 24, 2016, www.healthaffairs.org/do/10.1377/hblog20160324.054114/full.

151. Timothy Jost, "Zubik v. Burwell Briefs Explore Potential Compromise (Update)," *Health Affairs Blog*, April 13, 2016, www.healthaffairs.org/do/10.1377/hblog20160413.054470/full.

152. Adam Liptak, "Justices, Seeking Compromise, Return Contraception Case to Lower Courts," *New York Times*, May 16, 2016, www.nytimes.com/2016/05/17/us/supreme-court-contraception-religious-groups.html; Timothy Jost, "Seeking Compromise, Supreme Court Remands Contraceptive Coverage Case to Lower Courts," *Health Affairs Blog*, May 16, 2016, www.healthaffairs.org/do/10.1377/hblog20160516.054884/full.

153. Timothy Jost, "Government Requests Input on Possible Contraceptive Coverage Compromises (Updated)," *Health Affairs Blog*, July 21, 2016, www.healthaffairs.org/do/10.1377/hblog20160721.055916/full.

154. Timothy Jost, "Judge Rules Against Administration in Cost-Sharing Reduction Payment Case," *Health Affairs Blog*, May 12, 2016, www.healthaffairs.org/do/10.1377/hblog20160512.054852/full.

155. Timothy Jost, "House Seeks Pause in Cost-Sharing Reduction Litigation (Updated)," *Health Affairs Blog*, November 22, 2016, www.healthaffairs.org/do/10.1377/hblog20161122.057670/full.

156. Richard Fausset and Abby Goodnough, "Louisiana's New Governor Signs an Order to Expand Medicaid," *New York Times*, January 12, 2016, www.nytimes.com/2016/01/13/us/louisianas-new-governor-signs-an-order-to-expand-medicaid.html.

157. Abby Goodnough, "With Health Care Switch, Kentucky with Health Care Switch, Kentucky Ventures into the Unknown," *New York Times*, January 13, 2016, www.nytimes.com/2016/01/14/us/affordable-care-act-kentucky-insurance-exchange.html.

158. Jack Healy, "Colorado Weighs Replacing Obama's Health Policy with Universal Coverage," *New York Times*, April 28, 2016, www.nytimes.com/2016/04/29/us/colorado-weighs-replacing-obamas-health-policy-with-universal-coverage.html; Sy Mukherjee, "Colorado Voters Reject Universal Health Care Measure," *Forbes Magazine*, November 8, 2016, https://fortune.com/2016/11/08/election-colorado-amendment-69-coloradocare.

159. Timothy Jost, "Alaska Reinsurance Plan Could Be Model for ACA Reform, Plus Other ACA Developments," *Health Affairs Blog*, June 16, 2016, www.healthaffairs.org/do/10.1377/hblog20160616.055420/full.

160. Heather Howard and Dan Meuse, "State Interest in 1332 Waivers Gaining Steam," *Health Affairs Blog*, November 2, 2016, www.healthaffairs.org/do/10.1377/hblog20161102.057390/full.

161. Timothy Jost, "The 2017 Benefit and Payment Parameters Final Rule: Drilling Down (Part 1)," *Health Affairs Blog*, March 2, 2016, www.healthaffairs.org

/do/10.1377/hblog20160302.053603/abs; Timothy Jost, "The 2017 Benefit and Payment Parameters Final Rule: Drilling Down (Part 2)," *Health Affairs Blog*, March 2, 2016, www.healthaffairs.org/do/10.1377/hblog20160302.053628/full.

162. Timothy Jost, "New Guidance on SHOP Online Enrollment Requirements," *Health Affairs Blog*, April 19, 2016, www.healthaffairs.org/do/10.1377/hblog20160419.054538/full.

163. Margot Sanger-Katz, "Budget Office Lowers Its Forecast for Obamacare Enrollment," *New York Times*, January 25, 2016, www.nytimes.com/2016/01/26/upshot/budget-office-lowers-its-forecast-for-obamacare-enrollment.html.

164. Liz Hamel et al., "Survey of Non-Group Health Insurance Enrollees, Wave 3," Kaiser Family Foundation, May 20, 2016, www.kff.org/health-reform/poll-finding/survey-of-non-group-health-insurance-enrollees-wave-3.

165. Reed Abelson and Margot Sanger-Katz, "Obamacare Marketplaces Are in Trouble. What Can Be Done?," *New York Times*, August 29, 2016, www.nytimes.com/2016/08/30/upshot/obamacare-marketplaces-are-in-trouble-what-can-be-done.html.

166. Timothy Jost, "Obama Administration Acts to Stabilize Marketplaces, Implement Expatriate Coverage Legislation (Updated)," *Health Affairs Blog*, June 9, 2016, www.healthaffairs.org/do/10.1377/hblog20160609.055261/full.

167. Anna Wilde Mathews, "Sales of Short-Term Health Policies Surge," *Wall Street Journal*, April 10, 2016, www.wsj.com/articles/sales-of-short-term-health-policies-surge-1460328539.

168. Timothy Jost, "New Rule on Excepted Benefits, Short-Term Coverage; Mental Health and Substance Use FAQs," *Health Affairs Blog*, October 30, 2016, www.healthaffairs.org/do/10.1377/hblog20161030.057301/full.

169. Timothy Jost, "ACA Final Rule Omits Opt-Out Payment Provisions; CMS Extends Coverage Deadline," *Health Affairs Blog*, December 16, 2016, www.healthaffairs.org/do/10.1377/hblog20161216.057990/full.

170. Robert Pear, "House Republicans Unveil Long-Awaited Replacement for Health Law," *New York Times*, June 22, 2016, www.nytimes.com/2016/06/22/us/politics/house-republicans-unveil-affordable-care-act-replacement.html.

171. Joseph Antos and James Capretta, "The House Republicans' Health Plan," American Enterprise Institute, June 22, 2016, www.aei.org/articles/the-house-republicans-health-plan; "Proposals to Replace the Affordable Care Act—Speaker Paul Ryan Proposal," Kaiser Family Foundation, March 2017, http://files.kff.org/attachment/Proposals-to-Replace-the-Affordable-Care-Act-Speaker-Paul-Ryan.

172. Nate Silver, "2016 Election Forecast," *FiveThirtyEight*, https://projects.fivethirtyeight.com/2016-election-forecast.

173. Christine Eibner, Sarah Nowak, and Jodi Liu, "Hillary Clinton's Health Care Reform Proposals: Anticipated Effects on Insurance Coverage, Out-of-Pocket Costs, and the Federal Deficit," Commonwealth Fund, September 23, 2016, www.commonwealthfund.org/publications/issue-briefs/2016/sep/hillary-clintons-health-care-reform-proposals-anticipated.

174. Evan Saltzman and Christine Eibner, "Donald Trump's Health Care Reform Proposals: Anticipated Effects on Insurance Coverage, Out-of-Pocket Costs, and the Federal Deficit," Commonwealth Fund, September 23, 2016, www.commonwealthfund.org/sites/default/files/documents/___media_files_publications_issue_brief_2016_sep_1903_saltzman_trump_hlt_care_reform_proposals_ib_v2.pdf.

175. Robert Pear, "Senate Republican Leaders Vow to Begin Repeal of Health Law Next Month," *New York Times*, December 6, 2016, www.nytimes.com/2016/12/06/us/politics/senate-republican-leaders-vow-to-begin-repeal-of-health-law-next-month.html.

176. Reed Abelson, "Donald Trump Says He May Keep Parts of Obama Health Care Act," *New York Times*, November 11, 2016, www.nytimes.com/2016/11/12/business/insurers-unprepared-for-obamacare-repeal.html.

177. Robert Pear, Jennifer Steinhauer, and Thomas Kaplan, "G.O.P. Plans Immediate Repeal of Health Law, Then a Delay," *New York Times*, December 6, 2016, www.nytimes.com/2016/12/02/us/politics/obamacare-repeal.html.

178. Barack Obama, "United States Care Reform: Progress to Date and Next Steps," *Journal of the American Medical Association* 316, no. 5 (August 2, 2016): 525–532, https://jamanetwork.com/journals/jama/fullarticle/2533698.

179. Joseph Antos and James C. Capretta, "The Future of the ACA's Exchanges," *Health Affairs Blog*, October 11, 2016, www.healthaffairs.org/do/10.1377/hblog20161011.057024/full.

180. Robert Moffitt, "Year Six of the Affordable Care Act: Obamacare's Mounting Problems," Heritage Foundation, April 1, 2016, www.heritage.org/health-care-reform/report/year-six-the-affordable-care-act-obamacares-mounting-problems.

181. Jonathan Oberlander, "Implementing the Affordable Care Act: The Promise and Limits of Health Care Reform," *Journal of Health Politics, Policy and Law* 41, no. 4 (August 2016): 803–826, https://read.dukeupress.edu/jhppl/article/41/4/803/13901/Implementing-the-Affordable-Care-Act-The-Promise.

182. Timothy Jost, "Taking Stock of Health Reform: Where We've Been, Where We're Going," *Health Affairs Blog*, December 6, 2016, www.healthaffairs.org/do/10.1377/hblog20161206.057800/full.

183. Adele Shartzer, Sharon K. Long, and Nathaniel Anderson, "Access to Care and Affordability Have Improved Following Affordable Care Act Implementation; Problems Remain," *Health Affairs* 35, no. 1 (January 2016): 161–185.

184. Jones, *Exchange Politics*, 134–161.

185. Daniel Beland, Philip Rocco, and Alex Waddan, *Obamacare Wars: Federalism, State Politics, and the Affordable Care Act* (Lawrence: University of Kansas Press, 2016), 155–162.

186. Bowen Garrett and Anuj Gangopadhyaya, "Who Gained Health Insurance Coverage Under the ACA and Where Do They Live?," Urban Institute, December 2016, www.urban.org/sites/default/files/publication/86761/2001041-who-gained-health-insurance-coverage-under-the-aca-and-where-do-they-live.pdf.

187. Matt Broaddus and Edwin Park, "Affordable Care Act Has Produced Historic Gains in Health Coverage," Center on Budget and Policy Priorities, December 15, 2016, www.cbpp.org/sites/default/files/atoms/files/12-15-16health.pdf.

188. Sherry Glied, Stephanie Ma, and Sarah Verbofsky, "How Much of a Factor Is the Affordable Care Act in the Declining Uninsured Rate?," Commonwealth Fund, December 2016, www.commonwealthfund.org/sites/default/files/documents/___media_files_publications_issue_brief_2016_dec_1920_glied_aca_and_uninsured_rate_rb_v3.pdf.

189. Robert J. Blendon, John M. Benson, and Logan S. Casey, "Health Care in the 2016 Election—a View Through Voters' Polarized Lenses," *New England Journal of Medicine* 375, no. 17 (October 27, 2016), www.nejm.org/doi/pdf/10.1056/NEJMsr1606159.

190. May, "Implementation Failures Revisited"; note: May's 2015 article examines the troubled first months of the ACA rollout. His framework is a useful conceptual approach to policy implementation, but the conclusions here differ in some significant ways from those of May.

4

The Dog Caught the Car: Now What?

I used to tweet, but it's an act of futility.

—Sylvester Stallone

On New Year's Day 2017 few observers would have made a large wager on the survival of the Affordable Care Act (ACA). House Republicans had been passing repeal bills since 2011, and Senate Republicans had passed repeal legislation in late 2016. President-elect Donald Trump campaigned on a clear message of opposition. This chapter relates the story of how, against all odds, the ACA emerged alive and mostly well at the end of the year.

The Senate's first move was procedural. It set in motion the process to include an ACA repeal as part of the annual reconciliation process to assure Democrats could not filibuster the expected bill.[1] After his inauguration President Trump immediately issued an executive order that instructed departments to waive or defer ACA provisions creating a fiscal burden for states, individuals, or providers. This order was largely a symbolic statement of presidential intent. Most real changes required regulatory modifications or statutory changes.[2]

However, no "repeal-and-replace" plan emerged from the White House. The opening move belonged to the House. At the January Republican retreat, Speaker Paul Ryan told House Republicans to expect a floor vote on the ACA by early March.[3]

The House Bill

In its basic outlines, the American Health Care Act (AHCA) was similar to the bills passed by House Republicans several times in previous years. It embodied the same policy approach found in a bill introduced by Representative Tom Price of Georgia, who had been appointed head of Health and Human Services (HHS), and contained the ideas from Speaker Ryan's "Better Way" proposal. It was a leadership bill drafted in secret without hearings and the typical rollout fanfare. Democrats criticized the lack of an open process and created a media event by "searching" for the draft bill they had not been allowed to view.[4]

On March 6, Representatives Kevin Brady and Greg Walden, ranking members, respectively, of the Ways and Means and the Energy and Commerce Committees, introduced the AHCA, which was a reconciliation bill designed to bypass a Senate filibuster. Three days later, on March 9, the two committees approved the AHCA. A week later the House Budget Committee voted 19–17 to advance the bill. The close vote, with three GOP defections, was a sign of pending trouble. The Congressional Budget Office (CBO) score followed quickly and indicated 24 million people would lose health insurance coverage by 2026.[5]

Repeal of Obamacare had been a Republican campaign pledge since 2010, but the party lacked a consensus on what, if anything, should replace the ACA. As a floor vote approached, the provisions of the repeal bill became more contentious among House Republicans because this vote was likely to impact the entire health system, not just represent a political statement.

Conservative Freedom Caucus members immediately voiced their opposition because they didn't believe the AHCA went far enough in repealing the ACA. They met with the president but didn't find a path to negotiation over specific provisions.[6] Personal lobbying by the White House eventually brought about half of the three dozen members of the Freedom Caucus to support Ryan's bill.[7] Nearly two dozen GOP moderates were in opposition because they worried about the increase in uninsured as well as the impact of Medicaid changes beyond repeal of ACA's expansion.[8]

As the White House and the House leadership made concessions to the Freedom Caucus, they continued to lose support among moderates. In the lead-up to the scheduled vote, several amendments were added. For conservatives they included Medicaid provisions, such as work requirements, quicker ending of expansion, and a block grant option. For moderates, additional funding for maternal care and aid for elderly were intended to sweeten the pot. Representative Charles Dent of Pennsylvania, a moderate leader, said, "I believe this bill, in its current form, will lead to the loss of coverage and make insurance unaffordable for too many Americans, particularly for low-to-moderate income and older individuals. . . . This legislation misses the mark."[9]

Appropriations Committee chair Rodney Frelinghuysen declared his opposition as the floor vote approached. Then hours before the scheduled vote, Speaker Ryan announced he was withdrawing the bill because it didn't have the votes to pass.[10] It became evident that "Repeal Obamacare" was a successful political slogan as long as Republicans didn't actually have to find a majority to vote for the bill. They were learning that health policy is hard.

The main provisions of AHCA were as follows:[11]

- Repeal the individual and employer mandates
- Replace premium and cost-sharing subsidies with an age-adjusted flat tax credit
- Add a late penalty for not maintaining continuous coverage
- Eliminate most of the tax provisions of the ACA, including the Medicare Hospital Insurance tax
- Create "Patient & State Stability Fund" grants to create high-risk pools
- Establish per capita caps on federal Medicaid spending
- Allow states to establish Medicaid work requirements

The bill retained popular insurance market rules, such as a ban on pre-existing conditions and allowing children to remain on family coverage until age twenty-six. It maintained the basic structure of the marketplaces with the provision of tax credits to assist in the purchase of insurance for those not part of the employment-based system. Some of the Republican critics referred to it as "Obamacare lite."[12]

After the vote cancellation, the House Republican leadership and President Trump continued to search for votes but found consensus elusive. The Freedom Caucus was most vocal in its opposition to the basic approach of AHCA, but with each concession moderates became more apprehensive.[13]

Vice President Mike Pence met with the Republican caucus in early April in an attempt to revive the AHCA but found conservatives and moderates still far apart.[14] However, by mid-April a compromise was negotiated by Representative Tom MacArthur of New Jersey, one of the moderate leaders, and Representative Mark Meadows of North Carolina, a leader of the Freedom Caucus. The MacArthur amendment would retain essential health benefits, age rating, and community rating but allow states to request a waiver as long as the state formed a high-risk pool and penalized an individual with a lapse in coverage of more than sixty-three days. The maximum age rating was increased from 3:1 to 5:1, which allowed a greater premium differential for older individuals.[15]

With this concession Freedom Caucus members began to sign on to support the AHCA, but moderates became more reluctant.[16] By early May, Speaker Ryan believed he had cobbled together enough yes votes with the changes. On May 4, the AHCA bill passed with a slim 217–213 majority.[17]

All Democrats were in opposition, and most Freedom Caucus members who had opposed the March version voted yes in May. The moderate Tuesday Group was split between support and opposition.[18]

The Senate's Turn

Next it was the Senate's turn to attempt repeal and maybe replace. Republicans in the Senate were not happy with the AHCA and immediately moved to create their own bill.[19] The House bill was formally received by the Senate on June 7 and placed on the calendar. The Senate Budget Committee, chaired by Mike Enzi of Wyoming, presented a "discussion draft" on June 22. The legislative strategy was to substitute the Senate bill for the House-passed AHCA. The draft had been put together by a group of thirteen GOP Senate leaders without participation of key moderates, such as Senator Susan Collins. There were also no hearings or opportunities for public and interest group comments.[20] Updates to the draft appeared on June 26, July 13, and July 20.

Many of the basic policy ideas contained in the AHCA were retained in the draft Better Care Reconciliation Act (BCRA). The core ideas were as follows:[21]

- Repeal the individual and employer mandates and cost-sharing subsidies
- Modify premium tax credits as follows:
  - Extend them to those below 100 percent of the federal poverty level (FPL)
  - Set an upper limit for subsidies of 350 percent of FPL
  - Link subsidies to actuarial value benchmark of 58 percent
- Retain private market rules, such as prohibiting preexisting conditions
- Retain health insurance marketplaces
- Establish a State Stability and Innovation Program
- Encourage health savings accounts
- Phase out enhanced funding for Medicaid expansion
- Convert federal Medicaid funding to a per capita allotment
- Allow Medicaid work requirements as a state option

As the BCRA moved from initial draft to floor vote, some changes were made to accommodate senators essential in assembling a majority, but the core ideas in both the House and Senate versions were similar. Both repealed the mandates and cost-sharing subsidies, shifted the basis for the tax credits, retained popular private market rules, ended enhanced federal Medicaid expansion funds, and placed per capita funding limits on the federal Medicaid formula. The CBO scores for both projected massive increases in the uninsured and declines in Medicaid enrollment and funding.[22]

As with the House struggle to find an AHCA majority in the GOP caucus, the Senate path to a BCRA majority was arduous. We will summarize the Senate Republican effort to find a majority coalition, then offer thoughts on why the effort failed.

The Republican Senate leadership initially hoped the Senate would vote on the BCRA bill before the early-July recess, but opposition emerged, and the CBO score on June 26 projected a significant increase in the number of uninsured.[23] The next day the vote was postponed until senators returned from the Fourth of July recess. Opposition from within the GOP Senate caucus grew in the interim, with hospitals and state officials in many states expressing their opposition to the Senate bill.[24] Majority Leader Mitch McConnell announced a delay in the start of the August recess to allow more time for a vote on BCRA and stated a vote would not take place until Senator John McCain returned from his eye surgery in Arizona.

On July 13 the Senate Republican leadership released the latest version of BCRA. Among other changes the bill included an amendment by Senator Ted Cruz allowing the sale of insurance in the marketplace that did not meet essential health benefit standards. Other changes allowed use of tax credits to purchase catastrophic plans, provided new money for substance abuse programs, and targeted stability fund money for Alaska. The massive long-term cuts to Medicaid remained in the bill.[25]

A few days later Majority Leader McConnell announced that Republicans were not in agreement on BCRA, and there would be a vote to *repeal, but not replace* the ACA. But he changed course after a meeting with President Trump.[26] The vote hesitation reflected a series of divisions among Senate Republicans. Conservatives, such as Senators Rand Paul and Ron Johnson, wanted to eliminate premium subsidies and reduce insurance market regulations. Moderates, such as Senators Susan Collins and Lisa Murkowski, sought to protect ACA's insurance access by maintaining subsidies and retaining critical regulations. Several senators from Medicaid-expansion states were concerned with loss of future Medicaid funds.[27] The CBO estimated 22 million additional people would be uninsured under the BCRA.[28]

Finally, on July 25 the Senate took a procedural vote for floor consideration of the AHCA with the intent of substituting the BCRA for the House-passed bill. The motion passed 51–50, with Vice President Pence breaking a tie. Senator McCain, who had just returned from Arizona, voted for the motion to proceed.

The revised BCRA bill on the floor required sixty votes to break a filibuster because the Senate parliamentarian had ruled that its Planned Parenthood funding suspension and abortion provision disqualified the bill as a reconciliation measure.[29] Nine Republicans joined with Democrats to defeat the motion 43–57. Democratic opposition was unanimous, and

Republican no votes came from both moderates, such as Senator Collins, and conservatives, such as Senator Paul.[30]

The next day another bill was proposed *to repeal and delay*; it would have formally repealed the ACA but delayed the effective date of repeal by two years on the presumption that Congress could fashion a replacement before then. Seven Republicans were opposed, mostly from the moderate wing but including Senator McCain. The vote was 45–55.[31]

The final act of the July ACA repeal performance took place on July 28. Majority Leader McConnell offered the "skinny bill," which only repealed the individual and employer mandates and the medical device tax, three of the most unpopular provisions of the ACA.[32] The rationale was to keep the process going through a negotiation between the House and Senate, with each having passed a bill related to ACA repeal. This was rejected 49–51, with Senator McCain dramatically casting the decisive vote and joining Senators Murkowski and Collins in opposition. Senator McCain implored his colleagues to pursue a bipartisan effort to change the ACA.[33]

After the failure of all three attempts, Majority Leader McConnell indicated the Senate could not reach agreement and would move to consider a tax bill where more consensus existed among Republicans. However, one last effort was made to save the ACA repeal crusade. Republican senators Lindsey Graham and Bill Cassidy had introduced an alternative approach in mid-July as the vote on BCRA approached, but their amendment never received a vote.[34] After the failure of the three options in late July, Graham continued to argue his bill was the last chance to repeal Obamacare in 2017.[35]

In mid-September Majority Leader McConnell indicated the Senate would vote on the Graham-Cassidy proposal. This long-shot last chance came days before the deadline on the reconciliation approach. After October 1, votes would be needed to overcome a filibuster.

The Graham-Cassidy proposal embodied many of the same policy ideas found in the BCRA and AHCA but was more radical in its approach.[36] Federal premium and cost-sharing subsidies were eliminated in the bill and replaced with a grant program for the states, which could be used for the same purpose. The grant program was authorized only until 2026. The Medicaid provision repealed extra funding for Medicaid expansion and converted all federal Medicaid funding to a per capita limit with the goal of transforming it into a block grant. It is likely Graham-Cassidy, if passed, would have increased the uninsured by millions and destabilized insurance markets. It also substantially reduced federal Medicaid spending by the mid-2020s.[37]

Senator Cassidy lobbied his colleagues relentlessly in September, arguing that failure to enact some type of ACA repeal would damage the Republican Party in 2018, but the hasty process, with constant bill-language modifications, contributed to continued opposition from both moderates and conservatives, as well as provider and consumer interest groups.[38] On September 26 Senator Cassidy said the votes were not present and the effort would be dropped. At a minimum Senators Paul, Collins, and McCain were all in opposition, guaranteeing the lack of a majority.[39]

Since early summer Republican senator Lamar Alexander and Democrat Patty Murray had been developing a bill to stabilize the nongroup insurance market. With the Republican effort to repeal the ACA a failure, they hoped their bill represented a bipartisan effort to solve one of the pressing ACA-related problems. At first, they seemed to have the support of President Trump, and Majority Leader McConnell indicated he would bring the bill to a vote, if the president endorsed it. But when the White House conditioned support on more fundamental changes to the ACA, the effort collapsed.[40]

There was one more arrow in the anti-ACA quiver. As Republicans moved to enact a major tax reduction using the reconciliation process, an amendment was added to remove the tax penalty in the individual-mandate section of the ACA. This allowed Republicans to claim at least one small victory in their long attempt to repeal the ACA and had the added bonus of increasing the savings in the tax bill, thus allowing an additional tax reduction.[41] The mandate itself could not have been removed under reconciliation rules, but changing the penalty to zero was permissible.

The individual mandate was the most unpopular part of the ACA. Supporters of the ACA had for years claimed this was an essential piece necessary for the functioning of the individual market. It was assumed that without the mandate, younger, healthier individuals would opt out of purchasing insurance, leading to adverse selection and higher prices in the ACA marketplaces and resulting in a "death spiral."[42] The CBO and others in their analytic studies assumed the number of uninsured would rise dramatically without the individual mandate. In November the CBO estimated the immediate impact would be 4 million more uninsured and a 10 percent increase in premiums in the nongroup market.[43] Others were less pessimistic. Timothy Jost argued the most critical parts of the ACA remained in place and suggested the CBO estimate of uninsured without the mandate might be too high.[44]

What Happened When the Dog Caught the Car?

We have all watched a dog futilely chasing a car down the street and speculated about what the dog might do if he actually caught it. For more than six years the Republican Party had chased the ACA, barking loudly and proclaiming their intent to repeal and perhaps replace it with something better. In January 2017 they caught the car with the unexpected victory of President Trump. As the 115th Congress opened, there was a determination to repeal the ACA, but 2017 ended without successful repeal legislation.

After an initial failure, the House barely passed the AHCA in May. Over the summer various Senate approaches each fell short.

For this quick overview of what went wrong, we will use John Kingdon's model as a conceptual framework. Kingdon conceptualizes the policy process as occurring in three parallel streams: problems, policies, and politics. Successful policy adoption occurs when the streams converge, creating a window of opportunity.[45]

In the problem stream, ACA repeal occupied a high place on the congressional agenda, but not because of intense public pressure or a catastrophic event. In fact, by early 2017 public opinion on the ACA was more favorable than ever before, and many individual parts of it had always enjoyed more public support than the label "Obamacare."[46] The public pressure to repeal came predominantly from Republican voters and donors, and this negative attitude had been fostered by GOP politicians and conservative activists. The constant condemnation of the ACA created the sense of mandate among congressional Republicans to place repeal high on the agenda.

The policy stream was more complicated. Policy ideas are discussed, debated, and filtered in the policy stream long before an issue has a high place on the agenda. This vetting of policy ideas for addressing problems is not the province of legislators and instead involves academics, interest groups, think tanks, and others devoted to policy analysis. The conservative and market-oriented health policy analysts had been engaged with this work in the policy stream for decades and had filled a large bookshelf with proposals on the subject. In fact, several policy ideas embodied in the ACA, such as the individual mandate and tax credits to purchase insurance in an exchange, had emerged from the conservative segment of the policy stream.[47]

The dilemma for Republican legislators was the fact that many conservative health policy ideas, if enacted, were likely to increase the number of uninsured and make health insurance premiums more, not less, expensive for many families. Even some conservative analysts were critical of aspects of the bills because of potential future coverage gaps.[48] The Republican bills embodied three fundamental policy ideas:

- Reducing federal subsidies for purchasing health insurance in the individual market
- Relaxing insurance regulations around elements such as preexisting conditions, thereby allowing provision of less adequate insurance at a lower price
- Significantly reducing federal funding for Medicaid, thus reducing the scope of the program

For the most conservative Republicans, the three ideas taken together would over time reduce health coverage subsidy by the federal government and force greater reliance on a free market approach to health insurance. Even if the trade-off was a larger uninsured population, reduction in federal responsibility and spending was worth the decline in coverage.

Many Republicans in Congress seemed to believe there was no such trade-off, but independent analysts, such as the CBO, argued otherwise. The ideological framework emphasizing market-based approaches to all issues creates a bias against government-funded solutions. Also, reduced federal health spending provided budget space for future tax cuts.

In retrospect it appears the conservative-oriented policy community didn't produce effective ACA policy alternatives that found their way into the GOP bills. Since at least the early 1980s, the central policy idea among Republicans for Medicaid has been to reduce federal government spending by transforming the program into a block grant rather than an open-ended entitlement program. Republican presidents since Ronald Reagan have unsuccessfully sought to significantly reduce federal Medicaid spending with this approach.

Decades of experience with health insurance in the individual market have demonstrated that without market rules, adverse selection will occur, driving up cost and limiting access. Many insurance companies supported the ACA market rules in exchange for the opportunity to increase customers. Without market rules applied to all companies, none could afford to unilaterally follow constraints, such as not employing preexisting conditions to screen insurance applicants.

The rhetoric around the various 2017 bills was anti-ACA but sought more radical change by moving beyond termination of the ACA expansion to include the long-sought goal of transforming the entire Medicaid program. The inclusion of this policy idea in the legislation increased the scope of opposition.

In both the House and the Senate there were struggles to build majority coalitions to pass ACA repeal legislation. A sharp division existed between moderates, who were concerned about coverage impact, and conservatives, who wanted ACA repeal with or without a replacement. Conservatives were satisfied to return to the 2009 status quo before the enactment of the ACA. They were willing to venture even further by significantly reducing all Medicaid funding in the future. House and Senate leadership tried to finesse the divide with minor modifications of the bills, because they understood no Democrats would be willing to join them.

Interest groups, media, and other stakeholders are also instrumental in building a majority legislative coalition. In this instance, many provider and consumer interest groups, as well as business leaders, opposed the legislation. Opponents included governors of both parties concerned about Medicaid cuts, insurance plans, the American Medical Association, the American Hospital Association, and AARP.[49]

Public opinion remained divided with a heavily partisan tilt, but opinion had marginally shifted by early 2017, with a slight majority having a favorable opinion of the ACA. Republicans favored repeal; Democrats opposed it. Most Americans (60 percent) didn't believe the ACA had a personal impact on their lives. A majority of Republicans supported ACA repeal, but only a quarter approved of the replacement plans.[50] Public opinion, even among Republicans, did not clearly support the Republican repeal effort.

The House leadership was barely able to assemble a majority in favor of the AHCA. The Senate failed to pass any of the several repeal bills brought to the floor, but most failed by a narrow margin. Why did the effort fail despite House and Senate majorities and negative public opinion within the ranks of Republican voters? The window of opportunity slammed shut because a viable alternative was not developed in the policy stream, and leadership strategies in the political stream were flawed and poorly executed, preventing the emergence of a majority coalition.

For at least two decades conservative policy analysts have developed ideas for a different approach to organizing and financing the health insurance system. Using tax credits to purchase insurance is one key element. Limiting public programs, especially Medicaid, but restraining federal funding by transforming an entitlement into a block grant is the other. The core ideological premise is a better system with a predominant market approach rather than a large government role. But legislation built on this premise is likely to be analyzed as reducing rather increasing the number of uninsured. The CBO and other analytic scorekeepers found each of the bills as significantly increasing the ranks of the uninsured. With inclusion of all of Medicaid for significant reduced funding, not just the ACA expansion, providers, governors, and other interest groups joined the opposition. This was especially problematic for House and Senate moderates.

Both Speaker Ryan and Majority Leader McConnell opted to bypass the normal legislative process and write bills with minimal discussion and little opportunity for critique by outside groups or even members. They seemed to initially believe their majority and the several years of repeal as a campaign slogan assured Republican legislators would vote for anything carrying the repeal label. They appeared to underestimate conservatives' desire for complete repeal irrespective of the consequences and moderates' unwillingness to be responsible for increased uninsured and decimation of the entire Medicaid program.

We have seen that President Barack Obama played a critical leadership role in the passage of the ACA. President Trump wished to repeal Obamacare but didn't appear to have either interest in or a sense of what a viable alternative might be. He constantly pushed for a vote on repeal but vacillated between enthusiasm for and critique of the actual bills with little interest in the details.[51]

Republican ACA critics often complained the ACA was not drafted using the regular legislative process. Compared with the process here, however, the ACA passage entailed a more extended and inclusive process. The 2009–2010 ACA legislative process demonstrated more skillful and effective leadership in the face of similar internal differences of opinion. We don't know what would have happened if Senator McCain had voted yes instead of no on that July evening. Would the House and Senate Republicans have been able to meld and reconcile differences and find a majority in both houses to pass the end product? Perhaps, but the fault lines were evident. One factor driving a swift and closed process to produce a bill was the realization that the repeal effort was becoming increasingly unpopular.

When the ACA passed, many of its supporters expected a path to acceptance similar to those of Social Security and Medicare, which were both opposed by conservatives at the time of passage but became popular programs and politically untouchable. They were often referred to as the third rail of American politics. Why didn't this happen with the ACA? Jacob Hacker and Paul Pierson have demonstrated that retrenchment of the welfare state has not generally occurred, but it almost happened with the ACA. They attribute this to *asymmetric polarization*, with the Republican Party moving sharply to the right. This might seem to doom the opportunity to retrench popular social programs, but a loyal electoral base, conservative activist donors, and a geographical institutional advantage provided a sense of immunity from election retaliation for eliminating a large-scale social program.[52]

Eric Patashnik and Jonathan Oberlander arrive at a similar set of conclusions about the motives of Republicans in attempting to repeal the ACA in 2017 as well as in their seven-year opposition campaign. They observe that the diversity of policy approaches within the ACA, combined with radicalization of Republicans, created only modest feedback effects, thus limiting support for the program, even among beneficiaries.[53]

Kingdon has observed windows of opportunity do not stay open indefinitely. When the Republicans in the House and Senate failed to find a set of policy ideas to replace the ACA capable of gaining support from a majority coalition in 2017, the window closed. A year later Democrats had regained a majority in the House, and the window closed for the remainder of Trump's term in office. But the Trump administration did pursue several strategies for sabotage, which is the topic in our next section.

Administrative Sabotage

Despite the roller-coaster ride of the legislative process for most of 2017, there was an expectation of ACA repeal. Nevertheless, the Trump administration also pursued a sabotage strategy, employing the executive powers of the president to diminish the effectiveness of the law. During 2017 there were three types of actions for pursuing the sabotage strategy. One was to drastically reduce funding for various outreach and enrollment efforts. A second was to threaten and eventually eliminate cost-sharing reduction (CSR) payments, which compensated insurance plans for reimbursement of deductibles and copayments for low-income individuals who purchased insurance in the marketplace. The third was to use waivers to weaken the regulations in the insurance market and allow states to reduce Medicaid eligibility.

Opening Salvo: First-Day Executive Order

During the campaign President Trump had frequently proclaimed Congress would send him a repeal-and-replace bill on his first day in office, and he would sign it.[54] This stump-speech boast was obviously not going to happen, but he did sign an executive order on the first day directing administration officials to dismantle the ACA to the maximum extent possible under the law.[55] This was largely a symbolic action. Significant administrative change usually requires an extended process involving budgets and rules.

Rule Changes

Just days after the Senate confirmed Tom Price as Health and Human Services secretary in early February, HHS announced a notice of proposed rule making to modify existing rules to stabilize the market. Many of the provisions of the proposed rule changes had been sought by insurance plans. The proposed changes involved reducing the length of enrollment periods, limiting coverage upgrades, changing the calculation of actuarial values, and allowing states to determine network adequacy.[56] The final rule was adopted in April with few changes from the proposed rule.[57] In general these changes had the effect of enhancing the financial position of insurance companies in the individual market and making it more difficult for some consumers to purchase insurance.

Outreach Funding Reduction

From the beginning various forms of outreach and customer assistance were an integral part of the ACA marketplace enrollment strategy. Those eligible to purchase insurance under the ACA were often unaware of the availability of subsidized premiums or uncertain about how to evaluate their options and sign up for coverage. An elaborate system had been developed during the Obama administration to offer outreach assistance in the lead-up to each open enrollment period. Advertising in various media and providing a system of navigators to assist individuals with the process had been shown to increase enrollment among previously uninsured individuals.[58]

As part of the concerted effort to diminish the ACA, the Trump administration slashed federal funding for both media outreach and navigator programs. The first step in this sabotage strategy came days after the January executive order as the White House issued directives to halt all advertising and outreach in the final days of the 2017 open enrollment period.[59] These attempts to drastically reduce outreach and enrollment assistance were part of an overall strategy to depress enrollment.[60] Many states with their own marketplaces continued to fund these efforts and experienced somewhat better 2017 enrollment.[61] This financial squeeze continued later in 2017 with additional reductions in the months before the 2018 enrollment period.[62] These actions included last-minute budget requests, cutting support for navigator groups, prohibiting HHS regional offices from participating in outreach, and reducing mail outreach.[63] The reductions were likely to make it harder to enroll in 2018 coverage, potentially leading to a decline in market participation.[64]

Threats to CSR Payments
The cost of health insurance for most Americans can be measured in two ways. First, there is the insurance premium, which is paid even if no services are required during the year. Those with employment-sponsored insurance probably pay some portion of the total premium but usually a relatively small share. Second, most plans have cost-sharing provisions in the form of deductibles, coinsurance, and copayments. *Deductibles* represent the amount paid by an insured person before the plan begins to cover services. *Coinsurance* is the percentage of the bill the patient pays after the deductible is covered. *Copayments* are flat fees associated with each unit of service. To prevent these cost-sharing mechanisms from becoming too burdensome, most plans have out-of-pocket limits beyond which the insured person is not responsible for any additional payments.

When the ACA was enacted, the rules governing purchase of insurance plans in the marketplace were categorized by their actuarial value as platinum, gold, silver, and bronze. Actuarial value is the average expense level that an insurance plan meets. Under the ACA, platinum plans cover 90 percent, gold 80 percent, silver 70 percent, and bronze 60 percent. The higher the actuarial value, the higher the premium and the lower the insured's total cost share.

The ACA calculates the amount of the premium tax credit based on the second least expensive, silver plan, and the size of the credit is a function of the family income. The higher the income, the smaller the tax credit, with 400 percent of FPL being the ceiling. For those between 100 and 250 percent of FPL, the ACA also makes cost-sharing reductions available. Without those, the family in this range would potentially have to pay a large share of income for its part of the premium, deductibles, coinsurance, and copays.

The ACA mechanism for cost-sharing reductions was to require insurance companies to cover these expenses for families in the eligible income category, with the federal government responsible for reimbursing the insurance plan. However, the text of the statute was not clear about whether the CSR payments were to be an integral part of the premium tax credits or require a separate annual appropriation. The Obama administration offered the former interpretation, but the Republican House majority contended the latter. This led to a lawsuit by the House Republicans alleging the administration's improper use of funds for this purpose.[65] The lawsuit was still pending in the courts when the Trump administration took office.

Throughout the early part of 2017, President Trump frequently threatened to stop these payments but didn't follow through while repeal-and-replace legislation was pending in the House and Senate, confident that the new law would eliminate the disputed provision. The president seemed to regard the threat to withhold the payments as a bargaining chip in negotiations around new legislation.[66] However, in October, with bleak prospects for new legislation, President Trump formally announced an intention to stop the payments for 2018 and beyond.[67] The lawsuit brought by the House was still pending in the appeals court. The states and insurance companies were likely to continue to argue for CSR payments as a legal obligation.

The halting of payments did not, however, eliminate the obligation of insurance plans to provide the CSR subsidies to those eligible. In response most insurance companies, with the approval of state regulators, increased the premiums for their silver plans to cover the unreimbursed CSR expenses. For those eligible for CSRs, the higher premium cost increased the size of their premium credit. This has been called "silver loading." For most, the end result was a lower out-of-pocket cost, but for some of those not eligible for CSRs, the result was a higher cost.[68] The Trump administration sought to characterize the CSR payments as a subsidy for the insurance companies, but this was another example of flawed legislative language opening the door for an extended legal and political battle that Congress was unable to resolve, with some families suffering higher costs or less choice in the insurance market.

Waivers

The third sabotage strategy of the Trump administration was to aggressively employ waivers to weaken or effectively eliminate various provisions of the ACA. For decades the federal government had the legal authority under Section 1115 of the Social Security Act to waive some Medicaid requirements as part of demonstration projects. Beginning with the Bill Clinton administration, this Section 1115 waiver authority had been used more aggressively to expand the scope of Medicaid coverage.[69] With the ACA, Medicaid expansion requests for such waivers grew. The Obama administration approved several waivers to encourage requesting states to adopt Medicaid expansion.[70]

Section 1332 of the ACA was inserted at the urging of Senator Ron Wyden of Oregon. It permitted states in 2017 and thereafter to request innovation waivers to modify elements of the individual insurance market. The ACA statute stated waivers could not reduce the comprehensiveness of benefits, affordability of insurance, or number of people covered or increase the federal deficit. With a Section 1332 waiver, a state may use innovative approaches in the individual market with the same level of federal funding to achieve the health insurance goals of the ACA.[71] We will examine the 2017 Trump administration approach to each of these waiver authorities.

Medicaid

In March 2017 Secretary Price and Centers for Medicare and Medicaid Services (CMS) administrator Seema Verma invited states to resubmit rejected Section 1115 waivers or propose new ones with policy ideas not accepted in the past.[72] The invited waiver areas applying to Medicaid beneficiaries included work requirements, use of insurance premiums, and financial penalties for recipients failing to follow program rules.[73] Medicaid Section 1115 waivers prior to the Trump administration typically were used as a tool to increase state flexibility and allow for expansion of coverage beyond the original statutory provisions. Frank Thompson concluded the waivers were historically not vehicles for policy retrenchment. The flexibility increased coverage and contributed to the durability of Medicaid from the Clinton through the Obama administrations.[74]

The ACA modified and clarified the Section 1115 waiver process as applied to Medicaid. CMS now had to take new procedural steps before it could approve an 1115 waiver, which now required public notice, a comment period, and posting of the terms and conditions of the waiver approval. These new transparency provisions would also provide a record for judicial review.[75]

The Obama administration had been open to considering 1115 waivers as part of a state plan to accept Medicaid expansion. In September 2013 Arkansas was the first to receive a Medicaid expansion waiver. The state sought to place the whole expansion population in a "private option" with the use of premium support to subsidize the purchase of health insurance in the marketplace. This was a concession to the anti-Obamacare sentiment in the state as well as a way of strengthening the marketplace with the addition of more participants.

Michigan's approach of charging limited premiums for the expansion population was approved in December 2013. Iowa's waiver for a private insurance option was similar, but not identical, to Arkansas's and was approved in December 2014. Pennsylvania's premium plan was also approved in 2014 but never implemented because of a change in governorship, with the commonwealth adopting regular expansion. The Indiana and Montana premium plans were approved in 2015, as was a private option for New Hampshire.[76] These represented a negotiated path to Medicaid expansion.

The typical approach in these waivers was to either charge beneficiaries a premium or give beneficiaries a private option to perchance insurance in the marketplace with a premium subsidy. This had not previously been allowed under the Medicaid statute. By 2017 seven states had such waivers, although the Obama administration had rejected some requests, notably including those seeking work requirements.[77]

As the Trump administration began, five states had 1115 waivers pending with CMS.[78] Massachusetts sought a different type of expansive waiver and withdrew its request. The others sought a variety of changes, with work requirements being a common denominator.[79] Most of the waiver requests would likely reduce the number of people covered. The waiver process often featured a negotiation between CMS and the state, with the state modifying elements of its request to obtain approval.

The Obama administration had held the line on approvals extending limits to the entire Medicaid adult population and had rejected work-requirement proposals. CMS had signaled that the Trump administration would be open to such changes, and some states moved to take advantage of the policy modification. The use of Medicaid 1115 waivers to sabotage the ACA only worked in those states seeking to constrain rather than expand Medicaid. Waivers could only be initiated by the states. By the end of 2017, the Trump administration had followed up its March letter with a November information bulletin inviting states to submit waivers with work requirements. By late 2017 eight states had applications pending, with work requirements featuring prominently.[80]

Section 1332 Waivers

According to John McDonough, the Section 1332 waivers emerged from the initial competition between Senators Ron Wyden and Max Baucus for leadership on health reform. Wyden's 2007 bill envisioned a more radical reform converting employer-sponsored policies into employer-subsidized insurance purchased in a marketplace. The Senate Finance Committee's ACA version was emerging as the winning approach, and Wyden asked Baucus for two amendments.

One would allow workers with unaffordable employer insurance to take the employer contribution into the marketplace. Both business and labor groups opposed this. Baucus accepted the second amendment instead. This was a waiver for state innovation with language identical to that of Wyden's earlier bill. Thus Section 1332 was born. Originally it was to take effect in 2014, but the CBO warned the Wyden waiver would complicate the fiscal analysis of ACA, and the Senate changed the effective date to 2017. Both before and after ACA passage, Senators Wyden and Bernie Sanders attempted to move the date back to 2014. They were unsuccessful.[81]

The statutory waiver language provided guardrails to prevent states from using 1332 waivers to dilute ACA consumer protections. A 2015 Obama administration guidance document details how, under waiver changes, coverage must be comprehensive and affordable, insure comparable numbers, and not increase the federal deficit. Furthermore, 1332 waivers cannot change Medicaid or the Children's Health Insurance Program, although it is possible to combine a 1332 waiver with a Medicaid 1115 waiver to integrate a set of changes.[82]

The Obama administration did not approve any 1332 waivers, since they were not allowed prior to 2017. The Trump administration immediately perceived 1332 waivers as a vehicle to undermine and weaken various provisions of the ACA. In March 2017 Secretary Price wrote to all governors soliciting waivers to apply for a 1332 waiver but did caution them about the legal limits.[83]

The Trump administration approved Hawaii's waiver request in January 2017, allowing that state to reinstate a decades-old employer-mandate plan. It approved an Alaska proposal for a reinsurance program to help stabilize the individual insurance market in July. Minnesota, Oklahoma, and Oregon followed with reinsurance-based waiver applications. By late 2017, Iowa, New Hampshire, and Massachusetts were also working on waiver proposals.[84] Oregon's reinsurance program was approved in late 2017, and in September part of Minnesota's reinsurance plan was approved.[85]

The approval process slowed later in the year and apparently became more onerous. California, Iowa, and Oklahoma all withdrew their proposals. The proposals of Massachusetts, Ohio, and Vermont were deemed incomplete and not approved.[86]

The Trump administration would continue to approve 1332 waivers designed to establish reinsurance programs, and by late 2019 eleven more states had been approved. Most of them were liberal states.[87] In October 2018 CMS revised the guardrail guidance document, opening the door for more comprehensive waivers that would likely reduce comprehensive insurance.[88] However, the use of 1332 waivers as a sabotage strategy had not been successful. As with Medicaid 1115 waivers, action by the Trump administration required that states take the initiative. Many were reluctant to do so.

State Actions

As the fate of the ACA hung in the balance during 2017, states that had not expanded Medicaid tended to wait and see. These remaining states were Republican dominant and had resisted expansion during the Obama administration. Expansion advocates in Maine developed a new strategy, which involved using the initiative process to place the question directly before the voters. In November 2017 the voters approved a ballot initiative authorizing expansion. However, Republican governor Paul LePage refused to implement expansion, and it was delayed a year until a new governor took office in January 2019.[89] The Maine approach had been watched by expansion advocates in several other states that would pursue it in 2018.

The heavy cloud looming over most states was the concern about market stability. An Urban Institute study in January 2017 found state concerns that premiums would escalate, insurers would exit the market and leave some counties with no insurance plan in the ACA marketplace, and total enrollment would plummet. Many insurers had experienced early losses but improved their financial position in 2016. Additionally, there was fear that the great uncertainty about the future of the ACA would destabilize the individual market.[90]

As the year progressed state exchanges appeared to be more successful in stabilizing the market with enrollment growth, and the anticipated freefall decline did not materialize. Minnesota developed a successful reinsurance program.[91] Several other states began to pursue the reinsurance idea by developing Section 1332 waivers with a reinsurance focus. By the end of summer 2017, the last county without an insurance plan in the marketplace for 2018, Paulding County, Ohio, had gained coverage. Thus, there were no "bare" counties for the next year.[92]

A Kaiser Family Foundation study of the individual insurance market in 2017 found continued improvement in medical loss ratios, gross margins per patient, and premiums outpacing claims. The study authors concluded that overall the market was stabilizing, but some parts of the country were more fragile.[93] In some markets there were fewer participating plans, with state exchanges more successful. This was probably due to more active recruitment of plans by state exchanges.[94] In 2017 there were few major ACA changes at the state level. The accomplishment was the maintenance of the status quo with the failure of repeal legislation and the stabilization of the individual markets.

Legal Issues

While various legal battles continued throughout 2017, there were no major court decisions upholding or weakening the ACA. Legal disputes continued around the question of the appropriate accommodations for religious organizations on the ACA requirement for contraceptive coverage. The Trump administration in October 2017 issued new interim final rules on the subject, which provided a much broader exemption from the ACA requirement.[95] There were legal challenges to the interim final rule, and it would be late 2018 before the Trump administration's rule was finalized.[96] The legal challenges ultimately went to the Supreme Court, which in 2020 upheld the Trump administration rule.[97]

The other continuing legal issues surrounded risk-corridor payments and cost-sharing reduction payments. With risk-corridor payments various insurance companies continued their legal fight to receive full reimbursement, even if the government didn't collect enough program revenue to cover the payments. The Trump administration moved to halt these payments in October 2017. Nineteen state attorneys general filed suit for an injunction to require the Trump administration to continue making the payments.[98] Both of these legal issues were not resolved in 2017 and would continue into the new year and beyond.

2017: Wrap-Up

As President Trump took office in January 2017, ACA supporters feared the law's significant expansion of health insurance would not survive into 2018. The GOP majorities in Congress could not quite pass legislation repealing the law but came close. The Trump administration sabotage of the program caused marginal harm but was not fatal. Court challenges to the administrative rules delayed or halted the full impact of administrative efforts to weaken the program. Despite state anxiety, massive insurance company withdrawal from ACA marketplaces did not occur. Several states began to fashion Section 1332 waivers designed to stabilize the individual market. Timely adjustments overcame the end of CSR payments, and the devastating impact on the market did not happen.[99]

Finally, the source of legal challenges began to flip. During the Obama administration opponents used continuing legal challenges by state attorneys general and others as a strategy of resistance. In 2017 it was the Trump administration's turn to have state attorneys general leading the charge against actions to sabotage the ACA.

In the following chapter we trace the survival of the ACA in 2018 and beyond.

Notes

1. Timothy Jost, "ACA Repeal Process Begins in Congress," *Health Affairs Blog*, January 3, 2017, www.healthaffairs.org/do/10.1377/hblog20170103.058214/full.

2. Timothy Jost, "Trump Executive Order on ACA: What It Won't Do, What It Might Do, and When," *Health Affairs Blog*, January 21, 2017, www.healthaffairs.org/do/10.1377/hblog20170121.058405/full.

3. Rachael Bade, "Ryan: GOP Will Replace Obamacare, Cut Taxes and Fund Wall by August," *Politico*, January 25, 2017, www.politico.com/story/2017/01/republican-agenda-retreat-obamacare-wall-tax-cuts-23417.

4. Robert Pear, "G.O.P. Accused of Playing 'Hide-and-Seek' with Obamacare Replacement Bill," *New York Times*, March 2, 2017, www.nytimes.com/2017/03/02/us/politics/obamacare-aca-repeal-replace.html.

5. "American Health Care Act: Budget Reconciliation Recommendations of the House Committees on Ways and Means and Energy and Commerce," Congressional Budget Office, March 13, 2017, www.cbo.gov/system/files/115th-congress-2017-2018/costestimate/americanhealthcareact.pdf; Timothy Jost, "CBO Projects Coverage Losses, Cost Savings from AHCA; Administration Signals Flexibility to Governors on Waivers," *Health Affairs Blog*, March 14, 2017, www.healthaffairs.org/do/10.1377/hblog20170314.059186/full.

6. Jennifer Steinhauer, "G.O.P. Health Bill Faces Revolt from Conservative Forces," *New York Times*, March 7, 2017, www.nytimes.com/2017/03/07/us/politics/affordable-care-act-obama-care-health.html.

7. Maggie Haberman and Robert Pear, "After Halting Start, Trump Plunges into Effort to Repeal Health Law," *New York Times*, March 9, 2017, www.nytimes.com/2017/03/09/us/politics/health-bill-clears-house-panel-in-pre-dawn-hours.html.

8. Tim Alberta, "Inside the GOP's Health Care Debacle: Eighteen Days That Shook the Republican Party—and Humbled a President," *Politico*, March 24, 2017, www.politico.com/magazine/story/2017/03/obamacare-vote-paul-ryan-health-care-ahca-replacement-failure-trump-214947.

9. Russell Berman, "Republicans Can't Find the Votes for Their Health-Care Bill," *The Atlantic*, March 23, 2017, www.theatlantic.com/politics/archive/2017/03/trump-republicans-scramble-gop-health-care-bill/520560.

10. Robert Pear, Thomas Kaplan, and Maggie Haberman, "In Major Defeat for Trump, Push to Repeal Health Law Fails," *New York Times*, March 24, 2017, www.nytimes.com/2017/03/24/us/politics/health-care-affordable-care-act.html.

11. "Summary of the American Health Care Act," Kaiser Family Foundation, May 2017, http://files.kff.org/attachment/Proposals-to-Replace-the-Affordable-Care-Act-Summary-of-the-American-Health-Care-Act.

12. David Weigel, "'Obamacare Lite,' 'RINOcare': Conservatives Rebel Against GOP's ACA Bill," *Washington Post*, March 7, 2017, www.washingtonpost.com/news/powerpost/wp/2017/03/07/obamacare-lite-rinocare-conservatives-rebel-against-gops-aca-bill.

13. Robert Pear and Thomas Kaplan, "Ceding to One Side on Health Bill, Trump Risks Alienating Another," *New York Times*, April 4, 2017, www.nytimes.com/2017/04/04/us/politics/president-trump-health-care.html.

14. Mike DeBonis and John Wagner, "Republicans Try to Revive Health-Care Effort as Leaders Seek to Temper Expectations," *Washington Post*, April 4, 2017, www.washingtonpost.com/powerpost/with-help-from-pence-house-republicans-suddenly-rekindle-health-care-talks/2017/04/04/91cf1c74-192f-11e7-855e-4824bbb5d748_story.html.

15. Margot Sanger-Katz, "What Changed in the Health Repeal Plan to Win Over the Freedom Caucus," *New York Times*, April 26, 2017, www.nytimes.com/2017/04/26/upshot/what-changed-in-the-health-repeal-plan-to-win-over-the-freedom-caucus.html.

16. Dan Diamond, "What's in the GOP's Latest Deal to Repeal Obamacare," *Politico*, April 26, 2017, www.politico.com/tipsheets/politico-pulse/2017/04/whats-in-the-gops-latest-deal-to-repeal-obamacare-219988.

17. Thomas Kaplan and Robert Pear, "House Passes Measure to Repeal and Replace the Affordable Care Act," *New York Times*, May 4, 2017, www.nytimes.com/2017/05/04/us/politics/health-care-bill-vote.html.

18. Kim Soffen, Darla Cameron, and Kevin Uhrmacher, "How the House Voted to Pass the GOP Health-Care Bill," *Washington Post*, May 4, 2017, www.washingtonpost.com/graphics/politics/ahca-house-vote.

19. Matt Flegenheimer, "The Next Step for the Republican Health Care Bill: A Skeptical Senate," *New York Times*, May 4, 2017, www.nytimes.com/2017/05/04/us/politics/senate-health-care-bill.html.

20. Robert Pear, "13 Men, and No Women, Are Writing New G.O.P. Health Bill in Senate," *New York Times*, May 8, 2017, www.nytimes.com/2017/05/08/us/politics/women-health-care-senate.html.

21. Annie L. Mach, "Comparison of the American Health Care Act (AHCA) and the Better Care Reconciliation Act (BCRA)," Congressional Research Service, July 23, 2017, https://fas.org/sgp/crs/misc/R44883.pdf.

22. Timothy Jost, "The Latest CBO Score of the Better Care Reconciliation Act Leaves 22 Million Uninsured by 2026 (Update)," *Health Affairs Blog*, July 20, 2017, www.healthaffairs.org/do/10.1377/hblog20170720.061145/full.

23. Timothy Jost, "CBO Projects That 22 Million Would Lose Coverage Under Senate Bill," *Health Affairs Blog*, June 27, 2017, www.healthaffairs.org/do/10.1377/hblog20170627.060839/full.

24. Jennifer Steinhauer and Robert Pear, "G.O.P. Support of Senate Health Repeal Erodes During Break," *New York Times*, July 7, 2017, www.nytimes.com/2017/07/07/us/politics/republicans-health-care-bill.html.

25. Sara Rosenbaum, "Medicaid and the Latest Version of the BCRA: Massive Federal Funding Losses Remain," *Health Affairs Blog*, July 14, 2017, www.healthaffairs.org/do/10.1377/hblog20170714.061061/full; Timothy Jost, "Senate GOP Leadership Unveils Latest Version of Health Reform Legislation," *Health Affairs Blog*, July 14, 2017, www.healthaffairs.org/do/10.1377/hblog20170714.061057/full.

26. Julie Hirschfeld Davis, Thomas Kaplan, and Maggie Haberman, "Trump Demands That Senators Find a Way to Replace Obamacare," *New York Times*, July 19, 2017, www.nytimes.com/2017/07/19/us/politics/donald-trump-obamacare-health-care-republicans-senators.html.

27. Anjali Singhvi and Alicia Parlapiano, "What's Dividing Republican Senators on the Health Care Bill," *New York Times*, July 12, 2017, www.nytimes.com/interactive/2017/07/11/us/politics/republicans-change-senate-health-care-bill.html.

28. "Estimate for HR 1628, the Better Care Reconciliation Act of 2017," Congressional Budget Office, www.cbo.gov/system/files/115th-congress-2017-2018/costestimate/52941-hr1628bcra.pdf.

29. Timothy Jost, "Senate Parliamentarian Rules Several BCRA Provisions Violate the Byrd Rule," *Health Affairs Blog*, July 21, 2017, www.healthaffairs.org/do/10.1377/hblog20170721.061166/full.

30. Thomas Kaplan and Robert Pear, "Senate Votes Down Broad Obamacare Repeal," *New York Times*, July 25, 2017, www.nytimes.com/2017/07/25/us/politics/senate-health-care.html.

31. Joe Williams, "Senate Rejects Obamacare 'Repeal and Delay' Proposal," *Roll Call*, July 26, 2017, www.rollcall.com/2017/07/26/senate-rejects-obamacare-repeal-and-delay-proposal.

32. Margot Sanger-Katz, "'Skinny' Obamacare Repeal Would Clash with Republicans' Health Care Promises," *New York Times*, July 25, 2017, www.nytimes.com/2017/07/25/upshot/skinny-obamacare-repeal-would-clash-with-republicans-health-care-promises.html.

33. Carl Hulse, "McCain Provides a Dramatic Finale on Health Care: Thumb Down," *New York Times*, July 28, 2017, www.nytimes.com/2017/07/28/us/john-mccains-real-return.html.

34. Burgess Everett, "Graham Introduces Repeal Back-Up Plan," *Politico*, July 13, 2017, www.politico.com/story/2017/07/13/lindsey-graham-health-care-proposal-240503.

35 Jennifer Haberkorn, Burgess Everett, and Seung Min Kim, "Inside the Life and Death of Graham-Cassidy," *Politico*, September 27, 2017, www.politico.com/story/2017/09/27/obamacare-repeal-graham-cassidy-243178.

36. Sarah Kliff, "I've Covered the GOP Repeal Plans Since Day One. Graham-Cassidy Is the Most Radical," *Vox*, September 20, 2017, www.vox.com/health-care/2017/9/20/16333338/obamacare-repeal-graham-cassidy.

37. Jacob Leibenluft et al., "Like Other ACA Repeal Bills, Cassidy-Graham Plan Would Add Millions to Uninsured, Destabilize Individual Market," Center on Budget and Policy Priorities, September 20, 2017, www.cbpp.org/research/health/like-other-aca-repeal-bills-cassidy-graham-plan-would-add-millions-to-uninsured.

38. Haberkorn, Everett, and Kim, "Inside the Life and Death of Graham-Cassidy."

39. Juliet Eilperin, Sean Sullivan, and Amy Goldstein, "Senate GOP Abandons Latest Effort to Unwind the Affordable Care Act," *Washington Post*, September 26, 2017, www.washingtonpost.com/powerpost/senate-gop-effort-to-unwind-the-affordable-care-act-faces-critical-test-tuesday/2017/09/26/097b2dc2-a25f-11e7-b14f-f41773cd5a14_story.html.

40. Nicholas Fandos, "McConnell Signals Willingness to Hold Vote on Health Deal if Trump Approves," *New York Times*, October 22, 2017, www.nytimes.com/2017/10/22/us/politics/mitch-mcconnell-trump-bipartisan-health-proposal.html.

41. Timothy Jost, "Senate GOP Tax Cut Bill Heads to Full Senate with Individual Mandate Repeal," *Health Affairs Blog*, November 17, 2017, www.healthaffairs.org/do/10.1377/hblog20171117.748105/full.

42. J. B. Silvers, "How the G.O.P. Tax Bill Will Ruin Obamacare," *New York Times*, December 4, 2017, www.nytimes.com/2017/12/04/opinion/gop-tax-bill-obamacare.html.

43. "Repealing the Individual Health Insurance Mandate: An Updated Estimate," Congressional Budget Office, November 2017, www.cbo.gov/system/files/115th-congress-2017-2018/reports/53300-individualmandate.pdf.

44. Timothy Jost, "The Tax Bill and the Individual Mandate: What Happened, and What Does It Mean?," *Health Affairs Blog*, December 20, 2017, www.healthaffairs.org/do/10.1377/hblog20171220.323429/full.

45. John Kingdon, *Agendas, Alternatives, and Public Policies*, 2nd ed. (New York: Harper Collins, 1995).

46. Ashley Kirzinger et al., "US Public Opinion on Health Care Reform, 2017," *Journal of the American Medical Association*, April 18, 2017, https://jamanetwork.com/journals/jama/fullarticle/2614802.

47. Michael Cooper, "Conservatives Sowed Idea of Health Care Mandate, Only to Spurn It Later," *New York Times*, February 14, 2012, www.nytimes.com/2012/02/15/health/policy/health-care-mandate-was-first-backed-by-conservatives.html.

48. Joseph R. Antos and James C. Capretta, "Republicans Should Take the Time Necessary to Improve the American Health Care Act," *Health Affairs Blog*, March 10, 2017, www.healthaffairs.org/do/10.1377/hblog20170310.059127/full.

49. Jonathan Martin and Alexander Burns, "Governors from Both Parties Denounce Senate Obamacare Repeal Bill," *New York Times*, July 14, 2017, www.nytimes.com/2017/07/14/us/politics/governors-oppose-senate-affordable-care-act-repeal.html; Robert Pear and Thomas Kaplan, "Republican Leaders Defy Bipartisan Opposition to Health Law Repeal," *New York Times*, September 19, 2017, www.nytimes.com/2017/09/19/us/politics/obamacare-act-fix-collapses-repeal

-trump.html; Robert Pear, "Insurers Come Out Swinging Against New Republican Health Care Bill," *New York Times*, September 20, 2017, www.nytimes.com/2017/09/20/us/politics/insurers-oppose-obamacare-repeal.html.

50. Robert J. Blendon and John M. Benson, "Public Opinion About the Future of the Affordable Care Act," *New England Journal of Medicine* 377, no. 12 (August 31, 2017): e12(1)–(7), www.nejm.org/doi/full/10.1056/NEJMsr1710032; Kirzinger et al., "US Public Opinion on Health Care Reform, 2017."

51. Glenn Thrush and Maggie Haberman, "Inspiring Little Fear in Senators, Trump Struggles to Sell Health Bill," *New York Times*, July 20, 2017, www.nytimes.com/2017/07/20/us/trump-republicans-obamacare.html.

52. Jacob Hacker and Paul Pierson, "The Dog Almost Barked: What the ACA Repeal Fight Says About the Resilience of the American Welfare State," *Journal of Health Politics, Policy and Law* 43, no. 4 (August 2018): 551–577.

53. Eric M. Patashnik and Jonathan Oberlander, "After Defeat: Conservative Postenactment Opposition to the ACA in Historical-Institutional Perspective," *Journal of Health Politics, Policy and Law* 43, no. 4 (August 2018): 651–682.

54. Philip Bump, "It's True Trump Didn't Pledge Obamacare Repeal in 64 Days. He Pledged It in One," *Washington Post*, March 24, 2017, www.washingtonpost.com/news/politics/wp/2017/03/24/its-true-trump-didnt-pledge-obamacare-repeal-in-64-days-he-pledged-it-in-one.

55. Jost, "Trump Executive Order on ACA."

56. Timothy Jost, "Unpacking the Trump Administration's Market Stabilization Proposed Rule," *Health Affairs Blog*, February 16, 2017, www.healthaffairs.org/do/10.1377/hblog20170216.058794/full.

57. Timothy Jost, "Examining the Final Market Stabilization Rule: What's There, What's Not, and How Might It Work? (Updated)," *Health Affairs Blog*, April 14, 2017, www.healthaffairs.org/do/10.1377/hblog20170414.059646/full.

58. Karen Pollitz, Jennifer Tolbert, and Ashley Semanskee, "2016 Survey of Health Insurance Marketplace Assister Programs and Brokers," Kaiser Family Foundation, June 8, 2016, www.kff.org/report-section/2016-survey-of-health-insurance-marketplace-assister-programs-and-brokers-section-2-in-person-assistance-during-open-enrollment; Lori Lodes, "I Ran ACA Outreach Under Obama. Trump's Funding Cuts Could Ruin the Health Care Law," *Vox*, September 12, 2017, www.vox.com/the-big-idea/2017/9/12/16294784/aca-outreach-advertising-sabotage-funding.

59. Amy Goldstein, "White House Stops Ads, Outreach for Last Days of 2017 ACA Enrollment," *Washington Post*, January 26, 2017, www.washingtonpost.com/national/health-science/white-house-stops-ads-outreach-for-last-days-of-aca-enrollment/2017/01/26/a2f92682-e420-11e6-ba11-63c4b4fb5a63_story.html.

60. Maura Calsyn and Nicole Rapfogel, "Administrative Actions to Reverse Sabotage and Lower Costs in the ACA Marketplaces," Center for American Progress, July 14, 2020, www.americanprogress.org/issues/healthcare/reports/2020/07/14/487610/administrative-actions-reverse-sabotage-lower-costs-aca-marketplaces.

61. Emily Curran et al., "2017 Federal and State Marketplace Trends Show Value of Outreach, to the Point," Commonwealth Fund, May 4, 2017, www.commonwealthfund.org/blog/2017/2017-federal-and-state-marketplace-trends-show-value-outreach.

62. Shelby Gonzales, "Trump Administration Slashing Funding for Marketplace Enrollment Assistance and Outreach," Center on Budget and Policy Priorities, September 1, 2017, www.cbpp.org/blog/trump-administration-slashing-funding-for-marketplace-enrollment-assistance-and-outreach.

63. Timothy Jost, "CMS Cuts ACA Advertising by 90 Percent amid Other Cuts to Enrollment Outreach," *Health Affairs Blog*, August 31, 2017, www.healthaffairs.org/do/10.1377/hblog20170901.061790/full.

64. Shanoor Seervai, "Cuts to the ACA's Outreach Budget Will Make It Harder for People to Enroll," Commonwealth Fund, October 11, 2017, www.commonwealthfund.org/publications/other-publication/2017/oct/cuts-acas-outreach-budget-will-make-it-harder-people-enroll.

65. Timothy Jost, "Rapid Developments in House v. Burwell," Health Affairs Blog, December 29, 2016, www.healthaffairs.org/do/10.1377/hblog20161229.058172/full.

66. Nicholas Bagley, "Trump's Ominous Threat to Withhold Payment from Health Insurers, Explained," *Vox*, August 2, 2017, www.vox.com/the-big-idea/2017/3/29/15107836/lawsuit-aca-payments-reimbursement-unconstitutional.

67. Timothy Jost, "Administrations Ending of Cost Sharing Reduction Payments Likely to Roil Individual Markets," *Health Affairs Blog*, October 13, 2017, www.ncmedsoc.org/wp-content/uploads/2017/10/Health-Affairs-Article-on-CSRs.pdf.

68. Margot Sanger-Katz, "Trump's Attack on Insurer 'Gravy Train' Could Actually Help a Lot of Consumers," *New York Times*, October 18, 2017, www.nytimes.com/2017/10/18/upshot/trumps-attack-on-insurer-gravy-train-could-actually-help-a-lot-of-consumers.html.

69. Frank J. Thompson, *Medicaid Politics: Federalism, Policy Durability, and Health Reform* (Washington, DC: Georgetown University Press, 2012), chap. 5.

70. "1115 Medicaid Waivers: From Care Delivery Innovations to Work Requirements," Commonwealth Fund, April 2018, www.commonwealthfund.org/sites/default/files/documents/___media_files_publications_explainer_2018_apr_explainer_1115waivers.pdf.

71. Jennifer Tolbert and Karen Pollitz, "Section 1332 State Innovation Waivers: Current Status and Potential Changes," Kaiser Family Foundation, July 6, 2017, www.kff.org/health-reform/issue-brief/section-1332-state-innovation-waivers-current-status-and-potential-changes.

72. Judith Solomon and Jessica Schubel, "Medicaid Waivers Should Further Program Objectives, Not Impose Barriers to Coverage and Care," Center on Budget and Policy Priorities, August 29, 2017, www.cbpp.org/sites/default/files/atoms/files/8-28-17health.pdf.

73. David K. Jones et al., "Undermining the ACA Through the Executive Branch and Federalism: What the Trump Administration's Approach to Health Reform Means for Older Americans," *Journal of Aging and Social Policy* 30, no. 3–4 (2018): 282–299, https://doi.org/10.1080/08959420.2018.1462684.

74. For an excellent historical summary of Section 1115 waivers, see Thompson, *Medicaid Politics*, 134–166.

75. Sidney D. Watson, "Out of the Black Box and into the Light: Using Section 1115 Medicaid Waivers to Implement the Affordable Care Act's Medicaid Expansion," *Yale Journal of Health Policy, Law, and Ethics* 15 (2015), https://digitalcommons.law.yale.edu/yjhple/vol15/iss1/12.

76. Jane B. Wishner et al., "Medicaid Expansion, the Private Option, and Personal Responsibility Requirements," Urban Institute, May 2015, www.urban.org/sites/default/files/publication/53236/2000235-Medicaid-Expansion-The-Private-Option-and-Personal-Responsibility-Requirements.pdf.

77. Arizona, Arkansas, Indiana, Iowa, Michigan, Montana, and New Hampshire. Samantha Artiga et al., "Current Flexibility in Medicaid: An Overview of Federal Standards and State Options," Issue Brief, Kaiser Family Foundation, January 2017,

http://files.kff.org/attachment/Issue-Brief-Current-Flexibility-in-Medicaid-An-Overview-of-Federal-Standards-and-State-Options.

78. Arkansas, Indiana, Iowa, Kentucky, and Massachusetts.

79. MaryBeth Musumeci, Elizabeth Hinton, and Robin Rudowitz, "Section 1115 Medicaid Expansion Waivers: A Look at Key Themes and State Specific Waiver Provisions," Kaiser Family Foundation, August 2017, https://nationaldisabilitynavigator.org/wp-content/uploads/news-items/KFF_Section-1115-Waivers_Aug-2017.pdf.

80. Sara Rosenbaum, "The Trump Administration Re-Imagines Section 1115 Medicaid Demonstrations—and Medicaid," *Health Affairs Blog*, November 9, 2017, www.healthaffairs.org/do/10.1377/hblog20171109.297738/full.

81. John E. McDonough, "Wyden's Waiver: State Innovation on Steroids," *Journal of Health Politics, Policy and Law* 39, no. 5 (October 2014): 1099–1111.

82. Sarah Lueck and Jessica Schubel, "Understanding the Affordable Care Act's State Innovation ('1332') Waivers," Center on Budget and Policy Priorities, September 5, 2017, www.cbpp.org/sites/default/files/atoms/files/2-5-15health1.pdf.

83. Brad Wright et al., "The Devolution of Health Reform? A Comparative Analysis of State Innovation Waiver Activity," *Journal of Health Politics, Policy and Law* 44, no. 2 (2019): 315–331.

84. Justin Giovannelli and Kevin Lucia, "States See Opportunities for Flexibility in the ACA's Innovation Waiver Program," Commonwealth Fund, September 15, 2017, www.commonwealthfund.org/blog/2017/states-see-opportunities-flexibility-acas-innovation-waiver-program.

85. Wright et al., "The Devolution of Health Reform?"

86. Billy Wynne and Taylor Cowey, "Navigating the Section 1332 Waiver Process: For States, a Treacherous Road Ahead," *Health Affairs Blog*, November 29, 2017, www.healthaffairs.org/do/10.1377/hblog20171128.217593/full.

87. Frank J. Thompson, Kenneth K. Wong, and Barry G Rabe, *Trump, the Administrative Presidency, and Federalism* (Washington, DC: Brookings Institution Press, 2020), 60–61.

88. Katie Keith and Chris Fleming, "CMS Releases New 1332 Waiver Concepts: Implications," *Health Affairs Blog*, November 29, 2018, www.healthaffairs.org/do/10.1377/hblog20181129.845780/full; Timothy Jost, "Using the 1332 State Waiver Program to Undermine the Affordable Care Act State by State," Commonwealth Fund, October 30, 2018, www.commonwealthfund.org/blog/2018/using-1332-state-waiver-program-undermine-affordable-care-act-state-state.

89. Sarah Kliff, "Maine Just Became the 33rd State to Expand Medicaid," *Vox*, November 7, 2017, www.vox.com/policy-and-politics/2017/11/7/16619270/maine-medicaid-expansion-obamacare.

90. Sabrina Corlette et al., "Uncertain Future for Affordable Care Act Leads Insurers to Rethink Participation, Prices," Urban Institute, January 2017, www.urban.org/sites/default/files/publication/87816/2001126-uncertain-future-for-affordable-care-act-leads-insurers-to-rethink-participation-prices_1.pdf.

91. Robert Pear, "Minnesota Finds a Way to Slow Soaring Health Premiums," *New York Times*, September 2, 2017, www.nytimes.com/2017/09/02/us/politics/minnesota-health-care-reinsurance.html.

92. Timothy Jost, "ACA Round-Up: Last Bare County Covered, Oklahoma Waiver Application Complete, and More," *Health Affairs Blog*, August 25, 2017, www.healthaffairs.org/do/10.1377/hblog20170825.061677/abs.

93. Cynthia Cox, Ashley Semanskee, and Larry Levitt, "Individual Insurance Market Performance in 2017," Issue Brief, Kaiser Family Foundation, May 17, 2018, www.kff.org/health-reform/issue-brief/individual-insurance-market-performance-in-2017.

94. E. Curran, J. Giovannelli, and K. Lucia, "Insurer Participation in ACA Marketplaces: Federal Uncertainty Triggers Diverging Business Strategies," Commonwealth Fund, January 5, 2018, www.commonwealthfund.org/blog/2018/insurer-participation-aca-marketplaces-federal-uncertainty-triggers-diverging-business.

95. Katie Keith and Timothy Jost, "Trump Administration Regulatory Rebalancing Favors Religious and Moral Freedom over Contraceptive Access," *Health Affairs Blog*, October 7, 2017, www.healthaffairs.org/do/10.1377/hblog20171021.317078/full.

96. Katie Keith, "Religious, Moral Exemptions from Contraceptive Coverage Mandates: Second Verse, Same as the First," *Health Affairs Blog*, November 9, 2018, www.healthaffairs.org/do/10.1377/hblog20181109.87594/full.

97. Katie Keith, "Supreme Court Upholds Broad Exemptions to Contraceptive Mandate—for Now," *Health Affairs Blog*, July 9, 2020, www.healthaffairs.org/do/10.1377/hblog20200708.110645/full.

98. Timothy Jost, "State Attorneys General Ask Court for Injunction Reversing CSR Payment Halt," *Health Affairs Blog*, October 18, 2017, www.healthaffairs.org/do/10.1377/hblog20171022.15020/full.

99. Joann Volk et al., "Loss of Cost-Sharing Reductions in the ACA Marketplace: Impact on Consumers and Insurer Participation," Commonwealth Fund, March 30, 2017, www.commonwealthfund.org/blog/2017/loss-cost-sharing-reductions-aca-marketplace-impact-consumers-and-insurer-participation.

5

The Trump Administration's Sabotage Strategies

> *Only Burnside could have managed such a coup,*
> *wringing one last spectacular defeat from the jaws of victory.*
>
> —Abraham Lincoln

As 2018 began, the midterm election was eleven months away. The Republican leadership was unwilling to embark on a new round of Affordable Care Act (ACA) repeal legislation after confidence in a quick 2017 victory was shattered. The ACA legislative story for 2018 is simple. No further serious efforts at ACA repeal were undertaken. In mid-2018 a coalition of conservative groups and health policy analysts released a plan similar to the 2017 Graham-Cassidy bill.[1] Senator Lindsey Graham and others voiced support for the idea, but the congressional leadership was not interested in a 2017 rerun.[2]

Congress, in an effort to marginally impact premiums, did pass legislation in January 2018 to suspend the tax on insurance companies for 2019. Oliver Wyman estimated this would save 2.2 percent in premiums. Since the law only applied to 2019 reinstatement of the tax, Wyman projected an increase in premiums in 2020 and beyond.[3] This and other ACA-related taxes were permanently repealed in 2019.

The story of 2018 entails the administrative actions of the Donald Trump administration and the continued legal battles initiated by both those opposed to and those supporting the ACA.

Administrative Sabotage Actions

One of the major accomplishments of the ACA was to strengthen individual insurance plans in the marketplace by requiring all plans to follow a set of consumer-friendly rules, such as prohibition of preexisting-condition screens and provision of standard benefit coverage. But the individual insurance market remained fragile, especially in some parts of the country. One feature of the Trump administration sabotage effort was the use of regulatory authority to weaken the segment of the market in which customers could purchase individual policies with a tax credit. If healthy customers could be lured out of the marketplace by cheaper but lower-quality coverage, ACA marketplace prices would escalate, and insurers might abandon the ACA market. In January and February 2018, the Trump administration began this strategy with the Labor Department proposing relaxed rules for association health plans and short-term plans.[4]

Association Health Plans

For decades some individuals had purchased health insurance through an association typically for members of a similar trade or profession. Prior to the ACA some of these association health plans (AHPs) were rampant with fraud and abuse. After the ACA enactment, the Barack Obama administration regulation specified AHPs had to follow individual market rules. There was a limited exception for AHPs for small employers sharing a common interest, which were regulated by large group rules. However, individual sole proprietors were not eligible for this category.[5]

The new Trump administration rule, proposed in January 2018 and finalized in June, weakened the federal regulation of AHPs. Under the new rules AHPs would function under the more lenient standards applied to large-employer plans. For example, essential health benefit standards would not apply, preexisting-condition screens were not prohibited, and premiums could be segmented.[6] The ostensible rationale for relaxing regulation of AHPs was to lower premium costs. However, actuarial studies projected this move would peel from the ACA individual marketplace a number of low-risk individuals, leaving the risk pool less healthy with higher premiums.[7]

Short-Term Plans

In the 1996 Health Insurance Portability and Accountability Act, Congress defined as "short-term" plans with a duration of less than a year. These were to be regulated by the states and exempt from federal rules. The ACA statute and initial rules did not treat short-term policies as requiring minimum essential coverage; nor did they meet the individual-mandate requirement.[8] Under both statutes short-term plans were treated as temporary health insurance for individuals in transition from one policy to another.

By 2016 the Obama administration was aware of abuses in the issuance of short-term policies. Some were being issued for just short of a year, and the ACA consumer protections did not apply. The Obama administration responded by promulgating a rule limiting short-term policies to three months without the option to renew. The purpose of the rule was to preclude healthy individuals from purchasing cheaper short-term policies and thus weakening the individual-market risk pool. The Obama regulation took effect in April 2017, but the Trump administration moved in early 2018 to replace the rule with a new one that again allowed short-term plans to last for a year and to be renewed. However, states retained the authority to regulate a lower limit.[9]

The new Trump administration rule became effective October 2, 2018. An estimated 160,000 individuals had short-term plans during 2016 prior to the rule limiting such plans to three months. However, the ending of the individual-mandate penalty, the new Trump administration rule, and more aggressive marketing by insurance companies were expected to exponentially increase the number of people opting for the cheaper short-term plans.[10]

The problems with short-term plans included both the threat that they might destabilize the ACA individual market by luring out healthy individuals and the hazards they posed for individuals who may not understand the low value of the coverage and likelihood of high out-of-pocket costs in the event of serious illness.[11] A Melman research report estimated 2020 ACA market decline of 6 percent and subsequent premium increase of 4 percent attributed to the Trump administration's regulatory changes for short-term and association policies.[12] These changes were not likely to generate a death spiral for the ACA marketplace but served to increase premiums and weakened consumer protections.

Section 1332 Waiver Encouragement and State Waivers

Section 1332 waivers offered the greatest potential for ACA sabotage in those states controlled by Republicans. Several waivers had been approved by the Trump administration in 2017, and four more were approved during the summer of 2018. These were all for reinsurance programs in Maine, Maryland, New Jersey, and Wisconsin. An Ohio application submitted in March 2018 requested waiver of the individual-mandate requirement. The Centers for Medicare and Medicaid Services (CMS) indicated the request did not comply with the requirements.[13]

State Section 1332 waiver requests during 2018 all focused on reinsurance plans and were not numerous. In an attempt to stimulate additional requests and farther-reaching proposals, the CMS in October 2018 issued a new guidance for states considering applying for 1332 waivers. This replaced the Obama administration's 2015 guidance. The "guardrails" in the law itself limit the extent of the waivers by requiring that coverage be comprehensive, protect against excessive costs, insure a comparable number of residents, and not increase the federal deficit. The state must also enact a law to allow action under the waiver. The Trump administration guidance provided a weaker interpretation of the guardrails and introduced new waiver concepts: account-based subsidies, state-specific premium assistance, adjusted plan options, and risk-stabilization strategies.[14]

The guidance implied a 1332 waiver would be favorably reviewed if it only provided comparable access, not actual coverage. An acceptable waiver might make some individuals better off, even as vulnerable populations were worse off. States might increase coverage by use of short-term policies that failed to meet ACA consumer-protection standards. Marketplace subsidies for noncompliant plans might even be approved.[15]

Timothy Jost concluded that the late 2018 guidance represented an effort to achieve by administrative fiat what could not be accomplished legislatively in 2017. It opened a wide door to legitimizing, and perhaps subsidizing, insurance plans that deviated from ACA standards in explicit fashion. He forecasted significant legal challenges if some states received waivers consistent with the Trump administration guidance.[16]

Medicaid Waivers

In 2017 Congress was unable to pass legislative proposals to radically reduce the size and scale of the Medicaid program, but the Trump administration effort to shrink Medicaid enrollment continued in 2018 with aggressive use of the Section 1115 waiver authority. As with 1332 waivers, the initiative must come from the state. Some Republican-dominated states sought damaging waivers. There is a long history of states using 1115 waivers to modify their Medicaid programs. Typically, this has been a strategy to expand coverage in some fashion. The Bill Clinton administration began a more aggressive approach to granting waivers, and this continued for two decades. The Obama administration approved waivers for Iowa and Arkansas to allow the states to arrange private insurance for the expansion population as part of an agreement to expand Medicaid.[17]

In the early days of the Trump administration, governors were told the new administration was open to 1115 waivers that reduced the number of beneficiaries by use of work requirements and other conditions. This represented a clear departure from previous use of waivers. A number of states began to develop 1115 waiver proposals involving work requirements in 2017 and early 2018. By the end of 2018, sixteen states had proposals either approved or pending.[18]

By early 2018 Kentucky, Indiana, and Arkansas had received waiver approval to apply a Medicaid work requirement. Approvals for New Hampshire and Wisconsin came later in the year. Arkansas was the first to implement its work requirements in June 2018. The Kentucky waiver was challenged in federal court and blocked just prior to July implementation. The narrow district court decision didn't address the broad question of whether work requirements are allowed but rather found the waiver rationale failed to address the central issue of the impact on coverage.[19] The administration appealed the decision and immediately began a new round of comments on a second waiver from Kentucky, which had no major changes in approach. CMS approved the new waiver in late November 2018 with a scheduled effective date of April 1, 2019.[20]

By the end of 2018, only Arkansas had actually started imposing work requirements. An initial projection estimated that 20 to 30 percent of the Arkansas Medicaid expansion population would lose coverage in the first year as a consequence of the work requirement.[21] It appeared that 2019 would be a pivotal year for the Medicaid work-requirement issue.

Legal Issues

The ACA had disappeared from the congressional agenda in 2018, and the courts became a central battleground for both sides. In February 2018, nineteen Republican attorneys general initiated a lawsuit in a Texas federal district court contending the reduction of the individual-mandate penalty to zero rendered the entire ACA invalid.[22] The Trump administration responded in June, not by defending the law but by agreeing the individual mandate was unconstitutional. It contended that several provisions of the law should be invalidated but not the entire ACA. The Department of Justice argued for striking the guaranteed-issue and community-rating provisions as inseparable from the individual mandate.[23]

Seventeen Democratic attorneys general intervened to defend the ACA, since the Trump administration failed to do so.[24] Thus, state officeholders were battling in court over the future of the federal law. Judge Reed O'Connor ruled in favor of the Republican attorneys general in late December and found the whole ACA to be invalid but delayed implementation of his ruling until an appeal was resolved. Both the Trump administration and the Democratic attorneys general appealed the decision, with a Fifth Circuit decision expected in 2019.[25] No matter which side prevailed in the appellate court, the loser in *Texas v. Azar* was expected to ultimately appeal to the Supreme Court.

Meanwhile, the state of Maryland filed a countersuit in a different district court hoping to have the ACA declared fully constitutional. In December the district court judge affirmed Maryland's right to bring suit and scheduled hearings for early 2019 for the related suit.[26]

New York and eleven other states filed a lawsuit in July to invalidate the Trump administration's rule on association health plans. The states argued the rule was intended to undermine the ACA. The district court was expected to hear the case in early 2019.[27]

Patient advocacy groups and a health-plan association filed suit in September 2018 to invalidate the Trump administration rule on short-term health plans. They argued the rule was inconsistent with the statute and contrary to congressional intent and contended it was arbitrary and capricious.[28] That hearing was set for early 2019 as well.[29]

Several cities filed suit challenging the Trump administration's 2019 benefit and payment parameters rule as undermining the navigator program and regulation of health plans, contending the president did not faithfully execute the law.[30] Both sides in the dispute over ACA protections of transgender individuals sought court intervention to uphold their positions. Section 1557 of the ACA prohibited discrimination, and the Obama rules had been challenged. During 2018 several district courts had ruled on the question, and the Trump administration was rewriting the regulations.[31]

The court battles over religious objections to contraception-coverage requirements continued. Democratic attorneys general in California and Pennsylvania had challenged the 2017 interim Trump administration revised rules. Federal judges issued injunctions to halt the new rules, and the appeal process had begun. The promulgation of final rules moved the cases back to the judicial docket for 2019.[32]

The final set of legal ACA legal issues in 2018 pertained to the ongoing disputes over cost-sharing reduction (CSR) payments to insurance plans and risk-corridor payments. The Trump administration 2017 decision to discontinue the payments effectively ended the suit over CSRs and resulted in a 2018 settlement among all the parties, although other litigation continued. This included cases before the court of claims.[33]

The risk-corridor program was a temporary effort to induce hesitant insurance plans to participate in the marketplace in the early years. Payments were collected from profitable firms and shared with those that lost money in the individual market. However, insufficient funds were collected to fully reimburse those eligible. The companies sued for full payment. In January 2018 oral arguments were heard on the cases, with a three-judge panel ruling in June that only partial payments could be made because the program was required to be budget neutral. The plaintiffs requested a rehearing but were denied. It was anticipated they would appeal to the Supreme Court.[34]

The Election

The most significant event of 2018 for the ACA was the outcome of the midterm election. Republicans gained two Senate seats to increase their margin but lost control of the House. Democrats gained forty seats and thus assured a congressional firewall against any attempt to repeal or legislatively revise the ACA until after the 2020 presidential election. It appeared the unpopular 2017 effort to repeal the ACA may have cost the Republicans a House majority.[35]

2019: Chipping Away Administratively

In modern American politics the day after the midterm election marks the beginning of the next campaign for president. As we look at events surrounding the ACA in 2019, the next presidential election is always part of the background. Republican efforts to repeal and replace the ACA before the 2020 presidential election ended when Democrats regained control of the House. The new House majority could now play the same game as Republicans did in 2011 by passing ACA enhancement legislation with no expectation of Senate approval or a presidential signature.

By May 2019, House Democrats had passed the Strengthening Health Care and Lowering Prescription Drug Costs Act. With little prospect of Senate approval, this bill was an early salvo in the 2020 election battle. The bill included additional money for ACA marketplace outreach, new funds for states seeking to establish their own marketplaces, limits on short-term plans, and requirements for more transparency on ACA progress reports.[36] Other provisions of the bill aimed at reducing the cost of prescription drugs. Public opinion polls showed greater support for the ACA since 2017 and substantial concern with the cost of prescription drugs.[37]

Even with a fierce partisan division in Congress, passing annual budget bills requires cooperation and accommodation. The spending bills passed in December 2019 included several ACA-related provisions, including some sought by Democrats. There was bipartisan support for repeal of three ACA taxes. The health insurance, Cadillac, and medical device taxes each had a history of delayed or suspended enforcement and opposition.

Other ACA provisions were intended to safeguard insurance markets against Trump administration threats to destabilize. These included assuring silver loading continued, maintaining automatic reenrollment, and requiring reporting of the costs of implementing the ACA.[38] A successful repeal bill or major expansion of the ACA was not going to pass until after the 2020 election.

Administrative Rules

At the other end of Pennsylvania Avenue, the Trump administration continued its efforts to sabotage both of the key foundations of the ACA goal of increasing high-quality health coverage. The line of attack had two prongs. First, efforts continued to weaken the ACA marketplaces for subsidized purchase of individual insurance. Second, Medicaid 1115 waivers were used aggressively to diminish Medicaid enrollment in Republican-dominated states, especially by promoting work requirements to reduce enrollment among the expansion population.

In January the Department of Health and Human Services proposed a rule to adjust the tax-credit payment formulas. The rule was finalized in April to be effective for the 2020 enrollment period. The out-of-pocket annual maximum was also modified.[39] An analysis of these changes estimated over 80 percent of marketplace customers would pay higher premiums, and as a result 70,000 people would drop coverage. The change in the out-of-pocket maximum applied to those with employer-sponsored insurance as well.[40]

In May the administration proposed an even farther-reaching new rule. The rule was technical and not likely to have a great deal of immediate impact. The poverty line measure had been adjusted each year using the Consumer Price Index (CPI). The administration proposed using the chained CPI instead in the future. This alternative measure is derived from consumer spending patterns. While many argued such a change would require legislation, the Trump administration was proceeding through regulation.[41] If approved, the change would over time reduce the number of people eligible for Medicaid and reduce tax credits as well as CSR payments in the marketplace.[42]

Throughout 2019 the Trump administration additionally sought, in a variety of ways large and small, to limit or depress enrollment in both marketplace plans and Medicaid. They encouraged consumers to consider insurance plans with fewer consumer protections. In June the administration finalized a rule allowing employers to substitute health reimbursement arrangements for group coverage, thus driving individuals to seek short-term plans. In August navigator funding was again cut for the 2020 enrollment period, leaving this critical element unavailable to many seeking insurance coverage in the marketplace.

In September the administration invited up to ten states to apply for a program allowing insurers to modify premiums and cost sharing based on health outcomes, meaning that healthy individuals would be charged less. In a move consistent with broader Trump efforts to discourage immigration and make life difficult even for legal immigrants, an October proclamation required immigrants to have health insurance.

This mandate could not be met with ACA marketplace plans or Medicaid but could be fulfilled with skimpy short-term plans. In November a new rule was proposed to make it more difficult for states to pay their share of Medicaid expenses by restricting provider assessments and intergovernmental transfers. In some states this might lead to a reduction in benefits or eligibility. A December rule was finalized modifying premium payments for abortion coverage, which was estimated to increase the likelihood individuals would lose complete coverage because of billing confusion.[43] Not all of these efforts ultimately succeeded, but the attempts created uncertainty and potential disruption of the ACA coverage-expansion strategy.

Medicaid

Work-requirement 1115 waivers were the principal Medicaid sabotage strategy of the Trump administration in 2019. The political climate in several states made this an attractive approach. Rarely were cost savings from declining enrollment cited as the rationale, but the objective of both federal and state governments seeking these work-requirement waivers was clearly to reduce the coverage impact of Medicaid expansion by excluding a segment of eligible beneficiaries. The argued objective was that work requirements would discourage dependence on welfare. This was the contention when Temporary Assistance for Needy Families and the Supplemental Nutrition Assistance Program added work requirements in the 1990s.[44] In oral arguments before the appeals court in 2019, the administration conceded holding down costs was a factor in the support for work requirements.[45]

The Obama administration had not approved work requirements, even as a condition for expansion. As noted above, it had been willing to try other experiments, for example, with premiums. However, the Trump administration not only was willing to authorize work requirements but actively encouraged states to submit such waivers. In 2018 work-requirement waivers were approved for Arkansas, Indiana, Michigan, New Hampshire, Kentucky, and Wisconsin. This was followed in 2019 by approvals for Arizona, Ohio, South Carolina, Utah, and Kentucky for a second time.

However, the 2019 implementation was very limited for two reasons. First, court challenges seeking to overturn the 1115 work-requirement waiver approvals caused them to grind to a halt. Second, in some states newly elected Democratic governors withdrew or halted the work-requirement waivers.

Arkansas was the first state to begin implementation of a 1115 work-requirement waiver. It lasted from June 2018 to March 2019, when a federal district court ruling halted it. Kentucky experienced a more complex path. The start of the Kentucky work requirement was blocked by federal district court in June 2018 and reapproved by CMS in November 2018. Its start was again stopped by the federal court in March 2019 and reapproved in November 2019. But in December the new Democratic governor terminated the Kentucky work-requirement program.[46]

Other Democratic governors took similar actions. Maine withdrew from the waiver in early 2019, and Virginia did the same with its pending request in December 2019. In Arizona, New Hampshire, and Indiana Republican governors suspended their waivers.[47] In Michigan the new

Democratic governor did not have the authority to suspend the waiver, although she opposed work requirements.[48] The federal district court in March 2020 vacated the Michigan waiver.

During this time Arkansas was the only state to fully implement a 1115 work-requirement waiver for a period. A Harvard School of Public Health study of the Arkansas experiment found 18,000 beneficiaries had lost coverage. Employment was not increased. There were negative medical implications for those who lost coverage, and recipients were often unaware of the paperwork requirements necessary to maintain coverage.[49] If the Trump administration, in concert with some states, wished to depress enrollment among the expansion population, work requirements were obviously an effective tool. The Arkansas experience demonstrated how the daunting paperwork involved for recipients, as well as the fragile nature of marginal part-time employment, depressed Medicaid enrollment.

Several lawsuits brought to the federal district court resulted in vacating the waivers because they did not meet the statutory requirements and would result in loss of coverage. In October 2019 a set of these lower-court decisions reached the federal court of appeals. Oral arguments were heard, and the subsequent decision upheld the lower-court rejection of the work requirements.[50] In late 2020 the Supreme Court agreed to hear an appeal to be argued in 2021.

In late 2019 Tennessee sought a 1115 waiver to create a Medicaid block grant within the state by fixing the amount of federal funding, potentially reducing benefits or denying eligibility and providing significant administrative flexibility for the state to use the annual Medicaid funds. By the end of the year, the administration had certified the application as complete and opened an additional comment period.[51] However, consideration was suspended in 2020, and the application was not acted on.

Medicaid expansion continued its slow evolution during 2019. Voters in Idaho and Maine had earlier approved expansion and began enrolling beneficiaries in 2019. Montana passed legislation in April 2019 to continue expansion until 2025.[52]

Utah took a more serpentine path in 2019. The legislature amended the voter-approved expansion in February 2019 by requiring the submission of an 1115 waiver limiting the new population to up to 100 percent, rather than 138 percent, of the federal poverty level (FPL), with a work requirement for the expansion population.[53] The waiver was quickly approved, and another was submitted in July to employ a per capita cap and an enrollment cap. This was not approved by CMS, but a November fallback waiver request increased the expansion population back to 138 percent of the FPL with a work requirement for the expansion group. This was approved in December, but the request for enrollment caps and premiums was not approved.[54]

1332 Waiver

The 1332 waiver option also presented opportunities for states to substantially reshape the ACA within their borders. The Trump administration continued in early 2019 to encourage states to submit 1332 proposals to radically change the ACA insurance markets, but the proposals received had focused on reinsurance plans. Idaho submitted a proposal to modify the separation between marketplace- and Medicaid-eligible individuals by allowing those between 100 and 138 percent of FPL to choose between Medicaid and a subsidized marketplace plan. In August CMS rejected the proposal as incomplete.[55]

The state of Georgia in late 2019 submitted a proposal for more radical change in the ACA within its state. In addition to requesting a reinsurance plan, Georgia proposed moving in 2022 to eliminate the healthcare.gov marketplace and instead allow enrollment through individual brokers and insurers. The future state subsidy structure would combine federal with state funds, but only to a cap. The state would determine the subsidy system to include plans that did not meet all ACA standards. If approved this plan would eliminate the central function of sorting beneficiaries into either Medicaid or marketplace plans, depending on their eligibility. It appeared to violate the basic guardrails required for 1332 waivers.[56]

Legal Issues

Once again lawyers and judges were at the center of legal battles around parts of the ACA, and a new challenge emerged as a threat to the whole law. As in the two previous years, the challenges came from both sides. Trump administration rules designed to undercut the ACA were challenged by supporters or those with a vested interest in the original provisions or rules. Conservative opponents of the law or Obama-era regulations sought to have them overturned. In 2019 there was greater action at the appeals court level as lawsuits brought in previous years began to be appealed.

Insurance plans continued to be involved in several suits as they proceeded through the federal court system. The 2014–2016 risk-corridor payments to insurance plans were only partially paid because dedicated revenue for this purpose was not adequate. A 2018 court of appeals decision ruled the additional payments were not required.[57] The Supreme Court agreed to accept the case in June 2019, and oral arguments were heard in December, with a 2020 decision anticipated.[58]

A similar issue dealt with the government's obligation to make CSR payments. In several suits across the country insurance plans sought reimbursements for CSRs. The heart of the issue continued to be whether these payments required specific appropriations or were to be treated as integral to the tax credits and not to require appropriation. Appeals court oral arguments were expected in early 2020.

Various parties had challenged the Trump administration's new rules on association health plans and short-term plans in federal court. In March the Democratic attorneys general who brought suit against AHPs won a victory in district court.[59] There was an expedited appeal, with oral arguments heard in November.[60] But the challenge to short-term plans was rejected in July, a decision appealed by the plaintiffs.[61]

The seemingly endless legal battles over the ACA requirement that contraceptive services be available as an insurance plan benefit continued. Various religious organizations had challenged the Obama rules and won some concessions. The Trump administration expanded exemptions, and this brought a different set of plaintiffs to court in a challenge to the new and broader exceptions. In June a federal court judge in Texas issued a nationwide injunction on enforcement of the contraceptive mandate.[62] With several appeals court decisions with varied outcomes, the Supreme Court agreed to hear the cases, with oral arguments likely in 2020.[63]

These cases were, by comparison, sideshows to the *Texas v. United States* suit, which was heard in the Texas federal district court. In 2018 eighteen Republican attorneys general, two Republican governors, and two individual Texas residents initiated the legal action, attempting to have the ACA declared unconstitutional. They claimed that when Congress in late 2017 reduced the individual-mandate tax penalty to zero, the mandate was no longer a tax and was therefore unconstitutional. As this key provision was an integral and inseparable part of the law, they argued the whole statute was unconstitutional.

The Department of Justice partially supported the plaintiffs and did not plan to defend the entire law. The full defense came from sixteen Democratic attorneys general whom the court allowed to be parties to the case. In late December 2018 the district court ruled in favor of the plaintiffs, finding the entire law unconstitutional.[64]

This set the stage for the 2019 battle among the parties before the Fifth Circuit Court of Appeals. In the January appeal, four additional attorneys general joined the case on the side of those defending the ACA, and two plaintiff states withdrew as a result of 2018 election changes. In March the Department of Justice informed the appeals court that it had changed its position and now supported the plaintiffs. However, when briefs were filed in May, the administration again modified its views and stated that only the provisions of the ACA actually injuring the plaintiffs should be struck. Over twenty amicus briefs were filed by a wide range of organizations and institutions in support of the ACA, and only a handful supported the plaintiffs' position.[65]

The three-judge appeals court panel heard oral arguments in July. In December 2019 the panel announced its 2–1 decision with a dissenting opinion. The judges determined the intervening states could be parties to the case because they would lose significant federal funds if the ACA was found unconstitutional. They also ruled the two individual plaintiffs had standing to sue. On the central issue the court determined the individual mandate was unconstitutional, not because of the removal of the penalty but under the commerce clause. On the key issue of severability, the court punted. It remanded the case back to the district court for additional analysis of the question.[66] The ACA defenders did not wish for the case to remain unresolved for an extended period and appealed to the Supreme Court, which agreed in March 2020 to hear the case.[67]

Doubts about the viability of the plaintiff's arguments came not only from strong defenders of the ACA but also from conservative legal scholars, such as Jonathan Adler, who was one of the legal architects of earlier challenges to the health law. Adler referred to the district court's decision as "the deployment of judicial opinions employing questionable legal arguments to support a political agenda."[68]

The appeals court decision in late December 2019 to return *Texas v. United States* to the district court for further review is perhaps symbolic of the ACA in 2019. Congress was divided and the Trump administration inconsistent in its approach; as a result state attorneys general took the lead on both sides in a variety of ACA-related cases. Through it all the health law survived, with both Medicaid expansion and the marketplaces continuing to provide health coverage for millions of Americans. The Texas case was expected to be argued before the Supreme Court in the fall of 2020 and probably decided in 2021, with the November 2020 election perhaps the largest influence on the future of the ACA.

2020: A Pandemic and Another Election

The year 2020 was like no other in living memory. The Covid-19 virus dominated all facets of life. This 2020 case study of the ACA will examine the continuing role of the courts, congressional attempts at expansion, Trump administration sabotage, and state endeavors to strengthen or weaken the law. The November election marked the impending end of the Trump administration. We will conclude this chapter with an assessment of the fortunes of the ACA during this four-year period.

Courts

As in the previous two years, much of the conflict around the ACA took place in the courts. In the last days of 2019, the Fifth Circuit Court of Appeals upheld the district court's determination that the individual mandate was unconstitutional, but it referred the critical question of severability back to the lower court for more in-depth consideration. This caused the ACA defenders to appeal to the Supreme Court for a final determination.

They first asked the Supreme Court for an expedited review, which was denied.[69] On March 2, 2020, the Supreme Court accepted the appeal, but there was no time to hear the oral arguments before the fall term.[70]

The parties to *California v. Texas*, as the case was renamed, filed their briefs beginning in May with the final replies in August. The oral arguments were scheduled for November 10, 2020, notably a week after the election. In the briefs the parties asked the Supreme Court to consider several questions. First, the ACA defenders challenged the appeals court's affirmation that individual and state plaintiffs had standing to sue. Second, the defenders disputed the appeals court's determination that the individual mandate was unconstitutional after the penalty was set at zero. The third and most critical question pertained to severability. The plaintiffs argued the individual mandate was inseparable from the rest of the statute, and therefore the whole law was unconstitutional. The defenders contended that even if the mandate was deemed unconstitutional, the rest of the law should stand.[71]

At this point in the briefs, the administration took a somewhat different view than the plaintiffs, who contended the entire ACA should be found unconstitutional on a nationwide basis. Throughout the process the Trump administration had taken various positions on the proper remedy. In court they argued only the insurance-regulation provisions of the ACA, such as preexisting-conditions protection, should be invalid, with the rest of the law severed. On appeal they shifted position to contend the entire ACA was linked to the individual mandate but simultaneously stated the proper remedy was to prohibit enforcement for only those provisions injuring the plaintiffs and only in the plaintiff states. This ambiguous legal argument was repeated in the briefs before the Supreme Court.[72]

Amicus briefs are submitted to a court to allow interested parties who are not case participants to bring facts and opinions to the attention of the judges. A wide range of organizations filed thirty-eight such briefs supporting the California position with the Supreme Court. Insurers, provider organizations, consumer advocates, service employee unions, scholars, and public health experts were among those filing briefs.[73]

The Supreme Court heard oral arguments in *California v. Texas* on November 11, 2020, a week after the election, probably not an accident of scheduling. The arguments were made in a virtual setting due to Covid-19 restrictions, with a decision expected in spring 2021. Based on the comments and questions during the oral arguments, legal scholars guessed the Court would, at a minimum, find the individual mandate severable from the rest of the ACA. The Court had recently, in similar cases, ruled a single unconstitutional provision in a statue did not automatically render the rest of the law invalid.[74]

Other ACA-related lawsuits were the subject of Supreme Court action in 2020. On April 27, 2020, the Supreme Court ruled 8–1 in *Maine Community Health Options v. United States* that the government was obligated to pay insurance plans what was owed under the temporary risk-corridor payment program. Congressional limits on risk-corridor payments set by appropriation riders did not limit the obligation. If the contested payments could not be settled, the insurance plans could sue in the court of claims.[75]

On July 8, 2020, the Supreme Court upheld the Trump administration rule revisions on the ACA contraceptive mandate as within the authority to allow religious- and moral-objection exemptions. But the Court's ruling did not address all of the questions about the legitimacy of the new rules, which meant additional cases were likely to be argued in the lower courts. As with other major cases, the plaintiffs were Democratic attorneys general from several states.[76]

On June 15 the Court, in a 6–3 decision, found civil rights law protections extended to gay and transgender individuals. This case was not directly related to the ACA but cast doubt on the validity of the new ACA Section 1557 rule finalized by the Trump administration, which revised the Obama administration rule enforcing the antidiscrimination section of the ACA. The Supreme Court ruling gave new life to the ongoing litigation around the Section 1557 rule, including a district court decision vacating the new administration rule.[77]

In July the court of appeals upheld the Trump administration rule, which broadened access to short-term plans, by concluding the rule was not prohibited by statute language.[78] In August the court of appeals ruled in favor of insurance plans seeking reimbursement for CSR payments from the federal government but limited the amount because of silver loading. The legal basis of the decision relied on the Supreme Court risk-corridor decision earlier in the year.[79]

Trump Administration Sabotage

During 2020 the Trump administration continued its strategy of administrative sabotage, even with the devastating impact on the health system of the worst epidemic in a century. In April the administration refused to allow a special enrollment period in response to the growing economic distress caused by Covid-19. Many state exchanges opened a special enrollment period to accommodate those losing employer-sponsored health insurance because of Covid layoffs. Insurance plans, state officials, and even many within the Trump administration argued for a special enrollment period, but President Trump rejected the idea.[80]

In late April CMS did announce a series of enforcement and rule-change delays in response to Covid, including suspension of the controversial double-billing rule related to abortion insurance coverage.[81]

As in previous years, the Trump administration sought to weaken various parts of the ACA with new rules or revisions of existing rules, as well as waivers for states whose officials were antagonistic to the health law. In late January they invited states to submit radical waiver proposals to convert Medicaid into a block grant in the state for the Medicaid expansion population. Transforming Medicaid into a block grant program had been a decades-long Republican goal that was never achieved legislatively.[82]

In June a final rule was promulgated that changed the interpretative rule in the Section 1557 antidiscrimination provision of the ACA to remove gender-identity protections.[83] In November a rule was finalized weakening Medicaid managed-care standards, including defining network adequacy. Since the rule was finalized, the incoming Joe Biden administration could only modify it with an entirely new revision process.[84]

Throughout 2020 the Trump administration continued to propose regulations designed to diminish the role of the ACA in providing health coverage. A June rule proposal provided tax advantages for health care sharing ministries, which often appear to consumers to be health insurance but in fact do not offer comprehensive coverage.[85] A July proposed rule weakened the criteria for allowing employers to continue offering "grandfathered" plans without some ACA consumer protections. Such plans were in effect prior to the ACA enactment. The proposed rule allowed some to continue that under the previous rule would have not qualified.[86] A postelection proposed rule announced in late November invited states to submit proposals to allow marketplace consumers to select plans only through brokers or insurance agents, replacing the healthcare.gov website.[87]

The rule-making process can present serious roadblocks to a new administration attempting to change what the previous administration has put in place. The drafting takes time, the public-comment period delays finalization, and if the rationale for change is not appropriately documented, court challenges can be expected to again delay the new rule. The Trump administration found it difficult and time-consuming to weaken the ACA by regulation change.

States
In 2020 the states continued to play a pivotal role in various phases of the ACA's evolution. Medicaid expansion continued its incremental movement in states that were initially resistant. The Trump administration persisted in encouraging states to adopt 1115 waivers designed to undermine the ACA. The waivers continued to be mostly utilized for reinsurance programs despite Washington's encouragement of more radical approaches.

Medicaid Expansion
Idaho and Nebraska began their Medicaid expansion in 2020 after voters approved the move with earlier ballot measures. During the summer voters in Missouri and Oklahoma approved expansion to be effective in July 2021.

The Medicaid expansion by ballot initiative was not an accident. The Fairness Group, a nonprofit associated with the California health workers union, provided critical support to local groups seeking expansion. They played an important role in the earlier expansion referendums in Utah, Idaho, and Nebraska as well as the 2020 efforts in Oklahoma and Missouri. Four nonexpansion states with referendum processes remain.[88] At the end of 2020 there were twelve remaining states without Medicaid expansion.

1115 Waivers and Work Requirements

Several states sought 1115 waivers, especially work-requirement waivers, as the Trump administration encouraged them. At the beginning of 2020 nine states had CMS approval for 1115 waivers allowing work requirements, and others were pending. But trial court decisions and changes in administration in some of the states had placed them in suspension.[89] As the scope of the Covid-19 pandemic became evident, others suspended the pending work requirements, and the Families First Coronavirus Response Act, which became law in March, froze disenrollment, which effectively suspended work-requirement provisions.[90] In February the court of appeals dealt a blow to the administration's efforts to promote 1115 work-requirement waivers with a unanimous decision upholding the lower court's overturning of the Arkansas waiver. The basis for the decision was not the idea itself but rather that the process leading to the waiver approval was deemed flawed.[91]

The administration requested a review of the decision, and in December the Supreme Court agreed to hear the case, with a decision likely in 2021.[92] Of course, the Biden administration was not expected to support future work-requirement waivers and attempt to reverse those already approved, even if the Supreme Court upheld their validity. Only Arkansas implemented a work-requirement waiver over several months, but the studies of its impact found significant loss of coverage without increased employment, additional hardship for those disenrolled, and a complex and costly reporting system.[93] The evidence from this brief experiment raises serious questions about the value of work-requirement waivers.

1332 Waivers

Section 1332 waivers were the other tool at the disposal of the Trump administration in its attempt to undermine the foundations of the ACA. As with Medicaid 1115 waivers, changes were only possible when a state took the initiative to propose a waiver change. Two additional reinsurance 1332 waivers were approved for New Hampshire and Pennsylvania in the summer of 2020. These were similar to other reinsurance waivers issued in the past and strengthened rather than weakened the ACA marketplace.

A radical 1332 waiver was issued to Georgia in November 2020. The first part was a reinsurance waiver similar to those issued to other states to take effect in 2022. The second part eliminates the healthcare.gov function in the state beginning in 2023 and allows individual brokers and agents exclusive authority to sell tax-credit-supported policies. This represented the third iteration of a proposal from Georgia. Earlier proposals envisioned ACA-noncompliant plans receiving tax credits. A Brookings Institution analysis estimated tens of thousands of Georgia residents would lose health insurance under the plan. This violates the statutory guardrails required for approval of a 1332 waiver and makes a court challenge likely to succeed.[94] Earlier Georgia also received an 1115 waiver for Medicaid expansion but only for those making less than 100 percent of FPL with premium payment and a work requirement. Thus, it is more limited than others states.[95]

A final, hollow action on 1332 proposals was a December 2020 proposed rule codifying the Georgia approach and encouraging other states to emulate Georgia's waiver.[96] The Biden administration is unlikely to approve a proposal similar to Georgia's, and other states will realize it is a futile effort.

Congress
In 2020 Democrats again introduced ACA enhancement legislation in the House in defining their goals for ACA expansion. Democrats, as in 2018 and 2019, passed the bill, but it had no chance in the Republican-controlled Senate.[97] Major provisions were aligned with the positions of Democratic presidential nominee Biden and included eliminating the 400-percent-of-FPL income cap for premium tax credits and replacing it with an 8.5 percent income ceiling, prohibiting short-term plans from exceeding three months, expanding funding for marketplace outreach, and offering financial incentives for the remaining states without Medicaid expansion.[98] While unsuccessful in 2018 these efforts created the template for success in 2021.

Despite the legislative barrier of divided government, House Democrats also attempted to highlight some of the ACA problems because of the Trump administration's obstruction tactics. One example is the House Energy and Commerce Committee study on the practices of companies selling short-term plans. The investigation found extensive denial of claims, rescinded coverage, discrimination against those with preexisting conditions, benefit limits, and misleading advertising.[99] They sought to make the case for future legislation limiting the expanded sale of short-term plans encouraged by the Trump administration.

2020: Conclusion
It is impossible to assess the ACA in 2020 without reference to the Covid-19 epidemic. Did the ACA make a difference? The complete answer will only be evident when there is a return to a normal economy. A Harvard Public Health study published in October 2020 compared the pre-ACA 2011–2013

recession to the 2014–2016 period. In the early period they found nearly 5 percent coverage loss associated with job loss, but in the post-ACA period, Medicaid (8.9 percent) and marketplace plan (2.6 percent) increases offset loss of employment insurance.[100]

September 2020 House testimony indicated Medicaid enrollment increased over 8 percent during the pandemic, especially in expansion states. State-based marketplaces with special enrollment periods also increased coverage. The administration's unwillingness to create a special enrollment period made federal marketplaces less responsive.[101] The ACA clearly helped many who lost employer-sponsored insurance maintain coverage.

The two major trends from 2018 and 2019 remained. Coalitions of state attorneys general continued to aggressively attack or defend the ACA, and the Trump administration pursued to the end a sabotage strategy, which featured waivers for states wishing to weaken the ACA in their jurisdictions. In response to suits challenging these administrative actions, the courts tended to insist on proper procedure in the development of rules meant to weaken ACA provisions. Finally, Medicaid expansion was adopted in additional Republican-dominated states, especially in response to ballot initiatives approved by the voters.

Trump Years Conclusion

The next chapters feature an in-depth examination of the ACA a decade after its enactment. The conclusion of this chapter briefly summarizes the ACA during the four years of the Trump administration. The Trump years began with a common expectation that the ACA would be repealed and replaced, probably with a law reflecting long-standing Republican health policy goals. With Republican control of both Congress and the White House, this was a reasonable estimation. The 2017 effort to do so failed by a few votes. Despite six years of loud condemnation of the ACA, the Republicans had not achieved consensus on a replacement policy. Evaluation of the proposed alternatives found they would lead to a significant decline in insurance coverage. President Trump never took a leadership role in the legislative struggle and did not produce an administration alternative. Republicans learned what Presidents Clinton and Obama had: health reform legislation is hard work.

In 2018 congressional Republicans were unwilling to renew the unpopular effort to repeal and replace the ACA in an election year. In November they lost their House majority, rendering the crusade over for the Trump presidency. In 2017 the Trump administration began a sabotage campaign to weaken and perhaps destroy parts of the ACA. In 2018, with the legislative option closed and the administration firmly in control of the relevant agencies, the campaign to diminish the ACA was aggressively pursued.

As with most modern and complicated statutes, Congress left large segments of daily operations to be defined in administrative regulations and guidance documents. What the Obama administration had developed to fully implement the coverage goals of the ACA, the Trump administration could unravel or change to thwart them. Waiver authority built into both the ACA and Medicaid could be utilized to weaken critical consumer-friendly protections in the law.

As this chapter has illustrated, there were multiple sabotage tactics. The Trump administration aggressively used rule changes to weaken ACA consumer protections and open the door for the sale of non-ACA-compliant plans. It also used budget powers to stop CSR payments and open enrollment assistance. Rule changes sought to weaken the mandated contraceptive services by allowing broad religious exemptions. States were encouraged to seek waivers designed to decrease Medicaid enrollment by use of work requirements. However, the courts overturned several of these efforts, often because of failure to follow mandated legal procedures or an inadequate rationale. Frank Thompson characterized the sabotage effort as an administrative war on the ACA, but one that did not succeed in exploding Obamacare.[102]

During the Trump era new rounds of lawsuits were filed, and older suits worked their way through the court system. With the Trump administration unwilling to defend the ACA against damaging lawsuits, Democratic state attorneys general took the lead in rebutting these challenges. They also acted as plaintiffs in bringing cases against Trump administration actions to weaken the ACA.

The most notable legal threat was the case of *California v. Texas* in which Republican attorneys general filed suit to have the entire ACA declared unconstitutional because of the individual mandate. Democratic attorneys general defended the law. The Supreme Court rejected the plaintiff's arguments in 2021. Medicaid expansion grew incrementally as several holdout states, some by voter referendum, accepted expansion.

The Trump administration departed after four years largely unsuccessful in its stated goal of repealing Obamacare. In January 2021 the ACA was more popular than it had been four years earlier. The number of uninsured has marginally increased, but the marketplaces continue to be viable and offer insurance plans of high quality at a reasonable price because of the tax credits. More states have expanded Medicaid, extending its safety net role.

In the next chapters we will assess the ACA a decade after its enactment.

Notes

1. Edmund F. Haislmaier, Robert E. Moffit, and Nina Owcharenko Schaefer, "The Health Care Choices Proposal: Charting a New Path to a Down Payment on Patient-Centered, Consumer-Driven," *Heritage Foundation Backgrounder*, July 11, 2018, www.heritage.org/sites/default/files/2018-07/BG3330_0.pdf.

2. Grace-Marie Turner, "Health Care Choices Proposal: A New Generation of Health Reform," *Forbes*, June 22, 2018, www.forbes.com/sites/gracemarieturner/?sh=2a8d6f536ec7.

3. Chris Carlson, Glenn Giese, and Thomas Sauder, "Analysis of the Impacts of the ACA's Tax on Health Insurance in Year 2020 and Later," Oliver Wyman, August 28, 2018, https://health.oliverwyman.com/content/dam/oliver-wyman/blog/hls/featured-images/August18/Insurer-Fees-Report-2018.pdf.

4. Katie Keith, "The Association Health Plan Proposed Rule: What It Says and What It Would Do," *Health Affairs Blog*, January 5, 2018, www.healthaffairs.org/do/10.1377/hblog20180104.347494/full; Katie Keith, "Administration Moves to Liberalize Rules on Short-Term, Non-ACA-Compliant Coverage," *Health Affairs Blog*, February 20, 2018, www.healthaffairs.org/do/10.1377/hblog20180220.69087/full.

5. Timothy Jost, "The Past and Future of Association Health Plans," Commonwealth Fund, May 14, 2019, www.commonwealthfund.org/blog/2019/past-future-association-health-plans.

6. Sarah Lueck, "Association Health Plan Expansion Likely to Hurt Consumers, State Insurance Markets," Center on Budget and Policy Priorities, March 7, 2019, www.cbpp.org/research/health/association-health-plan-expansion-likely-to-hurt-consumers-state-insurance-markets.

7. Sabrina Corlette, Josh Hammerquist, and Pete Nakahata, "New Rules to Expand Association Health Plans: How Will They Affect the Individual Market?," *Actuary*, May 2018, https://theactuarymagazine.org/new-rules-to-expand-association-health-plans/#en-4465-2.

8. Keith, "Administration Moves to Liberalize Rules."

9. Preethi Rao, Sarah Nowak, and Christine Eibner, "What Is the Impact on Enrollment and Premiums if the Duration of Short-Term Health Insurance Plans Is Increased?," Commonwealth Fund, June 5, 2018, www.commonwealthfund.org/publications/fund-reports/2018/jun/what-impact-enrollment-and-premiums-if-duration-short-term.

10. Ibid.

11. Sarah Lueck, "Key Flaws of Short-Term Plans Pose Risks to Consumers," Center on Budget and Policy Priorities, September 20, 2018, www.cbpp.org/research/health/key-flaws-of-short-term-health-plans-pose-risks-to-consumers.

12. Dane Hansen and Gabriela Dieguez, "The Impact of Short-Term Limited-Duration Policy Expansion on Patients and the ACA Individual Market," Milliman Research Report, Leukemia & Lymphoma Society, February 2020, www.lls.org/sites/default/files/National/USA/Pdf/STLD-Impact-Report-Final-Public.pdf.

13. "Tracking Section 1332 State Innovation Waivers," Kaiser Family Foundation, November 1, 2020, www.kff.org/health-reform/fact-sheet/tracking-section-1332-state-innovation-waivers.

14. Katie Keith, "Feds Dramatically Relax Section 1332 Waiver Guardrails," *Health Affairs Blog*, October 23, 2018, www.healthaffairs.org/do/10.1377/hblog20181023.512033/full; Katie Keith and Chris Fleming, "CMS Releases New 1332 Waiver Concepts: Implications," *Health Affairs Blog*, November 29, 2018, www.healthaffairs.org/do/10.1377/hblog20181129.845780/full.

15. Edwin Park, "New Guidance Reinterprets Section 1332 Waivers," Georgetown University Health Policy Institute, November 1, 2018, https://ccf.georgetown.edu/2018/11/01/new-guidance-on-section-1332-waivers-would-weaken-affordability-requirements-in-the-aca.

16. Timothy Jost, "Using the 1332 State Waiver Program to Undermine the Affordable Care Act State by State," Commonwealth Fund, October 30, 2018, www

.commonwealthfund.org/blog/2018/using-1332-state-waiver-program-undermine-affordable-care-act-state-state.

17. Anthony Albanese, "The Past, Present, and Future of Section 1115: Learning from History to Improve the Medicaid-Waiver Regime Today," *Yale Law Journal*, March 25, 2019, www.yalelawjournal.org/forum/the-past-present-and-future-of-section-1115.

18. Eliot Fishman and Dee Mahan, "Medicaid Waivers Restricting Adult Eligibility: A Legal and Political Update," *Health Affairs Blog*, January 24, 2019, www.healthaffairs.org/do/10.1377/hblog20190123.697954/full.

19. Sara Rosenbaum, "Medicaid Work Requirements: Inside the Decision Overturning Kentucky HEALTH's Approval," *Health Affairs Blog*, July 2, 2018, www.healthaffairs.org/do/10.1377/hblog20180702.144007/full.

20. MaryBeth Musumeci, Robin Rudowitz, and Elizabeth Hinton, "Re-Approval of Kentucky Medicaid Demonstration Waiver," Issue Brief, Kaiser Family Foundation, November 29, 2018, http://files.kff.org/attachment/Issue-Brief-Re-approval-of-Kentucky-Medicaid-Demonstration-Waiver.

21. Erin Brantley and Leighton Ku, "Arkansas's Early Experience with Work Requirements Signals Larger Losses to Come," Commonwealth Fund, October 31, 2018, www.commonwealthfund.org/blog/2018/arkansas-early-experience-work-requirements.

22. Katie Keith, "State Lawsuit Claims That Individual Mandate Penalty Repeal Should Topple Entire ACA," *Health Affairs Blog*, February 28, 2018, www.healthaffairs.org/do/10.1377/hblog20180228.852626/full.

23. Katie Keith, "Trump Administration Declines to Defend the ACA," *Health Affairs Blog*, June 8, 2018, www.healthaffairs.org/do/10.1377/hblog20180608.355585/full.

24. Katie Keith, "Democratic Attorneys Generals Allowed to Intervene in Individual Mandate Litigation," *Health Affairs Blog*, May 17, 2018, www.healthaffairs.org/do/10.1377/hblog20180517.968731/full.

25. Katie Keith, "Stay Granted in Texas v. Azar: Clears Way for Appeal, Keeps ACA in Place," *Health Affairs Blog*, December 30, 2018, www.healthaffairs.org/do/10.1377/hblog20191231.666628/full.

26. Katie Keith, "HealthCare.gov Enrollment Down Only Slightly; Maryland ACA Litigation Continues," *Health Affairs Blog*, December 21, 2018, www.healthaffairs.org/do/10.1377/hblog20181221.890621/full.

27. Katie Keith, "ACA Litigation Round-Up: CSRs, Risk Adjustment, AHPs, and Short-Term Plans," *Health Affairs Blog*, January 3, 2019, www.healthaffairs.org/do/10.1377/hblog20190103.188732/full.

28. Katie Keith, "Two New Lawsuits Challenge Trump Administration Actions on Health Reform," *Health Affairs Blog*, September 17, 2018, www.healthaffairs.org/do/10.1377/hblog20180917.479910/full.

29. Keith, "ACA Litigation Round-Up: CSRs, Risk Adjustment, AHPs, and Short-Term Plans."

30. Timothy S. Jost, "2018: The Year of Renewed Affordable Care Act Litigation," Commonwealth Fund, January 9, 2019, www.commonwealthfund.org/blog/2019/2018-year-renewed-affordable-care-act-litigation.

31. Katie Keith, "More Courts Rule on Section 1557 as HHS Reconsiders Regulation," *Health Affairs Blog*, October 2, 2018, www.healthaffairs.org/do/10.1377/hblog20181002.142178/full.

32. Katie Keith, "ACA Litigation Round-Up: Texas, Maryland, Short-Term Plans, and Contraceptive Coverage Mandate," *Health Affairs Blog*, November 20, 2018, www.healthaffairs.org/do/10.1377/hblog20181120.91642/full.

33. Katie Keith, "House v. Azar Nears Its End," *Health Affairs Blog*, May 17, 2018, www.healthaffairs.org/do/10.1377/hblog20180517.156095/full.
34. Katie Keith, "Federal Circuit Declines to Rehear Risk Corridors Case," *Health Affairs Blog*, November 7, 2018, www.healthaffairs.org/do/10.1377/hblog20181107.37909/full.
35. Dylan Scott, "Trump's Biggest Midterm Blunder: Embracing Obamacare Repeal," *Vox*, November 7, 2018, www.vox.com/policy-and-politics/2018/11/7/18070152/midterm-elections-2018-results-trump-obamacare-repeal.
36. Katie Keith, "House Passes Legislation to Strengthen the ACA," *Health Affairs Blog*, May 17, 2019, www.healthaffairs.org/do/10.1377/hblog20190517.626290/full.
37. Lunna Lopes et al., "KFF Health Tracking Poll—October 2019: Health Care in the Democratic Debates, Congress, and the Courts," Kaiser Family Foundation, October 2019, www.kff.org/health-reform/poll-finding/kff-health-tracking-poll-october-2019.
38. Katie Keith, "ACA Provisions in New Budget Bill," *Health Affairs Blog*, December 20, 2019, www.healthaffairs.org/do/10.1377/hblog20191220.115975/full.
39. Katie Keith, "The 2020 Final Payment Notice, Part 1: Insurer and Exchange Provisions," *Health Affairs Blog*, April 19, 2019, www.healthaffairs.org/do/10.1377/hblog20190419.213173/full.
40. Aviva Aron-Dine and Matt Broaddus, "Change to Insurance Payment Formulas Will Raise Costs for Millions with Marketplace or Employer Plans," Center on Budget and Policy Priorities, April 19, 2019, www.cbpp.org/sites/default/files/atoms/files/1-18-19health.pdf.
41. Dylan Matthews, "Trump Wants to Change How Poverty Is Calculated—to Make Fewer People Eligible for Benefits," *Vox*, May 11, 2019, www.vox.com/future-perfect/2019/5/11/18537012/trump-poverty-line-chained-cpi.
42. Aron-Dine et al., "Administration's Poverty Line Proposal Would Cut Health, Food Assistance for Millions over Time," Center on Budget and Policy Priorities, June 18, 2019, www.cbpp.org/sites/default/files/atoms/files/6-18-19pov.pdf.
43. "Sabotage Watch: Tracking Efforts to Undermine the ACA," Center on Budget and Policy Priorities, December 3, 2020, www.cbpp.org/sabotage-watch-tracking-efforts-to-undermine-the-aca.
44. Lola Fadulu, "Why States Want Certain Americans to Work for Medicaid," *The Atlantic*, April 12, 2019, www.theatlantic.com/health/archive/2019/04/medicaid-work-requirements-seema-verma-cms/587026.
45. Sara Rosenbaum et al., "Medicaid Work Experiments Meet the D.C. Circuit," *Health Affairs Blog*, October 28, 2019, www.healthaffairs.org/do/10.1377/hblog20191025.796704/full.
46. Arian Campo-Flores, "Kentucky's New Governor Ends Medicaid Work Requirement," *Wall Street Journal*, December 16, 2019, www.wsj.com/articles/kentuckys-new-governor-ends-medicaid-work-requirement-11576533315.
47. Jessica Schubel, "More States Reconsidering Medicaid Work Requirements," Center on Budget and Policy Priorities, January 9, 2020, www.cbpp.org/blog/more-states-reconsidering-medicaid-work-requirements.
48. Craig Mauger, "Emails: Michigan Health Director Sought to Suspend Medicaid Work Requirements," *Detroit News*, October 30, 2019, www.detroitnews.com/story/news/politics/2019/10/31/emails-michigan-health-chief-sought-suspend-medicaid-work-rules/4055782002.
49. Benjamin Sommers et al., "Medicaid Work Requirements in Arkansas: Two-Year Impacts on Coverage, Employment, and Affordability of Care," *Health Affairs* 39, no. 9 (September 2020): 1522–1530.

50. Sara Rosenbaum et al., "Medicaid Work Experiments Meet the D.C. Circuit."
51. Sara Rosenbaum and Alexander Somodevilla, "Looking Inside Tennessee's Block Grant Proposal," *Health Affairs Blog*, October 4, 2019, www.healthaffairs.org/do/10.1377/hblog20191002.734156/full.
52. "Status of State Medicaid Expansion Decisions: Interactive Map," Kaiser Family Foundation, November 2, 2020, www.kff.org/medicaid/issue-brief/status-of-state-medicaid-expansion-decisions-interactive-map.
53. Rachana Pradhan, "Utah GOP Shrinks Medicaid Expansion, Defying Voters," *Politico*, February 11, 2019, www.politico.com/story/2019/02/11/utah-medicaid-expansion-1163050.
54. MaryBeth Musumeci et al., "From Ballot Initiative to Waivers: What Is the Status of Medicaid Expansion in Utah?," Kaiser Family Foundation, November 15, 2019, www.kff.org/medicaid/issue-brief/from-ballot-initiative-to-waivers-what-is-the-status-of-medicaid-expansion-in-utah.
55. Katie Keith, "CMS Rejects Idaho Waiver as Incomplete," *Health Affairs Blog*, August 30, 2019, www.healthaffairs.org/do/10.1377/hblog20190830.458123/full.
56. Katie Keith, "Georgia Releases Broad 1332 Waiver Application," *Health Affairs Blog*, November 5, 2019, www.healthaffairs.org/do/10.1377/hblog20191105.878300/full.
57. Katie Keith, "Insurers Not Owed Risk Corridor Payments," *Health Affairs Blog*, June 15, 2018, www.healthaffairs.org/do/10.1377/hblog20180615.782638/full.
58. Katie Keith, "Justices Appear Sympathetic to Insurers in Risk Corridor Payment Oral Arguments," *Health Affairs Blog*, December 12, 2019, www.healthaffairs.org/do/10.1377/hblog20191212.691619/full.
59. Katie Keith, "Court Invalidates Rule on Association Health Plans," *Health Affairs Blog*, March 29, 2019, www.healthaffairs.org/do/10.1377/hblog20190329.393236/full.
60. Katie Keith, "Oral Arguments Held over AHP Rule," *Health Affairs Blog*, November 15, 2019, www.healthaffairs.org/do/10.1377/hblog20191115.817726/full.
61. Katie Keith, "ACA Litigation Round-Up: A Status Check," *Health Affairs Blog*, January 29, 2020, www.healthaffairs.org/do/10.1377/hblog20200129.210273/full.
62. Katie Keith, "Court Issues New Nationwide Injunction on Contraceptive Mandate," *Health Affairs Blog*, June 10, 2019, www.healthaffairs.org/do/10.1377/hblog20190610.936407/full.
63. Keith, "ACA Litigation Round-Up: A Status Check."
64. Lawrence O. Gostin, "Texas v. United States: The Affordable Care Act Is Constitutional and Will Remain So," *Journal of the American Medical Association Forum* 321, no. 4 (January 29, 2019): 332–333.
65. Katie Keith, "DOJ, Plaintiffs File in Texas v. United States," *Health Affairs Blog*, May 2, 2019, www.healthaffairs.org/do/10.1377/hblog20190502.780432/full.
66. Katie Keith, "Continued Uncertainty as Fifth Circuit Strikes Mandate, Remands on Rest of ACA," *Health Affairs Blog*, December 19, 2019, www.healthaffairs.org/do/10.1377/hblog20191219.863104/full.
67. Timothy Jost, "The Supreme Court Will Decide the Fate of the Affordable Care Act—Again," Commonwealth Fund, March 3, 2020, www.commonwealthfund.org/blog/2020/supreme-court-will-decide-fate-affordable-care-act-again.
68. Jonathan H. Adler and Abbe R. Gluck, "What the Lawless Obamacare Ruling Means," *New York Times*, December 15, 2018, www.nytimes.com/2018/12/15/opinion/obamacare-ruling-unconstitutional-affordable-care-act.html.
69. Keith, "ACA Litigation Round-Up: A Status Check."
70. Jost, "The Supreme Court Will Decide the Fate."

71. MaryBeth Musumeci, "Explaining California v. Texas: A Guide to the Case Challenging the ACA," Kaiser Family Foundation, September 1, 2020, www.kff.org/health-reform/issue-brief/explaining-california-v-texas-a-guide-to-the-case-challenging-the-aca.

72. Katie Keith, "DOJ, Republican AGs Ask Supreme Court to Strike Down ACA," *Health Affairs Blog*, June 26, 2020, www.healthaffairs.org/do/10.1377/hblog20200626.180922/abs.

73. Timothy S. Jost, "Amicus Briefs Flood In, Supporting the ACA," *Commonwealth Fund*, May 20, 2020, www.commonwealthfund.org/blog/2020/amicus-briefs-flood-supporting-aca.

74. Katie Keith, "Supreme Court Arguments: Even if Mandate Falls, Rest of Affordable Care Act Looks Likely to Be Upheld," *Health Affairs Blog*, November 11, 2020, www.healthaffairs.org/do/10.1377/hblog20201111.916623/full.

75. Katie Keith, "Supreme Court Rules That Insurers Are Entitled to Risk Corridors Payments: What the Court Said and What Happens Next," *Health Affairs Blog*, April 28, 2020, www.healthaffairs.org/do/10.1377/hblog20200427.34146/full.

76. Katie Keith, "Supreme Court Upholds Broad Exemptions to Contraceptive Mandate—for Now," *Health Affairs Blog*, July 9, 2020, www.healthaffairs.org/do/10.1377/hblog20200708.110645/full.

77. Katie Keith, "Supreme Court Finds LGBT People Are Protected from Employment Discrimination: Implications for the ACA," *Health Affairs Blog*, June 16, 2020, www.healthaffairs.org/do/10.1377/hblog20200615.475537/full; Katie Keith, "Court Vacates New 1557 Rule That Would Roll Back Antidiscrimination Protections for LGBT Individuals," *Health Affairs Blog*, August 18, 2020, www.healthaffairs.org/do/10.1377/hblog20200818.468025/full.

78. Katie Keith, "ACA Litigation Round-Up: Part II," *Health Affairs Blog*, July 21, 2020, www.healthaffairs.org/do/10.1377/hblog20200721.330502/full.

79. Katie Keith, "Federal Circuit: Insurers Owed Unpaid Cost-Sharing Reductions, Reduced by Higher Premium Tax Credits from Silver Loading," *Health Affairs Blog*, August 17, 2020, www.healthaffairs.org/do/10.1377/hblog20200817.609922/full.

80. Adam Cancryn, Nancy Cook, and Susannah Luthi, "How Trump Surprised His Own Team by Ruling Out Obamacare," *Politico*, April 3, 2020, www.politico.com/news/2020/04/03/trump-obamacare-coronavirus-164285.

81. Katie Keith, "ACA Round-Up: COVID-19 Delays, New COBRA Guidance, and More," *Health Affairs Blog*, May 5, 2020, www.healthaffairs.org/do/10.1377/hblog20200505.663518/full.

82. Michael Ollove, "Trump Administration Announces Shift to Medicaid Block Grants," Pew Charitable Trusts, January 30, 2020, www.pewtrusts.org/en/research-and-analysis/blogs/stateline/2020/01/30/trump-administration-announces-shift-to-medicaid-block-grants.

83. Katie Keith, "HHS Strips Gender Identity, Sex Stereotyping, Language Access Protections from ACA Anti-Discrimination Rule," *Health Affairs Blog*, June 13, 2020, www.healthaffairs.org/do/10.1377/hblog20200613.671888/full.

84. Elizabeth Hinton and MaryBeth Musukmeci, "CMS's 2020 Final Medicaid Managed Care Rule: A Summary of Major Changes," Kaiser Family Foundation, November 23, 2020, www.kff.org/medicaid/issue-brief/cmss-2020-final-medicaid-managed-care-rule-a-summary-of-major-changes.

85. Katie Keith, "New Proposed Rule on Health Care Sharing Ministries and Direct Primary Care," *Health Affairs Blog*, June 11, 2020, www.healthaffairs.org/do/10.1377/hblog20200611.714521/abs.

86. Katie Keith, "New Proposed Rule on Grandfathered Plans; Court Strikes Abortion Double Billing Rule," *Health Affairs Blog*, July 13, 2020, www.healthaffairs.org/do/10.1377/hblog20200713.885651/full.

87. Katie Keith, "The 2022 Proposed Payment Notice, Part 1: Exchange Provisions," *Health Affairs Blog*, November 27, 2020, www.healthaffairs.org/do/10.1377/hblog20201127.118789/full.

88. Sarah Kliff, "How Progressives Flipped the Script on Medicaid Expansion," *New York Times*, August 4, 2020, www.nytimes.com/2020/08/04/upshot/missouri-election-medicaid-expansion.html.

89. Schubel, "More States Reconsidering Medicaid Work Requirements."

90. Tricia Brooks, "Families First Coronavirus Response Act Freezes Disenrollment in Medicaid," Georgetown University Health Policy Institute, March 23, 2020, https://ccf.georgetown.edu/2020/03/23/families-first-coronavirus-response-act-freezes-disenrollment-in-medicaid.

91. Rachana Pradhan and Susannah Luthi, "Appeals Court Rejects Trump Approved Medicaid Work Requirements," *Politico*, February 14, 2020, www.politico.com/news/2020/02/14/appeals-court-rejects-trump-approved-medicaid-work-requirements-115221.

92. Adam Liptak, "Supreme Court to Hear Case on Trump's Medicaid Work Requirements," *New York Times*, December 4, 2020, www.nytimes.com/2020/12/04/us/supreme-court-medicaid-work-.html.

93. Jennifer Wagner and Jessica Schubel, "States' Experiences Confirm Harmful Effects of Medicaid Work Requirements," Center on Budget and Policy Priorities, November 18, 2020, www.cbpp.org/sites/default/files/atoms/files/12-18-18health.pdf.

94. Christen Linke Young and Jason Levitis, "Georgia's Latest 1332 Proposal Continues to Violate the ACA," Brookings Institution, September 1, 2020, www.brookings.edu/research/georgias-latest-1332-proposal-continues-to-violate-the-aca.

95. Joan Alker and Allexa Gardner, "Georgia's Medicaid Waiver Is Fiscally Foolish and Anti-Family," Georgetown University Health Policy Institute, October 28, 2020, https://ccf.georgetown.edu/2020/10/28/georgias-medicaid-waiver-is-fiscally-foolish-and-anti-family.

96. Tara Straw, "Trump Proposal Threatens Coverage of HealthCare.gov Enrollees," Center on Budget and Policy Priorities, December 7, 2020, www.cbpp.org/blog/trump-proposal-threatens-coverage-of-healthcaregov-enrollees.

97. Amy Goldstein, "House Democrats Push Through First Bill in a Decade Expanding Affordable Care Act," *Washington Post*, June 29, 2020, www.washingtonpost.com/health/house-democrats-push-through-first-bill-in-a-decade-expanding-affordable-care-act/2020/06/29/350d3046-ba0f-11ea-8cf5-9c1b8d7f84c6_story.html.

98. Katie Keith, "House Democrats Introduce New Coverage Bill," *Health Affairs Blog*, June 24, 2020, www.healthaffairs.org/do/10.1377/hblog20200624.197845/full.

99. Katie Keith, "New Congressional Investigation of Short-Term Plans," *Health Affairs Blog*, June 26, 2020, www.healthaffairs.org/do/10.1377/hblog20200626.227261/abs; US House of Representatives, Committee on Energy and Commerce, Subcommittees on Health and Oversight, "Shortchanged: How the Trump Administration's Expansion of Junk Short-Term Health Insurance Plans Is Putting Americans at Risk," June 2020, https://drive.google.com/file/d/1uiL3Bi9XV0mYnxpyaIMeg_Q-BJaURXX3/view.

100. Sumit D. Agarwal and Benjamin D. Sommers, "Insurance Coverage After Job Loss—the Importance of the ACA During the Covid-Associated Recession," *New England Journal of Medicine* 383, no. 17 (October 22, 2020): 1603–1606.

101. Aviva Aron-Dine, "Health Care Lifeline: The Affordable Care Act and the COVID-19 Pandemic," Center on Budget and Policy Priorities, September 23, 2020, www.cbpp.org/sites/default/files/atoms/files/9-23-20health-testimony.pdf.

102. For an excellent summary of the Trump administrative sabotage efforts, see Frank J. Thompson, Kenneth K. Wong, and Barry G. Rabe, *Trump, the Administrative Presidency, and Federalism* (Washington, DC: Brookings Institution Press, 2020), chap. 3.

6

An Assessment: What Has Been Achieved?

If you don't know where you are going, you'll end up someplace else.

—Yogi Berra

This chapter examines the Affordable Care Act (ACA) a decade after its enactment. Did the ACA achieve its primary goals by 2020? It is easy to be impatient and believe major social legislation ought to immediately solve a problem. This has not historically been the case. The Social Security program was enacted in 1935, but monthly benefits were not scheduled to begin until 1942, seven years later. Congress ultimately accelerated the timetable to start monthly payments in 1940 and included spouses and dependents as eligible. The amount was very low. Not until 1950 did Congress significantly increase monthly payments. Four years later disability protection was added. Other major expansion changes occurred in the early 1970s.[1]

Medicare, the other major social insurance program, was enacted in 1964. Eight years later, coverage included those with disabilities. Meaningful cost-control measures were introduced fifteen years after enactment.[2] For the ACA, ten years after enactment represents six years after implementation of major provisions. In our internet-dominated world of rapid change, a decade or even six years appears to be an eternity. If our perspective is the world of the two major social insurance programs of the twentieth century, we find the ACA today in about the same place as Social

Security and Medicare when the first major expansions occurred. This bit of history should be remembered as we attempt to assess ACA's coverage gains at age ten.

The principal goal of the ACA was to expand coverage to include people classified as uninsured, as well as to reduce their out-of-pocket costs. This was to be accomplished with three strategies. Medicaid was expanded to cover the uninsured whose income was less than 138 percent of the federal poverty level (FPL). State electronic marketplaces were to be created in which insurance companies would sell plans that met basic standards for those with incomes between 138 and 400 percent of FPL. Tax credits and cost-sharing reduction payments were to be used to reduce premium and out-of-pocket costs. Those with incomes higher than 400 percent of FPL could still purchase plans, but without premium assistance. Insurance regulations were intended to provide consumer protections. This chapter examines the impact of insurance marketplaces and Medicaid expansion.

In 2011 there were 266 million nonelderly individuals in the United States. Of these, 48 million (18 percent) were uninsured. The private nongroup market was the source of insurance for 6 percent, and employer-sponsored insurance (ESI) covered the largest segment at 56 percent. Medicaid covered 18 percent.[3]

Figure 6.1 illustrates the change in the number of uninsured in the nonelderly population from 2008 to 2019. It shows the sharp decline in those without health insurance beginning in 2014 with the full implementation of the ACA.

The conclusion of this chapter considers the relative roles of the marketplaces and Medicaid expansion in this decline. In 2016 the number of uninsured had dropped by almost 18 million from the 2013 pre-ACA baseline.

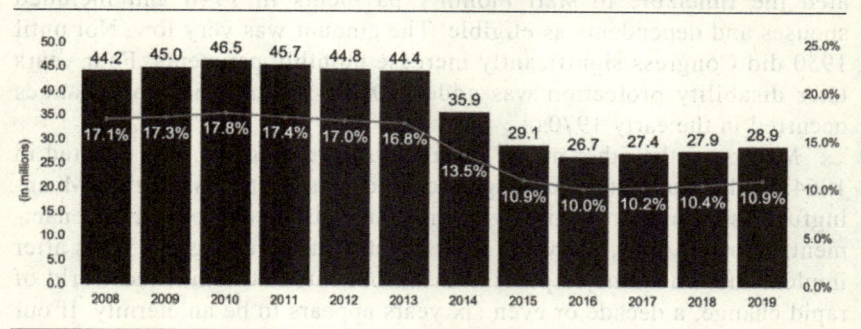

Figure 6.1 Number of Uninsured and Uninsured Rate, 2008–2019

Year	Uninsured (millions)	Uninsured Rate
2008	44.2	17.1%
2009	45.0	17.3%
2010	46.5	17.8%
2011	45.7	17.4%
2012	44.8	17.0%
2013	44.4	16.8%
2014	35.9	13.5%
2015	29.1	10.9%
2016	26.7	10.0%
2017	27.4	10.2%
2018	27.9	10.4%
2019	28.9	10.9%

Note: Includes nonelderly individuals age zero to sixty-four.
Source: Kaiser Family Foundation analysis of 2008–2019 American Community Survey, One-Year Estimates.

During the Donald Trump years, the number of uninsured climbed again, with 2 million more uninsured in 2019 compared to the low point of 2016, but the total share of uninsured remained well below the pre-ACA number. Given the widespread job loss and insurance disruption in 2020 due to the Covid-19 epidemic, 2019 is a better benchmark for the permanent coverage impact of the ACA.

Marketplaces

Both the marketplace insurance plans and Medicaid expansion were critical elements of the ACA strategy to increase coverage. We will first discuss the marketplace and then Medicaid. On the eve of the ACA passage, about 18 percent of the population was uninsured. Most were in families with at least one person working, but either in multiple part-time jobs or in a job that did not offer employer-sponsored health insurance. They did not meet the categorical requirements for Medicaid or the often very low income ceiling in many states.[4]

Elizabeth Rigby and Jake Haselswerdt characterized the ACA exchange approach as one-tailed devolution with partial preemption. This means states wishing to be more progressive could utilize state exchanges to do so, but federal preemptive rules precluded more conservative approaches. Thus, the incentive system for state exchanges favored Democratic-dominated states with a progressive agenda. Opposition to exchanges became a high-visibility, low-risk strategy for ACA opposition because of the federal platform default.[5]

This was not the only factor at work. David Jones reminds us there was also an intraparty divide among Republicans.[6] Gubernatorial leadership on the issue was often critical. Daniel Beland, Philip Rocco, and Alex Waddan cite institutional fragmentation, lack of state experience with this type of institution, and the absence of additional federal funding as barriers to legislative action creating exchanges.[7] The technical problems associated with creating a state exchange offered both a rationale and an excuse for deferring to the federal platform. It is likely we will see limited migration from the federal platform in the years ahead, but the path may not always be smooth or beneficial because barriers still exist.[8]

Irrespective of the choices made by states in their approach to the marketplaces, did they succeed in the fundamental goal of expanding coverage and reducing costs for beneficiaries? Here we will examine the overall success of the marketplace exchanges on these criteria.

Enrollment

When the law was enacted, the Congressional Budget Office (CBO) projected marketplace enrollments would be 24 million by 2019. As Figure 6.2

Figure 6.2 Total Marketplace Enrollment, State and Federal, 2014–2021

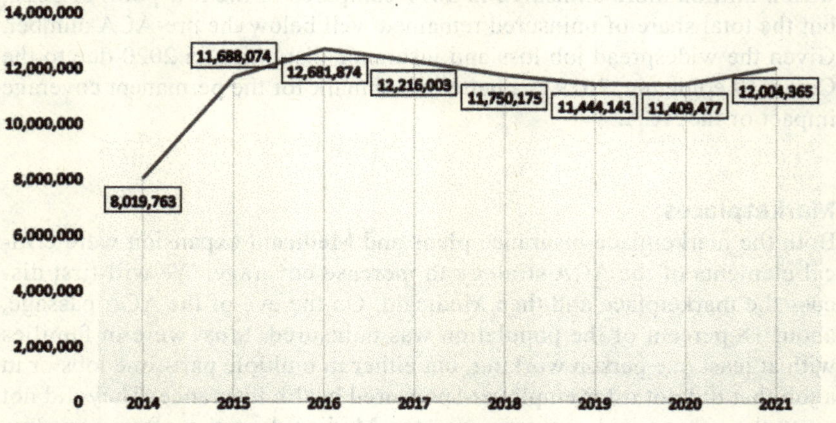

Year	Enrollment
2014	8,019,763
2015	11,688,074
2016	12,681,874
2017	12,216,003
2018	11,750,175
2019	11,444,141
2020	11,409,477
2021	12,004,365

Source: Kaiser Family Foundation.

illustrates, the actual number was half the CBO projection. However, nongovernmental projections also missed the mark. Sherry Glied, Anupama Arora, and Claudia Solís-Román in their 2015 assessment of the original projections found outside analysts, such as the Lewin Group and RAND, were also too high and attributed this first-year shortfall to the unexpectedly slow rollout.[9]

Aviva Aron-Dine two years later attributed much of the high enrollment estimate to an assumption that some employers would drop coverage, with employees migrating to the marketplace, which did not happen.[10]

The individual insurance market provided a source of coverage for nearly 11 million people in the years immediately prior to the ACA implementation. In 2014, the first year of the exchanges, the number increased nearly 50 percent to 15.5 million. For 2015 the number jumped to 17.4 million before declining but remaining higher than the pre-ACA totals (see Table 6.1).

The ACA marketplaces accounted for nearly 10 million enrollees, or about two-thirds of the individual market total. Of these, about 85 percent received premium subsidies. In 2015, enrollments within the exchanges accounted for slightly over 50 percent of the individual market but by 2018 had grown to over 70 percent. The individual market outside the exchanges is divided into ACA-compliant and -noncompliant plans, with about 60 percent of these being compliant plans.

Both categories of off-exchange plans declined over the four years, and off-exchange plans accounted for most of the decline in the individual

Table 6.1 Individual Market Enrollment, 2015–2018 (millions)

	2015	2016	2017	2018
Exchange, subsidized	8	8.4	8.2	8.6
Exchange, nonsubsidized	1.5	1.6	1.5	1.3
Exchange, total	9.5	10	9.7	9.9
Off-exchange, ACA compliant	4.9	4.8	3.6	2.6
Off-exchange, non–ACA compliant	3	2.3	1.9	1.3
Off-exchange, total	7.9	7.1	5.5	3.9
Total individual market	17.4	17	15.2	13.8

Source: Kaiser Family Foundation.

market between 2015 and 2018.[11] In 2019 an estimated 3.7 million were enrolled in individual market plans outside the exchanges, with 11.4 million purchasing in the marketplaces.[12]

There appear to be multiple reasons for off-exchange decline. Some of these plans had been grandfathered noncompliant plans and lost that status. Individuals without employer-sponsored insurance may have gained it. Probably cost was a barrier for many because subsidies do not exist for off-exchange purchases. The off-exchange ACA-compliant policies were part of the same risk pool as those within the exchanges and experienced sharp premium increases.

By 2020 new enrollees accounted for 25 percent of the total, and 87 percent were eligible for subsidies. A total of about 70 percent had incomes between 100 and 250 percent of FPL. Approximately 1 million of the 11.5 million were not eligible for subsidies. State marketplace enrollments generally increased in the last years of the Trump administration, whereas enrollments declined slightly in federal platform states. In 2020 state platforms increased enrollment by 3 percent.[13]

We can reasonably conclude that after the first seven marketplace years, enrollment remained stable and subsidies effective for those eligible, with room to grow enrollment utilizing aggressive outreach and stricter limits on noncompliant short-term policies.

Premiums

The monthly cost of a premium is a critical barometer for both enrollees and insurance companies. A premium that is too high is a purchase barrier for consumers. A premium that is too low may gain customers but not produce sufficient revenue to pay claims. A 2009 study found a third of those insured in the individual market were unemployed, and most of the remainder were either self-employed or worked for firms with fewer than twenty employees. Half spent more than 10 percent of their income on health care for less comprehensive benefits. In the pre-ACA era, the individual market was not financially hospitable for low- to moderate-income individuals.[14]

In 2014, the first year of ACA coverage, premiums tended to be lower than anticipated, with significant variations from state to state. Some carriers began with lower premiums in the hope of developing initial market share and assumed a growing pool of good risks. They may have also concluded the risk-corridor programs provided a safety net. Since over 80 percent of the marketplace participants received tax credits to assist with premium payments and many were eligible for cost-sharing reduction assistance, costs for most participants in the marketplace were considerably lower than before the ACA marketplaces.

Table 6.2 shows the average premium for the benchmark silver plan, as well as the premiums in the high and low states, for each year to provide some perspective.[15] The premium increase between the initiation of ACA exchanges in 2014 and 2021 was 66 percent, but the table illustrates that most of the premium growth came with the 60 percent growth between 2016 and 2018. Since 2018 the average cost has slightly declined.

A detailed Urban Institute study of premiums since 2017 found rural areas with limited insurance plan competition tended to have higher increases than urban areas in the same states. State actions can have an impact on premiums. Alaska's very high premiums declined sharply after the initiation of a state reinsurance program.[16]

The primary cause of the major 2017–2018 premium escalation appears to be a response to the ending of federal payments for the mandated cost-sharing reduction programs for low-income beneficiaries. This, combined with the pending demise of the individual mandate, caused insurance companies to conclude the future risk pool would be smaller and less healthy.

Table 6.2 Average, High, and Low Premiums for Second-Lowest-Cost Silver Plan

Year	Silver Plan Cost		
	Average	Low	High
2014	$273	MN $182	AL $426; WY $419
2015	$276	AZ $196	AL $488; VT $468
2016	$299	NM $212	AL $719; VT $468
2017	$356	WA $243	AL $926; NC $543
2018	$481	RI $311	WY $865; NB $767
2019	$478	MN $326	WY $865; NB $838
2020	$462	MN $309	WY $881; IA $742
2021	$452	MN $307	WY $791; NB $699

Source: Kaiser Family Foundation.
Note: For the high catergory, the highest and second-highest states are listed.

After substantial increases, companies adjusted premiums down to avoid losing competitive advantage, especially in markets in which Medicaid managed-care organizations entered to compete with traditional carriers.[17]

These major premium increases in the benchmark silver plan were utilized to allow for continuation of the cost-sharing reductions.[18] Indirectly the federal government paid for most of the increase because the higher premium resulted in greater spending on premium credits. This was called "silver loading."

The group especially hard-hit by these premium increases included those with income too high to qualify for premium credits. These individuals experienced significant premium and cost-sharing increases. The number of people purchasing a plan in the marketplace without subsidy has declined sharply, with state-by-state variations. Older adults with incomes slightly above the FPL are the most vulnerable. For these individuals short-term, non-ACA-compliant plans are an attraction.[19] Trump administration regulations stimulated the expansion of these plans.

By 2020 new enrollees accounted for 25 percent of the total, and 87 percent were eligible for subsidies. A total of about 70 percent had incomes between 100 and 250 percent of FPL. Approximately 1 million of the 11.5 million were not eligible for subsidies. State marketplace enrollments generally increased in the last years of the Trump administration, while they declined slightly in federal-platform states. In 2020 state exchanges increased enrollment by 3 percent.[20]

Stable enrollment and effective subsidies for those eligible, with room to grow enrollment by utilizing aggressive outreach along with stricter limits on noncompliant short-term policies, is a reasonable outlook after the first seven marketplace years.

Insurance Companies

Insurance companies offering plans in the ACA exchanges are the other side of the coin. The public-option idea did not make it into the final bill, and most of the co-ops struggled to succeed. To remake the individual market as a key element in expanding coverage and reducing the number of uninsured, it was essential for insurance companies to participate and succeed financially. As private corporations they had to prosper in this new environment. With the ACA there was potentially a much larger risk pool with many clients paying more in premiums than they were generating in claims expenses. The tax-credit public subsidy of premiums for those with incomes below 400 percent of FPL rendered private health insurance in the marketplace affordable for many.

We will briefly look at three elements of the ACA marketplace success from the perspective of the participating insurance companies in the period from 2014 to 2020. First, we consider the extent of and shifts in participation by companies. Second, we examine competition in the market with an eye to its impact on price and consumer choice. Third, we assess market stability as a function of insurance company financial success. The exchanges evolved in three phases: the new market rush occurred from 2014 to 2016, followed by retrenchment in 2017 and 2018 and a stabilizing period from 2019 to 2021.

Participation

In the first years of the ACA exchanges, companies rushed to participate. In 2015, 251 companies were offering plans in the marketplaces. This number had declined by nearly half, to 132, by 2018. Major companies, such as United Health Care, Cigna, and Aetna, withdrew from participation in the 2017 retrenchment period. However, a number of insurance companies expanded their presence, such as the Medicaid managed-care organization Centene, which had the highest number of clients in the individual market.[21]

Blue Cross Blue Shield in 2018, with 47 percent, had the largest enrollment share in the individual market. Medicaid managed-care organization insurers quickly captured a larger total enrollment, growing from 15 to 27 percent between 2016 and 2018. By 2020 Medicaid insurers were offering plans in half of the rating regions in the country, in twenty-nine states encompassing nearly two-thirds of the nation's population.

The number of enrollees with national and regional insurers fell by half to 14 percent in the 2016–2018 retrenchment period. Provider-sponsored insurers maintained about 10 percent of the market, and co-ops accounted for 2 percent. National enrollment numbers vary significantly by state. For example, co-ops had the largest market share in Montana and Maine. In Wisconsin provider-sponsored insurance plans and co-ops accounted for three-quarters of total enrollment.[22]

The most significant insurance company shift in the ACA marketplace was the withdrawal of many national insurance firms. They appeared to have priced their product higher, with fewer network restrictions, and began to lose market share in the retrenchment period. They were replaced by aggressive Medicaid insurance plans.

An Urban Institute study found the success of the Medicaid insurers was due to tighter networks, lower provider rates, and administrative cost control. The remaining national and regional insurance plans began to emulate the cost-saving approaches of the Medicaid insurers.[23] Blue Cross plans have for decades been dominant in the individual market, and they continued to be the major force in the ACA exchanges. Not only have Medicaid insurers grown into a strong second-place position, but the remaining national carriers have emulated their approach. The 2017 concern about massive insurer withdrawal from the ACA exchanges did not materialize.

Competition

Competition drives markets. The basic premise of the ACA marketplace is that competition among insurers will produce cost-effective plans and lower premiums. Government intervention created two features modifying the market. Rules prohibiting practices harmful to consumers, such as preexisting-condition screening, and tax credits to offset a significant part of the premium reshaped the previous market conditions to some degree. Was there still a basis for competition among insurance carriers? Did competition in the modified markets produce the expected results?

We noted above that the absolute number of insurance plans participating in the exchange markets declined significantly as the new market rush was followed by a period of retrenchment. In 2017 the number of insurers in the federal exchanges fell by half.[24] Kevin Griffins, David Jones, and Benjamin Sommers found 20 percent of counties had limited competition among insurers in 2016.

By 2018 this had jumped to 64 percent of counties, representing 40 percent of the population, with only one or two insurers in the marketplace. A third of these had only one insurer. This competitive decline was not evenly distributed across the country. Weak competitive areas tended to be concentrated in the upper Midwest and Southeast.[25]

A 2019 Urban Institute study found marketplace competition stabilized in 2019 but remained lower than in the original market rush phase. Blue Cross Blue Shield dominated markets with one insurer and was a major participant in those with two insurers.[26] Three percent of enrollees had only one insurer to choose from, and 20 percent had two. Thus, almost 80 percent of enrollees had three or more insurance providers available.[27]

If we define a competitive market as one in which three or more participants are offering plans, then four in five enrollees have the advantage of competition. Provider competition does appear to have the expected impact on premiums. Despite more expensive medical facilities, premiums in market-competitive urban areas are cheaper than in rural areas.[28]

Higher payment rates in rural areas may have reflected an inability to strike a better price with providers when narrow networks were not possible. The risk pool in urban areas may have been more diverse with a younger population. More sparsely populated areas may just be less able to support multiple insurance plans because of the size of the risk pool.[29] Jessica Van Parys found premiums grew more rapidly during the retrenchment period in areas with monopoly insurers. This may have been an exercise of monopoly power or a reflection of inadequately adjusted risk pool distortions.[30]

With different types of insurers in the marketplace and some movement as insurers departed to be replaced by others, we can point to no single, definitive determination of the cause of premium variation between those counties with limited insurers offering plans and more competitive markets. It does seem clear that greater market competition among insurers does reduce premiums.

Insurance Market Stability
If you manage a health insurance company, what is the most important thing to accomplish? The simple answer is to collect more revenue in premiums than you spend on claims. For insurers to maintain a presence in the ACA exchanges, they must be financially successful. Even nonprofit entities cannot indefinitely pay more out in claims than they collect in premiums. There are complex metrics to assess how well insurance companies meet this fundamental standard.

One such basic measure is the medical loss ratio, which defines the relationship of premiums to claims paid. In the years immediately prior to initiation of the ACA marketplaces, this ratio was in the mid-eighties. It sharply increased in the initial market rush period to a high point of 103 percent in 2015. Some insurers abandoned the market, and those remaining tended to increase premiums significantly. The ratios began to drop and returned to 79 percent by 2019.

The gross margins per member per month followed a similar pattern. They declined to a negative number in 2015 and then steadily increased from 2016 forward, with greater margin in 2019 than prior to the opening of the exchanges. Monthly premiums and claims per person demonstrated a similar pattern.[31]

Averages mask differences. Obviously all insurance companies were not able to collect more in premiums than they paid in claims in the early market rush period. During the retrenchment phase, some exited the market, and others were able to increase premiums. By the five-year anniversary of the exchanges, the market had stabilized for the companies. The various Trump administration sabotage actions, including elimination of the individual mandate and halting payments for the cost-sharing reduction program, had not been fatal blows to insurers in the exchanges.

Individual Mandate
The individual mandate was the most disliked feature of the ACA and perhaps the most overrated. In the 1990s the idea was part of a conservative alternative to more expansive government involvement in financing health insurance. The principal target was younger, healthier individuals who were reluctant to spend money on health insurance because they did not believe they were going to need it during the year. It was a private insurance approach to universal coverage.

When insurance companies were threatened with new regulations limiting their ability to underwrite risk by excluding or charging more based on risk, they insisted on the individual mandate. It was seen as a way for insurance plans to collect premiums from healthy individuals to help cover costs for individuals with higher-than-average claims. Many health policy analysts supported the proposition as essential for insurance plan stability. They argued it was essential for marketplace viability.

Political opposition led to the effective repeal of the mandate by reducing the penalty to zero. Did this cause the ACA marketplaces to collapse? It did not. Marketplace enrollment did decline after the elimination, but not by much. Was the mandate responsible for significantly increased coverage? Matthew Fiedler reviewed several analytic studies and concluded the mandate did increase insurance coverage, but not by nearly as much as the models had assumed.[32] The Congressional Budget Office continued to revise downward its projection of the impact of the mandate on coverage.[33] Even Jonathan Gruber, one of the intellectual architects of the ACA and a champion of the individual mandate, admitted it had not been as critical as initially estimated.[34]

The penalties were relatively low compared to premiums without subsidy, and exemptions were extensive. The almost 13 million who claimed exemptions in 2015 were twice as many as those who paid a penalty and the same number as purchased coverage in the individual market.[35] Fiedler attempted to ascertain how many individuals above 400 percent of FPL had obtained coverage because of the mandate and put the number at 1.2 million in 2016.[36]

ACA champions were convinced by econometric models, such as those by the CBO, that the individual mandate was essential for reducing the uninsured and stabilizing the individual insurance market. The Massachusetts experience seemed to confirm that conclusion. They sought to defend the mandate from political and legal attacks, which strengthened the resolve to assume it was absolutely essential.

The Supreme Court upheld the mandate, but a Republican majority in Congress ultimately eviscerated it by lowering the penalty to zero. Subsequent analysis indicated the mandate, as structured, only had a marginal impact on enrollment in the individual market. The point is probably moot since Congress will not likely restore the penalty because the mandate remains the most unpopular feature. The group most likely not to purchase coverage in the absence of the mandate includes those above 400 percent of FPL. Increasing the level of credits above the current cutoff would likely be a more popular approach.

Co-ops

Cooperatives have a long history in the American medical marketplace dating back to the 1920s. Medical cooperatives flourished for a time in Oklahoma and the state of Washington. Rural-area cooperatives were common across the Midwest in several areas of economic life.[37] Therefore, we should not be surprised that this organizational concept was ultimately part of the ACA. Liberal reformers, especially in the House, included a robust public option in their ACA bill.

The basic argument was a fusion of liberal and conservative ideas. More consumer-friendly competition was needed in the individual market, which could be provided by a quasi-public entity offering insurance plans at cheaper premiums because shareholder payments were not built into the rate structure. Opposition from the insurance industry and a few conservative Democratic senators killed the idea in the Senate bill.[38]

For decades cooperatives had existed in several segments of the economy, especially in the upper Midwest. As the public-option idea failed to gain consensus, Senator Kent Conrad of North Dakota offered an alternative proposal based on the cooperative concept. It was included in the final Senate bill. Originally, one co-op was envisioned in each state to serve the small-business and individual market. Consumer groups and other stakeholders could form a nonprofit co-op and receive start-up loans and grants from the federal government. There was a flourish of interest in co-ops, with twenty-four established before the opening of the marketplaces. In 2015 more than 1 million individuals were enrolled in co-op plans, but by 2020 only three co-ops remained, covering a little more than 100,000.[39]

What happened? Co-ops ran into a perfect storm of internal and external challenges. The Republican Congress, in budget negotiations from 2011 to 2013, ended the federal funds available for new entities and limited risk-corridor payments for co-ops.[40] Sabrina Corlette and colleagues suggested limits on use of federal funds for marketing, and for many the benefit design and pricing strategies led to bad risk pools. Generous coverage plans were offered at bargain rates.[41]

Scott Harrington concluded this led to a "winner's curse" as high enrollment generated by competitive premiums led to a less healthy risk pool.[42] Michael Sparer and Lawrence Brown identify the modifications and delays in the ACA's risk-stabilization programs as creating special financial challenges, even for those not plagued with risk pool challenges. They also describe the obstacles to creating new insurance companies with managers lacking deep experience in the industry and without the financial depth to absorb short-term setbacks.[43]

It is impossible to know if the public-option proposal in the House bill would have been more successful than the co-ops. For those who continue to champion a public-option approach to enhancing competition in the marketplaces, the co-op experience offers a valuable lesson on cliffs to be avoided.

Employer Mandate and the Small Business Health Options Program

Employer-sponsored insurance has been the keystone of health financing for decades. Since the 1970s many of the major reform proposals have envisioned extended ESI to cover most workers. This policy idea had been frequently discussed and analyzed in the policy stream. In one version, known as "play-or-pay," an employer either provides ESI or pays a percentage of each employee salary in a tax to offset public program coverage for the employee. This was a major feature of the 1991 Pepper Commission Report, a congressional report on expanding health coverage, and continued to be discussed as a tool for expanding employment-based insurance.[44]

This is primarily an issue with small to medium-size firms. In 2009, ESI covered 60 percent of the American public and 98 percent of full-time workers at firms larger than 200 employees. This share falls significantly for smaller firms: ESI covers only 60 percent of firms with less than 200 employees and less than half of firms with fewer than 10 employees.

The ACA was modeled on the Massachusetts health reform law, which included at modified employer mandate structured as a type of play-or-pay approach. The House ACA version required employers to pay at least 72 percent of the cost of insurance coverage for each employee or to pay between 2 and 8 percent of salary to an exchange trust fund to support tax credits in the exchanges for those employees.[45] The House approach was deemed unacceptable in the Senate. However, the idea of employer responsibility was borrowed from Massachusetts, and the Senate version embodied the provision that employers not providing ESI had to pay a penalty if at least one employee received a tax credit in an exchange.[46] A slightly modified Senate version was in the final bill.

In addition to coverage goals, there were two considerations related to the CBO score of the ACA favoring use of the employer mandate. The projected additional revenue from some employers helped pay for the ACA, and without an employer mandate the CBO was prepared to assume some employers would drop employee coverage and allow employees to purchase insurance in the exchange with tax credits. Thus, total program costs would rise.[47]

Since most large firms already offered ESI, small businesses were expected to experience the greatest impact of the new employer mandate. To facilitate small-business purchase of affordable ESI, the ACA established the Small Business Health Options Program (SHOP). Each state was to establish a SHOP exchange or incorporate a separate program for small businesses into its regular exchange. Otherwise an exchange facilitated by the federal government would serve as a backup.[48] A small business was also able to gain a tax credit to cover part of the cost of ESI for its employees for a two-year period when using the SHOP exchange.[49]

The employer mandate was not popular with business groups and not strongly supported by others before it was to be effective in 2013. The Barack Obama administration unilaterally postponed implementation of this provision for a year. An Urban Institute report in 2014 suggested the employer mandate might be usefully repealed. Its analysis indicated only a small coverage gain but likely labor market distortions.[50] Various ACA supporters were not committed to retaining the employer mandate as initiation neared.[51]

Nevertheless, both the mandate and the SHOP exchanges continued as features of the ACA. In 2017 Timothy Jost described how the Trump administration had effectively shut down the federal SHOP exchanges and allowed small businesses to deal directly with insurance companies or brokers. SHOP exchanges never worked as designed and covered only a small fraction of total small businesses.[52]

David Chase and John Arensmeyer, in a 2018 study, did find significant coverage gains for small-business employees because of the ACA. They attributed coverage expansion and premium stabilization to the ACA as a result of both the exchanges and Medicaid expansion. They calculated the rate of uninsured among small-business employees declined by 10 percent after initiation of the ACA.[53]

Some states continued their SHOP exchanges. A Commonwealth 2020 analysis found that state SHOP exchanges, such as those in California and Rhode Island, experienced success in helping small businesses expand employee coverage despite the failure of the federal SHOP exchanges. Changes in federal SHOP rules and support for the program contributed to the weak performance.[54]

How has the ACA impacted employer-sponsored insurance? What is the state of employer-sponsored insurance in 2020?

Prior to the opening of the ACA marketplaces, there was apprehension about an ESI decline as firms dropped employee coverage to allow them to purchase plans in the exchange.[55] The CBO projected an ESI coverage decline of 6 or 7 million individuals.[56] However, a 2018 Urban Institute study with a focus on workers and job categories found coverage gains between 2010 and 2016 without an adverse labor market effect.[57] The ACA coverage has not caused either a loss of jobs or a decline in ESI coverage leading to higher rates of lack of insurance among workers.

A 2020 Urban Institute report offered an insightful summary of ESI a decade after enactment of the ACA. There has been a modest increase in individuals covered by ESI in the last several years, but the absolute number is about the same as twenty years ago despite population growth. The percentage of nonelderly population covered by ESI declined to 58 percent compared to 66 percent two decades ago. The relative decline is mostly among those in the lower income categories, not individuals above 400 percent of FPL. At all income levels, the cost, as measured by employee share of premiums and cost, has increased substantially.[58]

A Commonwealth Fund study found differences in employee share of premiums and deductibles/coinsurance in various regions. In the South and Southwest employees paid a higher share of average state income in ESI cost sharing.[59]

Employer-sponsored insurance remains the most significant source of coverage for the nonelderly population. The ACA has contributed to the expansion of coverage for workers in small to medium-size businesses. Despite criticism, the employer mandate remains in effect and contributes to the stability of ESI and worker coverage. There is little evidence to suggest a large-scale decline in the role of ESI in the post-ACA implementation period.

Marketplace Conclusion

During the 2009 legislative crafting of the ACA, President Obama pledged during a speech to the American Medical Association, "And if you like your insurance plan, you will keep it."[60] He probably later regretted this pledge because some people did have to switch plans in the individual market. However, the fundamental premise was the core policy idea of the ACA. The ACA policy design idea was to leave existing employer-sponsored insurance in place and reduce the number of uninsured and underinsured by strengthening the individual private insurance market. Tax credits and consumer-friendly regulations were the tools, along with an individual mandate to enhance the risk pool and encourage insurance companies to participate.

Despite early technical missteps, states' reluctance to organize their own marketplaces, and the eventual dropping of the individual-mandate penalty, the ACA exchanges enabled millions to purchase affordable insurance with comprehensive coverage. For individuals with income slightly above the tax-credit-eligibility ceiling, the ACA promise of affordable insurance in the individual market remains out of reach.

The Trump administration attempted to sabotage the individual market by reducing enrollment outreach and authorizing the sale of short-term insurance with inadequate coverage. This only marginally diminished the role of the ACA exchanges in making health insurance coverage affordable for millions. The feared disruption of employer-sponsored insurance did not occur, as employers continued offering coverage to their workers.

The ACA marketplace does not advantage those with incomes above 400 percent of FPL who are not covered by employment-based insurance, such as contractors or individual entrepreneurs. They pay a high price for comprehensive coverage without a subsidy in the form of a tax credit or employer contribution. Outside the exchange some premiums may be cheaper, but they may encounter a "Wild West" of unregulated policies with uneven or inadequate coverage.

Medicaid Expansion

In 1965 Medicaid was an almost invisible element of the bill creating Medicare. The publicity buzz was dominated by the expansion of the social insurance idea to include public health insurance for the elderly. Medicaid expanded health access for the welfare poor, but it also made the enlargement of Medicare to cover a broader population less likely because some of the poor had gained coverage.

In the decades following its enactment, Medicaid did incrementally cover additional populations and lose some of its initial link to the cash welfare system. In 2003 Colleen Grogan and Eric Patashnik placed Medicaid at a crossroads. The two paths forward were a return to a narrow welfare medicine safety net program for the very poor or growth to become the key element for providing health coverage for those outside existing employment-sponsored insurance and public programs.[61]

The ACA clearly took Medicaid down the expansionist path. It was to be a critical piece of the strategy for expanding coverage. State Medicaid programs were to cover all individuals with incomes under 138 percent of FPL, with the federal government paying most of the cost. The marketplace exchanges with tax credits and the individual mandate garnered more attention as the law passed and implementation began. But the early coverage estimates projected a significant role for Medicaid expansion. The CBO estimate at the time forecasted coverage for 24 million through the exchanges and 16 million with Medicaid expansion.[62]

The 2012 Supreme Court decision, *National Federation of Independent Business v. Sebelius*, allowed individual states to reject Medicaid expansion, potentially diminishing the scope of its impact. Some states immediately accepted expansion, some did only later, and others still had not in early 2021. Medicaid expansion officially began in January 2014. In that year twenty-six states and the District of Columbia were expanding Medicaid; this included Michigan and New Hampshire, whose expansion began later in 2014. Twenty-four had either rejected expansion outright or hesitated to expand.

Twelve of the original twenty-four nonexpansion states had by 2021 opted to expand. Six of them did so as a result of a ballot initiative.[63] Florida and South Dakota may have ballot initiatives in 2022. Kansas and North Carolina have Democratic governors supporting expansion and negotiating with their legislatures on the issue. Eleven of the total expansion states did so as part of a Section 1115 waiver.[64] These waivers differed in their focus but often involved work requirements.[65] No state has rescinded its expansion decision, even with a shift in partisan control of the governor's office. Table 6.3 traces each state's Medicaid expansion history.

A variety of state political dynamics were at work in both the original and the later expansion dynamics. States with Democratic governors and legislatures were quick adopters. Others, such as Ohio and Arizona, had Republican governors who pushed through expansion over the reluctance of their legislatures. In Ohio Republican governor John Kasich went around the legislative opposition by having an obscure state board render the decision

Table 6.3 Medicaid Expansion

2014	AR, AZ, CA, CO, CT, DC, DE, HI, IA, IL, KY, MA, MD, MI, MN, ND, NH, NJ, NM, NV, NY, OH, OR, RI, VT, WA, WV
2015	AK, IN, PA
2016	LA, MT
2017	None
2018	None
2019	ME, VA
2020	ID, NE, UT
2021	MO, OK
None	AL, FL, GA, KS, MS, NC, SC, SD, TN, TX, WI, WY

Source: Kaiser Family Foundation.

to expand. Republican governor Jan Brewer in Arizona faced opposition from her party's majority in the legislature, but the partisan division was close. She convinced enough Republicans to join with Democrats to pass expansion. A similar dynamic occurred in North Dakota. Republican governors in Maryland, Nevada, and New Mexico had Democratic majorities in their legislatures and supported expansion.

Executive orders were employed to achieve expansion by four Democratic governors (Alaska, Arkansas, Kentucky, and Louisiana) and two Republican governors (Indiana and Iowa). In the case of Arkansas, the Democratic governor negotiated a 1115 waiver with the Obama administration allowing subsidized purchase of private insurance for the expansion population.[66]

In Montana and New Hampshire, Democratic governors with narrow Republican majorities in the legislature were able to combine Democratic legislators with a handful of Republicans to achieve majority support for expansion.[67] Kentucky was an original expansion state under a Democratic governor. His Republican successor attempted to scale back the program after an initial threat to terminate; he was succeeded by a Democrat who retained the original approach.

Most of the remaining nonexpansion states have solid Republican majorities in the legislature and the governorship. The most recent in this category of states, such as the 2020 Missouri and Oklahoma expansions, have come by way of ballot initiatives, with voters overriding the preference of state elected officials.[68]

Strong interparty competition has appeared to enhance the prospects for expansion in states with either divided government or Republican control.[69] This helps explain why Medicaid expansion occurred in Arizona but not Alabama. Major interest groups, often Republican-oriented ones, such as chambers of commerce and hospital associations, have often been strong and vocal supporters of expansion.[70] Beland, Rocco, and Waddan found policy legacies in the states led to very divergent Medicaid histories and institutions. Policy legacies are institutions and intergovernmental relationships predating the ACA. Entrepreneurial governors of both parties were able to maneuver the fragmented system to achieve expansion. Finally, public sentiment and the manipulation of it explain some of the variation in state response.[71]

Medicaid Enrollment

After the 2012 *National Federation of Independent Business v. Sebelius* Supreme Court decision rendered expansion optional, the CBO reduced its coverage projection from 16 million to 10 million. In 2015, 13.6 million were enrolled under the Medicaid expansion in thirty states. Over the next three years, expansion enrollment increased to 15.6 million, then decreased slightly to 15.3 million in 2019. Nationally the expansion population represented nearly 30 percent of Medicaid enrollment with a wide variation. For Maine the expansion population represented 10 percent of all Medicaid enrollees, but this is for the first year of that state's expansion. The 50 percent in Oregon represents the high outlier.[72] The Kaiser Family Foundation recently estimated another 2 million individuals live in states not expanding Medicaid and would be eligible if the state expanded.[73]

The expansion-state Medicaid enrollment surge contributed to greater decline in the uninsured compared to nonexpansion states. The uninsured rate for those under 200 percent FPL decreased in both, but it declined by half in expansion states, whereas nonexpansion states experienced much smaller declines.[74] For the uninsured poor Medicaid expansion was the most important factor in gaining coverage.

Spending and Budget Impact

The Medicaid expansion population has consistently incurred about 20 percent of total Medicaid spending in expansion states. There is variance, with a high of 40 percent in Montana and a low of 13 percent in Massachusetts.[75] Most of the money to cover the expansion population has come from the federal government, but the additional cost to state budgets has been a point of opposition, especially among Republicans.

Sommers and Gruber examined expansion states in the first years and found a sharp increase in Medicaid spending without commensurate reduction of other functions, such as education.[76] Bruce Ward in 2020 analyzed the budget impact of Medicaid expansion in several states for the 2014–2017 period.[77] He found a nearly 5 percent decline in traditional Medicaid spending during the expansion period.

Some individual states, such as Colorado, Washington, and Virginia, saw savings within traditional Medicaid equal to 85 percent of the state expansion costs. State budget categories outside Medicaid were also a source of savings as expansion covered some former state expenses in corrections, mental health, and substance abuse. In Michigan, for example, state mental health and substance abuse savings were shifted to Medicaid and represented 37 percent of the state expansion costs. Finally, in a number of expansion states, provider taxes or fees enhanced revenue due to expansion. A Louisiana health management organization fee was projected to cover 100 percent of the state's share of expansion costs.[78]

With the state budget savings associated with Medicaid expansion and the possibility of added financial incentives in the Joe Biden administration's Covid-19 relief package, additional states may abandon their opposition to Medicaid expansion in 2021 and 2022. It was nearly twenty years after enactment before the last holdout state, Arizona, agreed to participate in Medicaid. This piece of history might repeat.

Expansion has also benefited the financial position of hospitals. Fredric Blavin and Christal Ramos, in a study of expansion's impact on hospitals, concluded Medicaid revenue increased and uncompensated care decreased as a share of total expenses in expansion states but not in others. This left expansion-state hospitals in a better financial position.[79]

Health Effect of Medicaid Expansion

The fundamental purpose of Medicaid expansion was to cover the poor and near poor with the public health insurance program. An underlying assumption and rationale linked to expanded Medicaid coverage was improved health for those newly eligible. Did this happen? Were there measurable health-status improvements in Medicaid expansion states?

Madeline Guth, Rachel Garfield, and Robin Rudowitz, in an extensive Kaiser Foundation review of the literature on the health effects of Medicaid expansion, identified over 200 studies on the subject. They found the typical analysis confirmed better metrics in expansion states for early-stage cancer diagnosis, more listings for transplants, and additional medications for behavioral health and substance abuse disorder treatment.[80]

Recent studies found Medicaid expansion associated with fewer opioid deaths, fewer cardiovascular deaths, and improved diabetes management.[81] John Graves and colleagues compared older rural residents in the South and concluded those in expansion states experienced fewer health declines and better health baseline maintenance.[82]

Anuj Gangopadhyay and Emily Johnston, in an Urban Institute study, found a 14 percent reduction in the uninsured rate among young adults (ages nineteen to twenty-five) in expansion states. This was especially true for minority youth. There were also significant improvements in routine health care among this group.[83]

The evidence seems overwhelming. Expansion states have experienced health gains, especially within minority communities. Health disparities have also been reduced in expansion states. Madeline Guth, Samantha

Artiga, and Olivia Phan concluded in a Kaiser Foundation review of the literature that Medicaid expansion reduced but did not eliminate disparities. They found reduction in disparities especially in maternal and child health among Black and Hispanic beneficiaries.[84]

Medicaid Conclusion

On the eve of ACA passage, John Iglehart said of the coming Medicaid expansion, it "is one of the largely untold sagas of health reform." He went on to point out that nearly a quarter of the population would be receiving health coverage through Medicaid by 2019.[85] By 2019 Medicaid coverage for the nonelderly had grown from 18 to 21 percent, not quite reaching his projection.[86] But, with total expansion, the Urban Institute projects Medicaid coverage for 27 percent of the nonelderly population.[87] Intense Republican resistance to Medicaid expansion in several states, as well as the continuing opposition of conservatives to enlargement of public health insurance programs, has constrained the potential Medicaid impact.

The Trump administration continued to support fiscal limits to Medicaid with block grant and spending-cap legislation, as had both Presidents Ronald Reagan and George W. Bush. These efforts failed. The Trump administration efforts promoting work requirements to diminish eligibility were overturned by the courts.

Medicaid expansion was a key element in the ACA strategy to reduce the number of uninsured. Despite broad state opposition and Trump administration sabotage, Medicaid survived and grew significantly in the first decade of the ACA. It clearly continues down what Grogan and Patashnik called the "path to a more universal healthcare system for millions of Americans," as an essential piece of the ACA.[88] However, Medicaid barely survived the 2017 Republican attempt to not only repeal the ACA but cap federal funding for the entire program, not just the expansion segment. As more states embrace expansion, it seems less likely Medicaid will shrink in the future, but its position remains politically vulnerable as conservative ideological opposition remains strong.

Conclusion

For the Obama administration ACA passage was a top priority because the number of people uninsured was unacceptably high. In the previous decades several distinctive policy ideas had been offered to move the nation closer to universal coverage. The Massachusetts model became the basic framework for the bill. Medicaid expansion was crafted to move toward universal coverage through a public program for those whose income was less than 138 percent of FPL. The inadequacy of the individual market was the other target. Consumer-oriented regulation of insurance coverage provisions and tax credits for those with incomes below 400 percent of FPL, accompanied by cost-sharing reduction payments for those below 250 percent of poverty, were the key policy approaches to increase coverage and affordability.

We have seen in this chapter that both state and federal marketplaces were successful in contributing to an increase in the number of people covered by individual insurance policies. Trump administration policies contributed to a small marketplace decline, but the system survived the challenge. Fewer insurance companies are participating in the marketplaces today, but all counties have offerings available, and the firms have remained financially viable despite early concerns.

When the Supreme Court ruled Medicaid expansion was optional, it did not initially occur in nearly half the states. Partisan warfare over the ACA was a driving force of opposition in states dominated by Republicans. Gradually, reluctant states began to accept expansion, some because of election-driven changes and others because of ballot referendums endorsing expansion. Waivers and intergovernmental bargaining over the conditions of expansion were instrumental in some expansion acceptances. If all states agreed to Medicaid expansion, another 4 million individuals would be eligible, further reducing the number of uninsured.[89]

The ACA has achieved many of its coverage goals with tax credits in the marketplace and partial Medicaid expansion. Insurance companies have participated and prospered. No one lives in a county without at least one marketplace plan available. Employment-based insurance has been stable and remains the primary path to coverage for most working Americans. After six years of insurance expansion, the ACA has been successful but remains a work in progress for achieving close to universal coverage.

The following chapter will examine the shifting public perception of the ACA and legal challenges it faced in the first decade.

Notes

1. Martha A. McSteen, "Fifty Years of Social Security," *Social Security Administration*, www.ssa.gov/history/50mm2.html.

2. Jonathan Oberlander, *The Political Life of Medicare* (Chicago: University of Chicago Press, 2003), chap. 3.

3. "Health Insurance Coverage of the Nonelderly Population, 2011," Kaiser Family Foundation, 2012, www.kff.org/slideshow/health-insurance-coverage-in-america-2011.

4. "The Uninsured and the Difference Health Insurance Makes," Kaiser Family Foundation, September 1, 2012, www.kff.org/health-reform/fact-sheet/the-uninsured-and-the-difference-health-insurance.

5. Elizabeth Rigby and Jake Haselswerdt, "Hybrid Federalism, Partisan Politics, and Early Implementation of State Health Insurance Exchanges," *Publius: The Journal of Federalism* 43, no. 3 (summer 2013): 368–391.

6. David K. Jones, *Exchange Politics: Opposing Obamacare in Battleground States* (New York: Oxford University Press, 2013).

7. Daniel Beland, Philip Rocco, and Alex Waddan, *Obamacare Wars: Federalism, State Politics, and the Affordable Care Act* (Lawrence: University Press of Kansas, 2016).

8. Sarah Lueck, "Adopting a State-Based Health Insurance Marketplace Poses Risks and Challenges," Center on Budget and Policy Priorities, February 6, 2020, www.cbpp.org/research/health/adopting-a-state-based-health-insurance-marketplace-poses-risks-and-challenges.

9. Sherry Glied, Anupama Arora, and Claudia Solís-Román, "The CBO's Crystal Ball: How Well Did It Forecast the Effects of the Affordable Care Act?," Commonwealth Fund, December 2015, www.commonwealthfund.org/sites/default/files/documents/___media_files_publications_issue_brief_2015_dec_1851_glied_cbo_crystal_ball_forecast_aca_rb_v2.pdf.

10. Aviva Aron-Dine, "CBO Correctly Predicted Historic Coverage Gains Under ACA," Center on Budget and Policy Priorities, May 30, 2017, www.cbpp.org/blog/cbo-correctly-predicted-historic-coverage-gains-under-aca.

11. Rachel Fehr, Cynthia Cox, and Larry Levitt, "Data Note: Changes in Enrollment in the Individual Health Insurance Market Through Early 2019," Kaiser Family Foundation, August 21, 2019, www.kff.org/private-insurance/issue-brief/data-note-changes-in-enrollment-in-the-individual-health-insurance-market-through-early-2019.

12. "Current Trends in Individual Segment Enrollment," Mark Farrah Associates, August 20, 2019, www.markfarrah.com/mfa-briefs/current-trends-in-individual-segment-enrollment.

13. Katie Keith, "Final Marketplace Enrollment Data for 2020," *Health Affairs Blog*, April 2, 2020, www.healthaffairs.org/do/10.1377/hblog20200402.109653/full.

14. Michelle M. Doty et al., "Failure to Protect: Why the Individual Insurance Market Is Not a Viable Option for Most U.S. Families," Commonwealth Fund, July 2009, www.commonwealthfund.org/sites/default/files/documents/___media_files_publications_issue_brief_2009_jul_failure_to_protect_1300_doty_failure_to_protect_individual_ins_market_ib_v2.pdf.

15. "Marketplace Average Benchmark Premiums: Timeframe 2014–21" Kaiser Family Foundation, www.kff.org/health-reform/state-indicator/marketplace-average-benchmark-premiums.

16. John Holahan, Erik Wengle, and Caroline Elmendorf, "Marketplace Premiums and Insurer Participation: 2017–2020," Urban Institute, January 2020, www.urban.org/sites/default/files/publication/101499/moni_premiumchanges_final.pdf.

17. Ibid.

18. Sabrina Corlette, Kevin Lucia, and Maanasa Kona, "States Step Up to Protect Consumers in Wake of Cuts to ACA Cost-Sharing Reduction Payments," Commonwealth Fund, October 27, 2017, www.commonwealthfund.org/blog/2017/states-step-protect-consumers-wake-cuts-aca-cost-sharing-reduction-payments.

19. Rachel Fehr et al., "How Affordable Are 2019 ACA Premiums for Middle-Income People?," Kaiser Family Foundation, March 5, 2020, www.kff.org/health-reform/issue-brief/how-affordable-are-2019-aca-premiums-for-middle-income-people.

20. Keith, "Final Marketplace Enrollment Data for 2020."

21. "A Brief Analysis of the Individual Health Insurance Market," Mark Farrah Associates, August 6, 2018, www.markfarrah.com/mfa-briefs/a-brief-analysis-of-the-individual-health-insurance-market.

22. John Holahan, Caroline Elendorf, and Erik Wengle, "Which Types of Insurance Are Marketplace Enrollees Choosing?," Urban Institute, June 2020, www.urban

.org/sites/default/files/publication/102322/which-types-of-insurance-are-marketplace-enrollees-choosing_3.pdf.

23. Erik Wenale et al., "Effects of Medicaid Health Plan Dominance in Health Insurance Marketplaces," Urban Institute, June 17, 2020, www.urban.org/research/publication/effects-medicaid-health-plan-dominance-health-insurance-marketplaces.

24. Craig Garthwaite and John A. Graves, "Success and Failure in the Insurance Exchanges," *New England Journal of Medicine* 376, no. 10 (March 9, 2017): 907–910.

25. Kevin Griffith, David K. Jones, and Benjamin D. Sommers, "Diminishing Insurance Choices in the Affordable Care Act Marketplaces: A County-Based Analysis," *Health Affairs* 37, no. 10 (October 2018): 1678–1841.

26. Mark Hall, "Stabilizing and Strengthening the Individual Health Insurance Market: A View from Ten States," Brookings Institution, July 2018, www.brookings.edu/wp-content/uploads/2018/07/Stabilizing-and-Strenghtening-the-Individual-Health-Insurance-Market2.pdf.

27. "What Characterizes the Marketplaces with One or Two Insurers? An Update," Urban Institute, March 21, 2019, www.urban.org/research/publication/what-characterizes-marketplaces-one-or-two-insurers-update.

28. Erik Wengle, Linda J. Blumberg, and John Holahan, "Are Marketplace Premiums Higher in Rural Than in Urban Areas?," Urban Institute, November 2018, www.urban.org/sites/default/files/publication/99341/moni-ruralurban_-_final_1.pdf.

29. "What Characterizes the Marketplaces with One or Two Insurers?," Urban Institute.

30. Jessica Van Parys, "ACA Marketplace Premiums Grew More Rapidly in Areas with Monopoly Insurers Than in Areas with More Competition," *Health Affairs* 37, no. 8 (August 2018): 1243–1251.

31. Rachel Fehr, Daniel McDermott, and Cynthia Cox, "Individual Insurance Market Performance in 2019," Urban Institute, May 13, 2020, www.kff.org/report-section/individual-insurance-market-performance-in-2019-issue-brief.

32. Matthew Fiedler, "The ACA's Individual Mandate in Retrospect: What Did It Do and Where Do We Go from Here?," *Health Affairs* 39, no. 3 (March 2020): 429–435.

33. Glenn Kessler, "The CBO's Shifting View on the Impact of the Obamacare Individual Mandate," *Washington Post*, February 26, 2019, www.washingtonpost.com/politics/2019/02/26/cbos-shifting-view-impact-obamacare-individual-mandate.

34. Molly Frean, Jonathan Gruber, and Benjamin D. Sommers, "Premium Subsidies, the Mandate, and Medicaid Expansion: Coverage Effects of the Affordable Care Act," *Journal of Health Economics* 53 (May 2017): 72–86.

35. Fritz Busch and Paul R. Houchens, "The Individual Mandate Repeal: Will It Matter? (Yes, but Not as Much as You Might Think)," Milliman White Paper, Milliman, March 2018, www.milliman.com/-/media/Milliman/importedfiles/uploadedFiles/insight/2018/will-individual-mandate-repeal-matter.ashx.

36. Matthew Fiedler, "How Did the ACA's Individual Mandate Affect Insurance Coverage? Evidence from Coverage Decisions by Higher Income People," Brookings Institution, May 2018, www.brookings.edu/research/how-did-the-acas-individual-mandate-affect-insurance-coverage-evidence-from-coverage-decisions-by-higher-income-people.

37. Paul Starr, *The Social Transformation of American Medicine: The Rise of a Sovereign Profession and the Making of a Vast Industry* (New York: Basic Books, 1982), 302–306.

38. James Brasfield, "The Politics of Ideas: Where Did the Public Option Come from and Where Is It Going?" *Journal of Health Politics Policy and Law* 36, no. 3 (June 2011): 455–460.

39. Phil Galewitz, "Obamacare Co-ops Down from 23 to Final '3 Little Miracles,'" *Kaiser Health News*, September 9, 2020, https://khn.org/news/obamacare-co-ops-down-from-23-to-final-3-little-miracles.

40. Helen Levy, Andrew Ying, and Nicholas Bagley, "The Social, Political, and Economic Effects of the Affordable Care Act," *Russell Sage Foundation Journal of the Social Sciences* 6, no. 2 (July 2020): 42–66.

41. Sabrina Corlette et al., "Why Are Many Co-ops Failing? How New Nonprofit Health Plans Have Responded to Market Competition," Commonwealth Fund, December 2015, www.commonwealthfund.org/publications/fund-reports/2015/dec/why-are-many-co-ops-failing-how-new-nonprofit-health-plans-have.

42. Hoag Levins, "How 'Winner's Curse' Killed ACA Insurance Co-ops," Leonard Davis Institute of Health Economics, March 2016, https://ldi.upenn.edu/news/how-winners-curse-killed-aca-insurance-co-ops%23.

43. Michael S. Sparer and Lawrence D. Brown, "Why Did the ACA Co-op Program Fail? Lessons for the Health Reform Debate," *Journal of Health Politics, Policy and Law* 45, no. 5 (October 2020): 801–816.

44. Ken Jacobs and Jacob S. Hacker, "How to Structure a 'Play-or-Pay' Requirement on Employers: Lessons from California for National Health Reform," UC Berkeley Labor Center, June 2009, www.law.berkeley.edu/files/chefs/StructureEmployerPlayOrPay.pdf.

45. "Employer Mandate," Health Policy Brief, *Health Affairs*, January 15, 2010, www.healthaffairs.org/do/10.1377/hpb20100115.893036/full/healthpolicybrief_15.pdf.

46. "Penalties for Employers Not Offering Coverage Under the Affordable Care Act During 2019," Kaiser Family Foundation, June 10, 2019, www.kff.org/infographic/employer-responsibility-under-the-affordable-care-act.

47. John E. McDonough, *Inside National Health Reform* (Berkeley: University of California Press, 2011), 131–133.

48. "Small Business Insurance Exchanges," Health Policy Brief, *Health Affairs*, February 6, 2014, www.healthaffairs.org/do/10.1377/hpb20140206.80133/full/healthpolicybrief_108.pdf.

49. "Small Business Tax Credits," Health Policy Brief, *Health Affairs*, January 14, 2011, www.healthaffairs.org/do/10.1377/hpb20110114.474485/full/healthpolicybrief_38.pdf.

50. Linda J. Blumberg, John Holahan, and Matthew Buettgens, "Why Not Just Eliminate the Employer Mandate?," Urban Institute, May 9, 2014, http://webarchive.urban.org/publications/413117.html.

51. Paige Winfield Cunningham and Kyle Cheney, "Why Liberals Are Abandoning Obamacare Employer Mandate," *Politico*, July 6, 2014, www.politico.com/story/2014/07/obamacare-employer-mandate-108578.

52. Timothy Jost, "CMS Announces Plans to Effectively End the SHOP Exchange," *Health Affairs Blog*, May 15, 2017, www.healthaffairs.org/do/10.1377/hblog20170515.060112/full.

53. David Chase and John Arensmeyer, "The Affordable Care Act's Impact on Small Business," Commonwealth Fund, October 2018, www.commonwealthfund.org/sites/default/files/2018-10/Chase_ACA_impact_small_business_ib.pdf.

54. Rachel Schwab, Justin Giovannelli, and Kevin Lucia, "State-Based Marketplaces Find Value, Potential Opportunity for Growth in Small-Business Offering," Commonwealth Fund, March 18, 2020, www.commonwealthfund.org/blog/2020/state-based-marketplaces-find-value-potential-opportunity-growth-small-business-offering.

55. Gail R. Wilensky, "Employer-Sponsored Insurance: Is It Eroding Under the ACA, and Should We Care?" *Milbank Quarterly* 93, no. 3 (September 2015): 467–470.

56. Jessica Banthin and Sarah Masi, "Updated Estimates of the Insurance Coverage Provisions of the Affordable Care Act," Congressional Budget Office, March 4, 2014, www.cbo.gov/publication/45159.

57. Anuj Gangopadhyaya, Bowen Garrett, and Stan Dorn, "How Have Workers Fared Under the ACA?," Urban Institute, November 2018, www.urban.org/sites/default/files/publication/99310/how_have_workers_fared_under_the_aca.pdf.

58. Matthew Rae et al., "Long-Term Trends in Employer-Based Coverage," Urban Institute, April 3, 2020, www.healthsystemtracker.org/brief/long-term-trends-in-employer-based-coverage.

59. Sara R. Collins, "State Trends in Employer Premiums and Deductibles, 2010–2019," Data Brief, Commonwealth Fund, November 2020, www.commonwealthfund.org/sites/default/files/2020-11/Collins_state_premium_trends_2020_db_1.pdf.

60. Glenn Kessler, "Obama's Pledge That 'No One Will Take Away' Your Health Plan," *Washington Post*, October 30, 2013, www.washingtonpost.com/news/fact-checker/wp/2013/10/30/obamas-pledge-that-no-one-will-take-away-your-health-plan.

61. Colleen Grogan and Eric Patashnik, "Between Welfare Medicine and Mainstream Entitlement: Medicaid at the Political Crossroads," *Journal of Health Politics, Policy and Law* 28, no. 5 (October 2003): 821–858.

62. Douglas W. Elmendorf, "Letter to Honorable Nancy Pelosi," Congressional Budget Office, March 20, 2010, www.cbo.gov/sites/default/files/111th-congress-2009-2010/costestimate/amendreconprop.pdf.

63. Idaho, Maine, Missouri, Nebraska, Oklahoma, and Utah.

64. Arizona, Arkansas, Indiana, Iowa, Michigan, Montana, Nebraska, New Hampshire, New Mexico, Ohio, and Utah. Iowa initially expanded as part of a waiver but later abandoned in favor of regular expansion.

65. See footnote 2 in "Status of State Action on the Medicaid Expansion Decision," Kaiser Family Foundation, February 4, 2021, www.kff.org/health-reform/state-indicator/state-activity-around-expanding-medicaid-under-the-affordable-care-act.

66. Jane B. Wishner et al., "Medicaid Expansion, the Private Option, and Personal Responsibility Requirements," Urban Institute, May 2015, 5–8, www.urban.org/sites/default/files/publication/53236/2000235-Medicaid-Expansion-The-Private-Option-and-Personal-Responsibility-Requirements.pdf.

67. Philip Rocco, Ann C. Keller, and Andrew S. Kelly, "State Politics and the Uneven Fate of Medicaid Expansion," *Health Affairs* 39, no. 2 (March 2020): 494–501.

68. The Missouri legislature, in its 2021 session, refused to appropriate money for expansion, prompting a lawsuit, and in July 2021 the state supreme court upheld the constitutionality of the initiative referendum and ordered enrollment to begin.

69. Joshua Meyer-Gutbrod, "Between National Polarization and Local Ideology: The Impact of Partisan Competition on State Medicaid Expansion Decisions," *Publius: The Journal of Federalism* 50, no. 2 (spring 2020): 237–255.

70. For an early example of interest group effort, see James Brasfield, "Medicaid Expansion in a Litmus State: The Missouri Struggle," *Journal of Health Politics, Policy and Law* 41, no. 6 (December 2016): 1185–1196.

71. Beland, Rocco, and Waddan, *Obamacare Wars*, 122–123.

72. Madeline Guth et al., "Medicaid Expansion Enrollment and Spending Leading Up to the COVID-19 Pandemic," Kaiser Family Foundation, January 12, 2021, www.kff.org/medicaid/issue-brief/medicaid-expansion-enrollment-and-spending-leading-up-to-the-covid-19-pandemic.

73. Rachel Garfield, Kendal Orgera, and Anthony Damico, "The Coverage Gap: Uninsured Poor Adults in States That Do Not Expand Medicaid," Kaiser Family Foundation, January 21, 2021, www.kff.org/medicaid/issue-brief/the-coverage-gap-uninsured-poor-adults-in-states-that-do-not-expand-medicaid.

74. "Chart Book: The Far-Reaching Benefits of the Affordable Care Act's Medicaid Expansion," Center on Budget and Policy Priorities, October 21, 2020, www.cbpp.org/sites/default/files/atoms/files/10-2-18health.pdf.

75. Guth et al., "Medicaid Expansion Enrollment and Spending."

76. Benjamin Sommers and Jonathan Gruber, "Federal Funding Insulated State Budgets from Increased Spending Related to Medicaid Expansion," *Health Affairs* 36, no. 5 (May 2017): 938–944.

77. Bruce Ward, "Impact of Medicaid Expansion on State Budgets," Commonwealth Fund, May 2020, www.commonwealthfund.org/sites/default/files/2020-05/Ward_impact_Medicaid_expansion_state_budgets_ib_final.pdf.

78. Ibid.

79. Fredric Blavin and Christal Ramos, "Medicaid Expansion: Effects on Hospital Finances and Implications for Hospitals Facing COVID-19 Challenges," *Health Affairs* 40, no. 1 (January 2020): 82–90.

80. Madeline Guth, Rachel Garfield, and Robin Rudowitz, "The Effects of Medicaid Expansion Under the ACA: Updated Findings from a Literature Review," Kaiser Family Foundation, March 17, 2020, www.kff.org/report-section/the-effects-of-medicaid-expansion-under-the-aca-updated-findings-from-a-literature-review-report.

81. Nicole Kravitz-Wirtz et al., "Association of Medicaid Expansion with Opioid Overdose Mortality in the United States," *JAMA Open Network*, January 10, 2020, https://jamanetwork.com/journals/jamanetworkopen/fullarticle/2758476; Sameed Ahmed M. Khatana et al., "Association of Medicaid Expansion with Cardiovascular Mortality," *JAMA Cardiology* 4, no. 7 (June 5, 2019): 671–679; Jusung Lee et al., "The Impact of Medicaid Expansion on Diabetes Management," *Diabetes Care* 43, no. 5 (May 2020): 1094–1101.

82. John A. Graves et al., "Medicaid Expansion Slowed Rates of Health Decline for Low-Income Adults in Southern States," *Health Affairs* 39, no. 1 (January 2020): 67–76.

83. Anuj Gangopadhyay and Emily M. Johnston, "Impacts of the ACA's Medicaid Expansion on Health Insurance Coverage and Health Care Access Among Young Adults," Urban Institute, February 2021, www.urban.org/sites/default/files/publication/103673/impacts-of-the-acas-medicaid-expansion-on-health-insurance-coverage-and-health-care-access-among-young-adults_0.pdf.

84. Madeline Guth, Samantha Artiga, and Olivia Pham, "Effects of the ACA Medicaid Expansion on Racial Disparities in Health and Health Care," Kaiser Family Foundation, September 30, 2020, www.kff.org/medicaid/issue-brief/effects-of-the-aca-medicaid-expansion-on-racial-disparities-in-health-and-health-care.

85. John Iglehart, "Medicaid Expansion Offers Solutions, Challenges," *Health Affairs* 29, no. 2 (February 2010): 230–232.

86. "Health Insurance Coverage of the Nonelderly: Time Frame 2019," Kaiser Family Foundation, www.kff.org/other/state-indicator/nonelderly-0-64.

87. Michael Simpson, "Implications of Medicaid Expansion in the Remaining States," Urban Institute, June 2020, www.urban.org/sites/default/files/publication/102359/the-implications-of-medicaid-expansion-in-the-remaining-states-2020-update.pdf.

88. Grogan and Patashnik, "Between Welfare Medicine and Mainstream Entitlement," 822.

89. "Who Could Get Covered Under Medicaid Expansion?," Kaiser Family Foundation, February 10, 2021, www.kff.org/medicaid/fact-sheet/uninsured-adults-in-states-that-did-not-expand-who-would-become-eligible-for-medicaid-under-expansion.

7

The Verdict: Public Opinion, Legal Opinions

*I've been kicked around
Since I was born
And now it's alright, it's okay.*

—Bee Gees

These lyrics to the late-1970s hit by the Bee Gees might aptly describe the first decade of the Affordable Care Act (ACA). Despite being "kicked around" during its first decade, the ACA stayed alive. In this chapter we look at two critical elements of the survival. No public social welfare program is likely to have a high rate of survival unless the public approves of its goals and appreciates its success. We first look at the path of public opinion about the ACA and see that the law is more, not less, popular after a decade of challenges. From the day it was born, legal challenges have threatened its existence or bodily harm to critical parts. Despite some losses, the ACA has won more than lost in the courts, especially with regard to the critical threats.

Public Opinion: Hills and Valleys

A decade later probably the biggest surprise for the architects of the ACA has been its failure to achieve broader popularity given the scope of its benefits.[1] More individuals are now covered by Medicaid expansion or purchase their health insurance through a marketplace exchange with a tax credit. For many, their children remain covered until age twenty-six, preexisting conditions will not hang over a potential job move, and their insurance does not have narrow lifetime or yearly maximum benefits. However, these features may not be recognized as ACA benefits.

Figure 7.1 illustrates an answer to the simple question of whether support versus opposition to the ACA has remained constant over ten years. Those favoring the ACA slightly outnumbered those opposed at the time of enactment. The anticipated quick migration toward higher support did not materialize. A year later support and opposition were equal at 41 percent, with nearly 20 percent offering no opinion. In 2013, during the technical problems with marketplace rollout, opposition spiked to almost 50 percent and hovered for the next five years at about 45 percent. Meanwhile, favorable opinion rebounded as the ACA marketplaces recovered from the initial problems to settle in the low forties through 2016.

However, there was a sharp upturn in support by the end of the first year of the Donald Trump administration, with a 50 percent level of support for the first time. Opposition remained in the mid-forties, but the no-opinion responses decreased into the single digits. It appears this initial upward tick in support did not stem primarily from individuals changing their mind; rather the number of those with no opinion declined.

Support for the ACA increased throughout the Trump years and registered at 54 percent by early 2021. In 2018 unfavorable opinion declined to 40 percent and remained at that level, with the no-opinion response continuing in the single digits.

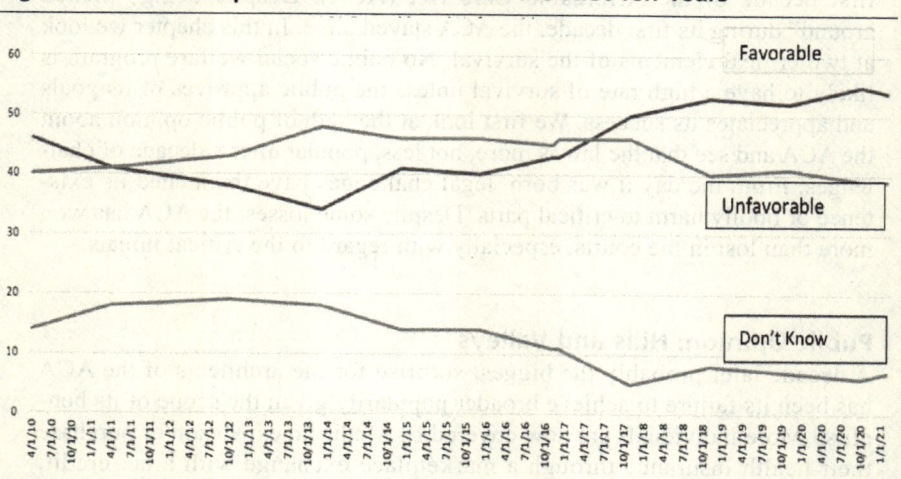

Figure 7.1 Public Opinion on the ACA over the First Ten Years

Source: Kaiser Family Foundation.

This shift of positive opinion occurred at the beginning of the Trump administration, when the threat to repeal the ACA had become a reality, not just a campaign slogan. An examination of key demographic factors helps to explain the shift in positive support.

Unsurprisingly, those who have examined public opinion on the ACA have found party identification to be a key predictor. Mollyann Brodie and colleagues, in a 2020 *Health Affairs* article summarizing the results of more than 100 polls on the ACA, concluded the partisan divide has grown over the decade because more Democrats now have a favorable view, not because Republican opposition has significantly declined.[2] Table 7.1 illustrates the stability of and marginal shifts in partisan division of opinion on the ACA.

The Kaiser tracking poll data show Republican opposition in the high seventies and Democratic support in the low eighties over the last few years. Democratic support declined during the marketplace rollout problems but substantially increased during the Trump administration. Among Independents, support was initially very low but grew steadily during the Trump administration years, with a decline in both unfavorable and no-opinion responses. By 2019 a majority of Independents reported a favorable view of the ACA.

The ACA is complex legislation. Early polls indicated large segments of the population reported lack of knowledge about the content of the law.[3] No doubt this lack of understanding contributed to a partisan divide, as respondents used their party identification as a proxy and cue for a response to pollsters. Democrats supported and Republicans opposed based on the stances of party leaders.

Other demographic variables are less predictive. Over 50 percent support for the ACA is now found among individuals in each income category with growth of support since 2017. The age categories, except those over sixty-five, have seen increased support and are currently at over 50 percent. Women are more supportive than men, but there is greater support than opposition among men. African Americans and Hispanics show higher favorable support than whites, but the latter do show slightly greater support than opposition.[4]

In this mix is the interesting phenomenon of liking the parts and opposing the whole. A 2016 Kaiser tracking poll survey found substantial support of 80 percent and above for various ACA provisions, such as children staying on parents' plan until age twenty-six, eliminating out-of-pocket costs for preventive services, tax credits to assist with insurance purchase, and Medicaid expansion. The only major provision with strong disapproval was the individual mandate.[5] It is possible to explain this riddle by realizing the ACA has become a partisan symbol with many opponents understanding little of its actual content.

Table 7.1 Division of Partisan Opinion on the ACA (percentage)

	4/10	4/11	10/12	12/13	12/14	12/15	11/16	11/17	11/18	11/19	10/20	2/21
Democrat												
Favorable	78	64	64	68	69	67	74	80	81	83	85	82
Unfavorable	13	17	15	13	18	19	19	17	16	12	9	10
Don't know	10	20	21	19	13	14	7	4	4	5	5	8
Independent												
Favorable	36	41	32	28	40	32	42	43	47	52	59	54
Unfavorable	46	44	49	56	46	53	48	50	48	43	35	40
Don't know	18	17	20	16	14	15	11	7	8	6	6	6
Republican												
Favorable	13	12	10	7	10	14	12	17	17	22	18	17
Unfavorable	78	74	77	80	79	79	79	81	76	73	79	75
Don't know	9	14	12	13	11	8	9	2	8	6	4	7

Source: Kaiser Family Foundation Tracking Poll.

Even among those purchasing marketplace plans, 40 percent expressed an unfavorable view of the ACA. Once again, Democrats who held non-group insurance plans were overwhelmingly in favor of the ACA, but 80 percent of Republicans in this category expressed an unfavorable view.[6] The partisan divide symbolized by the ACA appears to be a stronger pull on some Republicans' view of the act than its personal benefits. This simple fact may be the strongest explanation of why ACA approval has not grown as expected.

Lawrence Jacobs and Suzanne Mettler utilized a slightly different methodology to approach the question of response to the ACA over time. They employed a sample panel of the same individuals over the decade, interviewing them every two years. The Kaiser poll and others selected a different random sample for each set of interviews. Based on interviews through 2014, Jacobs and Mettler also found partisan affiliation to have the strongest association with favorable and unfavorable views of the ACA. They did find those in the panel who gained insurance coverage after 2010 were less likely to favor repeal.[7] This suggests that increased coverage due to the ACA resulted in the expected growth of support.

Three years later, after two more rounds of interviews, the share of respondents who reported the ACA made things better for their family had doubled since 2010 to include 20 percent of the sample. Those who said the ACA had a great deal of impact on access to health insurance had increased to nearly a quarter.[8] However, partisanship remained a dominating feature of the response to the ACA. Republicans, who resented government and taxes, had a stronger negative assessment of the ACA.[9]

The Affordable Care Act offers an interesting example of the impact of policy feedback on public-opinion shifts or stability for both specific pieces of legislation and political parties. Does major social legislation change citizens' political viewpoints and allegiance? Why didn't the ACA generate strong public support, as happened with Medicare?

Andrea Campbell has written extensively on policy feedback, putting forth several ideas in answer to these questions. First, the ACA offered different policy fixes aimed at various sets of people. The fractured policy design may have rendered the benefits less visible. Second, the actual benefits may have been too modest relative to the general problem of health care affordability, which is the greatest concern of citizens. Third, high levels of partisanship tend to distort and filter the information received. Republicans may have been much more exposed to negative information about the ACA, which filtered out understanding of the benefits. Fourth, even a decade after enactment, we may need more time to understand the full policy feedback impact of the ACA. The uptick in support during the last couple of years of the decade may be a harbinger of growing support in the coming years.[10]

Jacobs and Mettler found feedback was most prevalent among those who experience tangible benefits from the ACA, even in the high political noise surrounding the legislation. Also, for some, observation of positive impact for the country as a whole led to a more positive attitude toward the law.[11]

Eric Patashnik and Julian Zelizer examined the ACA in the context of a broader review of policy feedback on major pieces of legislation. They distinguished between enactment and postenactment decisions. In the former, policy design may fail to create incentives for constituency mobilization, and narrow adoption margins ultimately limit positive policy feedback. In the postenactment phase, there may be a failure to repair defects in the policy design. They cite the late-1930s major adjustments of Social Security as an example of increasing positive feedback with design modification. They cite the slow ACA phase-in, with major provisions effective four years after enactment, as limiting constituency building.[12] The contrast is Medicare's benefit effective date a year after enactment.

Unlike the 1988 Medicare Catastrophic Coverage Act, which was repealed a year after passage as public opinion turned sharply negative, the ACA has been a survivor. Despite a delayed and botched implementation, early public support decline, and a hostile Congress and administration, the ACA endured. A more positive public view emerged even as the ACA was threatened with repeal and partisanship grew more divisive. Campbell is no doubt correct in her assessment of the need for a more extended period to finally draw a conclusion on public opinion as policy feedback on the ACA.

Legal Issues

In 1937 the Supreme Court ruled 7–2 in *Helvering v. Davis*, rejecting a challenge to the constitutionality of the Social Security Act of 1935. The act provided for two taxes, one on employers and one on workers. Together the funds raised were to be used to pay benefits to eligible retirees. The legal challenge contended the taxes and related spending created an insurance program that was beyond the power of Congress under the Constitution. Speaking for the Court majority, Justice Benjamin Cordozo argued, following Alexander Hamilton, that the spending power of Congress is not limited as long as it is exercised for the general welfare.[13]

As an interesting note, the Court's conservative majority had struck down several New Deal programs by rejecting the commerce clause as their constitutional basis. After President Franklin Roosevelt threatened to expand the number of judges, Justice Owen Roberts began to side with the liberals, including in the *Helvering* case.[14] Perhaps the reader will anticipate the irony of later conservative Justice John Roberts's position on ACA legal challenges.

Conservative critics were initially opposed to both Social Security and Medicare, often deriding them as socialism. Legislative efforts were made over the years to weaken both programs. But after *Helvering*, few serious efforts were undertaken to terminate the programs with constitutional challenges. In recent decades legislative efforts to "privatize" both programs have met with political resistance. Both have broad public support.

With the ACA critics have made a consistent and ongoing effort to overturn or seriously weaken the law. They have more aggressively utilized the federal courts to achieve this end than critics of Social Security or Medicare did in earlier eras. The legal challenges have been an integral element of conservative opposition to the ACA.[15]

The following section briefly summarizes the series of legal challenges to the ACA, as well as court efforts to support the law during the Trump administration. The review begins with discussions of three serious efforts to overturn the law or major features of it, then examines cases challenging individual sections and assesses supporters' legal efforts to block Trump administration rule and policy changes. It concludes with thoughts on why the ACA has generated such a level of legal challenge.

The Big Ones

Three major cases threatened the very existence of the ACA. Table 7.2 summarizes the cases and their paths through the court system.

NFIB v. Sebelius (2012). The first and most significant legal challenge to the ACA began long before enactment and signing. In July 2009 a Federalist Society white paper raised questions about the constitutionality of the individual mandate.[16] As the ACA bill began to emerge from the House, Republican opposition initially focused on cost, but at the end of the summer David Rivkin and Lee Casey wrote op-ed pieces in the *Wall Street Journal* and *Washington Post* arguing the individual mandate was unconstitutional.[17]

Josh Blackman later recalled a November 2009 meeting of the Federalist Society in which a lobby conversation among several participants led to the drafting of a Heritage Foundation memo a month later contending the mandate was unconstitutional.[18] This paper became the starting point for the most serious legal challenge.

By the time the bill was signed in March 2010, conservative legal scholars and Republicans had mobilized a political and legal challenge. It was kicked off by the filing of a lawsuit in Florida federal district court by more than twenty Republican state attorneys general. At first major legal scholars were dismissive of the merits of the challenge and believed it posed little threat to the ACA.[19]

With Democrats in control of Congress and the White House, ACA opponents seized on what initially appeared to be a fringe constitutional

Table 7.2 Major Cases Seeking to Invalidate the ACA

Case	Year of Initial Suit	Legal Challenge	Path	Year of Supreme Court Decision	Conclusion
NFIB v. Sebelius	2010	Individual mandate is unconstitutional.	Suits in various jurisdictions; Florida district and appeals courts find mandate unconstitutional. Supreme Court accepts case in late 2011.	2012	Supreme Court upholds constitutionality of mandate as a tax. Supreme Court finds Medicaid expansion optional for states.
King v. Burwell	2012	Statutory interpretation: language implies subsidies only in state exchanges.	District court decisions mixed; appeals courts uphold subsidies. Supreme Court accepts case in November 2014.	2015	Supreme Court upholds ACA and interprets statute as allowing subsidy in both state and federal exchanges.
Texas v. California	2018	Since Congress reduced penalty to zero, it is not a tax and unconstitutional, thus whole ACA invalid.	Texas district court rules ACA unconstitutional. Appeals court agrees. Supreme Court accepts case in March 2020.	2021	Supreme Court finds the plaintiffs do not have standing to sue and dismisses the case.

issue as their path to stimulate public opposition and perhaps take down the whole law. This appeared to be a Hail Mary.[20] It would prove to be the first of many attempts to use the courts to accomplish what could not be achieved with the legislative process—namely, to weaken or dismantle the ACA.

Here we briefly summarize the path from initial suit to Supreme Court decision as well as review the legal issues. By the time the ACA was signed, conservative opponents had honed their legal strategy, and the state of Florida immediately filed suit in the federal district court. It was joined by twenty-five other states and eventually the National Federation of Independent Business (NFIB), as well as two uninsured plaintiffs. Various groups also filed suits in other jurisdictions.

Three were dismissed in federal district court, and the appeals court upheld those decisions. Two district courts found in favor of the constitutional challenge, but one of those decisions was overturned by the appeals court. The Florida district court's early 2011 decision finding the individual mandate unconstitutional was upheld in late 2011 by the appeals court, which also ruled the remainder of the law was constitutional.[21] The Supreme Court accepted the case in late 2011 and scheduled oral arguments for March 2012 with a decision anticipated by June.

Two major constitutional issues were before the Court. The plaintiffs argued the individual mandate was unconstitutional because the commerce clause did not permit Congress to require an individual to purchase something, in this case an insurance policy. The second issue was a challenge to the requirement that all states participate in Medicaid expansion or risk losing all their federal Medicaid funds.

Supporters feared the Court might rule the individual-mandate provision was unconstitutional and inseverable from the rest of law, thus striking down the whole ACA. This case was an existential threat. In June 2012 Justice Roberts spoke for a 5–4 majority in ruling the ACA individual-mandate provision was constitutional, but not based on the commerce clause. Rather, it was in effect a tax on those not purchasing insurance and permissible under the Constitution.

The surprise in the decision was the second part of the ruling, which found the loss of all Medicaid funds as the penalty for failure to enact expansion coercive. In effect this rendered Medicaid expansion optional for the states.[22] Defenders of the law were relieved by the decision preserving the individual mandate, which they perceived as critical to its success.[23]

King v. Burwell (2015). Conservative legal scholar Jonathan Adler's writings were integral to the *NFIB v. Sebelius* case. Adler later recounted how the next significant court challenge emerged. In a December 2010 American Enterprise Institute presentation, Tom Christina offered the view that a literal reading of the statute—four little words: "established by the state"—led to the conclusion that tax credits for the purchase of insurance could only be received in state-established exchanges, not federal exchanges.[24]

A few months later, Adler and coauthor Michael Cannon presented a paper with a more comprehensive legal argument making this point.[25] At first this was little more than a footnote to the constitutional argument underway in the *NFIB* case. Later, as the ACA survived the constitutional challenge and the Internal Revenue Service (IRS) issued preliminary rules allowing tax credits in both federal and state exchanges, conservative critics identified four words—"established by the state"—as the basis for their next major legal action against the ACA.

In September 2012, three months after the Supreme Court decision in *NFIB*, three separate cases were filed arguing the IRS rule was contrary to the ACA statutory language. Two of the cases with a group of citizens and businesses as plaintiffs were funded by the Competitive Enterprise Institute, a free market think tank. The other was filed by the Oklahoma attorney general. One of the district courts found the subsidies illegal, and two ruled the opposite. In July 2014 one appeals court ruled the subsidies to be legal, whereas a three-judge panel in a separate appeal reached a different conclusion, but reversed the decision on a rehearing by the full court. In November 2014 the Supreme Court agreed to hear the case.[26]

The Supreme Court heard oral arguments in early 2015. The discussion revolved around the intent of Congress in establishing exchanges. Did it seek to allow tax credits on state exchanges but not on fallback federal exchanges? Or was this a drafting error that created an ambiguity, in which case the Court should defer to the interpretation of the administrative agency?[27]

In June 2015 the Supreme Court, by a 6–3 majority, upheld the IRS statutory interpretation allowing tax credits in both federal and state exchanges. Again, Chief Justice Roberts wrote the majority opinion. In upholding the appeals court decision, he utilized a more favorable argument for the future of the ACA. The Chevron doctrine holds that when a statute is ambiguous, courts should defer to the administrative agency. The Court majority found the case to have deep economic and political significance, and Congress would not have intentionally left this question to be decided by the agency. The Court interpreted the statute to mean tax credits are available in both state and federal exchanges. Only Congress in the future could change the interpretation by amending the statute.[28] Little did anyone appreciate at the time that a new conservative administration would be in office sixteen months later. A different basis for the decision might have opened the door for a more restrictive administrative interpretation of the issue.

The *King* case did not present a constitutional threat, but if the Supreme Court had adopted the strict interpretation argument of Adler and others, a major feature of the ACA could have been decimated. If Democrats had retained congressional majorities, a simple language adjustment would have rendered the question moot. A Republican Congress did not opt to make such a change. Analytic assessments of the consequences of an adverse ruling determined a possible 8 million would lose health insurance, with premiums rising 35 percent.[29]

The cast of characters seeking to use *King v. Burwell* to eviscerate the ACA was substantially the same as in the *NFIB* case three years earlier. Conservative scholars such as Adler and Cannon were featured by think tanks such as the Heritage Foundation and the American Enterprise Institute to bolster the intellectual case for defeating the ACA. A phalanx of scholars on the other side, such as Timothy Jost and Nicholas Bagley made the legal case for sustaining the law.[30] Chief Justice Roberts, for a second time, was unwilling to lead the Supreme Court into overturning the central feature of the ACA: enabling individuals to purchase health insurance with tax credits.

The plaintiffs found a minor legislative drafting error and sought to magnify it into a death knell for a critical part of the law. Both Republican and Democratic legislative staff members, as well as Republican senators involved in the discussions, stated it was never the intent to limit subsidies to only state exchanges. It seems that the original Senate language envisioned tax credits used exclusively on state exchanges. Then, when the focus shifted to include a default to federal exchanges, some of the language in one section of the bill was not modified.[31] Had there been a conference committee instead of the House simply accepting the Senate bill, the error would likely have been caught and adjusted.

The ACA's *Perils of Pauline* existence survived another court test, as it would survive legislative efforts to repeal in the early Trump administration. We now turn to the third major attempt to overturn the ACA by judicial fiat.

Texas v. California (2018). *Texas v. California* challenged the individual mandate again. Perhaps because it was the most unpopular provision of the ACA, or because its legal status was contentious, the next major challenge to the ACA revisited the constitutionality of the individual mandate. In February 2018 the Texas attorney general, joined by twenty others and two individual plaintiffs, sued to have the individual mandate declared unconstitutional. The plaintiffs argued the provision was integral to the entire law, and therefore the whole ACA was invalid. The individual-mandate provision was not severable. At this point the reader can be forgiven for thinking the *NFIB* decision in 2012 had settled this issue. In 2017 Congress reduced the penalty for not purchasing insurance to zero, effectively eliminating its impact. The attorneys general contended the absence of a penalty meant the mandate was not a tax and was therefore unconstitutional.[32]

The plaintiffs selected a Texas district to file their case in anticipation of a friendly judge presiding. Judge Reed O'Connor lived up to their expectation.

In December 2018 he ruled the individual mandate was unconstitutional because it was no longer a tax since the penalty had been reduced to zero. He further found this provision to be integral to the entire law, which was wholly invalidated. The judge did not issue an immediate injunction, anticipating an appeal.[33] A year later the Fifth Circuit Court of Appeals, in a 2–1 decision, affirmed the mandate as unconstitutional but returned the case to the lower court for additional consideration of the severability issue. This became unnecessary when the Supreme Court in March 2020 agreed to hear the case and scheduled oral arguments for November.[34]

Like the *NFIB* case, this case was an existential challenge to the ACA. However, conservative ACA opponents did not line up in support as they had several years earlier. The defection of law professor Jonathan Adler was the most symbolic. His prolific legal arguments attacking the ACA and the individual mandate had been the heart of the *NFIB* case. This time he joined Abbe Gluck, an ACA-supportive law professor, in denouncing the case and Justice O'Connor's ruling.[35] Adler joined several other legal scholars in submitting an amicus brief arguing the individual mandate was severable from the rest of the ACA.[36] Yuval Levin, in the conservative *National Review*, said of Judge O'Connor's ruling, "The notion that this inoperative mandate is actually necessary for the functioning of the rest of the system created by the statute . . . doesn't even merit being called silly. It's ridiculous."[37]

Unlike in *NFIB* and *King*, the defense of the ACA rested with a hostile Trump administration. The Justice Department position on the case shifted several times. At the district court level, it had agreed the provision was unconstitutional but held that the only ACA provisions not severable were those related to consumer protection, such as guaranteed issue and prohibition of preexisting conditions. On appeal it maintained that the entire ACA was inseverable but the ruling applied only to the plaintiff states. In its brief to the Supreme Court, the Trump administration argued the remedy should only apply to the plaintiffs.[38] The attorney general of California, joined by several others, was allowed to enter the case to defend the ACA as the case developed.[39]

After observing the November 2020 oral arguments, most observers believed the Court would not overturn the ACA. The principal issues before the court were the standing of the plaintiffs, whether the elimination of the mandate penalty rendered it unconstitutional, and, if so, whether the mandate was separable from the rest of the law.[40] If a majority of the Supreme Court were to rule the entire ACA unconstitutional, an Urban Institute analysis found, 15 million covered with Medicaid expansion, 5 million with tax credits in the marketplace, and 2 million children covered until age twenty-six would likely become uninsured.[41] This huge negative impact is seen as a constraint on the Court's taking such a drastic step. Both precedent and the opinion of conservative legal scholars supported rejection of the plaintiff's argument. The Supreme Court issued a ruling in June 2021 that determined neither the states or the plaintiffs had standing to sue.

Religious Challenges: The Contraception Battles

In 2009, as the ACA was drafted in congressional committees, language related to paying for abortion was the subject of heated debate and nearly killed the bill in the House. But paying for contraception services was not a point of dispute. It seemed like public battles over birth control were a thing of the past. Prior to the ACA, most states required that insurance policies cover contraception services, but these were often subject to cost sharing, and state requirements did not extend to self-funded plans. The ACA expanded on these by requiring most individual market and employer plans to cover preventive services without cost, including coverage for women of preventive care and screening.[42]

At the time of enactment, little objection was raised. Law professor Helen Alvare, in a 2010 article on questions of conscience and the ACA, referred almost in passing to dissenting views on marginal issues such as contraception.[43]

The Barack Obama administration contracted with the Institute of Medicine (IOM) to recommend which services should be included in this requirement. The IOM recommended inclusion of the full range of contraceptives approved by the Food and Drug Administration. Health and Human Services (HHS) accepted the IOM recommendation in August 2011 and added a rule exempting churches from the requirement. Opponents objected, especially to the exclusion of institutions such as schools and hospitals from any exemption. The Catholic bishops called for broad exemption because contraception is not health care.[44]

In January 2012 the Obama administration announced a one-year delay in the application of the rule.[45] It offered a new accommodation in February. The insurance carriers, not the institutions, would be responsible for direct payment for contraceptive services. The Catholic bishops opposed the plan, but other groups supported the compromise.[46] Lawsuits were initiated by bishops in jurisdictions across the country.[47] In February 2013 the proposed rule was published but explicitly excluded for-profit entities. Initial compliance with the rule prohibiting cost sharing was uneven, and the rule was modified in 2015 to include a specific list of services covered by the requirement.[48]

A number of lawsuits had been filed in federal courts across the country, leading to several years of litigation on the subject, including multiple Supreme Court decisions. We will not attempt here to follow the winding road of court skirmishes on this issue but will focus our summary on the three Supreme Court decisions on the issue. The first was the *Hobby Lobby* case, followed by *Zubik* and *Little Sisters of the Poor*.

Burwell v. Hobby Lobby (2014). The Obama administration religious accommodation explicitly excluded for-profit entities. A number of them sued. The basis for the legal actions was not constitutional but statutory. The plaintiffs claimed the contraception mandate violated their religious rights under the 1993 Religious Freedom Restoration Act (RFRA). The Supreme Court in June 2014 ruled a privately held corporation, such as Hobby Lobby, is a person under the statute, and the mandate was a substantial burden. The accommodation process for nonprofit religion-based organizations should also be available to closely held corporations.

The Obama administration responded with a 2015 rule allowing an accommodation for closely held private corporations whose owners' religious beliefs opposed contraception.[49] Assessment was mixed, but even some who disagreed with the decision regarded it as narrowly decided and unlikely to be broadly applied to the contraceptive mandate.[50]

Zubik v. Burwell (2016). The second set of contraceptive-mandate court cases grew out of the Obama administration's distinction between exemption and accommodation. The exemption for churches was not extended to institutions with a religious affiliation, such as universities and hospitals. For the latter an accommodation was offered. After the *Hobby Lobby* decision, the accommodation was extended to some closely held corporations as well.

The accommodation allowed religiously affiliated nonprofits to submit a form indicating to HHS or their insurer or third-party health plan administrator their objection to all or some of the mandated contraceptive services. A late-2015 Kaiser Foundation survey found 10 percent of all nonprofits with over 1,000 employees had requested an accommodation.[51] Most, but not all, of these institutions were affiliated with the Catholic Church. This is not a surprise because of the church's theological objection to contraception.

The Becket Fund for Religious Liberty was the leading organization providing legal representation to religious nonprofits unhappy with the accommodation process. They argued the process continued to directly involve them with the provision of contraceptive services, which was a violation of their religious principles. This constituted a violation of the RFRA and the First Amendment.[52]

A number of institutions across the country filed lawsuits making a similar legal argument. Most of the district and appeals courts rejected the plaintiffs' contentions, but the Supreme Court did halt any penalties for failure to comply pending a resolution of the case. In November 2015 the Supreme Court combined several cases in accepting the issue for review. *Zubik v. Burwell* became the lead case. Oral arguments were heard in March 2016. At that point the Court had only eight members, with four liberals and four conservatives. In July, rather than ruling one way or the other, the

Supreme Court remanded the case back to the district court in an attempt to let the parties find a compromise solution.[53]

A settlement was not reached, but in May 2017 the Trump administration unilaterally issued an order to settle the issue to favor the plaintiffs.[54] This was followed later in the year with a new interim rule allowing almost any employer with religious or moral objections an exemption to the contraceptive mandate. The final rule released in November 2018 was identical to the interim rule.[55] This led to the next set of court cases on the issue.

Little Sisters of the Poor v. Pennsylvania (2020). The states of Pennsylvania and New Jersey immediately filed suit in federal court to halt implementation of the new rule. They succeeded in obtaining a nationwide injunction to halt implementation while the cases were working their way through the courts. The Little Sisters of the Poor, a religious nonprofit, was permitted to join the case in defense of the rule. It was already allowed an accommodation but was seeking full exemption under the new rule.[56]

The Supreme Court accepted the case and heard oral arguments on May 6, 2020. The main issues were whether the Administrative Procedures Act (APA) had been followed in the construction of the rules, whether the RFRA required or authorized broad exemptions, and whether a nationwide injunction halting implementation of the rule was valid.[57]

In July 2020 the Supreme Court, by a 7–2 margin, upheld the government's right under the ACA to exercise a broad set of religious and moral exemptions. The rule-making process did not violate the APA. The question of the application of RFRA to the case was not addressed; nor was the contention by the state of Pennsylvania that the rules were "arbitrary and capricious." This issue is still under litigation. Despite the decision margin, the justices offered differing views of the outcome. For example, Justice Roberts expressed concern that the rules might not adequately balance religious objections and health care access.[58]

The *Little Sisters* decision didn't settle key questions about the contraceptive mandate, such as the scope of the RFRA on this question or whether the Trump rule was arbitrary and capricious. At a minimum the Joe Biden administration is likely to seek to return to the Obama rule on accommodation, using the formal rule-making process. Unless a compromise can be found, as the Court sought in *Zubik*, this question will likely be the subject of legal battles for the entire Biden administration.

Sarah Lipton-Lubet captured the essential problem in describing dual narratives surrounding the issue of a contraception mandate. One side sees contraception as an evil practice and the government mandate to pay for it as part of a war on religion. The other side views the attempt to use a theological belief to force women to pay for or go without an essential health service as a war on women.[59] The best way to end wars is through diplomacy, not total victory. The problem flows from the unique characteristics of employer-based insurance. A minority, but still a significant number, of employers have sought an exemption. If a negotiated settlement in which neither side completely wins is not possible, the wars over contraceptive coverage will likely continue, with a Supreme Court majority appearing to lean in the direction of favoring religious claims.

Kelly v. Azar. This case is also before Judge Reed O'Connor in Texas. The plaintiffs contended in 2020 that not just the contraceptive mandate but the entire Section 2713 requiring insurance plans to cover a variety of preventive services without cost sharing is unconstitutional because it relies on outside groups for the listing of services. The case will be argued in the district court in 2022. It represents one more significant legal challenge to a provision of the ACA.[60] It is probably not the last.

Insurance Company Cases

The contraceptive-mandate cases were poster children for the ACA's place in the culture wars of the last few decades. The insurance company cases were invisible to all but ACA legal aficionados and involved disputes between the government and carriers over money. The cases emanated from two concerns when the ACA was drafted. The first was a fear that too many insurance companies might opt out of marketplace participation because the actuarial risk was uncertain. The second was the desire to protect low-income marketplace customers from excessive cost sharing, which might discourage them from purchasing an insurance policy.

Risk-Corridor Cases

The risk-corridor program was one of three ACA provisions designed to encourage initial insurance plan participation in the marketplaces. The other two were targeted reinsurance and permanent risk adjustment. The risk corridor was modeled after a permanent feature of the Medicare Part D prescription drug program and was to be in effect from 2014 through 2016.

It was established by Section 1342 of the ACA. The basic assumption was that some companies would generate significant profits from the marketplace business, and others would lose money in this new enterprise because of the inherent uncertainty of a new market. A formula was established for collection of excess profits and payments for unexpected losses. There was no statutory requirement of budget neutrality. Payments did not have to equal outlays. When the program began, the Republican Congress criticized it as a subsidy for insurance companies, and a 2014 appropriation rider prohibited use of other funds for payments. For 2014 HHS adopted a budget-neutral approach and was only able to pay 12 percent of the obligation under the formula. By 2016 more than $12 billion was owed.[61]

A number of lawsuits were filed by affected insurance companies, including Maine Community Health Options. The cases worked their way through the lower court system, and the Supreme Court agreed to hear the consolidated case with oral arguments scheduled for December 2019. The companies argued the statute did not require budget neutrality and that they had participated in the marketplaces in good faith despite the risks associated with a new venture. The government contended it was not obligated to make full payments because there were no appropriations and the rider prohibited the use of other funds.[62]

The Supreme Court decided in favor of the insurance plans in April 2020. The ruling found the government had an obligation to pay under the provisions of Section 1342 and the appropriations rider did not invalidate the responsibility. The plaintiffs could sue for damages in the federal court of claims.[63] This was a victory for the plaintiff companies and was expected to lead other companies, not only the parties to this case, to also seek damages in the court of claims.[64]

Cost-Sharing Reduction Cases

In order to reduce the financial burden for those in the individual insurance marketplace with an income less than 200 percent of the federal poverty level (FPL), the ACA required insurance plans to reduce cost sharing for these customers. The requirement had two parts. First, the annual cost-sharing limit was reduced. Second, the cost-sharing requirement, such as for the annual medical deductible, was lowered.[65] The ACA statutory language required the federal government to reimburse the insurance plans for this cost. However, House Republicans contended as early as 2011 that the ACA language did not include a continuing appropriation.

The House Republican majority refused to appropriate funds for this purpose and sued the Obama administration to prevent it from making the payments. A legal standoff ensued. In 2017 the Trump administration halted the payments, citing the absence of appropriations.[66] The insurance companies were still legally responsible for the payments, but without reimbursement there was a concern companies might exit the marketplaces.

It was estimated that this would cause 1 million people to drop coverage because of increased costs.[67] The states and insurance companies devised a work-around by allowing premium increases for "silver" plans, which allowed the companies to gain additional revenue to be used to offset the CSR payments. This was called "silver loading."[68]

Insurance companies brought lawsuits in federal court to restore the payments. With mixed results these cases have continued into 2021. Two August 2020 appeals court decisions found the companies were entitled to the CSR payments, but the amount should be adjusted to account for the silver-loading bonus. The Supreme Court has been asked to hear the case.

In early 2021 the Biden administration asked for additional time to present its briefs on the request. Paul Clement, who successfully argued the risk-corridor case, represented the insurance companies.

A negotiated settlement of past payments, which takes into account silver loading, seems likely. If the Biden administration resumes CSR payments, silver-loading premiums will need to be adjusted in the future. Congress could preclude future legal battles over CSR payments by adjusting the statutory language to make the appropriations permanent. To do so would probably require that such a change be part of a reconciliation bill to avoid a Senate filibuster.

Cases Challenging Trump Rules

President Trump's 2016 election created new participants in the ACA legal battles as the Obama administration had vigorously defended the ACA against various legal challenges. On the other hand, the Trump administration was determined to either repeal or sabotage the ACA to render it ineffective. Unable to repeal the law in 2017, the administration issued a variety of rule changes designed to sabotage it over the next three years.[69]

Republican attorneys general were in the forefront of legal challenges to the ACA rules or actions by the Obama administration. During the Trump administration, Democratic attorneys general were often major participants in challenges to new ACA rules. In early 2021, as the Biden administration took office, several of these cases were pending. The new administration began to change the government's position to one of support for the plaintiffs and to initiate the arduous process of modifying the rules.

Some of the major challenged rules included those allowing expansion of associated health plans and short-term plans. Another involved interpretations of the antidiscrimination ACA Section 1557 as it applies to gender identity and abortion issues. Maryland and other states challenged the Trump administration's actions related to the 2019 marketplace payment rules and won a partial victory in the district court, voiding some of the changes.[70]

The Section 1332 waiver issued to Georgia in the waning days of the Trump administration has also been contested. A lawsuit filed by Planned Parenthood contends the waiver process violated both the ACA provisions and the APA procedural requirements. The Biden administration will likely move to rescind the waiver.[71]

Medicaid Work Requirements

A significant pending legal challenge at the onset of the Biden administration concerned Medicaid work requirements. Conservative groups had, since the Ronald Reagan administration in the 1980s, sought to link income-based social programs to work requirements. In the mid-1990s the Republican congressional majority passed major changes to the cash welfare system, which included work requirements.[72] Work requirements for Medicaid beneficiaries were not part of the legislation at that time.

The Trump administration, despite Republican congressional majorities, was unable to achieve the goal of substantially shrinking the Medicaid population by reducing federal funding. In 2018 Centers for Medicare and Medicaid Services (CMS) director Seema Verma began an effort to impose work requirements, except for the elderly and disabled, on the Medicaid population for the first time. The tactic to achieve this goal was a substantial broadening of the scope of the Section 1115 waiver process, with the Medicaid expansion population a special target.

Verma issued a letter to state Medicaid directors in early 2018 inviting them to apply for 1115 waivers establishing Medicaid work requirements. All states were obviously not going to pursue this offer, but by late 2018 seven states had been approved for work-requirement waivers, and others had requests pending. Arkansas was the first and only state to actually implement work requirements. Opposition lawsuits quickly materialized, and injunctions halted implementation. A new governor withdrew Kentucky from the work-requirement waiver.

In the short time the Arkansas work requirements were in effect, more than 18,000 people were dropped from Medicaid eligibility. The Urban Institute and others analyzed the brief Arkansas experience with the work requirement. The studies found extensive dismissal of individuals from Medicaid coverage. The work-requirement process was found to be cumbersome, littered with errors, and lacking in clarity about the paperwork beneficiaries were required to submit.[73]

The legal challenges argued the idea of work requirements to determine eligibility was not lawful under the Medicaid statute. The waivers were outside the authority granted under Section 1115, and the experience of Arkansas demonstrated significant loss of coverage without the presumed benefits. The lower courts rejected the Trump administration's assertions of legality and value for Medicaid recipients.[74]

In December 2020 the Supreme Court agreed to consolidate the cases and consider *Becerra v. Gresham*, the challenge to Arkansas's Section 1115 work-requirement waiver. Oral arguments were set for the end of March 2021 but postponed at the request of the Biden administration.[75] Since the Biden administration is rescinding the waivers, the case is not expected to be further litigated.

What ensued in the waning days of the Trump administration and the beginning of the Biden administration was a spectacle of clashing bureaucratic actions surrounding Medicaid work requirements. As early as August 2020 Trump officials in HHS appeared to anticipate a November loss. They issued a good guidance rule to take effect in January 2021, which facilitated changes in existing guidance and made it more difficult to issue new guidance. Guidance refers to communications, such as letters to state Medicaid directors and frequently-asked-questions documents.

On January 4, CMS administrator Verma sent letters to all state Medicaid directors in an attempt to block termination of 1115 waivers for nine months and set a prolonged process for termination. States were requested to immediately send a letter to CMS agreeing to this directive. Additional pending work-requirement waivers were also approved.[76]

One day before President Biden's inauguration, HHS secretary Alex Azar published a sunset rule. This required HHS to review every rule more than ten years old and void any that were not reviewed. The incoming administration viewed this as little more than an effort to tie up resources in performing useless reviews.[77]

Unsurprisingly, the new Biden administration team responded quickly upon assuming office. On the first day, Chief of Staff Ron Klain issued a memorandum freezing last-minute regulations and set an administrative path for nullifying the sunset rule. At the end of January, President Biden issued an executive order designed to strengthen Medicaid and the ACA.[78]

This was followed by a series of actions in mid-February to overturn Verma's last-minute sabotage efforts. The states with approved work-requirement waivers were told the waivers would be canceled; they had thirty days to comment on the decision.[79] None of the states were actually implementing work requirements for two reasons. First, the work-requirement authority was suspended because of Covid-19. Second, the courts had halted several waivers until the legal issues were settled. Other waivers were awaiting ruling.

The Biden administration will not defend the work-requirement waivers in court and will utilize all its administrative powers to nullify the actions of the Trump administration.[80] This has been a contentious Medicaid issue directed mostly at the expansion population rather than traditional Medicaid beneficiaries. Court challenges to the Biden administration's termination of the waivers might be made, but the law appears clearly on the side of administrative discretion and work requirements being beyond the scope of Section 1115 waiver authority.

Legal Issues Conclusion

The ACA has generated a cornucopia of lawsuits in its short history, and more are likely in its second decade. The ACA has become the focus of deep partisan divide and the legal system the battleground. Timothy Jost and Katie Keith presume the legal confrontations will continue. They suggest three factors reinforce this trend: the active role of state attorneys general provides an easy plaintiff, judge shopping enables early victories, and nationwide injunctions enable a single case to achieve broad impact. The Trump administration aggressively appointed conservative judges at every level. It is anticipated many of them will be open to future ACA legal challenges, especially as the Biden administration unravels many of the Trump-era ACA policies and rules.[81]

Stayin' Alive in the Courts and the Court of Public Opinion: Conclusion After a Decade

If the ACA were a cat, we might speculate it had used about seven of its nine lives in the first decade. The hyperpartisan atmosphere of the last decade made it unlikely the ACA would achieve the high public support enjoyed by Social Security. ACA support declined in the first half of the decade. Then, early in the Trump term, ACA approval ratings began to climb above 50 percent for the first time, and they have remained there. Court cases both challenged and sustained the ACA. Opponents scored a few legal victories, but the courts never dealt a deathblow verdict, although the ACA had a few near-death experiences. In the growing partisan divide, each side has psychological filters screening out positive information about public programs championed by the other side. The state attorneys general have become legal gladiators for their partisan team. Think tanks and foundations encourage and fund legal challenges to kill or weaken the ACA. Despite the pitfalls and roadblocks, the ACA has survived the anti-ACA rhetoric and lawsuit sabotage throughout its first decade.

The formal ACA title is the Patient Protection and Affordable Care Act. This implies an emphasis on cost control as well as coverage expansion. The next chapter will examine the issue of health care costs and approaches to control.

Notes

1. Mollyann Brodie et al., "Partisanship, Polling, and the Affordable Care Act," *Public Opinion Quarterly* 83, no. 2 (summer 2019): 428.

2. Mollyann Brodie et al., "The Past, Present, and Possible Future of Public Opinion on the ACA," *Health Affairs* 39, no. 3 (March 2020): 462–470.

3. Brodie et al., "Partisanship, Polling, and the Affordable Care Act," 428.

4. "KFF Health Tracking Poll: The Public's Views on the ACA," Kaiser Family Foundation, March 3, 2021, www.kff.org/interactive/kff-health-tracking-poll-the-publics-views-on-the-aca; this is updated with each monthly poll.

5. Ashley Kirzinger, Elise Sugarman, and Mollyann Brodie, "Kaiser Health Tracking Poll: November 2016," Kaiser Family Foundation, December 1, 2016, www.kff.org/health-costs/poll-finding/kaiser-health-tracking-poll-november-2016.

6. Liz Hamel et al., "Survey of Non-Group Health Insurance Enrollees, Wave 3," Kaiser Family Foundation, May 20, 2016, www.kff.org/health-reform/poll-finding/survey-of-non-group-health-insurance-enrollees-wave-3.

7. Lawrence Jacobs and Suzanne Mettler, "Liking Health Reform but Turned Off by Toxic Politics," *Health Affairs* 35, no. 3 (May 2016): 915–922.

8. Lawrence Jacobs, Suzanne Mettler, and Ling Zhu, "Affordable Care Act Moving to a New Stage of Public Acceptance," *Journal of Health Politics, Policy and Law* 44, no. 6 (December 2019): 911–918.

9. Lawrence Jacobs and Suzanne Mettler, "What Health Reform Tells Us About American Politics," *Journal of Health Politics, Policy and Law* 45, no. 4 (August 2020): 581–594.

10. Andrea Louise Campbell, "The Affordable Care Act and Mass Policy Feedbacks," *Journal of Health Politics, Policy and Law* 45, no. 4 (August 2020): 567–580.

11. Lawrence Jacobs and Suzanne Mettler, "When and How New Policy Creates New Politics: Examining the Feedback Effects of the Affordable Care Act on Public Opinion," *Perspectives on Politics* 16, no. 2 (June 2018): 345–363.

12. Eric M. Patashnik and Julian Zelizer, "The Struggle to Remake Politics: Liberal Reform and the Limits of Policy Feedback in the Contemporary American State," *Perspectives on Politics* 11, no. 4 (December 2013): 1071–1087.

13. Eduard Lopez, "Constitutional Background of the Social Security Act," *Social Security Bulletin* 50, no. 1 (January 1987): 5–11.

14. "Constitutionality of Social Security Act," Social Security Administration, www.ssa.gov/history/court.html.

15. Ronald Collins, "Book Profile: A Conspiracy Against Obamacare—the Book Based on the Blog," *SCOTUS Blog*, June 30, 2014, www.scotusblog.com/2014/01/book-profile-a-conspiracy-against-obamacare-the-book-based-on-the-blog.

16. Peter Urbanowicz and Dennis G. Smith, "Constitutional Implications of an 'Individual Mandate,' in Health Care Reform," *Federalist Society*, July 10, 2009, https://fedsoc.org/commentary/publications/constitutional-implications-of-an-individual-mandate-in-health-care-reform.

17. David B. Rivkin and Lee A. Casey, "Constitutionality of Health Insurance Mandate Questioned," *Washington Post*, August 22, 2009, www.washingtonpost.com/wp-dyn/content/article/2009/08/21/AR2009082103033.html; David B. Rivkin Jr. and Lee A. Casey, "Mandatory Insurance Is Unconstitutional: Why an Individual Mandate Could Be Struck Down by the Courts," *Wall Street Journal*, September 18, 2009, www.wsj.com/articles/SB10001424052970204518504574416623109362480.

18. Josh Blackman, "How Randy Barnett Joined the Constitutional Challenge to Obamacare," *Josh Blackman's Blog*, September 10, 2013, http://joshblackman.com/blog/2013/09/10/how-randy-barnett-joined-the-constitutional-challenge-to-obamacare; Randy Barnett, Nathaniel Stewart, and Todd Gaziano, "Why the Personal Mandate to Buy Health Insurance Is Unprecedented and Unconstitutional," Heritage Foundation, December 9, 2009, http://s3.amazonaws.com/thf_media/2009/pdf/lm_0049.pdf.

19. Timothy S. Jost, "State Lawsuits Won't Succeed in Overturning the Individual Mandate," *Health Affairs* 29, no. 6 (June 2010): 1225–1228.

20. Josh Gerstein, "How the Health Case Went Mainstream," *Politico*, March 25, 2012, www.politico.com/story/2012/03/how-the-legal-assault-on-obamas-health-law-went-mainstream-074429.

21. "Legal Challenges in Health Reform," Health Policy Brief, *Health Affairs*, October 31, 2011, www.healthaffairs.org/do/10.1377/hpb20111031.546762.

22. Timothy Jost, "The Supreme Court on the Individual Mandate's Constitutionality: An Overview," *Health Affairs Blog*, June 28, 2012, www.healthaffairs.org/do/10.1377/hblog20120628.020762/full; Sara Rosenbaum and Timothy Westmoreland, "The Supreme Court's Surprising Decision on the Medicaid Expansion: How Will the Federal Government and States Proceed?," *Health Affairs* 31, no. 8 (August 2012), www.healthaffairs.org/doi/10.1377/hlthaff.2012.0766.

23. Adam Liptak, "Supreme Court Upholds Health Care Law, 5–4, in Victory for Obama," *New York Times*, June 28, 2012, www.nytimes.com/2012/06/29/us/supreme-court-lets-health-law-largely-stand.html.

24. Jonathan H. Adler, "How 'The Case That Could Topple Obamacare' Began," *Washington Post*, January 22, 2014, www.washingtonpost.com/news/volokh-confiled-spiracy/wp/2014/01/22/how-the-case-that-could-topple-obamacare-began.

25. Jonathan H. Adler and Michael F. Cannon, "Taxation Without Representation: The Illegal IRS Rule to Expand Tax Credits Under the PPACA," *Health Matrix: Journal of Law and Medicine*, July 16, 2012, https://papers.ssrn.com/sol3/papers.cfm?abstract_id=2106789.

26. Sarah Kliff, "A Short, Visual Guide to Every Ruling on Obamacare's Subsidies," *Vox*, March 2, 2015, www.vox.com/2015/3/2/8134189/obamacare-king-timeline-scotus.

27. Timothy Jost, "*King v. Burwell*: Unpacking the Supreme Court Oral Arguments," *Health Affairs Blog*, March 5, 2015, www.healthaffairs.org/do/10.1377/hblog20150305.045244/full.

28. Timothy Jost, "The Supreme Court Upholds Tax Credits in the Federal Exchange," Commonwealth Fund, June 25, 2015, www.commonwealthfund.org/blog/2015/supreme-court-upholds-tax-credits-federal-exchange.

29. Linda J. Blumberg, Matthew Buettgens, and John Holhan, "The Implications of a Supreme Court Finding for the Plaintiff in King vs. Burwell: 8.2 Million More Uninsured and 35% Higher Premiums," Urban Institute, January 2015, www.urban.org/sites/default/files/publication/49246/2000062-The-Implications-King-vs-Burwell.pdf.

30. Nicholas Bagley, "Three Words and the Future of the Affordable Care Act," *Journal of Health Politics, Policy and Law* 40, no. 3 (June 2015): 589–597.

31. Robert Pear, "Four Words That Imperil Health Care Law Were All a Mistake, Writers Now Say," *New York Times*, May 25, 2015, www.nytimes.com/2015/05/26/us/politics/contested-words-in-affordable-care-act-may-have-been-left-by-mistake.html.

32. Katie Keith, "Judge Hears Oral Arguments in Texas v. United States," *Health Affairs Blog*, September 10, 2018, www.healthaffairs.org/do/10.1377/hblog20180910.861789/full.

33. Katie Keith, "Federal Judge Strikes Down Entire ACA; Law Remains in Effect," *Health Affairs Blog*, December 15, 2018, www.healthaffairs.org/do/10.1377/hblog20181215.617096/full.

34. Ian Millhiser, "The Fate of Obamacare Is in the Supreme Court's Hands Yet Again," *Vox*, March 2, 2020, www.vox.com/2020/3/2/21147037/obamacare-supreme-court-texas-john-roberts.

35. Jonathan H. Adler and Abbe R. Gluck, "What the Lawless Obamacare Ruling Means," *New York Times*, December 15, 2018, www.nytimes.com/2018/12/15/opinion/obamacare-ruling-unconstitutional-affordable-care-act.html.

36. Jonathan H. Adler, "The Penalty-Less Individual Mandate Is Severable from the Rest of the ACA No Matter How You Look at It," *Volokh Conspiracy Blog*, May 14, 2020, https://reason.com/volokh/2020/05/14/the-penalty-less-individual-mandate-is-severable-from-the-rest-of-the-aca-no-matter-how-you-look-at-it.

37. Yuval Levin, "The Obamacare Ruling," *National Review*, December 18, 2018, www.nationalreview.com/corner/the-obamacare-ruling.

38. MaryBeth Musumeci, "Explaining California v. Texas: A Guide to the Case Challenging the ACA," Kaiser Family Foundation, September 1, 2020, www.kff.org/health-reform/issue-brief/explaining-california-v-texas-a-guide-to-the-case-challenging-the-aca.

39. Katie Keith, "Democratic Attorneys Generals Allowed to Intervene in Individual Mandate Litigation," *Health Affairs Blog*, May 17, 2018, www.healthaffairs.org/do/10.1377/hblog20180517.968731/full.

40. Adam Liptak, "Key Justices Signal Support for Affordable Care Act," *New York Times*, November 10, 2020, www.nytimes.com/2020/11/10/us/supreme-court-obamacare-aca.html.

41. "Potential Impact of California v. Texas Decision on Key Provisions of the Affordable Care Act," Urban Institute, September 22, 2020, www.kff.org/health-reform/issue-brief/potential-impact-of-california-v-texas-decision-on-key-provisions

-of-the-affordable-care-act; "Suit Challenging ACA Legally Suspect but Threatens Loss of Coverage for Tens of Millions," Center on Budget and Policy Priorities, February 18, 2021, www.cbpp.org/research/health/suit-challenging-aca-legally-suspect-but-threatens-loss-of-coverage-for-tens-of.

42. Victoria Killion, "The Federal Contraceptive Coverage Requirement: Past and Pending Legal Challenges," Congressional Research Service, April 28, 2020, https://fas.org/sgp/crs/misc/R45928.pdf.

43. Helen Alvare, "How the Health Care Law Endangers Conscience," *Public Discourse*, June 29, 2010, www.thepublicdiscourse.com/2010/06/1402.

44. Sarah Lipton-Lubet, "Contraceptive Coverage Under the Affordable Care Act: Dueling Narratives and Their Policy Implications," *Journal of Gender, Social Policy & the Law* 22, no. 2 (2014): 343–385.

45. Laurie McGinley, "Religious Institutions' Health Plans Must Offer Birth Control," *Los Angeles Times*, January 20, 2012, www.latimes.com/archives/la-xpm-2012-jan-20-la-na-obama-birth-control-20120121-story.html.

46. Laurie Goodstein, "Obama Shift on Providing Contraception Splits Critics," *New York Times*, February 14, 2012, www.nytimes.com/2012/02/15/us/obama-shift-on-contraception-splits-catholics.html.

47. Mary Ann Glendon, "Why the Bishops Are Suing the U.S. Government," *Wall Street Journal*, May 21, 2012, www.wsj.com/articles/SB10001424052702303610504577418201554329764.

48. Mary Tschann and Reni Soon, "Contraceptive Coverage and the Affordable Care Act," *Obstetrics and Gynecology Clinics of North America* 42, no. 4 (2015): 605–617.

49. Killion, "The Federal Contraceptive Coverage Requirement," 8–9.

50. David Nather and Josh Gerstein, "Hobby Lobby Decision: 5 Takeaways," *Politico*, June 30, 2014, www.politico.com/story/2014/06/hobby-lobby-supreme-court-decision-5-takeaways-108467.

51. Laurie Sobel, Matthew Rae, and Alina Salganicoff, "Data Note: Are Nonprofits Requesting an Accommodation for Contraceptive Coverage?," Urban Institute, December 1, 2015, www.kff.org/womens-health-policy/issue-brief/data-note-are-nonprofits-requesting-an-accommodation-for-contraceptive-coverage.

52. Mark L. Rienzi, "Fool Me Twice: Zubik v. Burwell and the Perils of Judicial Faith in Government Claims," *Cato Supreme Court Review*, 2016, www.cato.org/sites/cato.org/files/serials/files/supreme-court-review/2016/9/2016-supreme-court-review-chapter-5.pdf.

53. Jennifer Haberkorn, "SCOTUS Seeks New Birth Control Policy," *Politico*, March 29, 2016, www.politico.com/story/2016/03/supreme-court-birth-control-obamacare-221354.

54. Robert Pear, "White House Acts to Roll Back Birth-Control Mandate for Religious Employers," *New York Times*, May 29, 2017, www.nytimes.com/2017/05/29/us/politics/birth-control-trump-obamacare-religion.htm.

55. Anna North, "The Trump Administration's Anti–Birth Control Agenda, Explained," *Vox*, November 12, 2018, www.vox.com/policy-and-politics/2018/11/12/18076120/trump-birth-control-2018.

56. Killion, "The Federal Contraceptive Coverage Requirement," 17–18.

57. Katie Keith, "ACA Contraceptive Mandate Heads Back to Supreme Court," *Health Affairs Blog*, May 6, 2020, htps://www.healthaffairs.org/do/10.1377/hblog20200506.930300/full.

58. Katie Keith, "Supreme Court Upholds Broad Exemptions to Contraceptive Mandate—for Now," *Health Affairs Blog*, July 9, 2020, www.healthaffairs.org/do/10.1377/hblog20200708.110645/full.

59. Sarah Lipton-Lubet, "Contraceptive Coverage Under the Affordable Care Act," 2–3.

60. Ian Millhiser, "There's a New Lawsuit Attacking Obamacare—and It's a Serious Threat," *Vox*, April 2, 2021, www.vox.com/2021/4/2/22360341/obamacare-lawsuit-supreme-court-little-sisters-kelley-becerra-reed-oconnor-nondelegation; Nicholas Bagley, "The Next Major Challenge to the Affordable Care Act," *The Atlantic*, June 18, 2021, www.theatlantic.com/ideas/archive/2021/06/next-major-challenge-affordable-care-act/619159.

61. Katie Keith, "Justices Appear Sympathetic to Insurers in Risk Corridor Payment Oral Arguments," *Health Affairs Blog*, December 12, 2019, www.healthaffairs.org/do/10.1377/hblog20191212.691619/full.

62. Katie Keith, "Supreme Court Rules That Insurers Are Entitled to Risk Corridors Payments: What the Court Said and What Happens Next," *Health Affairs Blog*, April 28, 2020, www.healthaffairs.org/do/10.1377/hblog20200427.34146/full.

63. "Maine Community Health Options v. United States," *Harvard Law Review* 134 (November 2, 2020): 170–179, https://harvardlawreview.org/2020/11/maine-community-health-options-v-united-states.

64. Edward C. Liu and Sean M. Stiff, "Ripple Effects: Assessing Impacts of the Supreme Court's Risk Corridors Decision," Congressional Research Service, July 16, 2020, https:///crsreports.congress.gov/product/pdf/LSB/LSB10519.pdf.

65. Bernadette Fernandez, "Health Insurance Premium Tax Credits and Cost-Sharing Subsidies," Congressional Research Service, April 20, 2020, https://crsreports.congress.gov/product/pdf/R/R44425.

66. Robert Pear, Maggie Haberman, and Reed Abelson, "Trump to Scrap Critical Health Care Subsidies, Hitting Obamacare," *New York Times*, October 12, 2017, www.nytimes.com/2017/10/12/us/politics/trump-obamacare-executive-order-health-insurance.html.

67. Linda J. Blumberg and Matthew Buettgens, "The Implications of a Finding for the Plaintiff in House v. Burwell," Urban Institute, January 2016, www.urban.org/sites/default/files/publication/77111/2000590-The-Implications-of-a-Finding-for-the-Plaintiffs-in-House-v-Burwell.pdf.

68. Larry Levitt, Cynthia Cox, and Gary Claxton, "The Effects of Ending the Affordable Care Act's Cost-Sharing Reduction Payments," Kaiser Family Foundation. April 25, 2017, www.kff.org/health-reform/issue-brief/the-effects-of-ending-the-affordable-care-acts-cost-sharing-reduction-payments.

69. Frank J. Thompson, "Six Ways Trump Has Sabotaged the Affordable Care Act," Brookings Institution, October 9, 2020, www.brookings.edu/blog/fixgov/2020/10/09/six-ways-trump-has-sabotaged-the-affordable-care-act.

70. Katie Keith, "ACA Litigation Round-Up, Part 2: Which 2019 Payment Rule Changes Were Legal? Plus, More from Judge O'Connor on the ACA," *Health Affairs Blog*, April 20, 2021, www.healthaffairs.org/do/10.1377/hblog20210420.44231/full.

71. Katie Keith, "Lawsuit Challenges GA's 1332 Waiver, ACA in the Biden Pandemic Plan," *Health Affairs Blog*, January 21, 2021, www.healthaffairs.org/do/10.1377/hblog20210121.230640/full.

72. "Work as a Condition of Medicaid Eligibility: Key Take-Aways from TANF," Issue Brief, Medicaid and CHIP Payment and Access Commission, October 2017, www.macpac.gov/wp-content/uploads/2017/10/Work-as-a-Condition-of-Medicaid-Eligibility-Key-Take-Aways-from-TANF.pdf.

73. Ian Hill and Emily Burroughs, "Lessons from Launching Medicaid Work Requirements in Arkansas," Urban Institute, November 5, 2019, www.urban.org/sites/default/files/publication/101113/lessons_from_launching_medicaid_work

_requirements_in_arkansas_3.pdf; Benjamin D. Sommers et al., "Medicaid Work Requirements—Results from the First Year in Arkansas," *New England Journal of Medicine* 318, no. 11 (September 12, 2019): 1073–1082.

74. Sara Rosenbaum and Alexander Somodevilla, "The Medicaid Work Experiments and the Courts: Round Two," *Health Affairs Blog*, March 19, 2019, www.healthaffairs.org/do/10.1377/hblog20190319.563156/full.

75. MaryBeth Musumeci, "Medicaid Work Requirements at the U.S. Supreme Court," Kaiser Family Foundation, February 11, 2021, www.kff.org/policy-watch/medicaid-work-requirements-at-u-s-supreme-court. (The case was originally *Azar v. Gresham* in 2020, became *Cochran v. Gresham* in early 2021, and *Becerra v. Gresham* when Xavier Becerra became HHS Secretary.)

76. Joan Alker, "Trump Administration Tries Its Best to Knock Legs Out from Under Medicaid on the Way Out the Door," Georgetown Health Policy Institute, January 15, 2021, https://ccf.georgetown.edu/2021/01/15/trump-administration-tries-its-best-to-knock-legs-out-from-under-medicaid-on-the-way-out-the-door.

77. Ibid.

78. Andy Schneider, "Medicaid Wars: The Unwinding Begins (Episode I)," Georgetown Health Policy Institute, February 1, 2021, https://ccf.georgetown.edu/2021/02/01/medicaid-wars-the-unwinding-begins-episode-i.

79. Joan Alker, "Biden Administration Withdraws Medicaid Work Requirements Guidance and More," Georgetown University Health Policy Institute, February 17, 2021, https://ccf.georgetown.edu/2021/02/17/biden-administration-withdraws-medicaid-work-requirements-guidance-and-more.

80. Andy Schneider, "Medicaid Wars: Rescind and Withdraw (Episode II)," Georgetown Health Policy Institute, March 19, 2021, https://ccf.georgetown.edu/2021/03/19/medicaid-wars-rescind-and-withdraw-episode-ii.

81. Timothy Stoltzfus Jost and Katie Keith, "ACA Litigation: Politics Pursued Through Other Means," *Journal of Health Politics, Policy and Law* 45, no. 4 (August 2020): 485–499.

8

Cost Control: An Elusive Goal

You never quite find it, but the search for it is compulsive.
—Harold Pinter

Cost control has been the Holy Grail of health policy for decades. Ask a policy expert about health costs, and you are likely to get a detailed analysis of expenditures relative to gross domestic product (GDP), the Consumer Price Index (CPI), the federal budget, or how the United States spends more than other developed nations. Ask the average citizen, and you will probably hear a lament about how premiums, out-of-pocket costs, and prescription drug prices keep increasing. Several years before the ACA, polling expert Robert Blendon observed, "What concerns Americans is not aggregate spending but the perceived negative impact on American families of their direct payments for health care (insurance premiums, copays, deductibles, and the cost of services and products). When asked about average Americans' spending for health care in 2006, 65 percent said that they spend too much, and only 17 percent said too little."[1]

This is similar to our collective response to the problem of global warming. Experts tell us the problem is serious, but daily life is only marginally impacted. It is easier to identify the problem than to find unambiguous solutions. Employers have sought to control their health insurance benefit costs by better management of use of services and shifting more of the total costs to employees. Public officials have lamented the share of the budget consumed by government health programs, especially Medicaid and Medicare, and attempt to restrain budget growth.

The ideas for solutions require significant societal changes and economic disruption for many in the short to medium term. Washington policymakers have trouble finding agreement on the simplest of problems, much less one that requires asking many voters to sacrifice current consumption for the prospect of a solution for the next generation.

For regular consumers of the policy literature, the nature of the problem is clear and unequivocal. For decades the rate of increase of health care spending has each year risen faster than other measures of growth in the economy, such as GDP or the CPI. As a result, a larger share of total national economic activity is spent on health care. This puts pressure on government budgets, business bottom lines, and household spending. The typical middle-class household has seen real wage increases eclipsed by additional health costs in the form of higher insurance cost-sharing fees and out-of-pocket costs.[2] In an effort to place health reform high on the agenda, reformers often cited high health costs as part of the rationale for change.

Drew Altman, in the fall of 2008, said, "There is no question that the public is concerned about health care: People are focused on the costs of health care and especially their own health-care bills. But health-care reform has to rise on the national policy agenda for this issue to carry the political force needed to compel action."[3]

Comparisons with other countries and even the rate of growth of societal health costs are not relevant to average citizens' lives. Nor do budget forecasts about future deficits in the Medicare Trust Fund or projected increases in state Medicaid obligations cause undue alarm. These are abstract numbers. Increased premiums, greater cost sharing, and rising out-of-pocket or uncovered costs are what pinches the average pocketbook.

If voters typically believe their health cost problem can be solved by less greed on the part of insurance companies or a shift in employer attitudes resulting in lower employee cost sharing, then they will be less likely to support systemic change, which may result in some loss of benefits in the future. Political support for a major policy shift requires, at a minimum, a public perception that a condition—rising aggregate health expenses—is enough of a problem to require a major adjustment.[4]

The concentration of health expenses contributes to a false sense of "not my problem." In a given year a small percentage of the total population accounts for a large share of total expenses.[5] This is basis for the need for insurance risk pools in which healthy individuals contribute to pay for those with significant expenses on the supposition that in the future, when serious illness strikes, the insurance pool will pay for their cancer treatment or heart surgery. The controversy over the individual mandate reflects the difference of understanding between experts, who accept as obvious the concentration of expenses, and many citizens who wish to minimize their personal insurance pool contribution when healthy and expect full payment of medical bills by insurance companies or the government when serious illness strikes.

Did the policy architects of the ACA craft a set of provisions to effectively control either system or individual costs? This chapter examines the cost-control policy ideas embedded in the ACA and whether they have achieved the desired effect. First, we briefly examine the data and concepts used in a discussion of health costs. Then we describe the goals and policy ideas related to costs included in the ACA. Finally, we assess whether the goals have been achieved.

Health Costs: Concepts and Data

To understand and examine the data related to health-cost containment, we must consider both the systemic problem as articulated by the policy experts and the perspective of the average person about family health costs. We will first describe overall health system expenditures over the last decade and then review how the average family has been affected.

Health Costs: System Perspectives

One common approach to interpreting the growth of health expenditures is to compare them with the growth of GDP. Table 8.1 summarizes aggregate health expenditures, GDP, and the respective rates of growth between 2011 and 2019.[6]

Over the nine-year period, GDP grew by 38 percent and health expenditures by 51 percent. If we only look at the period since the full 2014 ACA implementation, we find the GDP growth of 22 percent exceeded by the health-expenditure growth of 33 percent. As Table 8.1 indicates, national health expenditure (NHE) grew from 17.2 to 17.6 percent of GDP from 2011 to 2019. We can conclude health expenditures as a share of GDP increased with ACA implementation but have leveled off in the last few years.

This represents a small increase but part of a pattern exemplified by the rise in NHE from 5 percent in 1960 to 8.9 percent two decades later. By 1990 it had increased to 12.1 percent. At the time of the ACA enactment in 2010, it had climbed to 17.2. A 2014 study projected an increase to 19 percent of GDP by 2023.[7] At this point the projection seems high, but the number could well reach 18 percent. Is 20 percent a tipping point? In the 1980s many saw 10 percent as a line not to be crossed.

Other developed countries provide comprehensive health care for their citizens and spend less as a share of GDP. The average developed country spends 8.8 percent of GDP on health care, with Switzerland the next highest behind the United States at 12 percent.[8]

Table 8.1 Health Expenditures and GDP Compared, 2011–2019

	2011	2012	2013	2014	2015	2016	2017	2018	2019
Health expenditures (billions $)	2,518	2,620	2,696	2,849	3,014	3,158	3,284	3,440	3,795
GDP (billions $)	15,543	16,197	16,785	17,527	18,238	18,745	19,543	20,612	21,433
Health expenditures as percentage of GDP	17.2	17.2	17.0	17.2	17.4	17.7	17.7	17.6	17.7
Annual growth of health expenditures (percentage)	3.3	4.1	2.9	5.6	5.8	4.8	4.0	4.7	4.6
Annual growth of GDP (percentage)	3.7	4.2	3.6	4.4	4.1	2.8	4.3	5.5	4.0

Source: US Bureau of Census and Department of Commerce, Bureau of Economic Analysis.

In 2013, the per capita health spending in the United States was $9,065. This had increased to $11,582 by 2019, which represents a 28 percent increase, compared to a 23 percent increase in per capita GDP over the period.

Breakdown of System Costs and Changes over Time

Table 8.2 reports another approach, comparing increases in NHE and the consumer price index.[9]

Across four decades, health expenditures rose more rapidly than the CPI. For businesses, government, and households, health care became more expensive relative to other goods and services. Everyone contributes to the financing of health services in one way or another with premium payments, taxes, and out-of-pocket costs. Each year a little more income is devoted to health care. Over time other activities are squeezed to accommodate growth in health expenditures. This is the essence of the argument for a systemwide policy for slowing the rate of growth, even if the level of spending cannot be dramatically reduced. This is often called "bending the cost curve."[10]

Physicians/clinics (20 percent), hospitals (30 percent), and prescription drugs (10 percent) account for 60 percent of total health expenditures.[11] Table 8.3 indicates the rate of growth in these categories since 1970. In the decade of ACA implementation, each of the sectors exhibited similar growth, although between 2018 and 2019 expenditures grew faster for hospitals than for physicians or prescription drugs.

Table 8.2 CPI and NHE per Capita Change

Year	CPI Change (%)	NHE Change per Capita (%)
1980	10.8	14.1
1985	3.5	8.5
1990	4.4	10.6
1995	2.1	4.6
2000	2.5	6.2
2005	2.8	5.9
2010	1.7	3.0
2011	2.5	2.7
2012	1.9	3.2
2013	1.3	2.1
2014	1.5	4.4
2015	0.2	4.9
2016	1.0	3.8
2017	1.8	3.6
2018	2.1	4.2
2019	1.5	4.1

Source: Kaiser Family Foundation Health System Tracker.

Table 8.3 Increase in Sector Cost by Decade (in percent)

Year	1970s	1980s	1990s	2000s	2010–2019	2017–2018	2018–2019
Physicians/clinics	12.8	12.8	6.1	5.9	4.7	4.0	4.6
Hospitals	13.9	9.6	5.2	6.9	4.4	4.2	6.2
Prescription drugs	8.2	12.8	11.7	7.6	4.3	3.8	5.7

Source: Kaiser Family Foundation Health System Tracker.

In 2019 businesses and households accounted for 55 percent of total revenue in the health system, of which just over half is household spending. Government contributes 45 percent of the total, with two-thirds of public funds spent by the federal government and the remainder by state and local governments.[12]

On a per-enrollee basis, private insurance spending increased 51 percent from 2008 to 2019, compared to 26 percent for Medicare and 16 percent for Medicaid in the same period. Since 2010 the average annual per-enrollee increase was 3.5 percent for private insurance, 2 percent for Medicare, and 1.6 percent for Medicaid.[13]

Our final system cost measure is a transition to the individual perspective. Figure 8.1 describes a consistent metric that helps explain why cost containment is politically and conceptually difficult. Over 50 percent of the population annually only incurs collectively 3 percent of total costs. Figure 8.1 illustrates distribution of health expenditures for individuals in a given year.

The top 1 percent of individuals incurred 22 percent of total costs. The top 5 percent were responsible for 50 percent of the total, and at the other end, 50 percent of the population accounted for 3 percent of total costs. The pattern is constant year after year; the expenditures for individuals within the categories are not.[14] No doubt many of the lower 50 percent pay more in premiums than they generate in expenses. What is not always appreciated is the movement of resources from premiums paid by the healthy to cover the cost of those in the category of high spenders. Of course, this is caused not by frivolous spending but by the inevitable high expenses of those with a serious illness.

Insurance companies segment the population into groups for whom they are responsible to cover the cost of care, which constitute their *risk pool*. They must collect enough in premiums to pay expenses for those within their risk pool. The larger and more diverse the risk pool, the greater the probability the insurance company will have many more insured individuals within the lower 50 percent than in the top 1 percent of spenders.

Figure 8.1 Contributions to Total Health Expenditures by Individuals, 2016

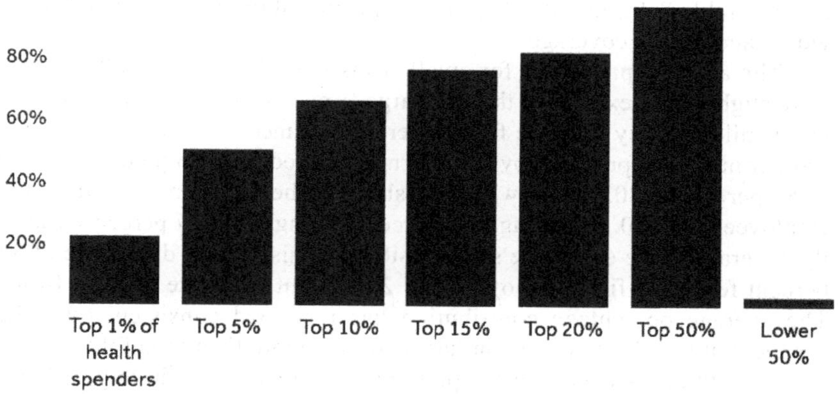

[Bar chart showing contributions by: Top 1% of health spenders (~22%), Top 5% (~48%), Top 10% (~62%), Top 15% (~72%), Top 20% (~78%), Top 50% (~97%), Lower 50% (~3%)]

Source: Kaiser Family Foundation Health System Tracker.

For families the pattern is only slightly different: 1 percent accounts for 15 percent of spending, and the top 5 percent incurs 37 percent. The top 50 percent generates 94 percent of the total. When examining out-of-pocket costs, the top 1 percent generates 19 percent of the total. The top 10 percent incur 63 percent of all out-of-pocket expenses. The top 50 percent generate 98 percent of all out-of-pocket costs. Even among the elderly, the top 50 percent incur 92 percent of costs in a given year.[15] The revenue to support the health system expenditures is distributed more evenly across the population. Many individuals pay more in premiums and taxes than they use in health resources in a given year. Voters among the 50 percent who incur only 3 percent of total health expenses may only perceive the problem of their high premiums and not understand why they keep rising.

The average citizen is not especially interested in health expenditure as share of GDP or the rate of growth relative to the CPI. How much have my premiums risen this year? How much more am I paying out of pocket for health care? This is their barometer for measuring health costs.

The majority of Americans receive health insurance as a benefit and pay part of the premium as well as cost sharing for the services utilized. These payments have risen sharply in the past decade.[16] Until the ACA, those without employment-based insurance or access to a public program paid the full premium for coverage in the individual market. The ACA marketplaces with premium tax credits and cost-sharing subsidies have assisted individuals whose incomes were below 400 percent of the federal poverty level.

The Cost of Insurance

The majority of Americans have health insurance through their place of employment. The cost of a premium has risen substantially in the past decade. Table 8.4 traces the rise in average annual premiums for both individual and family coverage.

The average premiums for small firms with fewer than 200 workers were slightly less expensive than for large firms, but the increase trajectory was similar. Nearly all large firms offered insurance for full-time workers. Worker insurance provided by small firms declined from 65 percent in 1999 to 55 percent in 2020.[17] How large a share of the premium is paid by the employee? In 2020, on average, 17 percent of single and 27 percent of family coverage is the employee's responsibility. This hides a difference of 35 percent for small-firm employees and 24 percent for those in large firms. The average percentage contribution has remained consistent over the decade, but the absolute amount has increased more than threefold.[18]

In addition to a share of the premium, employee cost sharing includes the annual deductible and copayments. In 2020 the average annual deductible for family plans ranged from $3,000 to $4,500, depending on the type of plan.[19] Physician copayments are also common.

The annual Kaiser Employer Health Benefit Survey for 2020 highlights the problem of health costs and the average family budget. Since 2010 earnings have increased 27 percent, which is slightly higher than the overall inflation rate increase of 19 percent. However, family premiums have risen 55 percent, with deductibles growing 111 percent over the decade. Total out-of-pocket costs have declined as a share of aggregate national health expenditures from one-third in 1970 to one-tenth in 2019. Of course total expenditures are much higher today, and out-of-pocket costs often still represent a major burden on family finances.[20]

In addition to expanding health insurance coverage, did the ACA have provisions designed to bend the systemic cost curve and reduce the burden

Table 8.4 Average Annual Premiums for Employment-Based Insurance

Year	Single Plan	Family Plan
1999	$2,196	$5,791
2005	$4,024	$10,880
2010	$5,049	$13,770
2013	$5,884	$16,351
2015	$6,251	$17,545
2018	$6,896	$19,616
2020	$7,470	$21,342

Source: Kaiser Family Foundation.

for individual families? This is part of the central topic of the chapter. Did the ACA succeed in slowing the rate of growth of health system costs in general? And did the ACA cause health expenditures for the average family to decline or at least stay the same?

Cost Containment Policy Ideas

Successful policy enactment requires the existence of a set of policy ideas that have a reasonable chance to achieve the desired objective. Advocacy coalitions are composed of participants with shared core policy beliefs, who loosely coordinate to influence an issue.[21] Coalition members share a similar worldview, likely sympathetic to the ideas of others within their coalition, but boundaries are not always clear. Some ideas rest on an ill-defined border between coalitions. Academic members emphasize the conceptual foundations of a policy idea, whereas the policy analysts focus more on the prospects of implementation. The space occupied by each coalition can be understood as a set of intersecting circles.

The section focuses on the policy ideas for restraining health costs. An idea may have emerged in response to a threat or opportunity or have been percolating for years in policy communities. There have been dozens of such ideas over the decades of health-cost discussions. Here we concentrate on those that have persisted over time, even as some elements have transformed.

The decades-long battle of opposing ideas about how to institute a health reform with the goal of expanding coverage can be seen as emerging from three major sets of advocacy coalitions within the health policy community.[22]

- *Social insurance reformers*, who favor universal coverage with a public system and a budget to control costs
- *Incremental tinkerers*, who favor a mixed public-private system to achieve broad coverage and system change to control cost
- *Consumer-choice champions*, who favor a market-based private insurance system with minimum involvement of government and employers and market mechanisms to control cost

Policy ideas to address cost have been a subsidiary element of reform debates, but expansion advocates perceived the need to consider the cost ramifications of their proposals. The worldview inherent in each advocacy coalitions reflects differences in perspective on both cost control and coverage expansion.

Below is a summary of the major cost-control policy ideas found within each advocacy coalition.

Social Insurance Reformers

Members of the social insurance reformers advocacy coalition view government's role in cost containment as positive and presume only public bodies have the leverage and incentive to place restrictions on the flow of revenue to health providers. They are pessimistic about effective cost control over the long term without a central role for government, especially the federal government.

Single-payer (budget) system. This is regarded as the gold standard of cost-control systems. Most health system revenue flows through this "single pipe" into the coffers of health providers and institutions. Government possesses substantial leverage in determining the level of payment, terms of payment, and annual rate of increase. It applies to health care the same budgeting principle governments use to control spending for education, roads, and the military. Health spending competes with other types of public service for the limited funds.[23] Advocates of this global budget approach cite the experience of Great Britain and Canada.

Administered price system. By the early 1980s two conclusions were widely drawn. First, national health insurance, with its single-payer cost-control model, was not likely to be enacted. Second, the Medicare cost-reimbursement payment system was unsustainable. The Ronald Reagan administration proposed and Congress quickly enacted legislation to create the Medicare Perspective Payment System (PPS). With the subsequent resource-based relative value scale (RBRVS) for physician fees, the two constituted a single-payer system for Medicare beneficiaries.[24]

With the 1980s enactment of a new Medicare reimbursement system, payment strategy shifted from cost reimbursement to an administered price system. If the price of services is indeed the critical factor in determining escalating costs, then for Medicare enrollees the federal government has the policy tools to slow the rate of increasing expenses. However, Congress has struggled to address the gap between recommended physician-fee adjustments and physicians' argument for a higher rate.[25]

The Medicare payment system has been the trendsetter for private insurance negotiation with providers. It serves as a benchmark against which payments are measured compared to private plans. However, to be fully effective, a price-control system must apply to all payers. Thus, an administered price system probably needs to be embedded in an all-payer approach to cover all providers to serve as an effective cost-containment approach.[26]

All-payer system. By the 1980s it was evident the single-budget approach was not likely to be enacted. A major source of provider payment continued to be insurance companies. Criticism of government for spawning "cost shifting" was growing. Health professionals and organizations complained that public programs did not pay their fair share, and thus providers were forced to charge private patients more to make up the difference.[27]

The all-payer model, especially for hospitals, sought to make certain all payers (government, insurance companies, private out-of-pocket payers) paid their fair and appropriate share of the cost to provide services. A long-standing example of an all-payer system was adopted in 1971 by the state of Maryland's Health Services Cost Review Commission. The system established yearly rates for hospitals. All payers—Medicare, Medicaid, and private plans—paid the same rate for the same service category. Costs incurred by the uninsured were spread across all hospitals and were not the sole responsibility of the serving institution. In 1976 Maryland hospital costs were 26 percent above the national average, but in 2007 they were 2 percent below.[28] Some scholars argue this system is not able to control total costs better than those of other states.[29] Since 2015 Maryland has moved to a budget system for hospitals but not extended this to other services.[30]

In 1992 Paul Ginsburg and Kenneth Thorpe made the case for all-payer-system rate setting utilizing the Medicare PPS and RBRVS methodology. They perceived this as accommodating competition among insurance plans and health management organizations (HMOs) because rates could still be negotiated below the established payment standards.[31]

Uwe Reinhardt in 2010 argued for an all-payer system to level the playing field since weaker payers were absorbing a disproportionate share of the total costs of services. His model looked to the negotiated approach of Germany, rather than PPS/RBRVS, as the best approach to determine the appropriate common rate for services.[32]

Joseph White, in his all-payer proposal, contended the system must be perceived as fair to both buyers and sellers of medical care. Rates should cover the cost of providing necessary services, reflect geographic differences, and be subject to regular adjustment.[33]

All-payer advocates differed on whether the rates should be derived from administered prices or negotiated.

Public option. In the realm of policy ideas, the public option was a relative newcomer in the years immediately preceding enactment of the ACA. Jacob Hacker is credited with bringing the idea into the health reform discussion. The House version of the ACA bill included a public option, but the final law did not because of Senate opposition. Progressives perceived the public option as a first step toward a single-payer approach.[34]

Hacker, in a 2009 report, argued the public-option proposal is similar to Medicare with a separate risk pool. A cost advantage is derived from lower administrative costs and the ability to bargain for lower prices using the Medicare rate structure. By restraining the rate of growth of its health expenditures over time, the public option contributes to slowing the excess growth of health spending relative to GDP.[35] A 2009 Urban Institute analysis was less optimistic but did conclude a strong public option would provide critical competition to private insurance companies in some markets. Competition helps offset increasing consolidation among both providers and insurance plans.[36]

Wrap-Up: Social Insurance Advocates

Universal coverage is the most important goal for social insurance reformers. A single national government health budget is the ideal method to control cost. This appears unlikely. An administered price system, like Medicare, is an alternative. Assuming a continued major role for private insurance, an all-payer system has seemed a logical approach. Recently, the idea of a public-option insurance company to compete with private insurance plans was suggested because it could pay lower rates of reimbursement.

The key cost-control principle is a significant role for government in determining reimbursements on the premise that the problem is inherently one of high prices and only the government has the leverage to reduce them.

Incremental Tinkerers

Members of this advocacy coalition accept the idea of a public-private partnership to pursue cost control. Since a majority of Americans will continue to receive workplace-based insurance, incremental tinkerers espouse policies that will enable public and private insurance programs to jointly pursue cost-containment goals in which they share a common benefit.

Many of the specific approaches envision fundamental changes in the organization of the health-delivery system to eliminate inefficiencies and reform payment incentives. Social insurance reformers tend to advocate for large-scale health system changes, but incremental tinkerers have promoted smaller changes with gradual system impact over time. Two common themes prevail across the coalition. First, there is the sense that we pay too much for health services, especially compared to other countries. Gerard Anderson famously remarked, "It's the prices, stupid."[37] Second, there is a pervasive impression that the decentralized and fragmented nature of the health system generates both excessive expenditures and lower-quality outcomes.

A wide range of policy ideas has emerged to address these problems. The policy proposals are distinct and incremental rather than comprehensive. Summarizing them can be a challenge. We will do so with two umbrella categories—organizational integration and payment incentives—but recognize the absence of a hard line between them.

Organizational integration: HMOs and managed care. Paul Starr traced the origins of the prepaid group practice concept from its early stages with the Kaiser system in California and Group Health Cooperative in Washington State.[38] They offered an alternative to the emerging system of stand-alone hospitals and independent physicians with separate reimbursements. In the post–World War II era, these integrated health service delivery organizations were a niche enterprise in the rapidly expanding world of employment-based insurance and private-hospital expansion.

Both conservative and liberal reformers rediscovered the idea in the 1970s as a solution to the explosion of costs. The Kaiser-Permanente HMO based in the San Francisco Bay Area appeared to be a viable model combining cost containment and quality service delivery. It employed physicians, owned hospitals, and assumed risk for its pool of patients. Liberals found this to be an organizational model better suited to a national health insurance system than the cost-reimbursement fee-for-service system. Conservatives also appreciated the efficiency of the Kaiser system and liked that it was a private organization, not a government agency.

The Richard Nixon administration's promotion of HMO development with federal grants did spawn the creation of additional HMOs, but the challenges of broad transformation of the organizational and financial structure of the health system proved too daunting.[39] In the 1980s Alain Enthoven, a Stanford professor and Kaiser enthusiast, promoted the idea of managed competition among HMOs as a basis for reorganizing health finance.[40]

By the late 1980s employers could no longer ignore and treat as just another business expense escalating health insurance costs. Managed care became the new model for employer-sponsored insurance (ESI) cost containment. White observed managed care came to have two elements.[41] First, it was a joint effort by businesses and their insurance plans to monitor and control utilization by requiring extensive preauthorization of procedures. This was a cost-control approach to expenses presumed to be driven by unnecessary or duplicative procedures and expensive tests. Public outrage and regulatory rules tended to blunt the cost savings associated with utilization review.[42]

Second, the term came to define a series of contractual arrangements between insurance plans and provider organizations featuring discounted prices for preferred providers. Those covered by managed-care plans incurred cost-sharing penalties if they were treated "out of network."[43] This approach has continued to be a predominant feature of employer-based insurance and many Medicaid programs.

By the 1990s HMOs had experienced fourfold growth but moved away from some elements of their origins. Half were owned by insurance companies. The preferred provider organization model was more attractive to some employers, and insurance plans had absorbed some of the HMO features.[44] Traditional HMOs did have a record of lower cost growth than insurance plans.[45] Managed care rather than HMO integrated health delivery systems became the preferred tool for employer cost containment in the 1990s. The ideal of an integrated delivery system joining hospitals and physicians in one organizational unit continued to be a compelling vision for reducing cost growth. Many delivery system reforms have their origins in the original HMO idea.

Accountable care organizations (ACOs). The HMO concept of system integration has long been a fascination among health policy scholars and administrators seeking to find a way to bring hospitals and physicians into the same organizational unit. If both are part of one bureaucracy with a single payment stream, more powerful incentives to avoid overutilization are assumed. The ACO is an incremental approach to the type of integration symbolized by HMOs, as both share the same premise. Closer integration of physicians and hospitals will lead to greater cost control and quality service delivery.

The Kaiser model HMO did not replace the deeply entrenched fee-for-service system of competitive hospitals and independent physicians, but the allure of the integrated system to include both physicians and hospitals has not disappeared. A 2006 article in *Health Affairs* by Elliott Fisher and colleagues is credited with the first use of the term *accountable care organization* in the literature.[46] A series of articles on this strategy for controlling Medicare expenses followed.[47] Physician groups and hospitals linked by common patients form an ACO, which coordinates care and receives bundled payments. When quality maintenance can be demonstrated, they share in Medicare savings.

The shared savings create an incentive for both physicians and administrators to seek cost-effective treatment systems. The required quality measures and the absence of a mandate for patients to seek care within the ACO protect patients against cost savings achieved at the expense of the best care. Unlike HMOs, ACOs do not assume all financial risk, except they will not receive a savings bonus if their effort does not lead to reduced expenses. This is referred to as "downside risk."[48]

Critics of ACOs argue the concept will flounder because it has inherent contradictions and the medical system culture will make the desired cooperation impossible outside limited experiments that are, in essence, special cases.[49] An early systematic study of ACOs found modest savings in physician-organized entities, but hospital-integrated ones on average did not produce savings.[50] Even ardent supporters concede it will be several years before the full impact of ACOs can be verified.[51]

It is presumed private insurance plans will follow the payment lead of Medicare financial incentives or penalties for ACOs. Rather than an all-payer system, it is an all-encouragement system and reflects the public-private partnership ideas with the presumption that a successful use of Medicare ACOs will cause the system to spread.

The promotion of electronic medical records is a key component. Cooperation without formal administrative integration probably requires at least a common information system for patient records, financial transactions, and record keeping. Thus, an effective electronic records system becomes a critical element in fostering the type of integration that is perceived as essential to cost control.

Payment incentives: value-based payment. In the years immediately preceding ACA enactment, Harold Miller articulated a cost-containment strategy centered on value-based payments, which provide incentives for efficient and quality services.[52] Whatever the financial/administrative system for organizing and delivering health services, providers will respond to the financial incentives of the payment system. This is true of a public health bureaucracy, a market system without regulation, or anything in between. Another means of cost containment has been value-based-payment incentive systems that seek to promote integrated and quality services as well as reduce inefficient and duplicative ones.

The Institute of Medicine held a set of workshops in 2009 and subsequently published them under the title *Roundtable on Value & Science-Driven Health Care*. Miller's paper was one of sixty-plus papers on the subject. A common theme was that the key to effective cost containment with quality improvement was an incremental modification of the entrenched fee-for-service system with its emphasis on service volume as the basis for payment.

The 800-page report defines the problem as provision of unnecessary services, inefficient delivery, excessive administrative costs flowing from fragmentation, high prices, and inadequate prevention efforts. Solutions offered include system reorganization and integration, especially for high-risk patients, electronic-records enhancement, reimbursement reform emphasizing value-based payments linked to illness episodes rather than service volume, focus on scientific understanding of effective treatments, and simplification of administration.[53]

In early 2008, health reform appeared likely to be high on the 2009 congressional agenda.

The Institute of Medicine roundtable was not the only venue with a robust set of cost-containment suggestions. A 2009 Commonwealth Fund study and a 2008 Medicare Payment Commission report to Congress echoed similar ideas.[54]

We will examine three value-payment ideas widely discussed in 2008. These were comparative effectiveness, bundled payments, and pay for performance (P4P). The ideas share the premise that incentives inherent in payment modifications will change the mind-set and practice routines of providers, leading to greater system efficiency with long-term cost savings.

Comparative effectiveness. A 2009 Institute of Medicine report observed that medical research aimed at finding the best treatment for a disease had been undertaken for more than a century, but the term *comparative effectiveness* had come to have more specific goals and definitions. Comparative effectiveness studies seek to inform health care decision-making by evaluating at least two treatment options for a given condition to discover what is best in actual practice.[55]

In the early twenty-first century in both the United States and Europe, the formal organization of efforts to produce systematic comparative effectiveness research was initiated. Britain created such a body in 1999, and other countries did the same.[56] The Dartmouth Atlas Project studied health costs over two decades, demonstrated significant regional variation in medical practice, and illustrated the need for systemic study of existing practices.[57] Carolyn Clancy in 2009 described the central role of the Agency for Healthcare Research and Quality in leading the effort to advance comparative effectiveness research.[58]

The early 2009 economic-recovery legislation provided over $1 billion for comparative effectiveness research to initiate a robust pursuit of these studies. A point of disagreement among advocates was the role of cost-effectiveness studies. While the potential relationship between cost and treatment decision is recognized, many argued premature cost-effectiveness studies could raise the specter of rationing.[59] Harold Sox and others stressed the importance of pursuing comparative effectiveness research to better inform clinical judgment.[60] There was a presumption this line of research would reduce clinical variations to produce quality outcomes and ultimately cost savings by reducing expensive treatments of little clinical value.

Bundled payments. Bundled payments occur when a payer combines a set of normal reimbursements for an episode of care into a single package. Providers are rewarded for providing quality care. The presumption is that bundled payment for both the physician and the hospital will reduce total spending by providing a disincentive for unnecessary and uncoordinated care. The result will be both cost reduction and higher quality.[61] Medicare demonstration projects have employed a bundled-services concept. The projects showed promise of both quality improvement and lower cost, but there has been strong resistance to the combination of physician fees and hospital payments into one bundle.[62]

The PROMETHEUS Payment Model is a Robert Woods Johnson Foundation–sponsored set of pilot projects using bundled payments to encourage physician-hospital collaboration and the reduction of avoidable complications. This seeks to shift payment to an episode-of-care model rather than a unit of service.[63] The Geisinger Health System in Pennsylvania developed its ProvenCare program for bundled payments involving all insurers and provided quality care with reduced costs. John Bertko argued this idea could be rapidly expanded to other hospital systems.[64]

The design of the bundled-payment system is key. If the payment does not account for disease severity, hospitals may be reluctant to care for patients with more serious problems or with multiple interrelated health issues. If postacute care is included in the bundle, there are additional cost- and quality-improvement opportunities. Yet postacute care may pose greater risk for providers because of uncertainty and also offer more opportunities to game the system by pushing some services beyond the time covered by the bundling.

A RAND Corporation study of the potential of bundled payments, reported in the *New England Journal of Medicine*, concluded that treatment of seven chronic conditions by bundling payments could save the system 5.5 percent in costs over ten years.[65] Any payment mechanism must produce new organizational arrangements to be truly effective. The record seems mixed with bundled-payment experiments.[66] A 2018 study did not find significant differences in payments between those hospitals using bundled payments and those not participating.[67]

The Patient-Centered Medical Home (PCMH) is a bundled-payment subset applied to primary care. It is a team-based model seeking to reduce costs and improve quality with better coordination focused on the patient. A meta-analysis of PCMH demonstrations found some cost savings and quality improvement but significant variation depending on the design and implementation.[68]

Pay for performance. In 2001 the Institute of Medicine released a report demonstrating systemic quality failures in the American health system and called for major changes to include realignment of payment incentives with quality improvements.[69] This call to action reinforced the contention of those who believed the fee-for-service payment system rewarded service volume and complexity rather than quality.

In the early 2000s a number of public- and private-sector pilot program experiments used the pay-for-performance idea. This was an umbrella term to categorize experiments with various financial incentives designed to emphasize quality measures as a partial basis for reimbursement. Rather than a single model, there were four general categories of approaches. Process, outcome, patient experience, and structure measures were the metrics employed as provider payment incentives.[70]

An evaluation of the Massachusetts Medicaid P4P special program found favorable trends but not large effects. Sandra Tanenbaum has traced the development of these concepts within Medicare over several years and found broad support for the idea, but a series of demonstration projects generated relatively little evidence that it makes a difference.[71] One of the early large-scale private-sector applications of P4P was the California Integrated Healthcare Association, which furnished physician groups with incentive payments for performance on quality benchmarks.[72]

Despite the absence of definitive evidence of P4P success in early efforts, reform advocates believed the idea of linking payments to quality metrics was sound. They argued these first efforts would gradually contribute to quality improvement by altering existing practices and routines. With higher service quality, greater cost efficiency is likely.[73]

Wrap-Up: Incremental Tinkerers

The incremental tinkerers advocacy coalition has tended to identify excessive and inappropriate use of services as the chief cause of high rates of health-expenditure growth. The policy ideas for solving the problem reflect this perspective and primarily involve reorganizing the administrative delivery system, the payment incentives, or both. The policy solutions include government, with Medicare as a trendsetter, combined with private-sector initiatives, and frequent joint efforts through pilot demonstration grants. There is a belief that both government and the private health sector, including employers sponsoring health coverage, have a stake and an incentive to control the cost growth rate. The policy ideas tend to presume a cooperative effort built around modifying organizational structure and incentives.

Paul Ginsburg summarized the incremental tinkerers' perspective:[74] "The best opportunity for cost containment is through provider payment reform that moves away from fee for service payment, which rewards greater volume and does nothing to support care coordination or chronic disease management, and towards models that engage and reward providers and patients for reducing costs and increasing quality."

Consumer-Choice Champions

Consumer-choice champions favor radical change in the financing and organization of the health system in order to foster cost containment. For them government, business, and insurance bureaucracies do not have appropriate incentives to control health-expenditure growth. There is an almost religious commitment to the belief that markets, properly organized, are the best way to cure the medical inflation of the past several decades. The policy ideas from this perspective include an emphasis on eliminating the favorable tax treatment of employment-based insurance, substituting a tax credit for the tax exclusion of employment insurance, and greater price transparency to aid consumer choice.[75]

Michael Porter proposed a set of radical changes in the organization and financing of health care to transform consumer health choices into individual determination of the cost and value of services.[76] In his managed-competition plan, Enthoven's approach to consumer choice was competition at the level of multiple integrated HMOs competing in a market for customers based on value and price.[77] The common denominator in all of these ideas is the cost-containment power of consumer choice based on viable options and a transparent price system.

Moving Medicare and Medicaid from social insurance programs to voucher systems has been a key policy goal. Substituting greater consumer choice for existing employment-based insurance is another. The favorable tax treatment of health insurance premiums paid by employers, leading to overinsurance, is seen as a major cause of health-expenditure growth. Shifting the role of government in a dramatic way is a major premise.

Public program vouchers. Moving a significant share of health system funding from the public sector to the private sector is a key premise. Eliminating traditional Medicare and replacing it with a premium support system is a major objective.[78] Transferring Medicaid financing from an entitlement program to a limited block grant to the states is a second feature.[79] Both moves clearly reduce the future liability of the federal government for health costs. Both shift greater levels of spending to individual households and away from larger risk pools. The Heritage Foundation has also argued for a premium support system for Medicaid.[80]

This approach presumes that greater spending by households without the intervention of third-party payers would cause individuals to pay greater attention to costs and thus to make more cost-effective choices about health services.

Consumer-directed insurance. That patient choice is just as important and applicable in making health treatment decisions as it is in purchasing bread or consumer electronics is a fundamental premise. In the world of employer-sponsored health insurance, this has led to the significant expansion of consumer-directed insurance. According to a 2012 RAND analysis, almost 20 percent of Americans with employer-provided insurance were enrolled in a consumer-directed plan. The study found that families in high-deductible plans spent less on health care than comparable families in a traditional plan. The study authors conceded that fewer screening tests might lead later to more significant episodes not captured in a single-year study.[81]

The consumer-directed approaches typically combine high-deductible insurance with some type of tax-exempt savings account that can be used to offset some of the out-of-pocket expenses. Greater patient awareness of the cost of a service, proponents argue, will create a reluctance to initiate a service unless it is clearly needed and presumed cost-effective.

A proposal to create health insurance plans that separate routine annual expenses from episodic occurrences of high expenses is another variation of this theme. John Cochrane states his fundamental presumption as follows:

"Free and competitive markets are the best way to spur innovation, provide better service, and reduce costs."[82] Amelia Haviland in a 2012 analysis concluded that if consumer-directed plans represented 50 percent of employer-provided insurance, an annual savings of $57 could be achieved, which would represent a 4 percent decline in total health spending for the nonelderly.[83]

Eliminate or reduce tax exclusion of health insurance. In the early 1950s, with the growing practice of employer-sponsored health insurance for workers, the IRS moved to treat the cash equivalent cost of the benefit as taxable income by issuing new rules. In the outcry that ensued Congress overturned the IRS ruling and exempted this benefit from taxation.[84]

Martin Feldstein, in a 1973 article, states, "American families are in general overinsured against health expenses. If insurance coverage were reduced, the utility loss from increased risk would be more than outweighed by the gain due to lower costs and the reduced purchase of excess care."[85] A similar theme is found in a widely cited paper published by the Joint Economic Committee in 1974. The paper makes two arguments against the tax exclusion:[86]

1. Without the tax exclusion there would be a significant increase in federal revenue, and the current benefit is greater for those with higher income.
2. The exclusion "encourages an excessive use of health insurance and inflates demand for hospital and medical care."

In the 1980s the policy idea that all or part of the tax exclusion for health insurance ought to be eliminated had gained acceptance in broad segments of the health policy community, but resistance among business and labor and fear of voter anger kept the provision out of the tax-reform legislation.[87]

In 1994 the Congressional Budget Office (CBO) released a report on the tax treatment of employment-based health insurance.[88] It concluded there is not a convincing rationale for the current exclusion.[89] The three options for change analyzed are limiting the exclusion, replacing it with a credit, and repealing the exclusion. The report was frequently cited in the years ahead by those who wished to modify the policy.[90]

Repeal of all or part of the tax exemption has become a strong policy preference of many because it fits with their desire to break away from the employment-based system and replace it with an approach that emphasizes individual consumer choice among alternative insurance arrangements as well as favoring less "first dollar" third-party payments as a way of introducing more consumer awareness of health costs as a method of cost saving.[91]

Eliminate state regulation of insurance. In the American federal system of government, the regulation of all types of insurance has been the responsibility of state governments. An insurance company wishing to sell individual health insurance policies across the country needs to gain approval from fifty different state regulators. Advocates conclude greater competition would exist in the market if an insurance company from one state were allowed to sell its policies in another state. Thus, a policy of preemption of state regulation of health insurance would produce greater competition in the insurance market and lead to low prices.[92]

Wrap-Up: Consumer-Choice Champions
The central health policy position of consumer-choice champions is the belief that markets and consumer choice represent the best approach to long-term cost control of health expenditures. They begin by rejecting a major role for government since they see public agencies as the problem rather than the solution and tend to align with budget deficit hawks, who warn that uncontrolled Medicare and Medicaid spending is a serious threat to the fiscal health of the country. They wish to reduce, but not eliminate, the total public spending for health care. They presume that reducing government outlays and shifting worker-based insurance into more consumer-directed spending will ultimately reduce aggregate health expenses.

Cost Containment and the ACA
As the House and Senate committees began the process of drafting the ACA, the primary objective was to expand coverage and reduce the number of uninsured. Cost containment was not ignored but was clearly a secondary objective. The cost-related element drawing the most attention was the CBO score of the bill, which served as a constraint on what could be included. The CBO score focus was the cost to the federal budget, not aggregate health system expenditures. If the total system costs were lowered, federal expenses might be projected to be less, but CBO scoring rules favored provisions directly tied to federal expenditures.

For those designing the legislation, there were three types of cost-containment provisions. The most important were those directly related to federal budget outlays. Potential savings for those individuals to be newly covered by the ACA in the marketplaces or by Medicaid expansion were also a concern because of the outcry about costs of individual insurance plans. Finally, various health reform stakeholder supporters continued to express concerns about unsustainable long-term growth of health expenditures.

Each category of cost-containment provisions was to some extent reflected in the final version of the ACA. Each category is briefly discussed below, noting the relevant provisions as well as the origin of the policy ideas guiding them.

Medicare Savings
Medicare savings projected for the first decade of the ACA were a critical element for the CBO score because they are firm and easy to count. They fall into the category of administered prices controlled by the government.

To some extent, less Medicare spending, unless offset by additional private-sector spending, also reduces health expenditures. Some of the major items in this category are as follows:[93]

- Reduction of disproportionate share hospital (DSH) payments
- Reduction in market basket reimbursement updates
- Reduction in hospital payments for high infection rates
- Penalties for excessive readmissions
- Expansion of competitive bidding for durable medical equipment
- Measures against fraud and abuse

Savings for the Individual
Individuals eligible for tax-credit subsidies spend considerably less of their own money for a comprehensive insurance plan. For low-income individuals this also includes cost-sharing reductions (CSRs). Medicare beneficiaries who purchase Part D prescription drug plans are beneficiaries of drug rebates and an eventual closing of the cost-sharing "donut hole."

Individuals with employer-sponsored insurance and those purchasing marketplace plans are beneficiaries of various insurance market reforms, including coverage of children until age twenty-six, restrictions on lifetime and annual limits, excessive age-related premiums, and premium savings from rate review.[94]

These are neither CBO-scored items nor likely to reduce the national health expenditure appreciably, but they do represent cost savings for many individuals. The individual, rather than system, savings were not a main focus of discussion around ACA cost containment, but they were a central concern for citizens pushing health reform onto the agenda.

Health System Reorganization Savings
In the health policy literature on the ACA and cost containment, most attention is devoted to this category of system savings. Three general types of provisions are usually cited as ACA cost-containment items:

New institutional arrangements
- Center for Medicare and Medicaid Innovation
- Patient-Centered Outcomes Research Institute (PCORI)
- Independent Payment Advisory Board (IPAB)
- Prevention and Public Health Fund
- Health Insurance Exchange

Pilot programs
- Accountable care organizations
- Bundled payments
- Value-based payments: pay for performance
- Medical homes

Administrative efficiencies
- Administrative simplification
- Medical records investments
- Waste, fraud, and abuse rules

Table 8.5 is a summary of cost-control ideas embedded in the ACA. Five sets of papers/reports released soon after enactment are used to illustrate the wide range of cost-control provisions as well as the lack of universal agreement on which of them are most significant. None of the reports explicitly cite all the provisions identified, which illustrates the breath of the provisions as well as their scattered nature. No article on coverage provisions would have failed to mention Medicaid expansion, for example, but no single provision or set of provisions was universally seen as the critical tool for cost containment.

Various cost-containment ideas found their way into the ACA. Use of Medicare reimbursement changes to reduce expenditures is an example of using an administered price system. Insurance exchanges to promote market competition among private insurance companies and the excise tax on high-cost plans are examples of market-based ideas.

The most dominant set of ideas flows from the incremental approach. David Cutler makes the distinction between short- and long-run savings.[95] He acknowledges the practical importance of near-term savings, such as Medicare reimbursement reductions, but emphasizes the essential significance of long-term cost-savings provisions, such as those embodied in bundled-payment and ACO pilot projects. He argues the many pilot approaches in the ACA could be taken as weak commitment to cost containment. "Rather the focus on experimentation along so many dimensions suggests a general desire to move forward rapidly on all possible fronts instead of predicting which direction will be most promising. Private-sector providers and large private payers must actively participate in the change to new models of care delivery."

Major legislation rarely embodies a single set of policy ideas. Various stakeholders and supporters agree on goals but differ on the policy paths to achieve them. ACA cost-containment goals are an example. Well over a dozen major ideas on how to "bend the cost curve" found their way into the ACA. Since most were not mutually exclusive, those crafting the legislation

Table 8.5 ACA Cost-Control Ideas

Cost Control Ideas	Orszag[a]	Urban Institute/Robert Wood Johnson Foundation[b]	Commonwealth Fund[c]	Oberlander[d]	Cutler[e]
PCORI	X	X	X		
IPAB	X	X	X	X	
Health insurance exchanges		X	X	X	X
ACOs		X		X	X
Provider incentive payment innovation	X	X	X	X	X
Excise tax on high-cost plans (Cadillac tax)	X	X		X	X
Electronic health records investment			X	X	
Administrative simplification	X				
Waste, fraud, and abuse rules		X			
Medicare payment reductions		X	X		X
Medicare readmission penalty	X	X	X		
Emphasis on prevention and wellness		X			
System redesign (e.g., medical homes)				X	X
Medicare Advantage reductions				X	

Source notes: a. Peter Orszag, "Health Care Reform and Cost Control," *New England Journal of Medicine*, August 12, 2010, https://www.nejm.org/doi/full/10.1056/nejmp10065. b. Stephen Zuckerman, "What Are the Provisions in the New Law for Containing Costs and How Effective Will They Be?," Urban Institute, August 2010; "How Does the ACA Control Health Costs," Health Policy Snapshot, Robert Wood Johnson Foundation, July 2011, https://www.rwjf.org/en/library/research/2011/07/how-does-the-affordable-care-act-attempt-to-control-health-care-.html; Stephen Zuckerman and John Holahan, "The Affordable Care Act Addresses Health Care Cost Containment," Urban Institute, October 2012, http://www.urban.org/UploadedPDF/412665-The-Affordable-Care-Act-Addresses-Health-Care-Cost-Containment.pdf. c. David Cutler et al., "The Impact of Health Reform on Health System Spending," Issue Brief, Commonwealth Fund and Center for American Progress, May 2010, https://www.commonwealthfund.org/sites/default/files/documents/_media_files_publications_issue_brief_2010_may_1405_cutler_impact_hlt_reform_on_hlt_sys_spending_ib_v4.pdf; Karen Davis, "Bending the Health Care Cost Curve: New Era in American Health Care?," Commonwealth Fund Blog, January 18, 2012, http://www.commonwealthfund.org/publications/blog/2012/jan/bending-the-health-care-cost-curve. d. Jonathan Oberlander, "Throwing Darts: Americans' Elusive Search for Health Care Cost Control," *Journal of Health Politics, Policy and Law* 36, no. 3 (June 2011): 477–484; Jonathan Oberlander, "Between Liberal Aspirations and Market Forces: Obamacare's Precarious Balancing Act," *Journal of Law, Medicine & Ethics* (winter 2014): 431–441; Jonathan Oberlander and R. Kent Weaver, "Unraveling from Within? The Affordable Care Act and Self-Undermining Policy Feedbacks," *The Forum* 13, no. 1 (2015): 37–62, https://www.degruyter.com/document/doi/10.1515/for-2015-0010/html. e. David Cutler, "How Health Care Reform Must Bend the Cost Curve," *Health Affairs* 29, no. 6 (June 2010): 1131–1135.

included many of the policy ideas prominent in the policy stream in the decade preceding the ACA.

Were the Cost-Control Ideas Successful?

If we concede cost containment was a secondary objective of the ACA, is it still fair to ask a decade later whether the law at least contributed to "bending the cost curve"? The answer is maybe, or it depends on whom you ask.

We will first look at assessments by those who have concluded the ACA contributed to slowing the rate of growth.

Ezekiel Emanuel contends the ACA's delivery system reforms are already paying dividends in the form of cost containment. He compares the Office of the Actuary's 2010 projections for 2017 with the actual expenditures and finds a cumulative savings of $2.3 trillion. Health expenditure as a percentage of GDP projection for 2017 was 20 percent but was actually less than 18 percent.[96]

Emanuel maintains the ACA reforms with modified financial incentives in pilot programs did not just produce a slower rate of growth but began to change the culture, which shifted away from a fee-for-service perspective to one of internalizing a value-based payment approach. He argues this cultural shift is better measured by the slowing of the aggregate growth rate than studies of individual pilot projects.[97]

David Blumenthal is less evangelistic in his assessment of the ACA's success in containing cost but points to the fact that health expenditures grew only slightly faster than GDP in the past decade. This a departure from the previous decade. He cites the ACA's Medicare cost savings as substantial.

Blumenthal views the value-based payment provisions as most significant. He concedes that system-changing efforts are not quickly accomplished. He divides the value-based payment experiments into two broad categories. Those in the pay-for-performance grouping involve rewards or penalties for behavior within the fee-for-service system. The second type address departures from the fee-for-service model to incentivize providers to be accountable for cost and quality. He concluded that the first type, P4P, lack clear efficacy, but those in the second category, such as ACOs, have had modest success.[98]

For Blumenthal the ACA's cost-containment strategy was clearly successful over the first decade, and like Emanuel he foresees the move from fee-for-service to a value-based payment system as accelerated by the ACA project initiatives, even if all of the pilot programs were not entirely successful. He urges a long and patient effort.

Joseph White might respond to Blumenthal by pointing out the significant Medicare cost reduction in the decade was possible because of the administrative pricing system. It did not require comprehensive system change or years-long experiments. At the time of enactment, White and Jonathan Oberlander contended that the set of ACA provisions touted as the keys to systemwide cost control were unproven.[99] Oberlander concedes the political appeal of delivery system reform as seemingly painless cost control but is unconvinced that a combination of ineffective reforms will somehow be effective.[100]

White and Oberlander doubt a single-payer system is politically feasible but endorse an all-payer system, such as that used in Germany.[101] White criticizes much of the ACA cost-control provisions as an "aspirational agenda" based more on hope than experience. He concedes there is broad institutional and incremental tinkerer coalition support for the concept of system transformation as the key to long-term cost control. White counters with the example of other countries with extensive private insurance, which do a better job of cost control by price setting using an all-payer approach.[102]

Voices from the market perspective also find the ACA's cost-control provisions lacking. Joseph Antos and James Capretta analyzed aggregate health-expenditure rates of increase in the decade since enactment and found the average annual rate of growth over a decade to be the same before and after the ACA. They contend spending per capita was greater after the ACA. They acknowledge the rate of uninsured has declined but see this as a cause of additional expenditures. Like White and Oberlander, they find the results of the ACA system-changing initiatives underwhelming. They stress the need for a revolution to address cost problems with a set of policy ideas.[103]

Charles Blahous also examines the trend lines and finds the decrease in aggregate expenditures began before ACA enactment and continued shortly thereafter. He attributes this to the economic downturn, not the ACA. Expenditures began to rise after the implementation of ACA coverage in 2014. His premise is that insurance coverage drives costs upward. Greater coverage increased expenditures, and savings did not offset the growth.[104]

The Cadillac Was Hard to Sell
The strangest ACA cost-containment tale may be the fancy Cadillac that became hard to sell. For four decades economists were convinced the favorable tax treatment of employment insurance had led to excessive insurance and higher costs. This idea overlapped advocacy coalitions and included some individuals supporting social insurance principles.

In the early months of 2009, a significant policy difference among Democrats concerned the tax exclusion of employer-sponsored insurance. Those who favored modifying the tax exclusion did so for two important policy reasons:[105]

1. It was a creditable way to raise additional revenue to offset program cost and produced a sizeable revenue score from the CBO.[106]

2. For decades health economists contended the tax exclusion led to excessive levels of insurance and contributed to escalating health costs and was of more value to the high-income taxpayer.[107]

The Senate Finance Committee bill had a partial limit on the tax preference for employer-sponsored insurance.[108] Neither the House version or the Senate Committee on Health, Education, Labor, and Pensions bill made changes to the tax exclusion. Liberal senators were not willing to accept exclusion changes.

By July proponents were referring to the insurance plans of Goldman Sachs executives as "gold-plated Cadillacs" that should be taxed.[109] Senator John Kerry suggested an excise tax on insurance company high-cost plans to achieve the same revenue goal without the political cost.[110] In September President Barack Obama endorsed the excise tax idea, but it was off the table for House leadership.[111] Majority Leader Harry Reid retained the excise tax in the Senate bill. When the Senate version became the primary bill, resistance by House leaders to the Cadillac tax was vigorous.

Opposition included both labor and business groups as well as many liberal House Democrats.[112] Some liberal policy organizations issued papers supporting the Cadillac tax plan.[113] Other liberal organizations, such as the Commonwealth Fund and the Employee Benefit Research Institute, took issue with the basic premise of the tax exclusion.

Health economists defended the excise tax compromise as essential for both revenue generation and cost control. They argued the greatest benefit for the tax exclusion was realized by those in higher income brackets, who had more generous first-dollar coverage. Conservatives advocated substitution of a universal tax credit for the tax exclusion. They found the ACA Cadillac tax provision weak and ineffective without the substitution of a tax credit that moved the system away from its employer-sponsored base toward individual choice of insurance plan.[114]

Throughout 2009 many liberals had objected to changes in the tax exclusion. They questioned whether it would only impact the insurance plans of executives at places such as Goldman Sachs. Cathy Schoen cautioned that workers in small firms, older workers, and those in industries with high claims were at risk with a policy limiting the tax exclusion.[115] Paul Fronstin warned of the complex administrative issues for employers raised by a cap on the tax exclusion and cited firm size and risk pool composition as more significant factors related to higher premiums than plan design.[116]

Jon Gabel, in January 2010, concluded that plan characteristics explained only a small part of premium variation, with industry and geographic cost differences the most powerful explanations.[117] Timothy Jost and Joseph White contended the Cadillac tax would have a broader and more negative impact on the beneficiaries of employer-sponsored insurance than proponents claimed. They also critiqued the premise that increased cost sharing spawned by the Cadillac tax would lower the health-cost trajectory in future years.[118]

The revenue-producing element was important for the White House and Senate Finance Committee since it generated a positive ten-year CBO score. All the parties recognized even a limited exclusion produced a significant revenue yield.

Jonathan Gruber, a key Obama advisor, made a comprehensive argument for capping the tax exclusion.[119] Paul Van de Water of the liberal Center on Budget and Policy Priorities in January 2010 argued the case on revenue and cost-control grounds with some protective adjustments for vulnerable workers.[120] Paul Krugman advocated an excise tax with some protective adjustments.[121] In late 2009 Henry Aaron and twenty-two other prominent health economists had signed a letter to President Obama calling an excise tax on high-cost plans one of the four key measures to include in the legislation.[122]

During January White House negotiations with organized labor leaders, adjustments were made to the Cadillac tax provisions, delaying the effective date until 2018, providing additional exemptions for high-risk groups, and increasing the trigger points. These modifications were included in a reconciliation bill passed by the House.[123]

The compromise satisfied labor and liberal opponents because it offered additional time to renew the argument without endangering the entire legislation. Proponents of the excise tax were disappointed it would not take effect sooner but happy the principle was established. Both sides felt they had achieved a partial victory. ACA opponents, unhappy with the entire ACA legislative approach, did not view the limited cap as even a partial victory.[124]

2015: Cadillac tax issue reemerges. The issue went into hibernation but reemerged in 2015. Corporations were assessing whether their health plans would pass the 2018 threshold. Analytic studies began to appear, interest groups started to mobilize, and the press discovered an old quarrel among ACA supporters.

This was an unresolved 2016 campaign issue. Harvard faculty economists were divided between those deeming the tax essential and those describing it as a tax on the sick.[125] Joseph Antos in April argued the elimination of the exclusion would not break the employer-sponsored insurance system but criticized the Cadillac tax as inefficient and regressive. He again advocated eliminating or capping the tax exclusion and replacing it with a tax credit.[126]

Business and labor began a push for repeal and formed a group, Alliance to Fight the 40.[127] David Wessel and Jared Bernstein argued against repeal in prominent op-ed pieces.[128] Hillary Clinton said she would modify or eliminate the tax. The Kaiser Foundation released a report concluding a third of the employer-sponsored plans could be subject to the tax by 2018.[129]

In September liberal Democratic senators introduced a bill to repeal the Cadillac tax after House Republicans had announced an intent to repeal several ACA-related taxes, including the Cadillac tax.[130] Economic heavyweights from left and right, Lawrence Summers and Gregory Mankiw, argued in a bipartisan op-ed for the retention of the tax as good public policy.[131] Earlier 101 health economists of varying political views had sent a public letter to congressional leaders urging retention of the tax.[132]

The Obama administration defended the Cadillac tax as an essential vehicle for cost control, but the revenue side of the original argument had receded. In October House Republicans moved toward passage of a bill to repeal many parts of the ACA, including the Cadillac tax.[133] It passed the House at the end of October. Some language in the House bill was not acceptable to the Senate, and a tug-of-war between GOP senators who sought a stronger repeal bill and those who wanted less cast doubt on its move forward.[134]

Minority leaders Harry Reid and Nancy Pelosi were working with labor leaders to develop a repeal strategy. They had met with President Obama and pressed for repeal, but he expressed concern about the lost revenue.[135]

Even with congressional agreement to repeal several elements of the ACA, including the Cadillac tax, there was little doubt it would be vetoed. By early December legislative leaders began to look at the pending "tax extender" legislative package under final negotiation with the White House. One of the technical attractions of using the tax extender bill was that the lost revenue from the Cadillac tax would not need an offset.[136]

By mid-December Senate negotiators were near an agreement on the tax as part of the larger tax extender bill.[137] The Cadillac tax and the medical device tax would be delayed for two years but not repealed.[138] President Obama signed the tax extender bill with its Cadillac tax provision. Repeal supporters were confident that with a new administration in 2017, the tax would ultimately go away. The bill extended the effective date of the tax until 2020, repealed a provision that specified the tax would not be a deductible business expense, and authorized a study of the appropriateness of the age and gender adjustments in the original law.[139] The compromise extension effectively took the controversial provision off the legislative agenda, but it had not disappeared.

Final round. As the 2020 Cadillac tax deadline approached, the drive for repeal began again. Stan Dorn referred to it as a zombie provision and argued employer-sponsored insurance was no longer too generous, requiring a cap on the exclusion. For many employees the opposite was true. New cost-sharing requirements rendered ESI inadequate.[140] The usual suspects continued their arguments for retention. Conservative Capretta and liberal Van de Water urged retention.[141] A group of health economists sent a letter to Congress supporting the Cadillac tax.[142]

It was really no contest. The House voted 419–6 to repeal. The Senate followed suit. The final repeal was included as part of the December 2019 budget bill.[143]

Vision is 20/20 in hindsight. Perhaps those promoting the Cadillac tax in 2009 really did believe it was the most important cost-control measure in the ACA. Or, when they delayed implementation to 2018, maybe they were just kicking the CBO score down the road to a point when repeal was inevitable. Many health economists were legitimately convinced of its value as an important cost-containment tool, but the combined opposition of labor and management made its demise inevitable.

The Cadillac tax was the most prominent symbol of the ACA's cost-control provisions. For decades it had been one of the few cost-containment ideas supported by economists of the Left and the Right. It was a hard sell to the average voter, who would see a visible tax increase. The idea of modifying the exclusion asked voters to pay more now in taxes on the unproven premise of insurance premium decline in the future. Its efficacy was more aligned with achieving a good CBO score than actually saving money. Because it would cost many average families higher premiums or additional taxes, or both, it was not a popular idea. Business and labor were strongly opposed. It persisted because policy experts believed in the idea as theory without real evidence to prove its aggregate cost-saving potential.

Consolidation

Health care markets presume competition within sectors, such as multiple hospitals within an urban area, and competition holding down prices, such as enhanced bargaining between insurance companies and hospitals. However, across the health system, institutional consolidation is accelerating.[144] Communities have multiple hospitals, various physician groups, many individual practitioners, and a variety of ancillary organizations providing services, such a home health agencies. Basic economic theory posits a positive role for market competition to hold down prices. If there is only one baker in town, we expect the price for a loaf of bread to be higher than if there are five competitive bakers.

Hospital consolidation has been occurring for several decades, especially in metropolitan areas. Brent Fulton found high levels of concentration in metropolitan areas, especially for hospitals.[145]

More recently insurance companies have also consolidated. Physician consolidation takes two forms. Group practices have expanded, leaving fewer solo practitioners. Hospitals and even some insurance companies have begun to purchase physician practices, which is an example of vertical integration.[146] Private equity has become the new player in the acquisition of physician practices, which appears to increase consolidation and add concerns about short-term profit seeking reducing quality of care.[147] The number of practices per year acquired more than doubled from 2013 to 2016.[148]

Medical marketplaces today typically have fewer competing entities than a decade or so ago. Does less market competition leads to higher prices. A 2020 Medicare Payment Advisory Commission review of the economic literature found a mixed picture of consolidation and prices.[149] Among its findings are the following:

- Hospitals with a large market share negotiate higher prices from commercial insurers; these prices are sometimes twice the Medicare reimbursement.
- Insurer market power has grown, but savings do not result in lower premiums for commercial patients.
- Market power may have greater long-term than short-term effects.
- Evidence is weak that insurer/provider vertical integration saves costs.
- Hospital-physician vertical integration is growing, and this often increases costs because of Medicare differential rates for the same service in hospital or office.
- Antitrust enforcement has been minimal in health markets.

Andrew Boozary and colleagues found higher ACA marketplace premiums in areas with high levels of market concentration.[150] Hannah Neprash and colleagues did not find hospital-physician vertical integration associated with ACO initiation.[151] Zack Cooper and colleagues, in a study of private insurance patients, discovered prices were 12 percent higher for monopoly hospitals compared with those in areas where four or more hospitals existed.[152]

Consolidation motives are not limited to revenue maximization. Hospital consolidation may be an attempt to improve quality and efficiency or occur when an entity's survival is at stake. Physicians may be attracted to the vertical integration of selling their practice to a hospital by more regular work hours and the escalating administrative expenses of a solo or small practice.

Whatever the initial motive, the consequences seem to be what economic theory predicts—namely, higher prices reflecting greater bargaining leverage. Since Medicare's administered-price system does not involve bargaining over rates, its costs are less impacted by consolidation.

Even aggressive antitrust action will not reverse consolidations already in place. The concentrated landscape of the health care marketplace is unlikely to unravel.[153] This may render a market-oriented approach moot in many parts of the country and influence what is perceived as the best approach to cost containment.

Conclusion

Has the ACA affected cost containment?

Melinda Beeuwkes Buntin and John Graves summarize their assessment by saying, "Disentangling the exact effects of a major piece of legislation from underlying trends is nearly impossible."[154]

Growth in per capita spending, perhaps a better measure than the frequently used percentage of GDP, declined sharply just before enactment of the ACA. It continued at a low rate until full implementation of the ACA in 2014, when there was a sharp one-year spike. By 2018 the annual rate was a little more than it had been a decade earlier, but growth was much lower than in the early 1990s or early 2000s.[155]

How much is enough? When is the cost curve bent sufficiently? A reasonable goal seems to be a long-term growth of health expenditures approximately equal to the annual growth of the economy. Thus, resources spent on health care would not increase annually more than in other sectors of the economy.

Since 1980 no Western country has experienced a rate of increase of health expenditures compared to GDP as steep as the United States, which went from 8 to 17 percent. The Organization for Economic Cooperation and Development (OECD) countries in 1980 were in a cluster between 5 and 8 percent, with the United States at the top of the grouping. In 2018 Germany had grown from 8 to 11 percent. Canada and France went from 7 to 11 percent. The United Kingdom, the best example of a pure single-payer system, moved from 6 to 10 percent. Over the forty years since 1980, no country has reduced its share. The cluster between 5 and 8 percent has become 10 to 12 percent, with the United States the outlier at 17 percent.[156] Other countries experienced less growth, but none had flattened the curve.

One might be tempted to assert the United States spends more to make us healthier. However, US life expectancy is seventy-nine compared to the low eighties in other countries that spend less. The OECD countries have fewer citizens who are obese or have multiple chronic conditions. The average length of hospital stay is greater. They have more physicians per 1,000 people and more physician visits per capita. The US rate of mortality amenable to health care is higher than for the others.[157]

These statistics reinforce the argument of those who contend a major system and culture reform is necessary to both improve quality and slow the expenditure rate of growth. However, several of the countries, such as Germany, employ some form of fee-for-service reimbursement without experiencing a high rate of growth. This strengthens the argument of those who claim an all-payer system of reimbursement is the best approach.

At the moment it seems unlikely the system-change/value-based payment model embedded in the ACA will be abandoned any time soon; nor does it appear the all-payer approach to include public and private insurance has the support of a congressional majority. Some of those skeptical of the value-based payment/system-change model and prefer instead a single-payer system seek to diminish the role of government and make greater use of markets with the assumption that cost savings will flow from greater consumer choice. There is even less evidence to support this proposition.

As long as health expenditures remain close to 17 percent of GDP over the next few years, the combination of system reform and Medicare administered prices is likely to be the most politically feasible cost-control strategy. In the early 1980s health expenditures exceeding 10 percent of GDP appeared to be a red line to trigger policy changes to control spending growth—hence a hesitancy now to declare 20 percent as the new crisis point.

Health policy experts and government officials worry about aggregate expenses; individuals are concerned about their personal costs in premiums and out-of-pocket charges. Outside the expert realm, the policy agenda is more driven by individual concerns. There is constant debate about cost-containment ideas. In the case of the value-based payment/system-reform set of ideas, these concepts were discussed, refined, and experimented with in the years leading up to the ACA enactment.

It is fair to say these cost-control ideas were the most well developed and broadly accepted among policy analysts and legislators. These concepts, especially as pilot project experiments, were less threatening to provider interest groups whose support was essential for ACA passage.

Despite mixed evidence of pilot project success, costs have moderated in the last few years. The ACA cost-containment provisions have to some extent contributed to slower growth at the end of the first ACA decade, and cost containment has not been pushed to the top of the agenda. Two health-cost issues with a high agenda priority and bipartisan interest are prescription drug costs and surprise billing.[158] These are not the major drivers of aggregate cost but are particularly visible for individuals.

The federal government, by use of administered prices, can exercise control over Medicare growth. Some of the pilot projects may marginally further the goal. This may be a constraint on the larger world of private-sector payments, but without a sense of crisis to drive cost containment higher on the agenda, the status quo is likely to continue. The ACA cost provisions will have some impact on aggregate expenses and incrementally modify provider system fee-for-service culture but not substantially bend the cost curve.

Notes

1. Robert Blendon et al., "Americans' Views of Health Care Costs, Access, and Quality," *Milbank Quarterly* 84, no. 4 (2006): 624–657.

2. David Auerbach and Arthur Kellermann, "A Decade of Health Care Cost Growth Has Wiped Out Real Income Gains for an Average US Family," *Health Affairs* 30, no. 9 (September 2011): 1630–1637; Edgar Peden and Mark Freeland, "A Historical Analysis of Medical Spending Growth, 1960–1993," *Health Affairs* (summer

1995): 235–245; Sara R. Collins et al., "Too High a Price: Out-of-Pocket Health Care Costs in the United States," Issue Brief, Commonwealth Fund, November 2014, www.commonwealthfund.org/~/media/files/publications/issue-brief/2014/nov/1784_collins_too_high_a_price_out_of_pocket_tb_v2.pdf; Sara R. Collins et al., "National Trends in the Cost of Employer Health Insurance Coverage, 2003–2013," Issue Brief, Commonwealth Fund, December 2014, www.commonwealthfund.org/~/media/files/publications/issue-brief/2014/dec/1793_collins_nat_premium_trends_2003_2013.pdf.

3. Drew Altman, "Beyond the Rhetoric," Stanford Medicine, fall 2008, http://sm.stanford.edu/archive/stanmed/2008fall/article4.html.

4. John Kingdon, *Agendas, Alternatives, and Public Policies*, 2nd ed. (New York: Harper Collins, 1995), chap. 5.

5. Anna Sommers and Mindy Cohen, "Medicaid's High Cost Enrollees: How Much Do They Drive Program Spending?," Kaiser Commission on Medicaid and the Uninsured, March 2006, www.kff.org/wp-content/uploads/2013/01/7490.pdf; "Medicare High Cost Beneficiaries," Congressional Budget Office, May 2005, www.cbo.gov/sites/default/files/109th-congress-2005-2006/reports/05-03-medispending.pdf; M. L. Berk and A. C. Monheit, "The Concentration of Health Expenditures: An Update," *Health Affairs* 11, no. 4 (winter 1992): 145–149; "Concentration of Health Care Spending in the U.S. Population," Kaiser Commission on Medicaid and the Uninsured, Slide 9 Topics Cost/Insurance, kff.org/health-costs/slide/concentration-of-health-care-spending-in-the-u-s-population-2010/.

6. Anne B. Martin et al., "National Health Care Spending in 2019: Steady Growth for the Fourth Consecutive Year," *Health Affairs* 40, no. 1 (January 2021): 14–24; "National Health Expenditure Accounts," Centers for Medicare and Medicaid Services, accessed on August 30, 2021, www.cms.gov/Research-Statistics-Data-and-Systems/Statistics-Trends-and-Reports/NationalHealthExpendData/NationalHealthAccountsHistorical.

7. Andrea Siskok et al., "National Health Spending Projections, 2013–23: Faster Growth Expected with Expanded Coverage and Improving Economy," *Health Affairs* 33, no. 10 (2014): 1841–5018.

8. Roosa Tikkanen and Melinda K. Abrams, "U.S. Health Care from a Global Perspective, 2019: Higher Spending, Worse Outcomes?," Issue Brief, Commonwealth Fund, January 30, 2020, www.commonwealthfund.org/publications/issue-briefs/2020/jan/us-health-care-global-perspective-2019.

9. "Health Spending Generally Grows Faster Than General Economic Inflation," Peterson-KFF Health System Tracker, www.healthsystemtracker.org/chart-collection/u-s-spending-healthcare-changed-time/#item-usspendingovertime_17.

10. David Cutler, "How Health Care Reform Must Bend the Cost Curve," *Health Affairs* 29, no. 6 (June 2010): 1131–1135.

11. "Hospital and Physician Services Represent Half of Total Health Spending," Peterson-KFF Health System Tracker, www.healthsystemtracker.org/chart-collection/u-s-spending-healthcare-changed-time/#item-usspendingovertime_17.

12. Martin et al., "National Health Care Spending in 2019," 18.

13. Rabah Kamal et al., "How Has U.S. Spending on Healthcare Changed over Time?," Peterson-KFF Health System Tracker, December 23, 2020, www.healthsystemtracker.org/chart-collection/u-s-spending-healthcare-changed-time/#item-usspendingovertime_1.

14. Bradley Sawyer and Gary Claxton, "How Do Health Expenditures Vary Across the Population?," Peterson-KFF Health System Tracker, January 16, 2019, www.healthsystemtracker.org/chart-collection/health-expenditures-vary-across-population/#item-start.

15. Ibid.

16. "Average Family Premiums Rose 4% to $21,342 in 2020, Benchmark KFF Employer Health Benefit Survey Finds," Kaiser Family Foundation, October 8, 2020, www.kff.org/health-costs/press-release/average-family-premiums-rose-4-to-21342-in-2020-benchmark-kff-employer-health-benefit-survey-finds.

17. Gary Claxton et al., "Employer Health Benefits—2020 Survey," Kaiser Family Foundation, 40, http://files.kff.org/attachment/Report-Employer-Health-Benefits-2020-Annual-Survey.pdf.

18. Ibid., 90.

19. Ibid., 113.

20. "Average Family Premiums Rose 4% to $21,342 in 2020," Kaiser Family Foundation.

21. Hank C. Jenkins-Smith et al., "The Advocacy Coalition Framework: An Overview of the Research Program," in *Theories of the Policy Process*, ed. Christopher M. Weible and Paul A. Sabatier, 4th ed. (New York: Westview Press, 2018), 148.

22. James Brasfield, *Health Policy: The Decade Ahead* (Boulder, CO: Lynne Rienner, 2011), 168–172.

23. For a full discussion of the single-payer idea, see "Exploring the Concept of Single Payer," special issue of *Journal of Health Politics, Policy and Law* 34, no. 4 (2009); Kip Sullivan, "Comment on Deborah Stone's 'Single Payer—Good Metaphor, Bad Politics,'" *Journal of Health Politics, Policy and Law* 35, no. 2 (2010): 277–288; for recent discussion of technical issue in design of single-payer system, see "Key Design Components and Considerations for Establishing a Single-Payer Health Care System," Congressional Budget Office, May 2019, www.cbo.gov/system/files/2019-05/55150-singlepayer.pdf.

24. For an excellent analysis of the origins of the Medicare administrative payment system, see Rick Mayes and Robert A. Berenson, *Medicare Prospective Payment and the Shaping of U.S. Health Care* (Baltimore: Johns Hopkins University Press, 2008).

25. "Medicare Payments to Physicians," Policy Brief, *Health Affairs*, February 13, 2013, www.healthaffairs.org/do/10.1377/hpb20130110.203020/full.

26. Uwe Reinhardt, "A Modest Proposal on Payment Reform," *Health Affairs Blog*, July 24, 2009, http://healthaffairs.org/blog/2009/07/24/a-modest-proposal-on-payment-reform; Paul Ginsburg, "All-Payer Rate Setting: A Response to a 'Modest Proposal' from Uwe Reinhardt," *Health Affairs Blog*, July 24, 2009, http://healthaffairs.org/blog/2009/07/24/all-payer-rate-setting-a-response-to-a-modest-proposal-from-uwe-reinhardt.

27. Jack Meyer and William Johnson, "Cost Shifting in Health Care: An Economic Analysis," *Health Affairs* 2, no. 2 (1983): 20–35.

28. Robert Murray, "Setting Hospital Rates to Control Costs and Boost Quality: The Maryland Experience," *Health Affairs* 28, no. 5 (2009): 1395–1404.

29. Mark Pauly and Robert Town, "Maryland Exceptionalism? All-Payers Regulation and Health Care System Efficiency," *Journal of Health Politics, Policy and Law* 37, no. 4 (August 2012): 697–707.

30. Robert Berenson, "Maryland's New All-Payer Hospital Demonstration," Urban Institute, November 2015, www.urban.org/sites/default/files/publication/73836/2000517-Maryland%27s-New-All-Payer-Hospital-Demonstration.pdf; Sarah Kliff, "All-Payer Rate Setting: America's Back-Door to Single-Payer?," *Vox*, February 9, 2015, www.vox.com/2015/2/9/8001173/all-payer-rate-setting.

31. Paul Ginsburg and Kenneth Thorpe, "Can All-Payer Rate Setting and the Competitive Strategy Coexist?," *Health Affairs* 11, no. 2 (summer 1992): 73–86.

32. Uwe Reinhardt, "The Many Different Prices Paid to Providers and the Flawed Theory of Cost Shifting: Is It Time for a More Rational All-Payer System?," *Health Affairs* 30, no. 11 (November 2011): 2125.

33. Joseph White, "Implementing Health Care Reform with All-Payer Regulation, Private Insurers, and a Voluntary Public Insurance Plan," and "Cost Control and Health Care Reform: The Case for All-Payer Regulation," Campaign for America's Future, 2009, www.researchgate.net/publication/237601584_Cost_Control_and _Health_Care_Reform_The_Case_for_All-Payer_Regulation; Joseph White, "Cost Control After the ACA," *Public Administration Review* 73 (September/October 2013): 524–533.

34. James Brasfield, "The Politics of Ideas: Where Did the Public Option Come From and Where Is It Going?" *Journal of Health Politics, Policy and Law* 36, no. 3 (June 2011).

35. Jacob Hacker, "The Case for Public Plan Choice in National Health Reform: Key to Cost Control and Quality Coverage," Berkeley Law, December 17, 2008, www.law.berkeley.edu/files/Hacker_final_to_post.pdf.

36. Robert Berenson, John Holahan, and Stephen Zuckerman, "Getting to a Public Option That Contains Costs: Negotiations, Opt-Outs and Triggers," Urban Institute, November 2009, www.urban.org/sites/default/files/publication/30756/411984-Getting -to-a-Public-Option-that-Contains-Costs-Negotiations-Opt-Outs-and-Triggers.PDF.

37. Gerard F. Anderson et al., "It's the Prices, Stupid: Why the United States Is So Different from Other Counties," *Health Affairs* 22, no. 3 (May/June 2003): 89–105.

38. Paul Starr, *The Social Transformation of American Medicine: The Rise of a Sovereign Profession and the Making of a Vast Industry* (New York: Basic Books, 1982), 320–331.

39. Lawrence D. Brown, *Politics and Health Care Organization: HMOs as Federal Policy* (Washington, DC: Brookings Institution, 1983).

40. Alain Enthoven, "Consumer-Choice Health Plan (Second of Two Parts): A National-Health-Insurance Proposal Based on Regulated Competition in the Private Sector," *New England Journal of Medicine* 298, no. 13 (March 30, 1978): 709–720.

41. Joseph White, "Targets and Systems of Health Care Cost Control," *Journal of Health Politics, Policy and Law* 24, no. 4 (1999), 653–695.

42. Mark Hall, "The Death of Managed Care: A Regulatory Autopsy," *Journal of Health Politics, Policy and Law* 30, no. 3 (June 2005): 427–450.

43. Jonathan P. Weiner and Gregory de Lissovoy, "Razing a Tower of Babel: A Taxonomy for Managed Care and Health Insurance Plans," *Journal of Health Politics, Policy and Law* 18, no. 1 (spring 1993): 75–103.

44. A preferred provider organization, or PPO, is a medical care arrangement in which medical professionals and facilities provide services to subscribed clients at reduced rates. Unlike the HMO it is not a single organization but a set of negotiated providers. Marsha Gold, "HMOs and Managed Care," *Health Affairs* 10, no. 4 (winter 1991): 189–206.

45. Humphrey Taylor and Michael Kagay, "The HMO Report Card: A Closer Look," *Health Affairs* 5, no. 1 (spring, 1986): 81–91.

46. Elliott Fisher et al., "Creating Accountable Care Organizations: The Extended Hospital Medical Staff," *Health Affairs* 26, no. 1 (2007); Elliott Fisher et al., "Fostering Accountable Care: Moving Forward in Medicare," *Health Affairs*, January 27, 2009, http://content.healthaffairs.org/content/28/2/w219.full.html.

47. See, for example, Elliott Fisher et al., "A Framework for Evaluating the Formation, Implementation, and Performance of Accountable Care Organizations," *Health Affairs* 31, no. 11 (November 2012): 2368–2378; American Hospital Association Committee on Research, *Accountable Care Organizations: AHA Research Synthesis Report*, American Hospital Association, June 2010, www.aha.org/ahahret -guides/2010-06-01-aha-research-synthesis-report-accountable-care-organizations;

Mark Shields et al., "A Model for Integrating Independent Physicians into Accountable Care Organizations," *Health Affairs* 30, no. 1 (January, 2011): 161–172.

48. "Accountable Care Organization Payment Systems," Medicare Payment Advisory Commission, revised October 2018, www.medpac.gov/docs/default-source/payment-basics/medpac_payment_basics_18_aco_final_sec.pdf.

49. Clayton Christensen et al., "The Coming Failure of Accountable Care," *Wall Street Journal*, February 18, 2013, http://online.wsj.com/article/SB10001424127887324880504578296902005944398.html; Gail Wilensky, "Lessons from the Physician Group Practice Demonstration: A Sobering Reflection," *New England Journal of Medicine* 365 (November 3, 2011): 1659–1661.

50. J. Michael McWilliams et al., "Medicare Spending After 3 Years of the Medicare Shared Savings Program," *New England Journal of Medicine* 379 (September 20, 2018): 1139–1149.

51. Fisher et al., "A Framework for Evaluating the Formation, Implementation, and Performance of Accountable Care Organizations."

52. Harold D. Miller, "Creating Payment Systems to Accelerate Value-Driven Health Care: Issues and Options for Policy Reform," Commonwealth Fund, September 1, 2007, www.commonwealthfund.org/publications/fund-reports/2007/sep/creating-payment-systems-accelerate-value-driven-health-care; Harold D. Miller, "Value-Based Payments, Outcomes, and Costs," in *The Healthcare Imperative: Lowering Costs and Improving Outcomes: Workshop Series Summary*, ed. Pierre L. Young, Leigh Anne Olsen, J. Michael McGinnis (Washington, DC: National Academies Press, 2010), 361–369, www.ncbi.nlm.nih.gov/books/NBK50929/pdf/Bookshelf_NBK50929.pdf.

53. Pierre L. Young, Leigh Anne Olsen, and J. Michael McGinnis, eds., *The Healthcare Imperative: Lowering Costs and Improving Outcomes: Workshop Series Summary* (Washington, DC: National Academies Press, 2010), www.ncbi.nlm.nih.gov/books/NBK50929/pdf/Bookshelf_NBK50929.pdf.

54. Rachel Nuzum et al., "Finding Resources for Health Reform and Bending the Health Care Cost Curve," Commonwealth Fund, July 2009, www.commonwealthfund.org/publications/fund-reports/2009/jul/finding-resources-health-reform-and-bending-health-care-cost; "Report to Congress: Reforming the Delivery System," Medicare Payment Advisory Commission, June 2008, www.medpac.gov/docs/default-source/reports/Jun08_EntireReport.pdf.

55. Institute of Medicine, *Initial National Priorities for Comparative Effectiveness Research* (Washington, DC: National Academies Press, 2009), 34, www.nap.edu/catalog/12648/initial-national-priorities-for-comparative-effectiveness-research.

56. Eric M. Patashnik, Alan S. Gerber, and Conor M. Dowling, *Unhealthy Politics: The Battle over Evidence-Based Medicine* (Princeton, NJ: Princeton University Press, 2017), 34–36.

57. Young, Olsen, and McGinnis, *The Healthcare Imperative*, 34.

58. Carolyn M. Clancy, "Comparative Effectiveness Research," in Young, Olsen, and McGinnis, *The Healthcare Imperative*, 270–272, www.ncbi.nlm.nih.gov/books/NBK50929/pdf/Bookshelf_NBK50929.pdf.

59. Alan Garber and Harold Sox, "The Role of Costs in Comparative Effectiveness Research," *Health Affairs* 29, no. 10 (October 2010): 1805–1801.

60. Harold Sox, "Defining Comparative Effectiveness Research: The Importance of Getting It Right," *Medical Care* 48, no. 6 (Suppl. 1) (June 2010): S7–S8.

61. Francois de Brantes et al., "Bundled and Fee-for-Episode Payments: An Example," in Young, Olsen, and McGinnis, *The Healthcare Imperative*, 370–375, www.ncbi.nlm.nih.gov/books/NBK50929/pdf/Bookshelf_NBK50929.pdf.

62. Jeff Goldsmith, "Analyzing Shifts in Economic Risks to Providers in Proposed Payment and Delivery System Reforms," *Health Affairs* 25, no. 1 (2010): 1301.

63. Francois de Brantes et al., "Building a Bridge from Fragmentation to Accountability—the Prometheus Payment Model," *New England Journal of Medicine* 361 (September 10, 2009): 1033–1036.

64. John Bertko, "Bundled Payments: A Private Payer Perspective," in Young, Olsen, and McGinnis, *The Healthcare Imperative*, 474–477, www.ncbi.nlm.nih.gov/books/NBK50929/pdf/Bookshelf_NBK50929.pdf.

65. Peter Hussey et al., "Controlling U.S. Health Care Spending—Separating Promising from Unpromising Approaches," *New England Journal of Medicine* 361, no. 22 (November 26, 2009): 2109–2112.

66. Tom Williams and Jill Yegian, "Bundled Payment: Learning from Our Failures," *Health Affairs Blog*, August 5, 2014, http://healthaffairs.org/blog/2014/08/05/bundled-payment-learning-from-our-failures.

67. Karen E. Joynt Maddox et al., "Evaluation of Medicare's Bundled Payments Initiative for Medical Conditions," *New England Journal of Medicine* 379, no. 3 (July 19, 2018): 260–269.

68. Anna Sinaiko, "Review of Medical Homes Shows Reduction in Spending for High-Risk Patients, but Design and Implementation Matter," *Commonwealth Fund Blog*, March 28, 2017, www.commonwealthfund.org/blog/2017/review-medical-homes-shows-reduction-spending-high-risk-patients-design-and.

69. Committee on Quality of Health Care in America, Institute of Medicine, *Crossing the Quality Chasm: A New Health System for the 21st Century* (Washington, DC: National Academies Press, 2001), www.ncbi.nlm.nih.gov/books/NBK222274/pdf/Bookshelf_NBK222274.pdf.

70. "Pay for Performance," Policy Brief, *Health Affairs*, October 11, 2012, www.healthaffairs.org/do/10.1377/hpb20121011.90233/full/healthpolicybrief_78.pdf.

71. Sandra J. Tanenbaum, "Pay for Performance in Medicare: Evidentiary Irony and the Politics of Value," *Journal of Health Politics, Policy and Law* 34, no. 5 (October 2009), 717–743.

72. "Pay-for-Performance: A Promising Start," Alliance for Health Reform, February 2006, www.allhealthpolicy.org/wp-content/uploads/2017/03/pub_4.pdf.

73. Suzanne F. Delbanco, Maclaine Lehan, and Roslyn Murray, "Performance: Not Strong Enough on Its Own?," *Health Affairs Blog*, October 24, 2018, www.healthaffairs.org/do/10.1377/hblog20181018.40069/full.

74. Paul Ginsburg, "Achieving Healthcare Cost Containment Through Provider Payment Reform That Engages Patients and Providers," *Health Affairs* 32, no. 5 (May 2013): 930.

75. Stuart Butler, "Containing Health Costs in a Consumer-Based Model," *Health Care Financing Review*, Annual Supplement, 1991, www.ncbi.nlm.nih.gov/pmc/articles/PMC4195138; Mark V. Pauly, "Competition in Health Insurance Markets," *Law and Contemporary Problems* 51, no. 2 (spring 1988): 237–271.

76. Elizabeth Teisberg, Michael Porter, and Gregory Brown, "Making Competition in Health Care Work," *Harvard Business Review* (July–August 1994), https://hbr.org/1994/07/making-competition-in-health-care-work.

77. Alain Enthoven, "The History and Principles of Managed Competition," *Health Affairs* 12 (Suppl. 1) (1993), www.healthaffairs.org/doi/pdf/10.1377/hlthaff.12.Suppl_1.24.

78. Robert Moffit, "Saving the American Dream: Comparing Medicare Reform Plans," Heritage Foundation, April 4, 2012, www.heritage.org/health-care-reform/report/saving-the-american-dream-comparing-medicare-reform-plans.

79. Nina Owcharenko, "Medicaid Reform: More Than a Block Grant Is Needed," Issue Brief, Heritage Foundation, May 4, 2012, http://thf_media.s3.amazonaws.com/2012/pdf/ib3590.pdf.

80. Brian Blasé, "How States Can Survive the Medicaid Crisis," Heritage Foundation, February 28, 2011, www.heritage.org/health-care-reform/report/how-states-can-survive-the-medicaid-crisis.

81. Amelia Haviland et al., "Growth of Consumer-Directed Health Plans to One-Half of All Employer-Sponsored Insurance Could Save $57 Billion Annually," *Health Affairs* 31, no. 5 (2012): 1009–1015; Amelia Haviland et al., *Skin in the Game: How Consumer-Directed Plans Affect the Cost and Use of Health Care* (Santa Monica, CA: RAND Corporation, 2012).

82. John Cochrane, "Health-Status Insurance: How Markets Can Provide Health Security," Policy Analysis no. 633, Cato Institute, February 18, 2009, www.cato.org/policy-analysis/health-status-insurance-how-markets-can-provide-health-security.

83. Haviland et al., "Growth of Consumer-Directed Health Plans," 1010.

84. S. Silow-Carroll et al., *In Sickness and in Health? The Marriage Between Employers and Health Care* (Washington, DC: Economic and Social Research Institute, 1995).

85. Martin Feldstein, "The Welfare Loss of Excess Health Insurance," *Journal of Political Economy* 81, no. 2 (1973): 251.

86. Martin Feldstein and Elisabeth Allison, "Tax Subsidies Private Health Insurance: Distribution, Revenue Loss and Effects," in *Hospital Costs and Health Insurance*, ed. Martin Feldstein (Cambridge, MA: Harvard University Press, 1981), 206–214.

87. William Brandon, "Health-Related Tax Subsidies," *New England Journal of Medicine* 307, no. 15 (October 7, 1982): 947–950; Paul Ginsberg, "Altering the Tax Treatment of Employment-Based Health Plans," *Milbank Memorial Fund Quarterly: Health and Society* 59, no. 2 (spring 1981): 224–255; Jonathan Fuerbringer, "President Said to Back Away from Tax on Fringe Benefits," *New York Times*, August 9, 1983, www.nytimes.com/1983/09/30/business/bill-would-keep-benefits-tax-free.html.

88. "The Tax Treatment of Employment-Based Health Insurance," Congressional Budget Office, March 1994, www.cbo.gov/sites/default/files/103rd-congress-1993-1994/reports/1994_03_taxtreatmentofinsurance.pdf.

89. "The Tax Treatment of Employment-Based Health Insurance," Congressional Budget Office, 11–16, https://www.cbo.gov/sites/default/files/103rd-congress-1993-1994/reports/1994_03_taxtreatmentofinsurance.pdf. It is notable that four of the ten footnotes cite Mark Pauley, a prominent advocate of changing the tax treatment.

90. In June 1995 MIT economist Jonathan Gruber published NBER Working Paper 5147, titled "Tax Subsidies to Employer-Provided Health Insurance." Gruber would, of course, fifteen years later be a key policy advisor to the Obama administration.

91. D. Eric Schansberg, "Envisioning a Free Market in Health Care," *Cato Journal* 31, no. 1 (2011): 27–58; John Cogan et al., "Making Markets Work: Five Steps to a Better Health Care System: Five Policy Reforms to Harness the Power of Markets," *Health Affairs* 24, no. 6 (2005): 1447–1457; Stuart Butler, "Will Employer-Sponsored Health Insurance Fade Away?," Brookings Institution, March 31, 2015, www.brookings.edu/research/opinions/2015/03/31-employer-health-insurance-aca-butler.

92. "The Competition Cure: A Better Idea to Make Health Insurance Affordable Everywhere," *Wall Street Journal*, August 23, 2009, www.wsj.com/articles/SB10001424052970203550604574360923109310680; Stephen Parente et al., "Consumer Response to a National Marketplace for Individual Health Insurance," *Journal of Risk and Insurance* 78, no. 2 (June 2011): 389–411.

93. "Cost Containment in the Affordable Care Act: An Overview of Policies and Savings," Center for Health Research and Transformation, May 2014, https://chrt.org/publication/cost-containment-affordable-care-act-overview-policies-savings.

94. Janet Weiner, Clifford Marks, and Mark Pauly, "Effects of the ACA on Health Care Cost Containment," Leonard Davis Institute of Health Economics, University of Pennsylvania, February 2017, https://ldi.upenn.edu/brief/effects-aca-health-care-cost-containment.

95. Cutler, "How Health Care Reform Must Bend the Cost Curve."

96. Ezekiel J. Emanuel, "Name the Much-Criticized Federal Program That Has Saved the U.S. $2.3 Trillion. Hint: It Starts with Affordable," *Stat*, March 22, 2019, www.statnews.com/2019/03/22/affordable-care-act-controls-costs.

97. Ezekiel J. Emanuel and Amol S. Navathe, "Delivery System Reforms: Evaluating the Effectiveness of the ACA's Delivery System Reforms at Slowing Cost Growth and Improving Quality and Patient Experience," in *The Trillion Dollar Revolution: How the Affordable Care Act Transformed Politics, Law, and Health Care in America*, ed. Ezekiel J Emanuel and Abbe R. Gluck (New York: Public Affairs Press, 2020), 225–249.

98. David Blumenthal and Melinda Abrams, "The Affordable Care Act at 10 Years—Payment and Delivery System Reforms," *New England Journal of Medicine* 382, no. 11 (March 12, 2020): 1057–1063, www.nejm.org/doi/full/10.1056/NEJMhpr1916092.

99. Jonathan Oberlander and Joseph White, "Systemwide Cost Control—the Missing Link in Health Care Reform," *New England Journal of Medicine* 361, no. 12 (September 17, 2009).

100. Jonathan Oberlander, "Throwing Darts, Americans' Elusive Search for Health Cost Control," *Journal of Health Politics, Policy and Law* 36, no. 3 (June 2011).

101. White, "Cost Control After the ACA," 524–533.

102. Joseph White, "Hypotheses and Hope: Policy Analysis and Cost Controls (or Not) in the Affordable Care Act," *Journal of Health Politics, Policy and Law* 43, no. 3 (2018): 455–481; Joseph White, "Costs Versus Coverage, Then and Now," *Journal of Health Politics, Policy and Law* 45, no. 5 (October 2020): 817–830.

103. Joseph Antos and James Capretta, "The ACA: Trillions? Yes. A Revolution? No." *Health Affairs Blog*, April 10, 2020, www.healthaffairs.org/do/10.1377/hblog20200406.93812/full.

104. Charles Blahous, "The Fiscal Effects of Repealing the Affordable Care Act," Mercatus Center, 2017, www.mercatus.org/publications/healthcare/fiscal-effects-repealing-affordable-care-act.

105. A good summary of the issues at the beginning of the postelection health reform debate is Bob Lyke, "The Tax Exclusion for Employer-Provided Health Insurance: Policy Issues Regarding the Repeal Debate," Congressional Research Service, November 21, 2008, www.policyarchive.org/handle/10207/19445.

106. For official estimates of revenue impact, see "Financing Comprehensive Health Care Reform: Proposed Health System Savings and Revenue Options," US Senate Committee on Finance, May 20, 2009, www.finance.senate.gov/imo/media/doc/051809%20Health%20Care%20Description%20of%20Policy%20Options.pdf; Joint Committee on Taxation, "Tax Expenditures for Health Care," JCX-66-08, US Senate Committee on Finance, July 30, 2008, www.finance.senate.gov/imo/media/doc/073108ektest.pdf; Lisa Clemans-Cope, Stephen Zuckerman, and Roberton Williams, "Changes to the Tax Exclusion of Employer-Sponsored Health Insurance Premiums: A Potential Source of Financing for Health Reform," Urban Institute, June 2009, www.urban.org/sites/default/files/alfresco/publication-pdfs/411916-Changes-to-the-Tax-Exclusion-of-Employer-Sponsored-Health-Insurance-Premiums-A-Potential-Source-of-Financing-for-Health-Reform.PDF.

107. Jason Roffenbender, "Employer-Based Health Insurance: Why Congress Should Cap Tax Benefits Consistently," Heritage Foundation, December 5, 2008, www.heritage.org/health-care-reform/report/employer-based-health-insurance-why-congress-should-cap-tax-benefits.

108. Max Baucus, *Call to Action: Health Reform 2009*, Senate Finance Committee, November 12, 2008, www.finance.senate.gov/imo/media/doc/finalwhitepaper1.pdf.

109. Wayne Herszenhorn, "A Bid to Tax Health Plans of Executives," *New York Times*, July 26, 2009, www.nytimes.com/2009/07/27/health/policy/27insure.html.

110. Jonathan Cohn, "How They Did It: The Inside Account of Health Reform's Triumph," *New Republic*, June 10, 2010, 23, https://newrepublic.com/article/75077/how-they-did-it; John E. McDonough, *Inside National Health Reform* (Berkeley: University of California Press, 2011), 88.

111. David Herszenhorn and Robert Pear, "Congress Is Split on Effort to Tax Costly Health Plans," *New York Times*, October 12, 2009, www.nytimes.com/2009/10/13/health/policy/13plans.html.

112. Allan Sloan, "Excise Tax on 'Cadillac' Health-Care Plans Is a Bad Idea," *Washington Post*, January 12, 2010, www.washingtonpost.com/wp-dyn/content/article/2010/01/11/AR2010011103591.html; Steven Greenhouse, "Unions Rally to Oppose a Tax on Health Insurance," *New York Times*, January 9, 2010, www.nytimes.com/2010/01/09/business/09union.html; Alec MacGillis, "Health-Care Reform Bill's Proposed Tax on High-Cost Plans Raises Questions," *Washington Post*, January 7, 2010, www.washingtonpost.com/wp-dyn/content/article/2010/01/06/AR2010010604931.html; Joseph White and Timothy Jost, "Cadillacs or Ambulances? The Senate Tax on 'Excessive' Benefits," *Health Affairs Blog*, December 3, 2009, http://healthaffairs.org/blog/2009/12/03/cadillacs-or-ambulances-the-senate-tax-on-excessive-benefits.

113. Paul Van de Water, "Excise Tax on Very High-Cost Health Plans Is a Sound Element of Health Reform," Center on Budget and Policy Priorities, November 10, 2009, www.cbpp.org/research/excise-tax-on-very-high-cost-health-plans-is-a-sound-element-of-health-reform.

114. Roffenbender, "Employer-Based Health Insurance"; Avik Roy, "Health Care and Profit Motive," *National Affairs*, no. 3 (spring 2010), www.nationalaffairs.com/publications/detail/health-care-and-the-profit-motive; Stuart M. Butler and Nina Owcharenko, "Making Health Care Affordable: Bush's Bold Health Tax Reform Plan," Heritage Foundation, January 22, 2007, www.heritage.org/research/reports/2007/01/making-health-care-affordable-bushs-bold-health-tax-reform-plan.

115. Cathy Schoen et al., "Progressive or Regressive? A Second Look at the Tax Exemption for Employer-Sponsored Health Insurance Premiums," Commonwealth Fund, May 2009, www.researchgate.net/publication/24434357_Progressive_or_regressive_A_second_look_at_the_tax_exemption_for_employer-sponsored_health_insurance_premiums.

116. Paul Fronstin, Employee Benefit Research Institute, "A Tax Cap on Health Benefits? Remember Sec. 89," *Wall Street Journal*, January 2009, http://online.wsj.com/ad/article/employeebenefits-cap.

117. Jon Gabel et al., "Taxing Cadillac Health Plans May Produce Chevy Results," *Health Affairs* 29, no. 1 (January 2010): 180.

118. Timothy S. Jost and Joseph White, "Cutting Health Care Spending: What Is the Cost of an Excise Tax That Keeps People from Going to the Doctor?," Institute for America's Future, https://ourfuture.org/files/Jost-White_Excise_Tax.pdf.

119. Jonathan Gruber, "A Win-Win Approach to Financing Health Care Reform," *New England Journal of Medicine* 361, no. 1 (July 2, 2009): 4–5.

120. Paul Van de Water, "Changes to Excise Tax on High-Cost Health Plans Address Criticisms, Retain Long-Term Benefits," Center on Budget and Policy

Priorities, January 26, 2010, www.cbpp.org/research/changes-to-excise-tax-on-high-cost-health-plans-address-criticisms-retain-long-term.

121. Paul Krugman, "The Health Insurance Excise Tax," *New York Times*, January 9, 2010, https://krugman.blogs.nytimes.com/2010/01/09/the-health-insurance-excise-tax.

122. Catherine Rampell, "Economists' Letter to Obama on Health Care Reform," *New York Times*, November 17, 2009, http://economix.blogs.nytimes.com/2009/11/17/economists-letter-to-obama-on-health-care-reform.

123. Laura Meckler and Naftali Bendavid, "Unions Cut Special Deal on Health Taxes," *Wall Street Journal*, January 15, 2010, www.wsj.com/articles/SB10001424052748704281204575003040695279432; Robert Pear and Steven Greenhouse, "Accord Reached on Insurance Tax for Costly Plans," *New York Times*, January 15, 2010, www.nytimes.com/2010/01/15/health/policy/15health.html.

124. Curtis S. Dubay, "Obamacare: Impact on Taxpayers," Heritage Foundation, April 14, 2010, http://s3.amazonaws.com/thf_media/2010/pdf/bg_2402.pdf.

125. Robert Pear, "Harvard Ideas on Health Care Hit Home Hard," *New York Times*, January 5, 2015, www.nytimes.com/2015/01/06/us/health-care-fixes-backed-by-harvards-experts-now-roil-its-faculty.html.

126. Joseph Antos, "Capping the Tax Exclusion Will Not Destroy Employer Health Insurance," American Enterprise Institute, April 26, 2015, www.aei.org/wp-content/uploads/2016/04/tax_exclusion_employer_health_insurance_obamacare_2020_500x293.jpg.

127. Reed Abelson, "Health Care Tax Faces United Opposition from Labor and Employers," *New York Times*, July 21, 2015, https://www.nytimes.com/2015/07/22/business/labor-and-employers-join-in-opposition-to-a-health-care-tax.html.

128. Jared Bernstein, "Obamacare's 'Cadillac Tax' Is an Important Part of the Plan So Don't Mess with It," *Washington Post*, July 15, 2015, www.washingtonpost.com/posteverything/wp/2015/07/15/obamacares-cadillac-tax-is-an-important-part-of-the-plan-so-dont-mess-with-it; David Wessel, "What the 'Cadillac Tax' Accomplishes—and What Could Be Lost in Repeal," *Wall Street Journal*, July 24, 2015, www.wsj.com/articles/BL-WB-56860.

129. Gary Claxton and Larry Levitt, "How Many Employers Could Be Affected by the Cadillac Plan Tax?," Kaiser Family Foundation, August 2015, https://files.kff.org/attachment/issue-brief-how-many-employers-could-be-affected-by-the-cadillac-plan-tax.

130. Sarah Ferrie, "House GOP Adds Healthcare Tax Bill to Fall Agenda," *The Hill*, August 24, 2015, https://thehill.com/policy/healthcare/251839-house-gop-adds-healthcare-tax-bill-to-fall-agenda.

131. Gregory Mankiw and Lawrence Summers, "Uniting Behind the Divisive 'Cadillac' Tax on Health Plans," *New York Times*, October 24, 2015, www.nytimes.com/2015/10/25/upshot/uniting-behind-the-divisive-cadillac-tax-on-health-plans.html.

132. Carolyn Johnson, "101 Economists Just Signed a Love Letter to the Obamacare Provision Everyone Else Hates," *Washington Post*, October 1, 2015, www.washingtonpost.com/news/wonk/wp/2015/10/01/101-economists-just-signed-a-love-letter-to-the-obamacare-provision-everyone-else-hates.

133. Peter Sullivan, "Obamacare Repeal Zips to House Floor," *The Hill*, October 9, 2015, https://thehill.com/policy/healthcare/256500-house-panel-advances-fast-track-obamacare-repeal.

134. Alexander Bolton, "GOP Searches for Obamacare Win," *The Hill*, November 2, 2015, https://thehill.com/homenews/senate/258920-gop-searches-for-obamacare

-win; Alexander Bolton, "ObamaCare Repeal Teeters in Senate," *The Hill*, November 16, 2015, https://thehill.com/homenews/senate/260153-obamacare-repeal-teeters-in-senate.

135. Peter Sullivan and Sarah Ferris, "Talk Grows of Repealing ObamaCare 'Cadillac Tax,'" *The Hill*, November 10, 2015, https://thehill.com/policy/healthcare/259727-talk-grows-of-repealing-obamacare-cadillac-tax.

136. Peter Sullivan, "Lawmakers Seek Late Deal to Scale Back 'Cadillac Tax,'" *The Hill*, December 1, 2015, https://thehill.com/policy/healthcare/261698-lawmakers-seek-late-deal-to-scale-back-cadillac-tax.

137. Alexander Bolton, "Senators Closing In on Major Tax Deal," *The Hill*, December 9, 2015, https://thehill.com/policy/finance/262665-senators-closing-in-on-major-tax-deal; Stephanie Armour and Richard Rubin, "Congress Pushes for Delay in 'Cadillac Tax' on Health Plans," *Wall Street Journal*, December 10, 2015, www.wsj.com/articles/congress-pushes-for-delay-in-cadillac-tax-on-health-plans-1449788386.

138. Alexander Bolton, "Congress on Verge of Major Deal Freezing ObamaCare Taxes," *The Hill*, December 15, 2015, https://thehill.com/homenews/senate/263255-congress-on-verge-of-major-deal-freezing-obamacare-taxes.

139. Timothy Yost, "How Does the Budget Agreement Affect the ACA," *Health Affairs Blog*, December 16, 2015, www.healthaffairs.org/do/10.1377/hblog20151216.052341/full.

140. Stan Dorn, "The Cadillac Tax: It's Time to Kill This Policy Zombie," *Health Affairs Blog*, June 18, 2019, www.healthaffairs.org/do/10.1377/hblog20190617.795057/full.

141. James C. Capretta, "Repeal of the Cadillac Tax Would Be a Strategic Mistake for Both Parties," American Enterprise Institute, August 13, 2019, www.aei.org/articles/repeal-of-the-cadillac-tax-would-be-a-strategic-mistake-for-both-parties; Paul N. Van de Water, "Why Congress Shouldn't Repeal the Cadillac Tax," Center on Budget and Policy Priorities, July 11, 2019, https://www.cbpp.org/sites/default/files/atoms/files/7-11-19health.pdf.

142. "Statement from Health Economists and Policy Analysts About Excise Tax on High-Cost Plans," Center on Budget and Policy Priorities, July 29, 2019, www.cbpp.org/sites/default/files/atoms/files/7-29-19health.pdf.

143. Katie Keith, "ACA Provisions in New Budget Bill," *Health Affairs Blog*, December 20, 2019, www.healthaffairs.org/do/10.1377/hblog20191220.115975/full.

144. Karyn Schwartz et al., "What We Know About Provider Consolidation," Issue Brief, Kaiser Family Foundation, September 2, 2020, www.kff.org/health-costs/issue-brief/what-we-know-about-provider-consolidation.

145. Brent D. Fulton, "Health Care Market Concentration Trends in the United States: Evidence and Policy Responses," *Health Affairs* 36, no. 9 (September 2017): 1530–1538.

146. Anna Wilde Mathews, "Physicians, Hospitals Meet Their New Competitor: Insurer-Owned Clinics," *Wall Street Journal*, February 23, 2020, www.wsj.com/articles/physicians-hospitals-meet-their-new-competitor-insurer-owned-clinics-11582473600.

147. Lovisa Gustafsson, Shanoor Seervai, and David Blumenthal, "The Role of Private Equity in Driving Up Health Care Prices," *Harvard Business Review*, October 29, 2019, https://hbr.org/2019/10/the-role-of-private-equity-in-driving-up-health-care-prices.

148. Jane M. Zhu, Lynn M. Hua, and Daniel Polsky, "Private Equity Acquisitions of Physician Medical Groups Across Specialties, 2013–2016," *JAMA Research Letter* 323, no. 7 (February 18, 2020): 663–665.

149. "Congressional Request on Healthcare Provider Consolidation," chap. 15 of Medicare Payment Advisory Commission, *Report to the Congress: Medicare Payment Policy* (Washington, DC: Medpac, March 2020), www.medpac.gov/docs/default-source/reports/mar20_entirereport_sec.pdf.

150. Andrew Boozary et al., "The Association Between Hospital Concentration and Insurance Premiums in ACA Marketplaces," *Health Affairs* 38, no. 4 (April 2019): 668–674.

151. Hannah Neprash et al., "Little Evidence Exists to Support the Expectation That Providers Would Consolidate to Enter New Payment Models," *Health Affairs* 36, no. 2 (February 2017): 346–354.

152. Zack Cooper et al., "That Price Ain't Right? Hospital Prices and Health Spending on the Privately Insured," Working Paper 21815, National Bureau of Economic Research, August 2017, https://zackcooper.com/sites/default/files/paper-files/w23748_0.pd.

153. Robert Berenson, "Addressing Pricing Power in Integrated Delivery," *Journal of Health Politics, Policy and Law* 40, no. 4 (August 2015): 725–729.

154. Melinda Beeuwkes Buntin and John A. Graves, "How the ACA Dented the Cost Curve," *Health Affairs* 39, no. 3 (March 2020): 403–412.

155. Ibid., 404.

156. Roosa Tikkanen, "Multinational Comparisons of Health Systems Data, 2019," Commonwealth Fund, January 30, 2020, www.commonwealthfund.org/publications/other-publication/2020/jan/multinational-comparisons-health-systems-data-2019.

157. Ibid.

158. Congress enacted surprise billing legislation in December 2020. This refers to "unanticipated out-of-network medical bills." For detailed explanation, see "Surprise Medical Bills: New Protections for Consumers Take Effect in 2022," Kaiser Family Foundation, February 4, 2021, www.kff.org/private-insurance/fact-sheet/surprise-medical-bills-new-protections-for-consumers-take-effect-in-2022. Prescription drug cost legislation has been on the congressional agenda, but no bill had been enacted by both houses of Congress as of late 2021.

9

The ACA Today...
and Tomorrow

Thus ends this year. . . . It's true we have gone through great melancholy because of the great plague.

—Samuel Pepys

Samuel Pepys chronicled in his diary the seventeenth-century plague in England. We begin this final chapter with a brief assessment of the role of the Affordable Care Act (ACA) in helping American society cope with its plague. Like the Black Death, Covid-19 arrived from China and caused death and economic dislocation. For more than a year, death, the threat of death, and economic hardship upended American society. Did the ACA, as a set of public policies, help the country cope with the health impact of Covid-19?

The existence of the ACA assisted many Americans in their attempt to cope with the medical complications of the disease by providing coverage for those who were uninsured because of Covid-related loss of employment. The ACA itself was transformed as a result of the various legislative actions designed to address the disruptions due to the pandemic.

The first cases appeared in the United States in early 2020. Clusters developed, and then Covid-19 appeared everywhere. Various types of economic activity shut down, especially in the service industries. Hospitals were overwhelmed. At first the Donald Trump administration treated it as a seasonal flu that would quickly disappear with the arrival of spring. State and local responses varied, and by late spring the plague had swept across the country.

Many employees who worked in offices were able to work from home and retained their employer-sponsored health insurance, but as segments of the economy shut down, millions lost their jobs and their insurance. The jobless rate climbed to almost 15 percent as 40 million filed for unemployment insurance—a number not seen since the Great Depression.

A June 2020 survey by the Commonwealth Fund found 40 percent of those laid off had been insured through the lost job. Of this group, two-thirds still retained insurance through the employer or COBRA, but a fifth became uninsured. Of these only 7 percent had regained coverage through a marketplace plan or Medicaid.[1] Thus, the ACA coverage backup did not work for all. In states without Medicaid expansion, this was unlikely to be a source of coverage for this cohort.

Most state-run exchanges reopened their enrollment period to accommodate individuals in this category, but the Trump administration refused to do the same for the federal exchanges.[2] In the federal exchanges some individuals who lost employment-based coverage were able to utilize the existing special enrollment period authorization to gain marketplace coverage, and nearly 1 million did so by July, which was nearly a 30 percent increase over the previous year. State exchanges were more active. California, for example, experienced new enrollments two and half times greater than the previous year.[3] Medicaid expansion states also experienced a rapid growth in enrollment, with a 15 percent increase in the first half of 2020.[4]

A person who lived in a state with its own exchange and Medicaid expansion was likely to be able to replace health insurance lost because of unemployment due to Covid-19. The effectiveness of the ACA as a backup for employment-based insurance often depended on state of residence.

Covid-19 Stimulus Bills and the ACA

Congress, in response to the Covid-19 crisis, enacted four major pieces of legislation intended to assist individuals and industries impacted by the epidemic: the Coronavirus Aid, Relief, and Economic Security (CARES) Act and the Families First Coronavirus Response Act in March 2020, the Coronavirus Response and Relief Supplemental Appropriations Act in December 2020, and in February 2021, with the Joe Biden administration in place, the American Rescue Plan Act (ARPA). All have provisions related to health policy, but only the ARPA significantly modified the ACA.

The CARES Act provided emergency funding to individuals, institutions, and corporations in response to rapid economic deterioration. Various public and private health organizations received funds, but the act did not expand health insurance coverage or address the cost of Covid treatment for the uninsured.[5]

A few weeks later Congress passed the Families First Coronavirus Response Act, which required all insurance plans to cover Covid testing and diagnosis without cost sharing. States received an additional 6 percent in Medicaid matching funds and were to cover testing without cost sharing.[6]

The Coronavirus Response and Relief Supplemental Appropriations Act was passed in late December 2020. It featured a number of ACA-related provisions. The No Surprises Act was part of this legislation. Large and unexpected charges for out-of-network services had become a frequent complaint, especially since the patient was often unaware that a provider was not part of the network. The bipartisan compromise legislation was attached to the appropriations bill.

The No Surprises Act limits patient cost-sharing responsibility for out-of-network providers to the same as for those in network, if the service takes place in a facility within the network—for example, if a patient at an in-network hospital is treated by an anesthesiologist who is not part of the insurance network. It also includes limits on air-ambulance fees. Providers and insurance companies have an arbitration process to settle disputes, and the patient cannot be billed beyond what the insurance paid.[7] This is an especially important protection for patients whose insurance is obtained in the marketplace, but it also applies to employer-sponsored insurance.

The appropriations act included a number of additional ACA provisions. Most related to items such as mental health parity, transparency rules, and continuity of care.[8] The act did not address expanding coverage for those newly uninsured because of Covid-related economic decline.

Wrapping Up After the First Decade

The actual state of our knowledge is always provisional and . . . there must be, beyond what is actually known, immense new regions to discover.

—Louis de Broglie

We begin a brief summary of what we know about the ACA early in its second decade with the sense of a provisional assessment. De Broglie won a Nobel Prize in physics but realized there was much yet to learn. This summary conclusion is at best an interim evaluation of the most comprehensive and significant health legislation in decades. The story of its ultimate impact, or lack thereof, will be written in the future.

There were dozens of tenth anniversary assessments in journals and books, but 2020 was only the seventh year of implementation for most major provisions. The 2020 election added a new facet to an ACA first-decade appraisal as Democrats regained control of Congress and the White

House for the first time since 2011, with an opportunity to make ACA changes large and small. We will draw on the previous chapters, as well as various assessments published in response to the tenth anniversary, to summarize a provisional assessment of the ACA.

We have three basic questions to ask in this final chapter:

1. Did the ACA endure the decade?
2. Was the ACA effective in achieving its goals?
3. What are the expectations for the ACA's second decade?

Did the ACA Endure the Decade?

How much of the ACA was left after a decade? Helen Levy, Andrew Ying, and Nicholas Bagley reminded us that the law was large and complex with many distinctive provisions.[9] Their analysis found most of the law was successfully implemented, but some parts were never put in place or were dropped. Legal challenges limited Medicaid expansion and modified some limits on cost sharing.

Some elements were born to fail. In this category they placed the Community Living Assistance Services and Supports (CLASS) Act, which was dropped before it went into effect, as was the business reporting requirement. The cooperatives are mostly gone, with a few barely surviving. Some failed elements had serious design flaws. Interest group pressure killed the Cadillac tax, as well as the tax on medical devices and health insurers. The Independent Payment Advisory Board was touted as a major cost-control feature, but members were never appointed, and the provision was repealed in 2018.[10]

Some provisions failed to thrive for various reasons. These included the Prevention and Public Health Fund and Section 1334, which envisioned the Office of Personnel Management contracting for at least two multistate plans in each exchange. The section providing a new pathway for biosimilar drugs did not meet the expectations of its champions.

Trump administration ACA sabotage efforts included allowing Medicaid work requirements, association health plans, and short-term insurance. Legal challenges from supporters slowed these attempts to weaken coverage expansion, and the Biden administration is rewriting the rules to nullify these efforts.

Their answer to what is left of the ACA? Most of it, despite some failures.

Was the ACA Effective in Achieving Its Goals?

Any major piece of legislation is likely to have multiple goals, some clear, others not. During the process, pieces are added reflecting preferences of a few legislators. Some parts are invisible to all but subject experts. For example, John McDonough cites Section 2001 of Title II as a resounding success. It established in Medicaid a new uniform national eligibility standard, which set a common definition of household income. This was a successful but under-the-radar provision.[11]

For our purposes, we focus on the two major goals most identified with the ACA:

1. Reduction in the number of uninsured by expansion of health insurance coverage and the consequent improvement of the health status of the population
2. Slowing the rate of growth of aggregate health costs for government and for individuals, especially through delivery system change

The expansion of Medicaid to cover all individuals with an income less than 138 percent of the federal poverty level (FPL) and the creation of insurance exchanges for the purchase of insurance with tax-credit assistance for those with income less than 400 percent of FPL were the main policy mechanisms designed to achieve the goal of reducing the number of uninsured.

In 2014 there were 44 million uninsured, and this was reduced to 29 million by 2019. The low point was 27 million in 2016. This represented a drop from 17 to 11 percent of the population uninsured.[12] Sommers estimated 60 percent of the reduction can be attributed to Medicaid and the rest to marketplace subsidies and the provision to allow children to remain on family coverage until age twenty-six.[13]

No one in 2010 expected the ACA to reduce the uninsured to zero or near zero, but the failure to universally adopt Medicaid expansion caused a shortfall in the coverage goal. A Kaiser Foundation analysis estimated coverage for slightly over 2 million additional people with universal Medicaid expansion.[14] About 10 percent of the population would remain uninsured after universal Medicaid expansion. Among the remaining uninsured are undocumented immigrants and those with non-ACA-compliant coverage.[15] These probably represent one-third of the residual uninsured.

Aparna Soni, Laura Wherry, and Kosali Simon reviewed the academic literature addressing the impact of the ACA on health outcomes. They found evidence to suggest improvements in early-stage cancer diagnosis and cardiovascular health, among others.[16] A similar Kaiser Foundation review also found mortality reduction and fewer disparities for black infants in expansion as opposed to nonexpansion states. They also identified more adults receiving consistent care for chronic conditions.[17]

Thomas Buchmueller and Helen Levy found racial and ethnic coverage and access differences continue to exist, but the ACA has reduced coverage disparities by widening the availability of insurance, especially for racial and ethnic minorities.[18]

Several years after full implementation of the ACA, the evidence clearly indicates health insurance coverage has significantly expanded with improved health outcomes. The benefits have not reached the entire population. The experience seven years after full implementation has identified the need for improvement in coverage with the expectation that additional coverage will result in more health-outcome advances.

For decades the cost of health care has risen exponentially. Whether this is measured as a percentage of gross domestic product (GDP) or in comparison with annual percentage increases in the consumer price index, the trend line has consistently moved upward. Public concern about health costs helped drive the politics of reform. The average voter viewed excessive health costs in terms of insurance premiums and cost sharing. Health policy experts tended to focus on systemwide cost increases on the premise these ultimately drove individual costs. However, every system saving approach did not return equal benefits to all individuals.

Melinda Beeuwkes Buntin and John Graves found the ACA reduced Medicare spending by modifying reimbursement rates, but this did not exceed the increases in Medicaid expenses and marketplace premium costs. Factors unrelated to the ACA contributed to the slightly slower rate of growth in total spending over the decade. They speculated delivery system reform contributed to slower growth.[19]

Joseph White is far more skeptical. He argues delivery system reform was long on hype and short on actual evidence of cost savings. He contends the average voter had health insurance and was probably more concerned about premiums and cost sharing than coverage expansion. The ACA architects needed interest group support to pass the ACA. They could not impose cost controls on private insurance without their assent or risked losing key support. Delivery system reforms, such as accountable care organizations, were either a cynical cost-control masquerade or, more likely, a case of wanting to believe these ideas were a path to control because they were popular among many reformers.[20]

Carrie Colla and Jonathan Skinner divided potential cost saving into micro and macro perspectives. In the micro-level view, they find a modest reduction in annual savings on the order of 0.14 percent in the decade after ACA enactment. They used Congressional Budget Office estimates compared to actual spending to derive the savings estimate with Medicare payment reductions constituting a major element. From a macro perspective they distinguish between aggregate spending and spending per covered individual. This accounts for spending changes over time purely attributed to more covered individuals after the ACA enactment. In this analysis Medicare and Medicaid spending per individual has remained flat. After an initial pause between 2010 and 2013, per covered individual, per-person spending growth continued for the rest of the decade. This was concentrated in the private insurance sector and apparently the result of rising prices and introduction of new technology.[21]

Sherry Glied, Sara Collins, and Saunders Lin, in their analysis, examined whether the ACA had in fact lowered financial barriers to health care for all Americans. From their examination of research studies since 2014, they found greater financial risk protection in both the individual and group markets as a result of coverage expansion and insurance market reforms, such as prohibition of annual or lifetime benefit limits.[22]

An early 2020 Commonwealth Fund survey explored the question of continued financial barriers a decade after the adoption of the ACA. It found as many as 40 percent inadequately insured, 15 percent with deductibles of $1,000 or more, and 25 percent with problems paying medical bills. Those with inadequate insurance or high deductibles were more likely to delay treatment. Thus, a decade after the ACA significantly expanded coverage, major financial problems and barriers continue to exist for many families.[23]

Has the ACA achieved its two major goals of expanded access and reduced cost a decade after enactment? The best answer may be partially. Insurance coverage has significantly reduced the number of uninsured, but serious gaps remain. Medicaid expansion has advanced but remains incomplete. The tax credits in the marketplace have enabled millions to become covered, but the cost remains too high for some, especially those with incomes marginally too high for eligibility. Cost sharing as a percentage of income is rising rapidly both with employment-based insurance and in the individual market.

Total system cost growth has abated slightly. Mostly this is the result of ACA-mandated Medicare payment reductions. After the ACA enactment, there was a pause in private-sector cost growth, but it has begun to climb again, whether measured on an aggregate or per-person basis.

The ACA has been successful to a point but has not resolved all the problems that led to its enactment. Our final section looks at the next ten years. These future scenarios assume the ACA will continue to be the subject of debate and scrutiny, with potential paths for change in the coming years. This will answer our third question, but first we undertake a quick review of the early Biden administration.

President Biden's First 300 Days

Since Franklin D. Roosevelt was president, the media has relished measuring the successes and failures of the first 100 days. In this assessment of the Biden administration and the ACA, we increase the length and select 300 days as our measure of progress, which brings us to November 2021.

ACA and Covid Relief

By the end of January 2021, the political alignment had drastically shifted. President Biden was in the White House, and the Democrats had the narrowest of margins in the Senate and House. A week after inauguration the president issued an executive order directing the Department of Health and Human Services (HHS) to take steps to broaden access to the ACA, especially for those adversely impacted by Covid, and to strengthen Medicaid. The order directed various agencies to review and change where necessary Trump administration rules, policies, and directives.[24] A first step in the directive was the establishment of a special enrollment period to facilitate use of the ACA to assist those without insurance because of Covid.[25]

The first congressional priority for Democrats was a new and larger stimulus bill. They quickly moved it forward without the need for Republican agreement because the reconciliation process was used, necessitating only a simple majority for passage in the Senate.[26] The American Rescue Plan Act (ARPA) was signed into law on March 11, 2021. We will only address its health-related provisions, which represented the most significant ACA changes since its enactment more than a decade earlier. It has both major cost-reduction assistance in the private insurance market and Medicaid provisions. Most of the coverage expansions only extend through 2022.

The ACA marketplace expansions include the following:[27]

- Extending premium tax credits to those with incomes above 400 percent of FPL. They will not need to spend more than 8.5 percent of family income on premiums. An estimated 3.6 million are eligible.
- For those with incomes between 100 and 400 percent of FPL, a lower percentage of income will be required for premium contribution. For some this will reduce premium cost to zero. An estimated 9 million people may benefit.
- In 2021 those receiving unemployment benefits will qualify for premium tax credits and cost-sharing reductions.
- For those who have been laid off, COBRA payments can be subsidized through the end of September 2021.

Medicaid provisions include the following:[28]

- Twelve states have not expanded Medicaid. As an inducement to do so, their federal Medicaid matching rate will be increased by 5 percent for two years.
- States have the option to extend postpartum coverage under Medicaid and the Children's Health Insurance Program (CHIP) from the current sixty days to one year. This provision is in effect for five years.
- Coverage will be provided with full federal funding for Covid testing, vaccination, and treatment under Medicaid for the uninsured.

These ACA modifications were intended to be short-term adjustments during the Covid epidemic. Additional legislation is necessary for them to become permanent.

A Kaiser Foundation analysis of the ARPA estimated the package of modifications will result in greatly reduced premium payments for many of the 15 million people now eligible for subsidies in the marketplace. The plight of those whose income is slightly above 400 percent of FPL has been called the "subsidy cliff." For the 3.4 million on the subsidy cliff, the modifications generated a significant savings. This group tends to be older and benefits the most from the ARPA adjustments to the ACA.[29]

Apart from the ARPA subsidy increases, the ACA itself has proven essential to the public Covid response. The marketplace has been available for many suddenly uninsured because of job loss. Medicaid expansion was also a safety valve for those who lost low-income employment. The ACA was not a perfect coverage response to the loss of employment-based insurance during the epidemic, but the ACA and its ARPA adjustments did provide a backstop for millions.

The special enrollment period expired in August, but more than 2.8 million had signed up for marketplace coverage since February in federal and state marketplaces. In conjunction with the tally of the regular enrollment period, this represented a record high. Medicaid enrollment also grew sharply in early 2021.[30]

Medicaid and the States

The Trump administration was unable to radically change Medicaid with legislative action but instituted sabotage strategies to weaken and diminish enrollment. The most notable of these was opening the door to Medicaid work-requirement requests from the states. Unraveling the legal position, rule making, and 1115 waivers surrounding work requirements became a high priority for the Biden administration.

In February the Centers for Medicare and Medicaid Services (CMS) notified states of a comprehensive review of approved work-requirement waivers, and in March it began by notifying Arkansas and New Hampshire of withdrawal. The legal case on the issue was before the Supreme Court, but the Biden administration Justice Department was no longer supporting the concept. The Court suspended consideration of the case but did not dismiss it.[31] By August CMS had notified nearly all affected states of the withdrawal of work-requirement waivers.[32]

A special case was the last-minute ten-year extension of the Texas 1115 waiver issued in the final days of the Trump administration. CMS contended the waiver approval process did not follow proper procedures and was therefore invalid. A major feature of the waiver was funding for an uncompensated care pool for payments to hospitals for services provided to uninsured patients.[33] In August a federal district judge enjoined CMS from proceeding with its rescission of the waiver. This legal battle will likely continue into the future. Revocation of the waiver would increase pressure on Texas to expand Medicaid.[34]

Another midnight-approval 1115 waiver targeted for review by the Biden administration was one granted to Tennessee in January 2021. The waiver transfers nearly all of the state's Medicaid participants to a new program that caps federal Medicaid funding in the state and allows the state to retain a share of federal savings.[35] It creates a strong incentive for the state to reduce service to beneficiaries.[36] Limited access to a wide range of prescription drugs is one possible consequence of the waiver. In August CMS reopened the public comment period on the waiver, which could be the first step in revoking it.[37]

1332 Waivers
The other waiver program the Trump administration sought to utilize to weaken Medicaid and ACA coverage provisions was the Section 1332 waiver. Trump administration changes to the guidance documents weakened the statutory guiderails. Most of the 1332 waivers approved during the Trump administration involved noncontroversial reinsurance programs. Fourteen states have such programs, and the Biden administration has begun to reapprove them as original approvals expire.[38] The August renewal of the Colorado program signals a positive view of these approaches by the Biden administration. Colorado expects a 20 percent reduction in premiums and a 2.5 percent enrollment increase as a result of the program.[39]

However, the Biden administration is taking a more hostile view toward the Trump administration's 1332 waiver for the state of Georgia, which eliminates use of the healthcare.gov marketplace website. In its place private insurance brokers are authorized to sell insurance plans, which are eligible for tax credits. In January two Georgia nonprofits sued CMS challenging the approval process for the waiver. The court allowed the state of Georgia to intervene as a party as it contends the waiver was legally appropriate. In June CMS requested additional information about the impact of the change for its review. Georgia refused to provide the requested information, and CMS has reopened a sixty-day comment period. It is likely the waiver will be administratively overturned with the action subject to continued legal challenge.[40]

Legal Issues
With a Biden administration Department of Justice, the government began to defend the ACA in court rather than supporting its challengers. There was little significant new litigation, although Nicholas Bagley called attention to a new suit filed in the Texas district court of Judge Reed O'Connor,

who sought to strike down the whole ACA in *California v. Texas*.[41] ACA Section 2713 requires health plans to offer coverage without cost sharing for certain preventive services. The suit claims a violation of the nondelegation doctrine, which posits Congress can only delegate power to agencies with adequate exercise instructions. The second claim relates to the constitutional provision requiring delegation of government power to officers of the United States—namely, those appointed by the president and department heads. The three entities to which Congress delegated authority to make recommendations on which services to cover may not be considered officers of the United States by the courts.[42] Timothy Jost contends longstanding precedent and practice supports the delegation of recommendations to advisory bodies, with the Senate-confirmed HHS secretary being the final decisionmaker.[43] Eventually this case may also reach the Supreme Court with its conservative majority.

The large court victory for the Biden administration was the 7–2 decision in *California v. Texas*, which rejected the attempt to invalidate the whole ACA because the individual-mandate penalty had been reduced to zero. In February the Biden Justice Department informed the Supreme Court it was formally changing the government position. The Trump administration had shifted position over time but ultimately supported the plaintiff position of unconstitutionality. The Biden letter stated the legal position that the individual mandate was constitutional and, if deemed unconstitutional, fully severable. It did not address the standing of the plaintiffs.[44]

In June, the Supreme Court dismissed the case on the grounds the plaintiffs did not have standing to sue. It was dismissed on procedural grounds without directly addressing the constitutionality of the mandate or its severability. This appears to mark the end of the decade-long attempts by conservative opponents to overturn the entire ACA.[45] Even the conservative Court majority signaled it was not prepared to overturn a law that provided health insurance for millions of Americans on a marginal constitutional challenge.

With the Biden administration's 2021 reversal of the government's position on various ACA legal issues, many pending cases were put on hold. The Supreme Court did reject an appeal on the risk-corridor cases, thus leaving the prior appeals court decision in place. The cases challenging the rules allowing expansion of association health plans and short-term plans were put on hold pending a Justice Department review of the government's position. In June the Supreme Court denied an appeal from insurers on the cost-sharing reduction cases, which left the earlier appeals court decision in place. The seemingly endless litigation over the contraceptive mandate continued in various courts.

The Medicaid work-requirement case pending before the Supreme Court was suspended in April, and it seems unlikely it will be taken up again because the Biden administration has systematically rescinded the Trump administration waiver approvals. The issue may return to the courts as lawsuits against the termination actions.[46]

In May the HHS Office for Civil Rights announced an interpretation of the Section 1557 prohibition on sex discrimination as including sexual orientation and gender identity. A Trump administration 2020 rule sought to narrow the protection. The Biden administration will likely develop a new rule, which will be further challenged.[47]

Build Back Better

After the 2020 election Democrats controlled both houses of Congress and the White House for the first time since 2010. Over the decade an extended legislative wish list had developed, but the internal division between the progressive and moderate wings of the party had grown. Consensus existed around the unmet needs to be addressed, but the particular policy approaches and scope of new initiatives remained a point of contention. For example, progressives advocated a Medicare for All approach to health policy reform, but moderates preferred to enhance the ACA.

The incoming Biden administration was clearly in the moderate camp but indicated support for a wide range of new social policy initiatives. The first priority was passage of an expanded Covid-19 relief. The ACA provisions of the ARPA were discussed above.

Early in the year a bipartisan group of senators fashioned an infrastructure spending plan that secured enough Republican votes to overcome a filibuster. The Infrastructure Investment and Jobs Act passed the Senate in August 2021 and the House in early November. This separated the infrastructure initiative from the reconciliation bill. The health policy agenda was part of a set of social policy initiatives. On a party line vote in August the Senate adopted a $3.5 trillion budget resolution that set the stage for the development of a reconciliation bill, the Build Back Better Act (BBBA).

The BBBA contains major initiatives related to climate change, child care, public housing, and several health policy initiatives. We will only address the ACA enhancement elements of the health policy provisions, and not discuss others, such as controlling prescription drug prices and expansion of Medicare benefits. Nor will we attempt to navigate the complex financial calculations and projections of program costs and tax increase offsets. Despite a Congressional Budget Office score of the House bill, cost and revenue projections are likely to significantly change before a final version is passed.

On. November 19, 2021, the House passed the BBBA reconciliation bill (HR 5376), and Senate action is anticipated in the near future. The Senate will not adopt the House version exactly as written. Additional negotiations and modifications will precede final passage. It is likely, but not certain, some form of the BBBA will become law in early 2022.

The origins of the ACA enhancement policy ideas in the BBBA began long before the Biden administration. Even prior to the Trump administration's efforts to repeal and sabotage the ACA, its supporters recognized shortcomings requiring a legislative fix.[48] Without a unified Democratic government, modifications were impossible. Major adjustments were identified to be fixed:

- Medicaid gap in which individuals below 100 percent of the federal poverty line in nonexpansion states were neither eligible for Medicaid coverage or marketplace tax credits
- Subsidy cliff in which those above 400 percent FPL were not eligible for tax credits even if they paid a high percent of income for insurance
- Need to reduce premiums and cost sharing for those receiving tax credits in the marketplaces, especially for low-income families
- Family glitch in which affordable employment-based insurance was measured for worker coverage only, not family coverage
- Create a state reinsurance plan to increase prospects for future lower premiums
- Establish a public option to provide increased affordable marketplace coverage
- Revise employer firewall to better define affordable employment-based insurance

The first legislative effort to address these ACA flaws was the House passage of the 2020 Patient Protection and Affordable Care Enhancement Act. It sought to expand eligibility for tax credits to those with incomes above 400 percent FPL, enhance tax credits by reducing the percentage of income an individual contributes toward premiums, and address the family glitch.[49] The Republican Senate majority did not take up the bill, but the package of changes became a template for future efforts.

In early 2021 the next step in the ACA modification effort was the ARPA, the Covid-19 relief bill passed by Congress in March. Its major provisions included extending premium tax credits for those above 400 percent FPL, a reduced share of income for premium contributions, premium tax credits, and cost-sharing reductions for unemployment compensation recipients.[50]

Subsequent analysis of the impact of the ACA provisions of the ARPA found the ACA adjustments prevented a significant increase in the number of the uninsured during the period of Covid job loss.[51] These provisions were time limited and set to expire in 2022.

By summer 2021 the BBBA reconciliation bill began to take shape. The Ways and Means and Energy and Commerce committees of the House drafted the health-related provisions of the bill. In July the Senate Budget Committee reached agreement on the budget limit, which was set at $3.5 trillion over ten years.[52] With this fiscal framework the House committees finalized the ACA-related provisions. The House proposal was released on September 15, and it contained the following major provisions:[53]

- Made permanent the enhanced marketplace subsidies in the ARPA
- Closed the Medicaid gap in two stages
- Individuals with unemployment benefits eligible for maximum tax credits until 2025

Other ACA-related provisions included: permanent authorization for the Children's Health Insurance Program (CHIP), requirement that Medicaid and CHIP provide continuous twelve-month eligibility for children, annual reinsurance program for states, adjustment to the employer firewall, and requirement for Medicaid twelve-month postpartum coverage. Some discussed reforms were not included, for example, addressing the family glitch and creating a public option.

The marketplace subsidy enhancements followed the ARPA template, which extended tax credits to those above 400 percent FPL calculated as a percentage of income. For those between 100 percent and 150 percent of FPL there would be zero premiums. For others, premium contributions would be on a scale relative to income until a maximum of 8.5 percent.[54]

There would be two steps taken to close the Medicaid gap for people between 100 percent and 138 percent FPL in nonexpansion states. These individuals were not eligible for Medicaid, nor did they qualify for marketplace tax credits. Under BBBA they would be eligible for marketplace tax credits with no premium and minimal co-pays until 2025. Low-income workers were also eligible and enrollment would be continuous. The second and permanent phase would create a new Medicaid program in which HHS contracts with third-party entities, such as managed care companies to provide coverage in nonexpansion states.[55]

By September there were two large roadblocks to swift consideration of the Build Back Better Act and its health provisions. The infrastructure bill had passed the Senate, but the Democratic progressive caucus was adamant about not taking a House vote on the infrastructure bill until the Senate supported the emerging Build Back Better bill. House moderates were demanding an immediate vote on the infrastructure bill.

Secondly, the estimated total cost of the Build Back Better bill was too high for some moderate Democrats in the Senate. Health provisions competed with other elements of the bill, as well as each other. With a smaller total budget, enhanced ACA tax credits and filling the Medicaid gap were not feasible if Medicare was expanded to include hearing, dental, and vision coverage.[56]

At the end of October, President Biden released a new compromise plan representing a consensus agreement among Democratic congressional leaders and the White House.[57] In early November Speaker Nancy Pelosi had secured enough votes to pass the infrastructure bill, and it was sent it to the White House for signature. Most House progressives accepted the leadership promise to quickly vote on the BBBA bill with assurances the Senate would take up and pass it.[58]

In order to bring the House reconciliation bill within the new fiscal limit in the budget resolution a number of modifications were made to the early September version. The reconciliation process incorporates a ten-year spending projection. Provisions that begin later or expire before the end of the ten-year period are scored by the Congressional Budget office to cost less over the decade. In 2010 ACA drafters employed a similar strategy to keep the ten-year fiscal estimate within the limit sought.

With the ACA enhancement provisions in the BBBA bill, this meant scaling back the scope of the September version. The major ACA-related changes in the final House version were:

1. The ACA marketplace tax credit enhancements were set to expire in 2025 rather than becoming permanent.
2. The Medicaid gap provision for creating a new national program after 2025 was dropped.

Even within the overall health provisions, congressional leaders needed to reduce the total cost of the bill.

The 2025 sunset for major ACA enhancement elements represents a serious risk. Major social programs tend to be insulated from repeal once many voters are beneficiaries.[59] The failed Trump administration attempt to repeal the ACA is a prime example. However, repealing a permanently authorized program is much more difficult than simply not reauthorizing a program set to expire. Unless there is a major change in attitude about the ACA among Republican leaders, reauthorization of ACA expansion provisions will be very difficult unless Democrats control the presidency and both houses of Congress in 2025.

300-Days Wrap
The first-300-days ACA record of the Biden administration receives a high mark. The administration moved swiftly to successfully support legislation and use executive action to expand the reach of the marketplaces and Medicaid in response to loss of coverage due to Covid.

There was a quick and systematic effort to replace Trump administration rules and guidance that sought to weaken ACA coverage. The *Texas v. California* case had already been argued before the Supreme Court, and the administration's formal notice of position change didn't address standing to sue, which became the salient issue. With other pending litigation the administration distanced itself from the legal positions of the Trump administration and successfully gained a pause.

The emerging Build Back Better Act contains several significant health provisions, especially continuation of the ARPA enhancements of the ACA to address the Medicaid gap, the subsidy cliff, and affordability of insurance in the marketplace for low-income families.

The following section assesses the future of the ACA and health policy during the Biden presidency and beyond. In the first 350 days, the Biden administration moved quickly and effectively to strengthen and expand the ACA. States refusing to expand Medicaid continue to limit the full scope of the act. Opposition groups are likely to continue legal challenges to the actions of the Biden administration with uncertain outcomes. Legislative corrections do not appear to have the support of any Republicans. With very thin margins in both Houses of Congress, it will be difficult to make significant adjustments to the nonbudgetary ACA provisions.

What Are the Expectations for the ACA's Second Decade?

Never make predictions, especially about the future.

—Casey Stengel

Scenarios

The ACA was enacted a little over a decade ago. We have traced its chronology, analyzed its various elements, and assessed its success to date. Where do we go from here? The ACA's second decade remains unknown but not unforeseeable. Path dependence has become a common concept in political science.[60] Once a policy is in place, its provisions shape what is likely and possible in the future. We have described the ACA's 2017 near-death experience and have watched a significant segment of Democratic party elites call for its replacement with something very different. Scenario planning enables us to examine possible futures in the face of an uncertain external environment.[61] This conclusion assesses three possible ACA scenarios over the next decade. What will be the likely status of the ACA as the country approaches the 2032 November election?

Our conceptual framework continues to be John Kingdon's model, which views the policy process as comprising three streams of activity: the *problem stream*, the *policy stream*, and the *political stream*.[62] The problem stream encompasses agenda setting, the policy stream involves the creation and refinement of policy ideas, and the political stream includes the building of majority coalitions at each stage.

Problem stream: agenda setting. Agendas expand and recede in the two-year election cycles and especially in presidential election years, with future general elections in 2024, 2028, and 2032. The outcomes are impossible to predict, but we know they will drive the agenda. There is no reason to conclude the partisan political divisions will radically change in the forthcoming election cycles.

There are two possible partisan configurations for each two-year period. Unified government exists when the same party controls the White House and both houses of Congress. In the forty years since 1980, unified government has only existed for six years for the Democrats and six years for the Republicans.[63] We don't know the precise configuration of the next decade, but mostly divided government is likely, with neither party controlling both the White House and both houses of Congress. Major legislation can be enacted during periods of divided government, but it is much harder. However, in a two-year period of unified government, high agenda policies have been passed. The ACA itself is such an example. Agendas in periods of divided government tend to be less ambitious.

Will the public and political elites regard health care problems as serious enough to justify a high place on the agenda? Will political leaders, especially the president, conclude additional health reform legislation is feasible enough to justify the political capital to place the issue high on the agenda? These will be the critical determinants of the place of health reform in the problem stream.

Policy stream: ideas are important. Chapter 1 described the long developmental history of policy ideas related to health reform. The national health insurance idea has persisted and been recycled as Medicare for All. The shift of the individual-mandate idea from conservative circles to a centerpiece of the liberal ACA is testament to the premise that there is little new under the sun in health policy. The public option was a new idea attempting to bridge the gap between those favoring more and those desiring less direct government involvement in financing and regulating health care.

It is unlikely major new health policy ideas will emerge in the policy stream in the coming decade. Rather, old ideas will be repackaged and minutely analyzed for effectiveness and feasibility. Think tanks across the political spectrum will generate reports, academic centers will construct even more sophisticated models, and advocates will be more inclined to shout across a philosophical divide than generate brand-new approaches. The health reform policy ideas currently on the table will be the ones debated in the decade to come.

Political stream: a majority coalition. During the second decade of the twenty-first century, American politics has been transformed into warring camps with few elected officials able to find firm political footing in the center. The liberal Republican and the conservative Democrat are endangered species, and voters are less likely to split their tickets than two decades ago. For the past several years majority coalitions have usually needed to come entirely from one party. It is hard to imagine a major change in health policy will be likely in any two-year period of divided government. For 2021 and 2022 the Democrats have extremely narrow majority margins in the House and Senate, as well as control of the White House. If the history of the last four decades is any guide, there might be one other two-year period over the next decade in which one party or the other has unified control and therefore a realistic opportunity to effect a significant health policy shift. In the current political environment, even minor policy modification is difficult to envision under divided government.

Three Scenarios for 2020s

Why three? We could do five or ten, but three captures the possible major alternatives for the ACA over the next decade. The three are labeled "the status quo," "a fundamental shift," and "incremental change."

Scenario One: The Status Quo

What does the status quo scenario look like? By the early 2030s the ACA is not much different than it is today. The BBBA with its ACA adjustments did not pass. A few holdout states have still not expanded Medicaid. There is a sharp dividing line at 400 percent of FPL for premium assistance. Those above the line without employment-based insurance continue to find ACA-compliant policies very expensive and tax credits unavailable. The share of the population uninsured remains at 10 to 12 percent.

Over the previous decade health reform legislation was not a high-priority agenda item for presidents and Congress. Neither the remaining uninsured nor the continued high system and rising out-of-pocket costs were sufficient to push additional health legislation high on the agenda.

Reform ideas continued to be analyzed and debated. Conservative scholars emphasized market-based reform approaches. Progressives argued the logic of expanding the social insurance principle for covering all citizens to achieve both comprehensive coverage and cost control. Other reformers sought modifications of the ACA. Breakthrough new ideas or even combinations of old ones never emerged.

A majority coalition to support any change never existed. The narrow window of opportunity in 2021 and 2022 closed and did not open again in the following decade.

Scenario Two: A Fundamental Shift

Scenario two envisions a fundamental shift in health policy. This may occur in one of two directions. We will first examine a form of Medicare for All representing a shift toward much greater government engagement. The second direction for major change is the opposite, with a focus on greater private market reliance and a diminished public-sector role, especially for the federal government.

Scenario two is predicated on significant changes in the health system and political environment causing reform to move to the top of the political agenda. In this scenario, both system costs and premium and out-of-pocket costs for individuals have risen to a perceived crisis level, and the uninsured share of the population has increased despite the existence of the ACA. Health financial and delivery system metrics are perceived as in crisis, as highlighted by newsworthy events.

The sharp partisan division of the early 2020s has continued, but one political party or the other managed to achieve unified government with congressional majorities for a period of two or four years. This allowed Congress to legislate a fundamental shift in health policy.

Scenario Two A: Medicare for All.

A strong unified government under the control of Democrats pushed a Medicare for All change expanding the role of government in the financing and delivery of health care during the decade. This policy idea builds on the Medicare principle of universal social insurance and replaces the ACA, Medicare, and Medicaid with a public financing and budgeting system while maintaining private ownership of medical facilities. Private health insurance is restricted. A Medicare-type administered payment system is utilized to control costs with out-of-pocket expenditure limits.

Jonathan Oberlander has referred to this as a pure Medicare for All reform.[64] It dramatically transforms the existing public-private mix. The federal government becomes the key financier and paymaster of all health delivery systems. The reorganized health system includes comprehensive benefits, limits cost sharing, provides universal eligibility, and eliminates most private insurance.[65] This is a basic reform model idea advanced since the early 1970s, when it was called national health insurance.

For decades Theodore Marmor has been a vocal advocate of a social insurance approach by expanding the idea beyond Medicare to include the entire population. He argues the fundamental principle of social insurance is to protect against financial risk and treat the entire population as the risk pool. Eligibility flows from citizenship, not income level.[66]

Jacob Hacker supports the basic idea of Medicare for All but cautions that the political hurdles are daunting. The shift from premiums, often mostly paid by employers, to a completely tax-funded system creates winners and losers, even if the ultimate level of spending is less. Interest group opposition would be fierce.[67]

Micah Johnson, Sanjay Kishore, and Donald Berwick analyzed various proposals and suggested a number of unresolved key design issues must be addressed before a bill might move forward. These include the role of private-sector insurance, payment methods, financing, and scope of covered services.[68]

What Oberlander called the hybrid model resembles actual Medicare today. A third of beneficiaries are in Medicare Advantage private plans, and all Part D prescription drug benefits are with private plans. The core idea is achievement of universal coverage utilizing a combination of public and private insurance similar to Medicare today rather than at its inception.[69] Sherry Glied and Jeanne Lambrew summarize the range of policy ideas in which Medicare or a Medicare-similar public option might exist in the marketplaces in competition with private plans. A key difference is the extent of eligibility for the public plan, including for those currently offered employment-based insurance.[70]

Either the pure or hybrid Medicare model represents a dramatic shift from the 2021 status quo. Progressives prefer the pure social insurance model but might settle for the hybrid in the hope it can be modified in the future. Both approaches have been widely debated, with the critical factor being the shape of a potential majority coalition in Congress. The success of Scenario Two A between 2021 and 2032 would be the result of progressives dominating the Democratic Party and achieving sufficient electoral success to create a majority coalition capable of supporting this change.

In the period leading to this fundamental shift, a consensus would be necessary among reformers around the exact nature of the proposal, in keeping with how the Massachusetts model became the consensus choice leading to the ACA in 2008.

Scenario Two B: market emphasis reform. The other fundamental-shift scenario envisions Republicans gaining strong unified control of the national government with an external environment conducive to health reform. In this scenario, the ACA remained unpopular among Republican core voters, even as a majority of voters viewed it positively. Without a resolution of fundamental cost and access problems, the various policy ideas found in the ACA replacement plans offered by Republicans in 2017, especially Graham-Cassidy, formed the nucleus of a market-centered approach with a sharply diminished role for government.

A Republican ACA replacement would transform Medicaid into a block grant rather than an entitlement, eliminate most of the insurance market regulations in the ACA, and fold Medicaid expansion and marketplace subsidy funds into a block grant for states to develop their own insurance marketplaces with little by way of federal rules or guidance. The health savings account rules would be modified to encourage major expansion of this use of pretax individual payment accounts.[71]

The Center for Health and Economy, a conservative think tank, offered an ACA alternative that aligns with previous Republican plans and could be a model for future legislation. It features replacement of ACA subsidies and Medicaid expansion funds with a grant to the states. It substitutes premium assistance for direct public program payments to providers. Most of the ACA insurance regulations are eliminated. The Center for Health and Economy analysis of the proposal projects more coverage and lower average premium cost.[72]

Opposition to the ACA was a central feature of Republican election campaigns since its enactment. The 2017 failure to repeal and replace the ACA was a debacle. The party had not coalesced around a single set of policy ideas for replacement. Conservative market-based policy ideas had been discussed for years, but a fundamental flaw exposed by the vetting of the proposals was that no plan seemed to leave most Americans better off than the ACA. Limiting the role of government, especially the federal government, and reducing federal health expenditures was the primary objective. It was difficult to shape an alternative approach with this constraint without leaving many in a worse financial or coverage position. Nevertheless, Republicans with unified government very nearly passed legislation that would not only repeal the ACA but make millions worse off than prior to the ACA enactment.

Before 2032 a return to unified Republican government could result in ACA repeal with a more market-based private insurance approach, significant reduction of the role of the federal government, and transformation of Medicaid into a block grant. Federal government health expenditures would decrease, but the number of uninsured would rise to greater than pre-ACA levels, with consumers paying more out of pocket. A stronger conservative elite consensus with public support would be needed to coalesce around a single market-oriented policy idea.

Both versions of the fundamental-shift scenario are politically feasible under conditions of strong unified government with consensus about the basics of a policy idea for replacing the ACA. Each fundamental-shift scenario is popular with a subset of the electorate and strongly opposed by others. Various provider interest groups are likely to oppose features of both, rendering approval difficult, even with unified majorities in Congress.

Scenario Three: Incremental Change
In the incremental change scenario, the ACA has solved just enough of the problems of insurance coverage and cost containment to show improvement in the key indicators. In the absence of a health policy crisis, it will be dif-

ficult to make the case for radical change. For Republicans, opposition to the ACA, rather than embrace of a clear set of policy alternatives, has been the driving force. For decades health reform has been a high agenda item for Democrats when they have enjoyed unified government. This has occurred in only three two-year periods in the past four decades. In 1993 and 1994 the Bill Clinton administration sought a comprehensive change, and congressional Democrats failed to agree among themselves on the best path forward. A decade and a half later, the Barack Obama administration successfully passed the ACA as reform legislation building on the existing system. The 2020 victory of President Biden is the third example.

For this scenario we assume divided, not unified, government will be the norm in the next decade. Interest in health reform legislation will remain high but difficult to achieve without unified government. Even incremental health policy initiatives only appear on the agenda under unified control of Congress and the presidency. With this constrained political environment, incremental change in the ACA is a feasible outcome and remains a satisfactory approach, if not the first preference, for many. Building a Democratic Party legislative majority coalition for ACA incremental changes is easier than effecting systemic change, such as Medicare for All.

The first two years of the Biden administration offered an opportunity for incremental change. If we assume passage of the Build Back Better Act in early 2022, much of the ACA incremental change agenda will have been accomplished with one major caveat. The key BBBA ACA provisions are scheduled to expire in 2025. The family glitch and the public option were not addressed. Permanent extension of the provisions will be the primary incremental strategy goal. If the BBBA does not become law in 2022, its provisions will constitute the core ACA incremental agenda for the rest of the decade.

With the Medicaid gap, the September 2021 BBBA draft envisioned a two-step process addressing the issue in nonexpansion states. Those in the gap would be able to purchase insurance in the marketplace with tax credits. Then, after 2025 special Medicaid program would be implemented for this population. Neither may be necessary if the remaining states accept Medicaid expansion. The final BBBA proposal approved by the House ended both the tax credit expansions and the Medicaid gap accommodation in 2025. Legislation to make the modifications permanent will be high on the reform agenda.[73]

Other potential incremental provisions include addressing the family glitch by basing eligibility for subsidies on cost of family member rather than individual plan, establishing continuous Medicaid eligibility for twelve months even if income changes, permanently extending CHIP, and extending full Medicaid postpartum benefits for a year.[74]

A second track is the use of administrative actions and rule-making authority to undo many of the Trump administration rules, such as those dealing with short-term policies and Medicaid work requirements. These include outreach expansion, modifying rules on topics, such as those dealing with short-term plans and Medicaid work requirements, and restoring original 1332 guiderail guidance.[75] New administrative rules do not require a legislative majority but are subject to easier modification by the next administration. A future Republican president might use rule-making authority to incrementally weaken the ACA.

Narrow majorities, the filibuster, limits on subjects for reconciliation, and the press of other agenda items may limit the ability to undertake even modest incremental adjustments in the first two years of the Biden term, despite a consensus on these ideas as important incremental ACA modifications.[76] The Build Back Better legislation contains a wide range of policy initiatives. Even with a consensus on the ACA provisions, the entire bill may fail in 2022.

Some or all of these incremental adjustments may not be enacted in the first two years of the Biden administration but will likely remain on the agenda for the next Congress, if Democrats retain majorities in both House and Senate. Without unified government, it seems unlikely any of the discussed legislative changes will occur during a period of divided control. These ACA incremental adjustment policy ideas will remain part of the ACA debate.

The public option. The establishment of a public option, not Medicare for All, will be the most debated issue in the coming decade. This modification sits on the border between incremental and fundamental change. A public option provision was not included in the BBBA.

Since the idea first emerged shortly before the ACA's enactment, there have been two versions. The initial conceptualization of the public option can be called the "competitive" version. This featured a public entity using Medicare rates and networks but remaining organizationally distinct. It was to be self-sustaining and open to anyone eligible for tax credits in the marketplace. While included in the House ACA bill in 2009, it was taken out of the Senate version. Proponents contended the public option could offer comprehensive coverage at lower premiums, because it was a nonprofit entity and utilized Medicare payment rates.

The "robust" version emerged in the 2020 presidential campaign as an alternative to Medicare for All proposals. Jacob Hacker characterized the reconstituted policy as "Public Option 2.0." It has the following features:[77]

- It creates a Medicare-like public insurance entity with similar networks and payments.
- It is available to anyone not covered by the existing public program with auto enrollment for the uninsured.
- Employers may enroll employees with payment to the entity based on payroll.

Advocates embraced the "trojan horse" characterization and contended it featured many of the positive elements of Medicare for All with a lower price tag and less political baggage.[78] Public Option 2.0 falls into the fundamental-shift scenario as a first cousin of the Medicare for All policy idea. While apparently more politically feasible, it carries many of the same enactment barriers.

The adoption of the "competitive" public option as part of the incremental change scenario is possible but a further political stretch. Critical design issues have emerged during discussion and analysis, casting some doubt on whether the "competitive" public option could achieve the cost-saving aspirations of its supporters. Matthew Fiedler contended the entity needed to set provider rates administratively, not by negotiation, and providers could not be allowed to accept private plan beneficiaries while excluding those from the public plan.[79]

In the coming decade Medicare for All advocates might see no reason to expend significant political capital to pass a competitive public option that they regard as a third-choice policy idea. In the past, provider interest groups opposed even the less robust competitive public option. The public option is a middle-ground compromise between the original ACA and Medicare for All, especially since the public option might eventually migrate to something close to Medicare. Sometimes middle-ground compromises are not satisfactory to either side, which is perhaps the case with the "competitive" public option. It will remain a subject of active discussion. Hacker argues a Public Option 2.0 is politically feasible if its advocates pursue a sophisticated advocacy campaign.[80]

States have been characterized as "laboratories of democracy." The ACA idea was first a state experiment in Massachusetts. Might states experiment with a public option as a stepping-stone to national use? The state of Washington has moved in this direction by establishing a state public option.[81] Nevada is close to adoption.[82] Colorado, New Mexico, and Oregon have considered a state public option. A 2021 study by Manatt Health Strategies compares various approaches states might undertake in adopting a public option. The authors conclude by pointing out the importance of understanding the affordability and access problems unique to the state and the type of public-option model best suited to address them.[83] A success story from one or two state public-option experiments might propel a national version. On the other hand, failure at the state level will cast doubt about the public option's viability.

Hacker and others will continue to advocate for a public option as part of an ACA incremental expansion, and while a supportive majority coalition will not likely be available in the first two years of the Biden Administration, it remains a viable addition at a later time.[84]

Which Scenario Is the Best Bet?

If you are prone to friendly wagers, which scenario should you pick as the most likely to describe the state of the ACA in 2032?

Majority coalitions are essential for policy enactment. If we define the decade by two-year cycles based on House elections, there will be ten from January 2021 to December 2032. Each will feature either unified or divided government. Major change is only likely to occur with unified government. How do we assess the probability of unified government existing over those ten cycles? Based on the history of the past four decades, divided government is likely most of the time.

Will health reform be high on the policy agenda with divided government? Rhetoric will continue, but the real agenda is shaped by what is possible. In the early 2010s, the GOP House majority regularly passed ACA repeal bills, but everyone recognized this as posturing, not real legislating. Kingdon observed that unresolved problems sometimes fade from prominence.[85] With many problems competing for attention, there are limits to the efforts exerted by groups and activists promoting solutions.[86] The very success of the ACA may limit the prospects for additional reform amid a crowded policy agenda.

We can expect the continued engagement of those in the health policy community with production of reports, books, and analyses. But if history is a useful guide, the focus will tend to be on advocating, defending, and criticizing existing ideas or minor variations of them. Twenty years ago, Hacker articulated a new idea for organizing and financing coverage: the public option. It was nearly included in the ACA and has been a central point of discussion among Democrats for the past decade. It has reached the status of an old idea. Maybe there will be a breakthrough new concept in the decade ahead, but the old ideas cover a wide range of possibilities. The short list of ideas is probably already on the table, although with most there is room for tinkering and refining.

What will happen in the political environment? This is a crucial unknown. Progressives foresee a demographic shift leading to a dominance of the national Democratic Party in the decades ahead.[87] Conservatives believe their current strength at the state and local levels outside major coastal metropolitan areas will enable them at a minimum to block progressive reform efforts.[88] Are both partially correct?

For progressives in the Democratic Party, Medicare for All is the Holy Grail. This represents a fundamental-shift scenario, and it is hard to foresee a transformation in the political environment over the next decade leading to its enactment. For conservative Republicans, a fundamental shift from a government-dominated health finance system to one organized by market principles is the ideal, but the analytic case for this idea has never demonstrated how it would leave the average citizen better off. Opposition to such a radical shift is likely to be overwhelming.

The ACA barely passed in 2010 when Democrats held a substantial majority in the House and a filibuster-proof majority in the Senate. It is a fair assumption the ACA in its current form would not have become law if the Democrats had only fifty-nine Senate votes in December 2009. Many reformers advocate a filibuster limit.[89] However, it is quite feasible to assume Republicans will have unified government at some point in the decade ahead. Without the filibuster, it would be easier for them to repeal the entire ACA and enact their fundamental-shift reform ideas.

Policy windows open infrequently and close quickly. They open as a result of a political shift creating the opportunity for a problem to be linked to a possible solution. As the legislative history of the ACA demonstrates, skillful leadership is often the essential catalyst for moving a bill through an open window in a timely fashion.

If you are going to make a bet on the future of the ACA, write your anticipated scenario on a piece of paper, seal it in an envelope, and mark it "Open in December 2032." Mine identifies number three, incremental change, as most likely. Eliminating the family glitch, subsidy cliff, and Medicaid gap, with broadened enrollment periods, will further significantly reduce but not eliminate the uninsured. For some, out-of-pocket costs will still be a burden. Surprise billing and some prescription drug costs may be restrained, releasing some of the pressure for larger changes.

There will still be some holdouts, but most states will have accepted Medicaid expansion. The public option is my question mark. Even a competitive public option requires legislation and cannot be accomplished by executive action. Interest group opposition will be fierce. The potential cost-containment features will probably not appear strong enough to overcome the resistance, unless Democratic unified government exists for at least another two-year window after 2024. The outcomes in state experiments might be a barometer of the public option's national acceptance.

A majority legislative coalition for even incremental ACA changes will require progressives and moderate Democrats to come to agreement on a path forward. The BBBA with its time-limited ACA enhancements may be perceived as a sufficient ACA enhancement, if the changes are made permanent by removing the 2025 expiration.

Campaign rhetoric often covers real differences with an assumption that everything is possible. Crafting legislation requires hard decisions on priorities. Among the choices may be expanding traditional Medicare by adding benefits and reducing the age of eligibility or incrementally increasing ACA benefits. In an ideal world, both are desirable. In the real world of budget constraints, both may not be possible in the short run.

The Affordable Care Act is an imperfect set of policies. It became law to expand health insurance coverage and restrain the growth of costs. It survived significant legal and political challenges in the first decade, made meaningful progress in achieving its goals, and ameliorated, but did not solve, the fundamental problems of health access and cost.

A policy window of opportunity requires sufficient interest in a perceived problem to propel an issue to a high place on the agenda. A set of policy ideas to address the problem needs to exist and be seen as viable. Finally, a legislative majority coalition must be present to enable legislation to emerge from Congress.

With Medicare and Medicaid, the Affordable Care Act is an essential part of the public policy structure for financing and organizing health care. Path dependence makes it likely debates and actions on health reform for the next decade will center on the Affordable Care Act, and it will be in place with some modifications in 2032.

Someone else will need to tell the continuing story in a decade.

Notes

1. Sara R. Collins et al., "An Early Look at the Potential Implications of the COVID-19 Pandemic for Health Insurance Coverage: Commonwealth Fund Health Care Poll: COVID-19, May–June 2020," Commonwealth Fund, June 23, 2020, www.commonwealthfund.org/publications/issue-briefs/2020/jun/implications-covid-19-pandemic-health-insurance-survey.

2. Rachel Schwab, Justin Giovannelli, and Kevin Lucia, "During the COVID-19 Crisis, State Health Insurance Marketplaces Are Working to Enroll the Uninsured," *Commonwealth Fund Blog*, May 19, 2020, www.commonwealthfund.org/blog/2020/during-covid-19-crisis-state-health-insurance-marketplaces-are-working-enroll-uninsured.

3. Katie Keith, "Access to ACA Coverage in the COVID-19 Crisis," *Health Affairs Blog*, July 1, 2020, www.healthaffairs.org/do/10.1377/hblog20200701.720915/full.

4. Aviva Aron-Dine, "Health Care Lifeline: The Affordable Care Act and the COVID-19 Pandemic: Testimony of Aviva Aron-Dine, Vice President for Health Policy, CBPP Before the House Energy and Commerce Subcommittee on Health," Center on Budget and Policy Priorities, September 23, 2020, https:///www.cbpp.org/sites/default/files/atoms/files/9-23-20health-testimony.pdf.

5. Tara Straw et al., "Health Provisions in House Relief Bill Would Improve Access to Health Coverage During COVID Crisis," Center on Budget Policies and Priorities, February 19, 2021, www.cbpp.org/sites/default/files/2-10-21health.pdf.

6. Kelly Moss et al., "The Families First Coronavirus Response Act: Summary of Key Provisions," Kaiser Family Foundation, March 23, 2020, www.kff.org/coronavirus-covid-19/issue-brief/the-families-first-coronavirus-response-act-summary-of-key-provisions.

7. Jack Hoadley, Katie Keith, and Kevin Lucia, "Unpacking the No Surprises Act: An Opportunity to Protect Millions," *Health Affairs Blog*, December 18, 2020, www.healthaffairs.org/do/10.1377/hblog20210104.961016/full.

8. Katie Keith, "Coverage Provisions in the 2021 Appropriations and COVID-19 Stimulus Package," *Health Affairs Blog*, January 4, 2021, www.healthaffairs.org/do/10.1377/hblog20210104.961016/full.

9. Helen Levy, Andrew Ying, and Nicholas Bagley, "What's Left of the Affordable Care Act? A Progress Report," *Russell Sage Foundation Journal of the Social Sciences* 6, no. 3 (July 2020): 42–66.

10. John E. McDonough, "Lost in the ACA: Bit Parts in a Landmark Law," *Journal of Health Politics, Policy and Law* 45, no. 4 (August 2020): 539–540.

11. Ibid., 535–536.

12. Jennifer Tolbert, Kendal Orgera, and Anthony Damico, "Key Facts About the Uninsured Population," Kaiser Family Foundation, November 6, 2020, www.kff.org/uninsured/issue-brief/key-facts-about-the-uninsured-population.

13. Benjamin Summers, "Health Insurance Coverage: What Comes After the ACA?," *Health Affairs* 39, no. 3 (March 2020): 453–461.

14. Rachel Garfield, Kendal Orgera, and Anthony Damico, "The Coverage Gap: Uninsured Poor Adults in States That Do Not Expand Medicaid," Kaiser Family Foundation, January 21, 2021, www.kff.org/medicaid/issue-brief/the-coverage-gap-uninsured-poor-adults-in-states-that-do-not-expand-medicaid.

15. Katherine Baicker and Benjamin D. Sommers, "Insurance Access and Health Care Outcomes," in *The Trillion Dollar Revolution: How the Affordable Care Act Transformed Politics, Law, and Health Care in America*, ed. Ezekiel J. Emanuel and Abbe R. Gluck (New York: Public Affairs Hachette Book Group, 2020), 209–224.

16. Aparna Soni, Laura R. Wherry, and Kosali I. Simon, "How Have ACA Insurance Expansions Affected Health Outcomes? Findings from the Literature," *Health Affairs* 39, no. 3 (March 2020): 371–378.

17. Madeline Guth, Rachel Garfield, and Robin Rudowitz, "The Effects of Medicaid Expansion Under the ACA: Updated Findings from a Literature Review," Kaiser Family Foundation, March 17, 2020, www.kff.org/medicaid/report/the-effects-of-medicaid-expansion-under-the-aca-updated-findings-from-a-literature-review.

18. Thomas Buchmueller and Helen Levy, "The ACA's Impact on Racial and Ethnic Disparities in Health Insurance Coverage and Access to Care," *Health Affairs* 39, no. 3 (March 2020): 395–402.

19. Melinda Beeuwkes Buntin and John A. Graves, "How the ACA Dented the Cost Curve," *Health Affairs* 39, no. 3 (March 2020): 403–412.

20. Joseph White, "Costs Versus Coverage, Then and Now," *Journal of Health Politics, Policy and Law* 45, no. 5 (August 2020): 817–830.

21. Carrie H. Colla and Jonathan Skinner, "Has the ACA Made Health Care More Affordable?" in *The Trillion Dollar Revolution: How the Affordable Care Act Transformed Politics, Law, and Health Care in America*, ed. Ezekiel J. Emanuel and Abbe R. Gluck (New York: Public Affairs, 2020), 250–263.

22. Sherry A. Glied, Sara R. Collins, and Saunders Lin, "Did the ACA Lower Americans' Financial Barriers to Health Care?," *Health Affairs* 39, no. 3 (March 2020): 379–386.

23. Sara Collins, Munira Z. Gunja, and Gabriella N. Aboulafia, "U.S. Health Insurance Coverage in 2020: A Looming Crisis in Affordability: Findings from the Commonwealth Fund Biennial Health Insurance Survey, 2020," Commonwealth Fund, August 19, 2020, www.commonwealthfund.org/publications/issue-briefs/2020/aug/looming-crisis-health-coverage-2020-biennial.

24. Timothy S. Jost, "President Biden Announces Priorities for Medicaid, the Affordable Care Act, Women's Health, and COVID-19," *Commonwealth Fund*

Blog, February 4, 2021, www.commonwealthfund.org/blog/2021/president-biden-announces-priorities-medicaid-affordable-care-act-womens-health-and-covid.

25. Katie Keith, "Biden Executive Order to Reopen HealthCare.gov, Make Other Changes," *Health Affairs Blog*, January 29, 2021, www.healthaffairs.org/do/10.1377/hblog20210129.998616/full.

26. The reconciliation process allows for expedited consideration of certain tax, spending, and debt-limit legislation. In the Senate, reconciliation bills aren't subject to filibuster, and the scope of amendments is limited, giving this process real advantages for enacting controversial budget and tax measures.

27. Katie Keith, "The American Rescue Plan Expands the ACA," *Health Affairs* 40, no. 5 (May 2021): 1–2.

28. Edwin Park and Sabrina Corlette, "American Rescue Plan Act: Health Coverage Provisions Explained," Georgetown Health Policy Institute, March 2021, https:///ccf.georgetown.edu/wp-content/uploads/2021/03/American-Rescue-Plan-signed-fix-2.pdf.

29. Daniel McDermott, Cynthia Cox, and Krutika Amin, "Impact of Key Provisions of the American Rescue Plan Act of 2021 COVID-19 Relief on Marketplace Premiums," Kaiser Family Foundation, March 15, 2021, www.kff.org/health-reform/issue-brief/impact-of-key-provisions-of-the-house-covid-19-relief-proposal-on-marketplace-premiums.

30. "2021 Final Marketplace Special Enrollment Period Report," US Department of Health and Human Services, September 15, 2021, www.hhs.gov/sites/default/files/2021-sep-final-enrollment-report.pdf.

31. Sara Rosenbaum, "Biden Administration Begins Process of Rolling Back Approval for Medicaid Work Experiments, but Supreme Courts Hangs On," *Commonwealth Fund Blog*, April 8, 2021, www.commonwealthfund.org/blog/2021/biden-administration-begins-process-rolling-back-approval-medicaid-work-experiments.

32. Christopher Brown, "HHS Revokes Medicaid Work Requirements in Three More States," *Bloomberg Law*, August 11, 2021, https://news.bloomberglaw.com/health-law-and-business/hhs-revokes-medicaid-work-requirements-in-three-more-states.

33. Dan Diamond, "Biden Officials Rescind Trump's Okay for Texas's $100 Billion-Plus Medicaid Plan," *Washington Post*, April 16, 2021, www.washingtonpost.com/health/2021/04/16/biden-rejects-texas-medicaid-plan.

34. Eli Kirshbaum, "Paxton's Judicial Victory Has Little Impact on Texas's Medicaid 1115 Waiver, Says Expert," State of Reform, August 25, 2021, https://stateofreform.com/featured/2021/08/paxtons-judicial-victory-has-little-impact-on-texass-medicaid-1115-waiver-says-expert.

35. Madeline Guth, Robin Rudowitz, and MaryBeth Musumeci, "Tennessee & Other Medicaid 1115 Waiver Activity: Implications for the Biden Administration," Kaiser Family Foundation, January 22, 2021, www.kff.org/medicaid/issue-brief/tennessee-other-medicaid-1115-waiver-activity-implications-for-the-biden-administration.

36. Andy Schneider and Allexa Gardner, "The Tennessee Waiver: Block Grant, Aggregate Cap, or Windfall?" Georgetown University Health Policy Institute: Center for Children and Families, January 21, 2021, https://ccf.georgetown.edu/2021/01/21/the-tennessee-waiver-block-grant-aggregate-cap-or-windfall.

37. Edwin Park, "Federal Government Accepting Public Comments on Tennessee Medicaid Block Grant Waiver Restricting Access to Prescription Drugs," Georgetown University Health Policy Institute: Center for Children and Families, August 19, 2021, https://ccf.georgetown.edu/2021/08/19/federal-government-accepting-public-comments-on-tennessee-medicaid-block-grant-waiver-restricting-access-to-prescription-drugs.

38. "State Innovation Waivers: State-Based Reinsurance Programs," CCIIO Data Brief Series, CMS Center for Consumer Information & Insurance Oversight, August 2021, www.cms.gov/CCIIO/Programs-and-Initiatives/State-Innovation-Waivers/Downloads/1332-Data-Brief-Aug2021.pdf.

39. Katie Keith, "Latest on Section 1332 Waivers: New Approvals, Impact of Reinsurance, and More," *Health Affairs Blog*, August 17, 2021, www.healthaffairs.org/do/10.1377/hblog20210817.894853/full.

40. Alexandra Gale and Stephanie Kennan, "The Courts and Healthcare Policy—August 2021," *JDSupra*, August 10, 2021, www.jdsupra.com/legalnews/the-courts-and-healthcare-policy-august-7729919; Katie Keith, "CMS Announces 60-Day Comment Period on Georgia's Section 1332 Waiver," *Health Affairs Blog*, November 12, 2021, www.healthaffairs.org/do/10.1377/hblog20211112.40785/full/.

41. The case is *Kelley v. Becerra*.

42. Nicholas Bagley, "The Next Major Challenge to the Affordable Care Act," *The Atlantic*, June 18, 2021, www.theatlantic.com/ideas/archive/2021/06/next-major-challenge-affordable-care-act/619159; Ian Millhiser, "There's a New Lawsuit Attacking Obamacare—and It's a Serious Threat," *Vox*, April 2, 2021, www.vox.com/2021/4/2/22360341/obamacare-lawsuit-supreme-court-little-sisters-kelley-becerra-reed-oconnor-nondelegation.

43. Timothy Jost, "Is the Affordable Care Act's Preventive Services Mandate Constitutional?," *Commonwealth Fund Blog*, September 13, 2021, www.commonwealthfund.org/blog/2021/is-aca-preventive-services-mandate-constitutional.

44. Katie Keith, "Biden Justice Department Formally Changes Positions in *California v. Texas*," *Health Affairs Blog*, February 12, 2021, www.healthaffairs.org/do/10.1377/hblog20210212.442587/full.

45. Lawrence O. Gostin and Alexandra Finch, "The Affordable Care Act Lives On: Now It Must Be Strengthened and Expanded," *Milbank Quarterly: Quarterly Opinion*, June 29, 2021, www.milbank.org/quarterly/opinions/the-affordable-care-act-lives-on-now-it-must-be-strengthened-and-expanded.

46. For useful summaries of pending cases, see Katie Keith, "ACA Litigation Round-Up, Part 1: Fight over Reimbursements for Cost-Sharing Reductions Continues," *Health Affairs Blog*, April 7, 2021, www.healthaffairs.org/do/10.1377/hblog20210407.782901/full; Katie Keith, "ACA Litigation Round-Up, Part 2: Which 2019 Payment Rule Changes Were Legal? Plus, More from Judge O'Connor on the ACA," *Health Affairs Blog*, April 20, 2021, www.healthaffairs.org/do/10.1377/hblog20210420.44231/full; Gale and Kennan, "The Courts and Healthcare Policy."

47. For in-depth assessment of the history of this issue, see Katie Keith, "HHS Will Enforce Section 1557 to Protect LGBTQ People from Discrimination," *Health Affairs Blog*, May 11, 2021, www.healthaffairs.org/do/10.1377/hblog20210511.619811/full.

48. For example, see Linda J. Blumberg and John Holahan, "After *King v. Burwell*: Next Steps for the Affordable Care Act," *The Urban Institute*, August 2015, https://www.urban.org/sites/default/files/publication/65196/2000328-After-King-v.-Burwell-Next-Steps-for-the-Affordable-Care-Act.pdf.

49. Katie Keith, "House Democrats Introduce New Coverage Bill," *Health Affairs Blog*, June 24, 2020, https://www.healthaffairs.org/do/10.1377/hblog20200624.197845/full/.

50. Katie Keith, "Final Coverage Provisions in the America Rescue Plan and What Comes Next," *Health Affairs Blog*, March 11, 2021, https://www.healthaffairs.org/do/10.1377/hblog20210311.725837/full/.

51. Michael Karpman and Stephen Zuckerman, "The Uninsured Rate Held Steady During the Pandemic as Public Coverage Increased," *The Urban Institute*, August 2021, https://www.urban.org/research/publication/uninsurance-rate-held-steady-during-pandemic-public-coverage-increased.

52. Tony Romm, Seung Min Kim, and Jeff Stein, "Senate Democrats Announce Plans for $3.5 Trillion Budget Package to Expand Medicare, Advance Biden Priorities," *Washington Post*, July 13, 2021, https://www.washingtonpost.com/us-policy/2021/07/13/infrastructure-senate-white-house/.

53. Katie Keith, "Unpacking the Coverage Provisions in the House's Build Back Better Act," *Health Affairs Blog*, September 12, 2021, https://www.healthaffairs.org/do/10.1377/hblog20210912.160204/full/.

54. Sarah Lueck, "House Bill's Permanent Marketplace Improvements Would Expand Affordable Coverage," *Center for Budget and Policy Priorities*, September 17, 2021, www.cbpp.org/blog/house-bills-permanent-marketplace-improvements-would-expand-affordable-coverage.

55. Judith Solomon, "Build Back Better Legislation Would Close the Medicaid Coverage Gap," *Center for Budget and Policy Priorities*, September 10, 2021, www.cbpp.org/research/health/build-back-better-legislation-would-close-the-medicaid-coverage-gap.

56. Dylan Scott, "Why Democrats' Ambitions for Health Care Are Shrinking Rapidly," *Vox*, May 7, 2021, www.vox.com/policy-and-politics/22422793/joe-biden-health-care-plan-obamacare-medicare-public-option.

57. Tony Romm, Sean Sullivan, and Tyler Pager, "Biden Unveils $1.75 Trillion Spending Plan, but Divisions Delay Economic Agenda," *Washington Post*, October 28, 2021, www.washingtonpost.com/politics/biden-to-announce-democratic-agreement-on-social-spending-deal/2021/10/28/2781863c-37d3-11ec-91dc-551d44733e2d_story.html.

58. Robert Baird, "Inside the Democrats' Battle to Build Back Better," *New Yorker*, November 8, 2021, www.newyorker.com/news/the-political-scene/inside-the-democrats-battle-to-build-back-better.

59. Jacob Hacker and Paul Pierson, "Policy Feedback in an Age of Polarization," *Annals of the American Academy of Political and Social Science* 685, no. 1 (September 2019): 8–28.

60. David Wilsford, "Path Dependency, or Why History Makes It Difficult but Not Impossible to Reform Health Care Systems in a Big Way," *Journal of Public Policy* 14, no. 3 (July 1994): 251–283.

61. Pierre Wack, "Scenarios: Uncharted Waters Ahead," *Harvard Business Review* (September–October 1985): 73–89.

62. John Kingdon, *Agendas, Alternatives, and Public Policies*, 2nd ed. (New York: Harper Collins, 1995).

63. Democrats: 1993–1994, 2009–2010, 2021–2023; Republicans: 2003–2007, 2017–2019.

64. Jonathan Oberlander, "Navigating the Shifting Terrain of US Health Care Reform—Medicare for All, Single Payer, and the Public Option," *Milbank Quarterly* 97, no. 4 (December 2019): 939–953.

65. Micah Johnson, Sanjay Kishore, and Donald Berwick, "Medicare for All: An Analysis of Key Policy Issues," *Health Affairs* 39, no. 1 (January 2020): 133–141.

66. Theodore R. Marmor, "Social Insurance and American Health Care: Principles and Paradoxes," *Journal of Health Politics, Policy and Law* 43, no. 6 (December 2018): 1013–1024.

67. Jacob Hacker, "From the ACA to Medicare for All?," in Emanuel and Gluck, *Trillion Dollar Revolution*, 333–348.

68. Johnson, Kishore, and Berwick, "Medicare for All," 133–141.

69. Mark Schlesinger and Jacob S. Hacker, "Secret Weapon: The 'New' Medicare as a Route to Health Security," *Journal of Health Politics, Policy and Law* 32, no. 2 (2007): 247–291.

70. Sherry A. Glied and Jeanne M. Lambrew, "How Democratic Candidates for the Presidency in 2020 Could Choose Among Public Health Insurance Plans," *Health Affairs* 37, no. 12 (December 2018): 2084–2091.

71. Jeff Wurzberg, "Republican Study Committee Releases Affordable Care Act Replacement Plan," *Health Law Pulse*, October 25, 2019, www.thehealthlawpulse.com/2019/10/republican-study-committee-releases-affordable-care-act-replacement-plan.

72. "The Health Care Choices Proposal," Center for Health and Economy, October 2020, https://healthandeconomy.org/the-health-care-choices-proposal-2.

73. Katie Keith, "House Passes Build Back Better Act,"*Health Affairs Blog*, November 23, 2021, www.healthaffairs.org/do/10.1377/hblog20211123.122022/full/.

74. Christina L. Goe and Dania Palanker, "ACA 'Family Glitch' Increases Health Care Costs for Millions of Low- and Middle-Income Families," Commonwealth Fund, April 22, 2021, www.commonwealthfund.org/blog/2021/aca-family-glitch-increases-health-care-costs-millions-low-and-middle-income-families; Jennifer Wagner and Judith Solomon, "Continuous Eligibility Keeps People Insured and Reduces Costs," Center on Budget and Policy Priorities, May 4, 2021, https://www.cbpp.org/sites/default/files/5-4-21health.pdf; Katie Keith, "Unpacking the Coverage Provisions in the House's Build Back Better Act." Health Affairs Blog, September 12, 2021, www.healthaffairs.org/do/10.1377/hblog20210912.160204/full.

75. Katie Keith, "The Affordable Care Act in the Biden Era: Identifying Federal Priorities for Administrative Action," Commonwealth Fund, May 28, 2021, www.commonwealthfund.org/publications/issue-briefs/2021/may/affordable-care-act-biden-era-federal-priorities.

76. Heather Caygle and Alice Miranda Ollstein, "Democrats Reopen Old Health Care Wounds with $3.5T Mega-Bill On the Line," *Politico*, September 8, 2021, www.politico.com/news/2021/09/08/democrats-medicare-spending-510456; Rachel Roubein, "The Health 202: Democrats Have Three Weeks to Get Their Health Game On," *Washington Post*, August 26, 2021, www.washingtonpost.com/politics/2021/08/26/health-202-democrats-have-three-weeks-get-their-health-game; Dylan Scott, "Why Democrats' Ambitions for Health Care Are Shrinking Rapidly," *Vox*, May 7, 2021, www.vox.com/policy-and-politics/22422793/joe-biden-health-care-plan-obamacare-medicare-public-option.

77. Jacob Hacker, "Between the Waves: Building Power for a Public Option," *Journal of Health Politics, Policy and Law* 46, no. 4 (August 2021): 535–547.

78. Ezra Tanen, "Will the Public Option Provide Universal Access to Affordable Health Insurance?," *Georgetown Journal on Poverty Law & Policy*, November 3, 2020, www.law.georgetown.edu/poverty-journal/blog/will-the-public-option-provide-universal-access-to-affordable-health-insurance.

79. Matthew Fiedler, "Designing a Public Option That Would Reduce Health Care Provider Prices," Brookings Institution, May 5, 2021, www.brookings.edu/essay/designing-a-public-option-that-would-reduce-health-care-provider-prices.

80. Hacker, "Between the Waves."

81. Sarah Kliff, "The Lessons of Washington State's Watered Down 'Public Option,'" *New York Times*, June 27, 2019, www.nytimes.com/2019/06/27/upshot/washington-state-weakened-public-option-.html.

82. Dylan Scott, "Nevada Is on the Verge of Passing a Public Option," *Vox*, May 19, 2021, www.vox.com/policy-and-politics/2021/5/19/22442477/nevada-public-option-health-care.

83. Manatt Health Strategies, "State Public Options: Comparing Models from Across the Country," California Health Care Foundation, March 2021, www.chcf.org/wp-content/uploads/2021/03/StatePublicOptionsComparingModelsAcrossCountry.pdf.

84. Jacob Hacker, "Medicare for More—Why We Still Need a Public Option and How to Get There," *New England Journal of Medicine* 385, no. 12: 1060–1062.

85. Kingdon, *Agendas, Alternatives, and Public Policies*, 103–104.

86. Scott, "Why Democrats' Ambitions for Health Care Are Shrinking Rapidly."

87. Paul Waldman, "Is the Emerging Democratic Majority Finally Coming to Pass?," *American Prospect*, August 11, 2019, https://prospect.org/power/emerging-democratic-majority-finally-coming-pass; Rob Griffin, William H. Frey, and Ruy Teixeira, "America's Electoral Future: The Coming Generational Transformation," Brookings Institution, October 19, 2020, www.brookings.edu/research/americas-electoral-future-the-coming-generational-transformation.

88. Ed Kilgore, "The Future Could Actually Be Bright for Republicans," *New York Magazine*, May 20, 2021, https://nymag.com/intelligencer/2021/05/the-future-could-actually-be-bright-for-republicans.html.

89. Mel Barnes et al., "Filibuster Reform Is Coming—Here's How," Brookings Institution, September 13, 2021, www.brookings.edu/research/fiilibuster-reform-is-coming-heres-how.

Bibliography

Agarwal, Sumit D., and Benjamin D. Sommers. "Insurance Coverage After Job Loss—The Importance of the ACA During the Covid-Associated Recession." *New England Journal of Medicine* 383, no. 17 (October 22, 2020): 1603–1606.
Alter, Jonathan. *The Promise: President Obama, Year One.* New York: Simon & Schuster, 2010.
Altman, Stuart, and David Shactman. *Power, Politics, and Universal Health Care: The Inside Story of a Century-Long Battle.* New York: Prometheus Books, 2011.
Anderson, Gerard F., Uwe E. Reinhardt, Peter S. Hussey, and Varduhi Petrosyan. "It's the Prices, Stupid: Why the United States Is So Different from Other Countries." *Health Affairs* 22, no. 3 (May/June 2003): 89–105.
Bagley, Nicholas. "Three Words and the Future of the Affordable Care Act." *Journal of Health Politics, Policy and Law* 40, no. 3 (June 2015): 589–597.
Bagley, Nicholas, and Helen Levy. "Essential Health Benefits and the Affordable Care Act: Law and Process." *Journal of Health Politics, Policy and Law* 39, no. 2 (April 2014): 445–449.
Beland, Daniel, Philip Rocco, and Alex Waddan. *Obamacare Wars: Federalism, State Politics, and the Affordable Care Act.* Lawrence: University of Kansas Press, 2016.
Blendon, Robert, Mollyann Brodie, John M. Benson, Drew E. Altman, and Tami Buhr. "Americans' Views of Health Care Costs, Access, and Quality." *Milbank Quarterly* 84, no. 4 (2006): 624–657.
Blumenthal, David. "Employer-Sponsored Health Insurance in the United States—Origins and Implications." *New England Journal of Medicine* 355 (July 6, 2006): 83.
Blumenthal, David, and Melinda Abrams. "The Affordable Care Act at 10 Years—Payment and Delivery System Reforms." *New England Journal of Medicine* 382, no. 11 (March 12, 2020): 1057–1063.
Blumenthal, David, and James A. Morone. *The Heart of Power: Health and Politics in the Oval Office.* Berkeley: University of California Press, 2009.

Brasfield, James. *Health Policy: The Decade Ahead.* Boulder, CO: Lynne Rienner, 2011.

Brasfield, James. "The Politics of Ideas: Where Did the Public Option Come From and Where Is It Going?" *Journal of Health Politics, Policy and Law* 36, no. 3 (June 2011): 455–460.

Brodie, Mollyann, Elizabeth C. Hamel, Ashley Kirzinger, and Drew Altman. "The Past, Present, and Possible Future of Public Opinion on the ACA." *Health Affairs* 39, no. 3 (March 2020): 462–470.

Brodie, Mollyann, Elizabeth C. Hamel, Ashley Kirzinger, and Bianca DiJulio. "Partisanship, Polling, and the Affordable Care Act." *Public Opinion Quarterly* 83, no 2 (summer 2019): 423–449.

Brown, Lawrence D., and Michael S. Sparer. "Poor Program's Progress: The Unanticipated Politics of Medicaid Policy." *Health Affairs* 22, no. 1 (January–February 2003): 31–44.

Buntin, Melinda Beeuwkes, and John A. Graves. "How the ACA Dented the Cost Curve." *Health Affairs* 39, no. 3 (March 2020): 403–412.

Butler, Stuart M. "Evolving Beyond Traditional Employer-Sponsored Health Insurance." Brookings Institution Hamilton Project. May 2007. www.hamiltonproject.org/assets/legacy/files/downloads_and_links/Evolving_Beyond_Traditional_Employer-Sponsored_Health_Insurance.pdf.

Campbell, Andrea Louise. "The Affordable Care Act and Mass Policy Feedbacks." *Journal of Health Politics, Policy and Law* 45, no. 4 (August 2020): 567–580.

Cannan, John. "A Legislative History of the Affordable Care Act: How Legislative Procedure Shapes Legislative History." *Law Library Journal* 105, no. 2 (2013): 131–173.

Cohen, Alan B., David C Colby, Keith Wailoo, and Julian E. Zelizer, eds. *Medicare and Medicaid at 50: America's Entitlement Programs in the Age of Affordable Care.* New York: Oxford University Press, 2015.

Cohn, Jonathan. "How They Did It: The Inside Account of Health Reform's Triumph." *New Republic.* June 10, 2010. https://newrepublic.com/article/75077/how-they-did-it.

Collins, Sara R., Cathy Schoen, Karen Davis, Anne K. Gauthier, and Stephen C. Schoenbaum. "A Roadmap to Health Insurance for All: Principles for Reform." Commonwealth Fund. October 2007. https://www.commonwealthfund.org/publications/fund-reports/2007/oct/roadmap-health-insurance-all-principles-reform.

Connolly, Ceci. "The Rescue: Obama's Last Chance." Chapter 4 in *Landmark: The Inside Story of America's New Health-Care Law and What It Means for Us All*, ed. Staff of the Washington Post. New York: Public Affairs Press, 2010.

Cutler, David. "How Health Care Reform Must Bend the Cost Curve." *Health Affairs* 29, no. 6 (June 2010): 1131–1135.

Davis, Karen. National Health Insurance: Benefits, Costs, and Consequences. Washington, DC: Brookings Institution, 1975.

Duffy, Thomas P. "The Flexner Report—100 Years Later." *Yale Journal of Biological Medicine* 84, no. 3 (September 2011): 269–276.

Enthoven, Alain. "The History and Principles of Managed Competition." *Health Affairs* 12 (Suppl. 1) (1993): 24–48.

Enthoven, Alain, and Richard Kronick. "A Consumer Choice Health Plan for the 1990s." Parts I and II. *New England Journal of Medicine* 320, no. 5, and 320, no. 12 (January 1989): 29–37 and 94–101.

Feder, Judith. "Medicare Implementation and the Policy Process." *Journal of Health Politics, Policy and Law* 2, no. 2 (summer 1977): 173–189.

Fiedler, Matthew. "The ACA's Individual Mandate in Retrospect: What Did It Do and Where Do We Go from Here?" *Health Affairs* 39, no. 3 (March 2020): 429–435.

Finbow, Robert. "Presidential Leadership or Structural Constraints? The Failure of President Carter's Health Insurance Proposals." *Presidential Studies Quarterly* 28, no. 1 (winter 1998): 169–189.

Frean, Molly, Jonathan Gruber, and Benjamin D. Sommers. "Premium Subsidies, the Mandate, and Medicaid Expansion: Coverage Effects of the Affordable Care Act." *Journal of Health Economics* 53 (May 2017): 72–88.

Furman, Jason, ed. *Who Has the Cure? Hamilton Project Ideas on Health Care.* Washington, DC: Brookings Institution, 2009.

Garthwaite, Craig, and John A. Graves. "Success and Failure in the Insurance Exchanges." *New England Journal of Medicine* 376, no. 10 (March 9, 2017): 907–910.

Gawande, Atkul. "Two Hundred Years of Surgery." *New England Journal of Medicine* 366, no. 18 (May 3, 2012): 1716–1723.

Ginsburg, Paul. "Altering the Tax Treatment of Employment-Based Health Plans." *Milbank Memorial Fund Quarterly: Health and Society* 59, no. 2 (spring 1981): 224–255.

Ginsburg, Paul, and Kenneth Thorpe. "Can All-Payer Rate Setting and the Competitive Strategy Coexist?" *Health Affairs* 11, no. 2 (summer 1992): 73–86.

Glied, Sherry A., Jacob Hartz, and Genessa Giorgi. "Consider It Done? The Likely Efficacy of Mandates for Health Insurance." *Health Affairs* 26, no. 6 (November–December 2007): 1612–1621.

Gordon, Robert J. *The Rise and Fall of American Growth: The U.S. Standard of Living Since the Civil War.* Princeton, NJ: Princeton University Press, 2016.

Griffith, Kevin, David K. Jones, and Benjamin D. Sommers. "Diminishing Insurance Choices in the Affordable Care Act Marketplaces: A County-Based Analysis." *Health Affairs* 37, no. 10 (October 2018): 1678–1684.

Grogan, Colleen. "Medicaid's Post-ACA Paradoxes." *Journal of Health Politics, Policy and Law* 45, no. 4 (August 2020): 617–632.

Grogan, Colleen, and Eric Patashnik. "Between Welfare Medicine and Mainstream Entitlement: Medicaid at the Political Crossroads." *Journal of Health Politics, Policy and Law* 28, no. 5 (October 2003): 829–836.

Gruber, Jonathan. "Taking Massachusetts National: Incremental Universalism for the United States." In *Who Has the Cure? Hamilton Project Ideas on Health Care*, ed. Jason Furman, 121–142. Washington, DC: Brookings Institution Press, 2008.

Hacker, Jacob. "Between the Waves: Building Power for a Public Option." *Journal of Health Politics, Policy and Law* 46, no. 4 (August 2021): 535–547.

Hacker, Jacob. "The Case for Public Plan Choice in National Health Reform: Key to Cost Control and Quality Coverage." Institute for America's Future. 2008. http://citeseerx.ist.psu.edu/viewdoc/download?doi=10.1.1.525.223&rep=rep1&type=pdf.

Hacker, Jacob. *The Road to Nowhere: The Genesis of President Clinton's Plan for Health Security.* Princeton, NJ: Princeton University Press, 1997.

Hacker, Jacob. "The Road to Somewhere: Why Health Reform Happened: Or, Why Political Scientists Who Write About Public Policy Shouldn't Assume They Know How to Shape It." *Perspectives on Politics* 8, no. 3 (September 2010): 861–876.

Hacker, Jacob, and Paul Pierson. "The Dog Almost Barked: What the ACA Repeal Fight Says About the Resilience of the American Welfare State." *Journal of Health Politics, Policy and Law* 43, no. 4 (August 2018): 551–577.

Himmelstein, David, and Steffie Woolhandler. "A National Health Program for the United States: A Physicians' Proposal." *New England Journal of Medicine* 320 (1989): 102–108.

Hussey, Peter, Christine Eibner, M. Susan Ridgely, and Elizabeth A. McGlynn. "Controlling U.S. Health Care Spending: Separating Promising from Unpromising Approaches." *New England Journal of Medicine* 361, no. 22 (November 26, 2009): 2109–2112.

Institute of Medicine. *Essential Health Benefits: Balancing Coverage and Cost*. Washington, DC: National Academies Press, 2012.

Jacobs, Lawrence, and Suzanne Mettler. "What Health Reform Tells Us About American Politics." *Journal of Health Politics, Policy and Law* 45, no. 4 (August 2020): 581–594.

Jacobs, Lawrence, and Suzanne Mettler. "When and How New Policy Creates New Politics: Examining the Feedback Effects of the Affordable Care Act on Public Opinion." *Perspectives on Politics* 16, no. 2 (June 2018): 345–363.

Jacobs, Lawrence, Suzanne Mettler, and Ling Zhu. "Affordable Care Act Moving to a New Stage of Public Acceptance." *Journal of Health Politics, Policy and Law* 44, no. 6 (December 2019): 911–918.

Jacobs, Lawrence R., and Robert Y. Shapiro. "Don't Blame the Public for Failed Health Care Reform." *Journal of Health Politics, Policy and Law* 20, no. 2 (summer 1995): 411–424.

Jacobs, Lawrence, and Theda Skocpol. *Health Care Reform and American Politics: What Everyone Needs to Know*. 3rd ed. New York: Oxford University Press, 2016.

Jones, David K. *Exchange Politics: Opposing Obamacare in Battleground States*. New York: Oxford University Press, 2013.

Jones, David K., Katharine W. V. Bradley, and Jonathan Oberlander. "Pascal's Wager: Health Insurance Exchanges, Obamacare, and the Republican Dilemma." *Journal of Health Politics, Policy and Law* 39, no. 1 (February 2014): 97–137.

Jones, David K., Michael K. Gusmano, Pamela Nadash, and Edward Alan Miller. "Undermining the ACA Through the Executive Branch and Federalism: What the Trump Administration's Approach to Health Reform Means for Older Americans." *Journal of Aging and Social Policy* 30, no. 3–4 (2018): 282–299.

Jost, Timothy Stoltzfus, and Katie Keith. "ACA Litigation: Politics Pursued Through Other Means." *Journal of Health Politics, Policy and Law* 45, no. 4 (August 2020): 485–499.

Joynt Maddox, Karen E., John Orav, Jie Zheng, and Arnold M. Epstein. "Evaluation of Medicare's Bundled Payments Initiative for Medical Conditions." *New England Journal of Medicine* 379, no. 3 (July 19, 2018): 260–269.

Kingdon, John. *Agendas, Alternatives, and Public Policies*. 2nd ed. New York: Harper Collins, 1995.

Law, Sylvia A. *Blue Cross: What Went Wrong?* 2nd ed. New Haven, CT: Yale University Press, 1976.

Lipton-Lubet, Sarah. "Contraceptive Coverage Under the Affordable Care Act: Dueling Narratives and Their Policy Implications." *Journal of Gender, Social Policy & the Law* 22, no. 2 (2014): 343–385.

Marmor, Theodore R. "Health Reform 2010: The Missing Philosophical Premises in the Long-Running Health Care Debate." *Journal of Health Politics, Policy and Law* 36, no. 3 (June 2011): 567–570.

Marmor, Theodore R. *The Politics of Medicare*. 2nd ed. New York: Aldine, 2000.

Marmor, Theodore R. "Social Insurance and American Health Care: Principles and Paradoxes." *Journal of Health Politics, Policy and Law* 43, no. 6 (December 2018): 1013–1024.

May, Peter J. "Implementation Failures Revisited: Policy Regime Perspectives." *Public Policy and Administration* 30, no. 3–4 (2015): 277–299.

May, Peter J., and Ashley E. Jochim. "Policy Regime Perspectives: Policies, Politics, and Governing." *Policy Studies Journal* 41, no. 3 (2013): 426–452.
Mayes, Rick. *Universal Coverage: The Elusive Quest for National Health Insurance.* Ann Arbor: University of Michigan Press, 2004.
Mazmanian, Daniel, and Paul Sabatier. *Implementation and Public Policy.* Glendale, IL: Scott, Foresman, 1983.
McDonough, John E. *Inside National Health Reform.* Berkeley: University of California Press, 2011.
McDonough, John E. "Lost in the ACA: Bit Parts in a Landmark Law." *Journal of Health Politics, Policy and Law* 45, no. 4 (August 2020): 539–540.
McDonough, John E., Brian Rosman, Mehreen Butt, Lindsey Tucker, and Lisa Kaplan Howe. "Massachusetts Health Reform Implementation: Major Progress and Future Challenges." *Health Affairs* 27, no. 6 (July–August 2008): 285–297.
Moon, Marilyn. *Medicare Now and in the Future.* 2nd ed. Washington, DC: Urban Institute Press, 1996.
"Moving Forward on Health Reform." *Health Affairs* 29, no. 6 (June 2010): 1092–1208.
Obama, Barack. "United States Care Reform: Progress to Date and Next Steps." *Journal of the American Medical Association* 316, no. 5 (August 2, 2016): 525–532.
Oberlander, Jonathan. "Implementing the Affordable Care Act: The Promise and Limits of Health Care Reform." *Journal of Health Politics, Policy and Law* 41, no. 4 (August 2016): 803–826.
Oberlander, Jonathan. "Navigating the Shifting Terrain of US Health Care Reform—Medicare for All, Single Payer, and the Public Option." *Milbank Quarterly* 97, no. 4 (December 2019): 939–953.
Oberlander, Jonathan. *The Political Life of Medicare.* Chicago: University of Chicago Press, 2003.
Oberlander, Jonathan. "Throwing Darts, Americans' Elusive Search for Health Cost Control." *Journal of Health Politics, Policy and Law* 36, no. 3 (June 2011): 477–484.
Oberlander, Jonathan, and Joseph White. "Systemwide Cost Control—the Missing Link in Health Care Reform." *New England Journal of Medicine* 361, no. 12 (September 17, 2009): 1131–1133.
Oliver, Thomas R., Philip R. Lee, and Helene L. Lipton. "A Political History of Medicare and Prescription Drug Coverage." *Milbank Quarterly* 82, no. 2 (2004): 283–354.
Olson, Laura Katz. *The Politics of Medicaid.* New York: Columbia University Press, 2010.
Patashnik, Eric M., Alan S. Gerber, and Conor M. Dowling. *Unhealthy Politics: The Battle over Evidence-Based Medicine.* Princeton, NJ: Princeton University Press, 2017.
Patashnik, Eric M., and Jonathan Oberlander. "After Defeat: Conservative Postenactment Opposition to the ACA in Historical-Institutional Perspective." *Journal of Health Politics, Policy and Law* 43, no. 4 (August 2018): 651–682.
Patashnik, Eric M., and Julian Zelizer. "The Struggle to Remake Politics: Liberal Reform and the Limits of Policy Feedback in the Contemporary American State." *Perspectives on Politics* 11, no. 4 (December 2013): 1071–1087.
Pauly, Mark V., and John Goodman. "Tax Credits for Health Insurance and Medical Savings Accounts." *Health Affairs* 14, no. 1 (spring 1995): 125–139.
Peterson, Mark A. "The ACA a Decade In: Resilience, Impact, and Vulnerabilities." *Journal of Health Politics, Policy and Law* 45, no. 4 (August 2020): 595–608.

Peterson, Mark A. "Reversing Course on Obamacare: Why Not Another Medicare Catastrophic?" *Journal of Health Politics, Policy and Law* 43, no. 4 (August 2018): 605–649.

Pressmen, Jeffrey L., and Aaron B. Wildavsky. *Implementation: How Great Expectations in Washington Are Dashed in Oakland*. Berkeley: University of California Press, 1973.

Quadagno, Jill. *One Nation Uninsured: Why the U.S. Has No National Health Insurance*. New York: Oxford University Press, 2005.

Quadagno, Jill. "Right-Wing Conspiracy? Socialist Plot? The Origins of the Patient Protection and Affordable Care Act." *Journal of Health Politics, Policy and Law* 39, no. 1 (February 2014): 35–56.

Reinhardt, Uwe. "The Many Different Prices Paid to Providers and the Flawed Theory of Cost Shifting: Is It Time for a More Rational All-Payer System?" *Health Affairs* 30, no. 11 (November 2011): 2125–2133.

Reinhardt, Uwe. "A Modest Proposal on Payment Reform." *Health Affairs Blog*. July 24, 2009. http://healthaffairs.org/blog/2009/07/24/a-modest-proposal-on-payment-reform.

Rigby, Elizabeth, and Jake Haselswerdt. "Hybrid Federalism, Partisan Politics, and Early Implementation of State Health Insurance Exchanges." *Publius: The Journal of Federalism* 43, no. 3 (summer 2013): 368–391.

Rose, Shanna. *Financing Medicaid: Federalism and the Growth of America's Health Care Safety Net*. Ann Arbor: University of Michigan Press, 2013.

Schlesinger, Mark, and Jacob S. Hacker. "Secret Weapon: The 'New' Medicare as a Route to Health Security." *Journal of Health Politics, Policy and Law* 32, no. 2 (2007): 247–291.

Sinclair, Barbara. *Unorthodox Lawmaking*. 5th ed. Thousand Oaks, CA: Sage Publications, 2017.

Skocpol, Theda. *Boomerang: Health Care Reform and the Turn Against Government*. New York: W. W. Norton, 1996.

Smith, David G., and Judith D. Moore. *Medicaid Politics and Policy*. 2nd ed. New York: Routledge, 2017.

Sparer, Michael. "Federalism and the Patient Protection and Affordable Care Act of 2010: The Founding Fathers Would Not Be Surprised." *Journal of Health Politics, Policy and Law* 36, no. 3 (June 2011): 461–468.

Sparer, Michael S., and Lawrence D. Brown. "Why Did the ACA Co-op Program Fail? Lessons for the Health Reform Debate." *Journal of Health Politics, Policy and Law* 45, no. 5 (October 2020): 801–816.

Starr, Paul. *The Social Transformation of American Medicine: The Rise of a Sovereign Profession and the Making of a Vast Industry*. New York: Basic Books, 1982.

Starr, Paul, and Walter Zelman. "Bridge to Compromise: Competition Under a Budget." *Health Affairs* 12 (Suppl. 1) (1993): 7–23.

Steinmo, Sven, and Jon Watts. "It's the Institutions, Stupid! Why Comprehensive National Health Insurance Always Fails in America." *Journal of Health Politics, Policy and Law* 20, no. 2 (summer 1995): 329–372.

Stevens, Robert, and Rosemary Stevens. *Welfare Medicine in America*. New Brunswick, NJ: Transaction Publishers, 2003.

Sullivan, Kip. "Comment on Deborah Stone's 'Single Payer—Good Metaphor, Bad Politics.'" *Journal of Health Politics, Policy and Law* 35, no. 2 (2010): 277–288.

Summers, Benjamin. "Health Insurance Coverage: What Comes After the ACA?" *Health Affairs* 39, no. 3 (March 2020): 453–461.

Thompson, Frank. *Health Policy and the Bureaucracy: Politics and Implementation.* Cambridge, MA: MIT Press, 1983.
Thompson, Frank J. *Medicaid Politics: Federalism, Policy Durability, and Health Reform.* Washington, DC: Georgetown University Press, 2012.
Thompson, Frank J., Kenneth K. Wong, and Barry G. Rabe. *Trump, the Administrative Presidency, and Federalism.* Washington, DC: Brookings Institution Press, 2020.
Tuohy, Carolyn. *Remaking Policy: Scale, Pace, and Political Strategy in Health Care Reform.* Toronto: University of Toronto Press, 2018.
Watson, Sidney D. "Out of the Black Box and into the Light: Using Section 1115 Medicaid Waivers to Implement the Affordable Care Act's Medicaid Expansion." *Yale Journal of Health Policy, Law, and Ethics* 15 (2015): 213–232.
Weiner, Jonathan P., and Gregory de Lissovoy. "Razing a Tower of Babel: A Taxonomy for Managed Care and Health Insurance Plans." *Journal of Health Politics, Policy and Law* 18, no. 1 (spring 1993): 75–103.
White, Joseph. "Cost Control After the ACA." In "The Health Care Crucible Postreform: Challenges for Public Administration," edited by Frank J. Thompson. Special issue of *Public Administration Review* 73, no. s1 (September/October 2013): S24–S33.
White, Joseph. "Costs Versus Coverage, Then and Now." *Journal of Health Politics, Policy and Law* 45, no. 5 (October 2020): 817–830.
White, Joseph. "Hypotheses and Hope: Policy Analysis and Cost Controls (or Not) in the Affordable Care Act." *Journal of Health Politics, Policy and Law* 43, no. 3 (2018): 455–481.
Wilensky, Gail R. "Employer-Sponsored Insurance: Is It Eroding Under the ACA, and Should We Care." *Milbank Quarterly* 93, no. 3 (September 2015): 467–470.
Wilsford, David. "Path Dependency, or Why History Makes It Difficult but Not Impossible to Reform Health Care Systems in a Big Way." *Journal of Public Policy* 14, no. 3 (July 1994): 251–283.
Wright, Brad, Anna Porter, Phillip M. Singer, and David K. Jones. "The Devolution of Health Reform? A Comparative Analysis of State Innovation Waiver Activity." *Journal of Health Politics, Policy and Law* 44, no. 2 (2019): 315–331.
Zedlewski, Sheila R., Gregory P. Acs, and Colin W. Winterbottom. "Play or Pay Employer Mandates: Potential Effects." *Health Affairs* 11, no. 1 (spring 1992): 60–83.

Index

Aaron, Henry, 248
abortion: ACA provisions, 57–58; BCRA provisions, 119; congressional Republican opposition to implementation, 73; pro-life faction holdouts, 46; Stupak Amendment, 43; Trump administration rules, 148–149
accountable care organizations: 2020 ACA assessment, 270
accountable care organizations (ACOs), 244(table); cost containment ideas, 54–55, 234, 243; delivery system reforms, 270; noncompliant plans, 75
Adler, Jonathan, 153, 203–204, 206
administered price system advocates, 230, 232
administrative rules, 147–149; daily operations of the ACA, 160–161
advocacy coalitions, 25, 229–230, 238–241
Agency for Healthcare Research and Quality, 236
Alaska: BCRA plan, 119; Medicaid expansion, 89, 93; premium costs, 174
Alexander, Lamar, 121
Alito, Samuel, 86
Alliance to Fight the 40, 248–249
all-payer systems, 230–231; feasibility of, 246

alternative plans to ACA, 91; cooperatives, 179–180
Altman, Drew, 222
Alvare, Helen, 207
American Association of Labor Legislation (AALL), 4–5
American Enterprise Institute, 97, 203–204
American Health Care Act (AHCA), 116–118, 122, 124
American Legislative Exchange Council (ALEC), 74–75
American Medical Association (AMA), 4–5, 7; opposition to Medicare, 10; prepayment associations, 7–8; resistance to Medicare, 9
American Rescue Plan Act (ARPA) (2021), 266, 272–273, 277
Anderson, Nathaniel, 98
antidiscrimination provision of the ACA, 156
Antos, Joseph, 97, 246
Arensmeyer, John, 182
Arizona: Medicaid expansion, 184–185; work requirements, 149–150
Arkansas: Medicaid expansion, 80, 89; Medicaid waivers, 144–145; Medicaid work requirement, 213; work requirements, 149; work-requirement waivers, 157

308 *Index*

Artiga, Samantha, 187–188
Azar, Alex, 214

Balanced Budget Act (1997), 24
ballot initiatives: Medicaid expansion, 132, 156–157, 185
Baucus, Max, 43–44, 53, 56, 130
Becerra v. Gresham, 213–214
Becket Fund for Religious Liberty, 208–209
Beebe, Mike, 89
Beland, Daniel, 98, 185–186
belief system: policy-politics intersection, 35
beneficiaries: Medicare, 2–3
Bernstein, Jared, 248–249
Bertko, John, 237
Beshar, Steve, 89
Better Care Reconciliation Act (BCRA), 118–121
Better Way proposal, Ryan's, 116
Bevin, Matt, 89
Biden administration: Build Back Better Act, 277–279; cost-sharing reduction, 212; Covid-19 stimulus bills, 266–267; gender-identity protections, 156; Medicaid expansion incentives, 187; Medicaid work requirement, 213–214; Section 1332 waivers, 158; 300-day assessment, 271–280; Trump's ACA sabotage, 268, 273–274
Blahous, Charles, 246
Blavin, Fredric, 187
Blendon, Robert, 99
block grant program, Medicaid as, 156
Blue Cross association, 7–8; Medicare expansion to universal health coverage, 15
Blue Cross Blue Shield insurance: enrollment share, 176; marketplace competition, 177
Blue Dog Democrats, 43, 63(n30)
Blue Shield plans, 8
Blumenthal, David, 87, 245
Boozary, Andrew, 251
Brady, Kevin, 116
Brewer, Jan, 185
Britain: universal health plan, 15, 236
Brodie, Mollyann, 197
Brookings Institution, 158; Hamilton Project, 37

Brown, Lawrence, 180
Brown, Scott, 45
budget: ACA financing debates in Congress, 51–52; the cost of insurance coverage, 228–229; the effect of risk-corridor payments, 146; impact of the Medicaid expansion, 186–187; Obama's ACA budget, 42
Build Back Better Act (BBBA), 276–280, 290
bundled payments, 235–237
Burr, Richard, 90–91
Burwell, Sylvia, 85
Burwell v. Hobby Lobby Stores, Inc., 86, 89, 207–208
Bush, George H.W.: health policy windows of opportunity, 27(table); health reform priorities, 26; Medicare expansion focusing on controlling costs, 16
Butler, Stuart, 38
Byrnes, John, 10

Cadillac tax: ACA cost containment elements, 54–57, 244(table); ACA implementation timeline, 71(table); ACA revenue and expense summary, 51–54; attempts at a bipartisan bill, 46; congressional pushback against, 246–248; death of, 268; delays, 91; the drive for repeal, 248–250; reemergence of, 248–249
California: ACA backup during Covid-19 pandemic, 266; litigation over Trump's health rules, 146; Section 1332 waivers, 131; SHOP exchanges, 182
California Integrated Healthcare Association, 238
California v. Texas, 153–154, 160, 274–275
Campbell, Andrea, 199
Cannon, Michael, 204
Capretta, James, 87, 97, 246, 250
Carter administration: employer mandate, 58; health policy windows of opportunity, 27(table); health reform priorities, 26; Kennedy-backed health insurance plan, 14–15; Medicare expansion to universal health coverage, 14–16
Casey, Lee, 201

Cassidy, Bill, 120–121
catastrophic coverage: consumer-choice plan, 19
Centene organization, 176
Center on Budget and Policy Priorities, 98; Cadillac tax, 248
Centers for Medicare and Medicaid Services (CMS): accommodation for Covid-19 cases, 155–156; Section 1115 waivers, 129–130; Section 1332 waivers, 143–144; states seeking work-requirement waivers, 157; Texas 1115 waiver invalidation, 273–274; Trump's Medicaid work requirement, 212–214
Chaffee, John, 51
Chase, David, 182
Chevron doctrine, 88, 204
child health, 188
childhood disease, 3
children: AHCA provisions, 117; demographics of ACA support, 197; provisions of the ACA, 46–48; State Children's Health Insurance Program, 23–24; *Texas v. California,* 206–207
Children's Health Insurance Program (CHIP), 76, 131, 278
Christie, Chris, 80
Christina, Tom, 203–204
Clancy, Carolyn, 236
clean-water technologies, 3
Clement, Paul, 212
Clinton, Hillary, 18, 20; Cadillac tax, 248–249; public option, 55; 2016 election, 95–96
Clinton administration, 18–25; employer mandate, 58; exchange model, 58–59; health policy failure, 36–37; health policy windows of opportunity, 27(table); health reform priorities, 26; individual mandate component, 51; Medicaid waivers, 144
coalitions: advocacy coalitions, 229–230; defeat of Clinton's health plan, 22; politics-policy intersection, 34
COBRA, 266
Cochrane, John, 239–240
Cohen, Wilbur, 1
coinsurance, 127
Collins, Susan, 118–120
Colorado: 1332 waivers, 274; universal health insurance system, 93

Committee of 100, 13–15
Committee on the Cost of Medical Care (CCMC), 6
Community Living Assistance Services and Supports (CLASS) Act, 75, 268
comparative effectiveness, 235–236
competition: cooperatives providing, 179–180; managed competition among HMOs, 233–234
computer crashes during implementation, 81–83
conceptual framework for implementation, 99–100
Congress: abortion debate, 57–59; ACA enduring despite hostility from, 200; ACA financing debates, 51–54; ACA legislative process, 38–39; AHCA, 116–118, 122, 124; BCRA, 118–121; Blue Dog Democrats, 43, 63(n30); Build Back Better, 276–278; Cadillac tax repeal, 249; calls for ACA repeal, 90–92, 95–96; Clinton's managed-care plan, 20–21; coalition-building for repeal efforts, 123; cooperative proposals, 179–180; cost containment measures for the ACA, 241–245; cost-sharing reduction cases, 211–212; Covid-19 stimulus bills, 266–267, 272–273; effect of 2010 midterm elections on ACA repeal, 87; eviscerating the individual mandate, 179; exchange rollout, 81–83; failure of Clinton's health plan, 21–24; the future of ACA, 289; gains and losses in the 2018 midterm elections, 146–147; House and Senate versions of the ACA, 45–46, 49–50; House passage of ACA, 42–43; Kerr-Mills bill, 10–11; *King v. Burwell,* 204–205; Kingdon's policy-streams framework, 25–26; Medicare expansion to universal coverage, 15; Medicare passage, 9–11; opposition to the Cadillac tax, 246–248; politics-policy intersection, 34–35; public option, 55–56; reliance on administrative regulations for ACA implementation, 159–160; Republican attempts at ACA repeal, 95; Republican repeal failure, 121–125; risk-corridor payments, 155, 210–211; Senate passage of ACA, 43–45; suspending

tax on insurance companies, 141; Trump's first moves towards repeal, 115–116; 2020 ACA enhancement legislation, 158. *See also* provisions of the ACA

Congressional Budget Office (CBO): ACA assessment in 2014, 84; ACA revenue and expense summary, 51–54; AHCA provisions, 116; attempts at a bipartisan bill, 44; BCRA provisions, 119; employer mandate, 181; marketplace enrollments, 171–173; Republican repeal proposals, 121, 123; tax exemption for ESI, 240

Conrad, Kent, 180

consolidation, institutional, 250–251

constitutional challenges to the ACA: individual mandate, 74; *King v. Burwell,* 203–205; *NFIB v. Sebelius,* 201–203; suits challenging the Trump administration's rules, 145–146; *Texas v. California,* 205–207; 2012 Court victory, 77–78. *See also* legal issues

Consumer Price Index (CPI), 148, 225–227

consumer-choice plan, 229, 238–239; Heritage Foundation, 19

consumer-directed insurance, 239–240

contraceptive mandate: employer responsibility provision, 80; *Kelly v. Azar,* 210; litigation over, 81, 85–86, 89, 92–93, 207–210, 275; *Little Sisters of the Poor v. Pennsylvania,* 209–210; Supreme Court ruling on, 155; Texas injunction, 152–153

Cooper, Jim, 19

Cooper, Zack, 251

cooperatives, 179–180; decline and failure, 92; 2020 ACA provisional assessment, 268

copayments, 127, 228

Cordozo, Benjamin, 200

core ideas of the ACA, 99–100

Corlette, Sabrina, 179–180

Cornhusker Kickback amendment, 44

Coronavirus Aid, Relief, and Economic Security (CARES) Act (2020), 266

Coronavirus Response and Relief Supplemental Appropriations Act (2020), 266

cost containment: ACA design and provisions, 241–245, 244(table); accountable care organizations (ACOs), 234–235; administered price systems, 230, 232; advocacy coalitions, 238–241; all-payer systems, 230–231; bundled payments, 236–237; consumer-directed insurance, 239–240; contributing elements of the ACA, 54–55; effectiveness of ACA in, 245–253; eliminating state regulation of insurance, 240–241; eliminating tax exemptions, 240; health system reorganization savings, 242–243; institutional consolidation, 250–251; Medicare savings, 252; nature of the problem and ideas for the solution, 221–223; organizational integration, 232–234; pay for performance model, 237–238; policy ideas, 229–241; public options, 231–232; public program vouchers, 239; public-private partnerships, 232; savings for the individual, 242; single-payer systems, 230; social insurance reform, 230, 232; value-based payment, 235–236. *See also* Cadillac tax

cost sharing measures: BBBA adjustments to ACA, 277; *California v. Texas* litigation, 274–275

cost shifting, 230–231

costs of health care: ACA cost containment, 55; the cost of insurance coverage, 228–229; early 20th-century CCMC recommendations, 6; Medicare expansion focusing on controlling, 16–18; public concern, 270; system costs and changes over time, 225–227; understanding the system, 223–225

cost-sharing reduction (CSR) payments: AHCA provisions, 117; effect on premium costs, 174–175; high income and, 175; legal challenges, 151–152; litigation over, 133, 211–212; small-business employer-sponsored insurance, 182–183; system costs over time, 227; ten-year ACA assessment, 174; Trump administration threatening,

127–128, 146
cost-sharing reductions, 91, 93
Covering America: Real Remedies for the Uninsured, 25, 37–38
Covid-19 pandemic: ACA assessment, 171; ACA assistance, 265–266; Biden policies assessment, 271–273; effect of the ACA on, 158–159; effect on ACA litigation, 153–155; stimulus bills, 266–267; Trump administration sabotage during, 155–159
critical interests, 99–100
Cruz, Ted, 119
Cutler, David, 243

Dartmouth Atlas Project, 236
decentralized models: Canada's universal coverage model, 19
deductibles, 127
delivery system reform, 245–246; 2020 ACA assessment, 270
denial of coverage: insurance company practices, 50; provisions of the ACA, 46–48
Dent, Charles, 116
developed countries: health care expenditures, 223–225
Dingell, John, 21
disabled individuals: Clinton's managed-care plan, 20–21
District of Columbia: Medicaid expansion, 81
Dorn, Stan, 249–250

econometric models of the ACA, 179
Economic and Social Research Institute, 25, 37
economic growth: early 20th century, 3
economic impacts: Covid-19, 265–266
economic projection of costs, 51–52
Edwards, John, 55
Eisenhower, Dwight D.: Medicare bill, 9
Elder Care bill, 10
elections (1980): Medicare expansion to universal coverage, 15
elections (2006): ACA assessment in 2014, 85; health policy as campaign issue, 36
elections (2008): diverse health reform models, 37; healthcare reform as Obama's legislative priority, 39–40
elections (2010): ACA implementation timeline, 71(table); legal challenges to the ACA, 72
elections (2012): Obama's reelection, 79
elections (2014): setbacks to ACA, 87
elections (2016), 95–96
elections (2018), 141, 146–147
elections (2020): ACA provisional assessment, 267–268; *California v. Texas* hearing, 154–155; partisan divide in Congress, 147
electronic medical records, 234–235
Emanuel, Ezekiel, 54, 245
Emanuel, Rahm, 40
employer mandate: ACA assessment in 2014, 84–85; ACA implementation timeline, 71(table); AHCA provisions, 117; BCRA provisions, 118; congressional policy development, 19, 21, 36, 38, 44; congressional skinny bill, 120; health policy windows of opportunity, 27(table); implementation delay, 79–80; play-or-pay systems, 38, 58; state waivers, 131; ten-year ACA assessment, 180–183
employer-sponsored insurance (ESI): ACA provisions, 58; average annual premiums, 228(table); BBBA adjustments to ACA, 277; consumer-choice plan, 19, 239–240; contraceptive mandate, 210; the cost of insurance coverage, 228–229; Covid-19 impact, 158–159, 266; Covid-19 stimulus bills, 267; effect on marketplace enrollments, 171–172; eliminating tax exemptions, 240; employer mandate, 180–183; health management organizations (HMOs), 232–234; industrial insurance, 7; Kennedy's universal coverage plan, 14–15; mandating coverage, 18; mixed private-public group insurance with shared responsibility, 37–38; negative impact of the Cadillac tax, 247–248; policy approaches from 1992–2008, 37; provisions of the ACA, 46–48; public programs coexisting with, 28; Section 1332 waivers, 130–131; small-business employer-sponsored insurance,

182–183; tax-credit approaches, 38; universal health plan financing, 15–16; wartime programs, 8. *See also* Cadillac tax
employment. *See* work requirement
employment, Covid-19 impact on, 266
Energy and Commerce Committee: ACA passage in the House, 42
enrollment figures, 82–83; effect of the individual mandate repeal, 179; employer-sponsored insurance, 181–183; individual market enrollment, 173(fig.); marketplace figures, 171–173; Medicaid expansion, 186; Trump administration attempts to limit, 148
Enthoven, Alain, 19, 58, 233
Enzi, Mike, 118
episodic expenses, 239–240
essential health benefits element, 76–77, 119
Europe: comparative effectiveness, 236
Ewing, Oscar, 9
Exchange Politics (Jones), 98
exchanges: ACA financing debates in Congress, 53(table); ACA implementation timeline, 71(table); ACA provisions, 58–59; accommodation for Covid-19 cases, 155; congressional challenges to tax credits in 2014, 88–89; Covid-19 pandemic response, 266; essential health benefits requirement, 76; litigation over premium tax credits, 86–87; provisions of the ACA, 46; rollout, 81–83; state vetoes for creation of, 78; states' resistance to ACA implementation, 74–75; 2016 assessment, 96, 99–100; 2016 assessment of the ACA, 98. *See also* marketplace insurance plans

Fairness Group, 157
Families First Coronavirus Response Act (2020), 266–267
family glitch, 95, 277–278, 286, 290
federal poverty level (FPL), 127–128, 150, 158; BBBA enhancements, 278; cost-sharing reduction cases, 211–212; health care expenditures, 227; 2020 ACA provisional assessment, 269

federalism: ACA provisions, 58–59; the theory of policy implementation, 69–72; 2016 assessment, 99–100
Federalist Society white paper, 201
federal-state programs: Medicaid, 3
fee-for-service payment model, 17, 234; ACA effectiveness, 245; value-based payment, 235
Feldstein, Martin, 240
Fiedler, Matthew, 179
filibuster, 115, 119, 289–290
financing health care plans: ACA financial structure design, 51–54; consumer-choice plan, 19; defeat of Clinton's health plan, 22–23; industrial sickness funds, 5; Kennedy/United Auto Workers plan, 15; Kerr-Mills bill, 12; Medicare, 2–3; Republican repeal policy ideas, 122–123; state health insurance programs, 7; 2020 ACA assessment, 271; universal public insurance, 27. *See also* cost containment; tax credits
Fisher, Elliott, 234
FiveThirtyEight, 95
Flexner Report, 4
Florida: ACA vetoes, 78; Medicaid expansion, 81, 90; *NFIB v. Sebelius*, 201–202, 202(table), 203
flu epidemic, 6
Forand, Aime, 9
Ford, Gerald: health policy windows of opportunity, 27(table); Medicare expansion to universal coverage, 14–15
Freedom Caucus, 116–118
Frelinghuysen, Rodney, 117
Fronstin, Paul, 247
Fuller, Helen, 9
Fulton, Brent, 250–251
fundamental shift in health policy, 282–283, 288–291

Gabel, Jon, 247–248
Gangopadhyay, Anuj, 187
Garamendi, John, 19
Garfield, Rachel, 187
Gawande, Atkul, 4
Geisinger Health System, 236–237
gender identity and sexual orientation, 155–156, 276

Georgia: radical ACA change proposals, 151; Section 1332 waivers, 157–158, 212; 1332 waivers, 274
Ginsburg, Paul, 231, 238
Gluck, Abbe, 206
goals of the ACA: of Medicaid and Medicaid expansion, 183–184; ten-year assessment, 170; 2020 provisional assessment, 268–269; 2020 ACA assessment, 271
government-funded approach: Clinton's health reform plan, 18–19
Graham, Lindsey, 120–121, 141
Graham-Cassidy bill, 120–121, 141
grandfathered plans, 156
Great Depression, 6
Grogan, Colleen, 184
gross domestic product (GDP) as percentage of health costs, 223–225
Groundhog Day legal issue, 92–93
Group Health Cooperative, Washington, 233
Gruber, Jonathan, 36, 56, 179, 186, 248
guardrails, 131, 143–144, 151, 158
Guth, Madeline, 187

Hacker, Jacob, 37, 55, 60, 231–232
Hamilton, Alexander, 200
Hamilton Project (Brookings Institution), 37
Harrington, Scott, 179–180
Hatch, Orrin, 90–91; State Children's Health Insurance Program, 23–24
Haviland, Amelia, 240
Hawaii: Section 1332 waivers, 131
Health Affairs, 98, 197, 234
Health and Human Services Department (HHS), 148; Biden broadening ACA access, 272; contraceptive recommendations, 207; Medicaid work requirement, 213–214; political challenges to ACA implementation, 73; regulation rollout, 78–79; *Zubik v. Burwell,* 208–209
health benefits of Medicaid expansion, 187–188
health management organizations (HMO), 232–234; controlling health care costs, 17–18; Kennedy's universal coverage plan, 14–15

health outcomes: 2020 ACA assessment, 269–270
health reform, 17–18
Health Services Cost Review Commission (Maryland), 231
health system reorganization savings, 242–243
healthcare.gov, 82–83, 151, 156–158, 274
HELP committee (Senate), 44, 52, 55
Helvering v. Davis, 200–201
Heritage Foundation, 19, 51, 97; political challenges to ACA implementation, 72–73
Hobby Lobby, 81, 86, 89, 207–208
hospital consolidation, 250–251
hospital coverage, 9; all-payer system, 231; benefits of Medicaid expansion, 187; Covid-19 stimulus bills, 267; Kerr-Mills bill, 12; Medicare passage, 10; SSA elements, 7; system costs over time, 225–227
House v. Burwell, 93
Hudson, Henry, 72
Hutchinson, Ira, 89
Hyde Amendment (1978), 57

immigrants: Trump efforts to discourage, 148–149; 2020 ACA provisional assessment, 269
implementation of the ACA: beginnings of coverage, 83–87; decline in uninsured numbers, 170–171; essential health benefits element, 76–77; exchange rollout, 81–83; first steps, 72–73; legal challenges by congressional Republicans, 73–74; May's conceptual framework, 99–100; Medicaid expansion, 80–81; Obama's last year, 92–96; postponing the employer mandate, 181–182; regulation rollout, 78–79; religious accommodation, 81; Republican Congress challenging ACA, 87–92; rule-making process, 75–76; state resistance, 74–75; Supreme Court victory, 77–78; ten-year assessment, 169–170; the theory of policy implementation, 69–72; timeline, 71(table); 2016 assessment, 96–100

incentives: ACA cost-control ideas, 244(table); value-based payment, 235–236
income bracket: determining ACA support, 197
income level: premium and cost-sharing increases, 175
income replacement: industrial sickness funds, 5; SSA debate, 6–7
incremental approach, 40, 58, 97–98, 234, 243
incremental tinkerers, 229, 232, 238, 246
Independent Payment Advisory Board (IPAB), 54–55, 244(table), 268
Indiana: Medicaid expansion, 89; Medicaid waivers, 144–145; work requirements, 149–150
individual mandate, 50–51; BCRA provisions, 118; legal challenges to, 72–74, 77–78, 81, 145–146; major cases seeking to invalidate the ACA, 202(table); *NFIB v. Sebelius,* 201–203; Republican repeal proposal, 121; short-term policies and, 143; states' resistance to ACA implementation, 74–75; ten-year ACA assessment, 178–179; *Texas v. California* challenging, 205–207; understanding the concentration of expenses, 222–223
individual savings, ACA provision for, 242
industrial sickness funds, 4–5
infant mortality, 3
infectious disease: decline during the 19th and 20th centuries, 5
Institute of Medicine (IOM): contraceptive recommendations, 207; cost containment, 235–237; essential health benefits, 76; women's health services, 85–86
institutional arrangements, 99–100
insurance market regulations: basic ACA elements, 50; importance of market rules, 123
insurance markets: Republican repeal proposals, 121
insurance providers: all-payer systems, 230–231; the cost of insurance coverage, 228–229; cost-sharing reduction cases, 211–212; individual mandate, 178–179; institutional consolidation, 250–251; legal cases, 210–212; market stability, 178; marketplace competition, 177–178; noncompliant policies, 82; participation levels, 176–177; system costs over time, 226–227; ten-year ACA assessment, 175–176
interim final rule, 132–133
Iowa: Section 1332 waivers, 131

Jacobs, Lawrence, 199–200
Johnson, Lyndon B.: health policy windows of opportunity, 27(table); health reform priorities, 26; Kerr-Mills bill, 11; Medicare bill signing, 1–2, 12–13; Medicare passage, 10
Johnson, Ron, 119
Johnston, Emily, 187
Joint Committee on Taxation, 65(n66); ACA financing, 54
Jones, David, 98
Jost, Timothy, 80–81, 98, 144, 182
Justice, Department of (DOJ): Biden administration defense of ACA, 274–276; Texas challenging the contraceptive mandate, 152–153

Kaiser-Permanente HMO, 233–234
Kasich, John, 184–185
Kelly v. Azar, 210
Kennedy, Edward: Clinton's health reform plan, 21; Committee of 100, 13–15; death of, 45; financing the ACA, 53; Senate passage of the ACA, 43; State Children's Health Insurance Program, 23–24
Kennedy, John F.: health policy windows of opportunity, 27(table); health reform priorities, 26; Medicare evolution, 9–10
Kennedy/United Auto Workers plan, 15
Kentucky: Medicaid expansion, 89, 93, 185; Medicaid waivers, 144–145; work requirements, 149
Kerr-Mills bill, 9–12
Kerry, John, 247
King v. Burwell, 86–88, 202(table), 203–205
King-Anderson bill, 10
Kingdon, John, 125, 280–281; policy-streams conceptual framework, 25–26

Klain, Ron, 214
Krugman, Paul, 92, 248

labor unions: Cadillac tax on gold-plated health plans, 56, 248; health insurance benefits of 1940, 8; industrial sickness funds, 4–5; support for Clinton's health plan, 21–22

legal issues: Biden's defense of ACA, 274–276; *Burwell v. Hobby Lobby Stores, Inc.,* 207–208; cases challenging Trump rules, 151–152, 212; challenging Medicaid waivers, 145; contraceptive mandate, 85–86, 89, 92–93, 207–210; cost-sharing reduction, 211–212; effect of the Covid-19 pandemic on, 153–155; first ACA implementation steps, 72; *Helvering v. Davis,* 200–201; individual mandate constitutionality, 145–146; *Kelly v. Azar,* 210; *King v. Burwell,* 86–87, 203–205; legal challenges by congressional Republicans, 73–74; *Little Sisters of the Poor v. Pennsylvania,* 209–210; major cases seeking to invalidate the ACA, 202(table); Medicaid work requirement, 212–214; *NFIB v. Sebelius,* 201–203; overturning Medicaid work requirement waivers, 149–151; risk-corridor cases, 210–211; *Texas v. California,* 205–207, 279–280; Trump's appointment of conservative judges, 214–215; against Trump's sabotage attempts, 133; 2017 ACA assessment, 132–133; *Zubik v. Burwell,* 208–209

legislative process for the ACA, 38–39; House and Senate versions of the ACA, 45–46; path from bill to law, 41–42. *See also* Congress

LePage, Paul, 132
Levin, Yuval, 206
LGBTQ individuals: civil rights protections, 155
Lieberman, Joe, 41(table), 44, 56
life expectancy, 3–4
Lipton-Lubet, Sarah, 209–210
Little Sisters of the Poor v. Pennsylvania, 92–93, 207–210
Long, Sharon, 98

long-run savings, 243
Louisiana: Medicaid expansion, 93
Louisiana Purchase amendment, 44
low-income individuals: basic elements of the ACA, 48–49; Clinton's managed-care plan, 20; Kerr-Mills bill, 11; Senate passage of the ACA, 43–44. *See also* Medicaid and Medicaid expansion

MacArthur, Tom, 117
Magaziner, Ira, 19–20
Maine: Medicaid expansion, 93, 132; work requirements, 149–150
Maine Community Health Options v. United States, 154–155, 211
managed-care approach, 18–20, 23, 232–234
managed-competition approach, 19, 23, 238–240
Mankiw, Gregory, 249
market reform: basic elements of the ACA, 48–51
market-based systems, 38, 46–48, 51, 123, 229, 243, 282, 285
marketplace insurance plans: ACA cost-control ideas, 244(table); ACA implementation timeline, 71(table); BBBA enhancement provisions, 279; BCRA provisions, 118; competition among insurers, 177–178; cooperatives, 179–180; declining competition and rising prices through consolidation, 251; employer mandate and small business health options, 180–183; enrollment figures, 171–173; expansions under ARPA, 272; Georgia's proposed radical changes, 151; individual mandate, 178–179; individual market enrollment, 173(fig.); insurance companies' participation, 175–177; insurance market stability, 178; marketplace enrollment, state and federal, 172(fig.); public opinion of the ACA, 199; risk-corridor cases, 210–211; state concerns over market stability, 132; system costs over time, 227; ten-year assessment of the ACA, 171–183; Trump administration sabotage attempts, 147–149; 2016 assessment, 94

Maryland: ACA constitutionality, 145; all-payer system, 231
Massachusetts Medicaid P4P program, 237–238
Massachusetts plan: ACA politics-policy intersection, 60; employer-sponsored insurance, 181; health reform legislation as national plan model, 36, 38–39; Medicare for All model, 284; Section 1332 waivers, 131; tax credits, 50
matching grant program, 9, 11
maternal health, 6–7, 116, 188, 278
May, Peter, 70, 99–100
McCain, John, 43, 72, 119
McConnell, Mitch, 119–121, 124
McDonough, John, 49, 52, 130
Meadows, Mark, 117
Medicaid and Medicaid expansion, 171; ACA backup during Covid-19 pandemic, 266; ACA implementation, 80–81, 89–90; ACA passage in the House, 42; ACA revenue and expense summary, 51–54, 53(table); AHCA provisions, 116–117; basic elements of the ACA, 48–51; BCRA plan, 118–119; changing the poverty line measure, 148; Clinton's managed-care plan, 20; effect of Covid-19 pandemic on enrollment, 158–159; enrollment assessment, 186; expansions under ARPA, 272; the future of ACA, 290–291; Graham-Cassidy bill, 120; health effect, 187–188; Hyde Amendment on abortion funding, 57; managed-care insurer enrollment, 176; origins of ACA, 2; partisan differences over, 90; per-enrollee costs, 226; provisions of the ACA, 46–48; purpose of the marketplace plans, 171; rules and guidance documents, 79; Section 1115 waivers, 128–130, 144–145; Section 1332 waivers, 130–131; Senate passage of the ACA, 43–44; spending and budget impact, 186–187; by state, 185(table); state actions in 2016, 93; state actions in 2017, 131–132; state administration, 12–13; State Children's Health Insurance Program, 24; Supreme Court decision, 77; ten-year ACA assessment, 183–188; Trump administration sabotage, 156, 273–274; 2016 assessment of the ACA, 96–100; 2020 ballot measures, 156–157; 2020 ACA provisional assessment, 268–269; voucher system replacing, 28, 239; work requirement waivers, 149–151. See also work requirement

Medicaid gap, 277, 279–280
medical loss ratio, 178
Medicare: ACA cost-control ideas, 244(table); administered price system, 230; all-payer system, 231; bill-signing ceremony, 1–2; as campaign issue of 1960, 9–10; Clinton's managed-care plan, 20; conservative criticism, 201; cost containment measures, 245–246, 252; evolution of, 2–3; failure of Clinton's health plan, 23; financing for prescription drug benefits, 52; impacts of consolidation, 251; implementation, 69; long-term achievements, 169–170; 1960s debate over, 9–10; per-enrollee costs, 226; the political future of the ACA, 289–291; political wrangling over, 9; public-option proposal, 231–232; 2020 ACA assessment, 270; universal health plan, 15; universal social insurance and, 13–16; voucher system replacing, 28, 239
Medicare Advantage plans, 3, 284; ACA cost-control ideas, 244(table); ACA implementation timeline, 71(table); ACA revenue and expense summary, 51–54
Medicare Catastrophic Coverage Act (1988), 16, 200
Medicare expansion: BBBA enhancements, 278; Clinton's health reform plan, 21, 24
Medicare Fee for Service: ACA revenue and expense summary, 51–54
Medicare for All scenario for ACA, 37, 282–284, 288–291
Medicare Part A, 2, 12; ACA implementation timeline, 71(table)
Medicare Part B, 12

Medicare PPS, 231
Medicare Prescription Drug Plan (Part D), 24–25, 284; ACA implementation timeline, 71(table)
Medicare Trust Fund, 10
Mettler, Suzanne, 199–200
Michigan: Medicaid expansion, 80; work requirements, 149–150
Miller, Harold, 235
Mills, Wilbur, 10–11; universal health coverage plan, 14
Minnesota: Section 1332 waivers, 131
missed opportunities, 15–16
Missouri: Medicaid expansion, 185
mixed private-public group insurance with shared responsibility, 37–38
Moffitt, Robert, 97
Montana: Medicaid expansion, 93, 185
Morone, James, 37
mortality rates, 5
Murkowski, Lisa, 119–120
Murray, Patty, 121

National Federation of Independent Business (NFIB) v. Sebelius, 77–78, 81, 184, 186, 201–203, 202(table), 205
national health expenditure (NHE), 223–227, 227(fig.), 242
national health insurance: administered price system, 230; Medicare for All, 281, 283. *See also* Medicare
Nelson, Ben, 44–45
New Deal programs, 6–7, 200
New Hampshire: Medicaid expansion, 185; Medicaid waivers, 144–145; Section 1332 waivers, 131, 157–158; work requirements, 149–150
New Jersey: *Little Sisters of the Poor v. Pennsylvania,* 209–210; Medicaid expansion, 80
New Mexico: veto for state exchange legislation, 78
New York: challenging Trump's ACA policies, 145–146
Nixon administration: employer mandate, 58; health policy windows of opportunity, 27(table); health reform priorities, 26; HMO development, 233; universal health coverage plan, 14

No Surprises Act (2020), 267
nondelegation doctrine, 274–275
North Dakota: Medicaid expansion, 185

Obama administration: ACA bill signing, 1–2, 33–34; Cadillac tax endorsement, 247–249; computer crashes during implementation, 82; contraceptive mandate, 207–208; healthcare reform as legislative priority, 39–40; House litigation against, 91; House passage of the ACA, 42–43; leadership role in ACA passage, 124; the legislative path from bill to law, 41(table); political challenges to ACA implementation, 73; postponing the employer mandate, 181–182; reconciliation bill, 46; reelection, 79; regulation rollout, 78–79; Republican Congress challenging ACA, 87–92; self-grade of the ACA, 97; short-term insurance policy abuse, 143; 2016 assessment, 92–96; work requirements, 149
Obamacare Wars (Beland, Rocco, and Waddan), 98
Oberlander, Jonathan, 54–55, 97–98, 125, 246
O'Connor, Reed, 134, 145, 205–206, 210, 274–275
off-exchange plans, 172–173
Office for Civil Rights: sex discrimination litigation, 276
Office of the Actuary, 245
Ohio: Medicaid expansion, 80, 184–185; Section 1332 waivers, 131; work requirements, 149
Oklahoma: Medicaid expansion, 185; Section 1332 waivers, 131
opposition groups: ACA implementation timeline, 71(table); ACA legislative process, 39; Clinton health plan, 21–22; legal challenges to the ACA, 72–73
Oregon: Section 1332 waivers, 131
organizational integration, 232–234
Orszag, Peter, 54
outreach funding reduction, 126–127

Pasteur, Louis, 4
Patashnik, Eric, 125, 184, 200

path dependence, 280–281
patient advocacy groups: challenging Trump's ACA rules, 146
patient choice in health treatment, 239–240
Patient Protection and Affordable Care Enhancement Act (2020), 277
Patient-Centered Medical Home (PCMH), 237
Paul, Rand, 119
Pauly, Mark, 50
pay for performance (P4P) model, 235–238, 245
payment incentives, 235–236
Pelosi, Nancy, 45; Cadillac tax repeal strategy, 249; Stupak Amendment, 43
penalties of the individual mandate, 179
Pence, Mike, 89, 117–118
Pennsylvania: litigation over Trump's health rules, 146; *Little Sisters of the Poor v. Pennsylvania,* 209–210; Medicaid expansion, 80–81, 89; Section 1332 waivers, 157–158
Pepys, Samuel, 265
per capital health spending, 225
Perry, Rick, 78, 81
Phan, Olivia, 187–188
physician costs, 10; changes over time, 225–227; the cost of insurance coverage, 228–229; Medicare coverage, 2
Planned Parenthood, 212
play-or-pay approach, 19–20, 58, 181
policy entrepreneurs, 27; building a majority coalition, 34–35
policy paradigm, 35
policy regimes: policy implementation theory, 70
policy-streams conceptual framework, 25–26, 280–282
political coalitions: the future of ACA, 289–291
political context of ACA, 2
political stream, 280–282
politics-policy nexus, 34–38, 59–61; ACA legislative process, 38–39; ACA repeal efforts, 122–125; addressing cost control, 221–223; cost containment, 226; the effects of the 2006 elections, 36; health reform policy approaches from 1992–2008, 36–38; House passage of ACA, 42–43; public opinion on the ACA, 196–200; Senate passage of ACA, 43–45
Porter, Michael, 238–239
potential cost saving: 2020 ACA assessment, 270
poverty line measure, 148
preexisting conditions, denial of coverage for: ACA assessment, 96–100, 195–196; ACA implementation, 72–73; ACA implementation timeline, 71(table); ACA provisions, 46–47, 58; AHCA provisions, 117; BCRA provisions, 118; insurance carrier competition, 177; repeal policy ideas, 122–123; Trump administration sabotage, 142, 154, 158, 206
preferred provider organizational model, 233–234
premium costs: BBBA enhancements, 278; benchmark silver plans, 174, 174(table); cost containment, 17–18; the cost of insurance coverage, 228–229; cost-sharing reductions, 127–128; effect of the individual mandate, 178–179; employment-based insurance, 228(table); insurance market stability, 178; marketplace competition, 177–178; Medicare funding, 2–3; provisions of the ACA, 46–47; small-business employer-sponsored insurance, 182–183; system costs over time, 225–227; ten-year ACA assessment, 173–175; Trump changes increasing, 143; voucher system, 28. *See also* subsidies
prepayment associations, 7–8, 232–233
prescription drugs: Clinton's managed-care plan, 20; Clinton's reform plan, 24; financing for Medicare, 52; Medicare Part D, 2–3, 24–25, 284; system costs over time, 225–227
Prevention and Public Health Fund, 268
preventive services, 98; ACA implementation, 71(table); *California v. Texas* litigation, 274–275; contraceptive services, 89, 207; cost-sharing, 210, 275; employer-sponsored insurance, 58;

objections to the mandate requiring, 85–86; provisions of the ACA, 46–47; public support for provision, 197
Price, Tom, 116
private equity in physician practices, 250–251
private insurance: accountable care model, 234–235; administered price system, 230; all-payer systems, 230–231; Georgia's 1332 waiver, 274; Medicare plans, 284; per-enrollee costs, 226; wartime programs, 8. *See also* employer-sponsored insurance
privatization efforts, 201
problem stream, 280–281
pro-life factions, 46
PROMETHEUS Payment Model, 236–237
ProvenCare program, 236–237
provider groups: financing the ACA, 52–53; HMO development for cutting costs, 233–234
provider incentive payment innovation, 244(table)
provisions of the ACA, 46–48; abortion, 57–58; basic elements, 48–51; Cadillac tax, 56–57; cost containment, 54–55; employer-sponsored insurance, 58; exchanges and federalist model, 58–59; financing, 51–54; policy design decisions, 48–59; public option, 55–56; 2016 assessment, 96–100. *See also* Cadillac tax; marketplace insurance plans
public hospitals, 5; ACA over the First Ten Years, 196(fig.)
public opinion: ACA failure to achieve broad popularity, 195–200; defeat of Clinton's health plan, 22–23; increase in ACA approval during the Trump term, 215; repeal versus ACA, 124; trust in government, 2; 2016 ACA assessment, 99
public option, 95; BBBA, 277–278; compromise over, 60; congressional passage, 44–46, 59; cooperatives, 92, 175, 180; cost containment, 231–232; future of the ACA, 284, 286–290; House passage of the ACA, 42–43; importance of, 55–56; policy-politics nexus, 281; role in ACA draft versions, 37, 41(table)
public-private partnerships, 232

race and ethnicity: 2020 ACA assessment, 269
Ramos, Christal, 187
Reagan administration: death of the national health program, 15; health reform priorities, 26; Republic opposition to Medicaid expansion, 49; the struggle for universal health coverage, 16
reconciliation process, 41(table), 292(n26); ACA repeal as part of, 115–116; AHCA, 116; attempts at a bipartisan bill, 45–46; Build Back Better Act (BBBA), 276–280, 290; partial repeal attempts in 2016, 95
regulatory guidance: ACA assessment in 2014, 84–85; BCRA provision, 119; eliminating state regulation of insurance, 240–241; importance of market rules, 123; Medicaid work requirement, 213–214; repeal policy ideas, 122–123; 2016 assessment of the ACA, 96–100
Reid, Harry, 41(table), 44–45, 55–56, 247, 249
Reinhardt, Uwe, 231
reinsurance, 76, 79.80, 278; BBBA, 277–278; 1115 waivers, 156; risk-corridor cases, 210; Section 1332 waivers, 157–158; state adjustments to ACA, 131–132, 143, 174; state changes to ACA, 93; 1332 waivers, 151, 157–158, 274. *See also* Section 1332 waivers
religious accommodation and religious exemption, 80–81, 85–86, 89, 92–93, 152–153, 207–210
Religious Freedom Restoration Act (1993), 81, 86, 208–210
repeal and delay strategy, 96, 120
repeal and replace strategy, 115–116; AHCA, 116–118, 124; BCRA, 118–121; lack of leadership in drafting, 124–125; policy ideas, 122–123; Republicans' lack of success, 121–125; Republicans' unwillingness to

pursue, 159–160; 2017 effects of Trump sabotage efforts, 133
repeal attempts, 90–92, 95; Cadillac tax, 248–250; causing an upturn in ACA support, 196–197; effect on the 2018 midterm elections, 146–147; of the employer mandate, 181–182; of the individual mandate, 179; public opinion on the ACA, 196–197, 199; Republican Congress calling for, 90–91; run-up to the 2020 presidential election, 147; Trump advocating for, 95–96; Trump's first moves towards, 115–116
resource-based relative value scale (RBRVS) methodology, 230–231
revenue in the health system, 225–227; impact of the Cadillac tax, 248
Rhode Island: SHOP exchanges, 182
risk adjustment, 105(n66), 222–223
risk corridor provisions, 85, 105(n66), 133, 146, 154–155, 210–211, 275
risk pool, 20, 94, 142–143, 173–175, 177, 180, 183, 222, 226–227, 231–232, 247
Rivkin, David, 201
Robert Woods Johnson Foundation, 236–237
Roberts, John, 77, 200, 204
Rocco, Philip, 98, 185–186
Roe v. Wade, 57
Roosevelt, Franklin D., 6–7, 27(table), 200
Roundtable on Value & Science-Driven Health Care, 235
routine medical expenses, 239–240
Rubio, Marco, 91
Rudowitz, Robin, 187
Ruether, Walter, 13
rule-making process, 75–76, 156; Trump administration changes, 126
rural areas: premium costs, 174–175
Ryan, Paul, 95, 115–116, 124

sabotage by the Trump administration, 160; in addition to repeal and replace strategies, 125–126; appointment of conservative judges, 214–215; CSR threats, 127–128; first-day executive order, 126; interim final rules, 132–133; investigation of short-term plans, 158; legal challenges to, 151–153; litigation over, 145–146; Medicaid work requirement, 144–145, 149–150, 212–214; outreach funding reduction, 126–127; response to Covid-19, 155–159; rule changes, 126; Section 1115 waivers, 128–130; Section 1332 waivers, 130–131, 143–144, 157–158; 2017 assessment, 133; weakening the marketplaces and promoting work requirements, 147–149
Sachs, Rachel, 88
sausage-making metaphor, 38–39
Schoen, Cathy, 247
Scott, Rick, 78, 81, 90
Sebelius, Kathleen, 82, 85
Section 1115 waivers, 128–129, 144–145, 149–151, 157, 214, 273–274. *See also* work requirement
Section 1332 waivers, 93, 128–131, 143–144, 151, 157–158, 212, 274
Senate Finance Committee, 11, 44; ACA's legislative path from bill to law, 41, 41(table); *King v. Burwell,* 88; opposition to healthcare reform, 21; public option, 55; Senate reform bill, 40, 55–56, 58
sexual orientation. *See* gender identity and sexual orientation
shared ideas, 70
Shartzer, Adele, 98
short-run savings, 243
short-term policies, 143, 145–146, 148–149, 158; court of appeals ruling on, 155; legal challenges, 152; ten-year ACA assessment, 175
Silver, Nate, 95
silver loading, 175, 211–212
silver plan costs, 174, 174(table)
single-payer plans, 37; advocacy coalitions, 230; cost containment, 252; feasibility of, 246; public option, 56, 231; Vermont's state plan, 90
skinny bill, 120
Skocpol, Theda, 22
Small Business Health Options Program (SHOP), 181–182
small businesses: ACA assessment in 2014, 84–85; employer mandate and small-business health options, 180–183
social context of ACA, 2

social insurance. *See* Medicare; Social Security
social insurance reformers, 229–230, 232
Social Security Act (1935), 6–7; conservative criticism, 201; *Helvering v. Davis*, 200–201; Medicare passage, 10. *See also* Section 1115 waivers
Social Security System: Medicare bill signing, 1–2
Sommers, Benjamin, 177, 186, 269
South Carolina: work requirements, 149
Sparer, Michael, 180
Spector, Arlen, 41(table)
stability in the insurance market, 121, 178; state concerns over, 132
Starr, Paul, 19–20, 232–233
state actions and programs, 7, 156; ACA assessment in 2014, 85; *California v. Texas* litigation, 274–275; Clinton's managed-care plan, 20; eliminating state regulation of insurance, 240–241; exchange model, 58–59; financial impact of Medicaid expansion, 186–187; health effect of Medicaid expansion, 187–188; incentives for marketplace plans, 171; Kerr-Mills bill, 9–10; marketplace enrollment, state and federal, 172(fig.); Medicaid expansion, 49, 80–81, 89–90, 93, 131–132, 184–185, 272–274; Medicaid expansion by state, 185(table); Medicaid work requirements, 212–214; regulation rollout, 78–79; resistance to ACA implementation, 74–75; Section 1115 waivers, 129–130; Section 1332 waivers, 129, 143–144, 151, 157–158; SHOP exchanges, 182; vetoes for state exchange legislation, 78. *See also* Medicaid and Medicaid expansion
State Children's Health Insurance Program (SCHIP), 23–24
status quo scenario for ACA, 282, 288–291
stimulus bills: Covid-19 bills, 266–267, 272–273
strategies of the ACA. *See* exchanges; marketplace insurance plans; Medicaid and Medicaid expansion; tax credits

Strengthening Health Care and Lowering Prescription Drug Costs Act (2019), 147
Stupak, Bart, 43
Stupak Amendment, 41(table), 43, 57
subsidies, 2; AHCA provisions, 117; BBBA enhancements, 278; BCRA plan, 119; BCRA provisions, 118; Georgia's proposed radical changes, 151; Graham-Cassidy bill, 120; *King v. Burwell*, 202(table), 203–205; major cases seeking to invalidate the ACA, 202(table); repeal policy ideas, 122–123; risk-corridor cases, 210–211
subsidy cliff, 273, 277, 280
Summers, Lawrence, 249
Supreme Court: *California v. Texas* litigation, 153–154, 275; challenges to the individual mandate, 79; constitutional challenges to the ACA, 77–78; contraceptive mandate, 92–93, 208; contraceptive mandate ruling, 155; cost-sharing reduction cases, 211–212; *Helvering v. Davis*, 200; individual mandate, 179; *King v. Burwell*, 86–87, 204–205; *Little Sisters of the Poor v. Pennsylvania*, 209–210; Medicaid work requirement, 213–214; *NFIB v. Sebelius*, 203; religious accommodation litigation, 81, 85–86; Republican Congress challenging ACA, 87–89; risk-corridor cases, 211; Texas injunction against the contraceptive ban, 152–153; *Texas v. California*, 206–207, 279–280; work-requirement waivers, 157; *Zubik v. Burwell*, 208–209
Switzerland: health care expenditures, 223

Taft, Robert, 8–9
Tanenbaum, Sandra, 237–238
Tavenner, Marilyn, 82
tax credits, 28; ACA revenue and expense summary, 51–54; basic elements of the ACA, 48–51; BBBA adjustments to ACA, 277; BCRA provisions, 118; congressional challenges in 2014, 88–89; consumer-choice plan, 19; consumer-directed

insurance, 239–240; eliminating to control costs, 240; employer-sponsored insurance, 38; exchanges rollout, 82; *King v. Burwell,* 86–87, 203–205; payment formula adjustments, 148; Republican repeal efforts, 124; system costs over time, 227; ten-year ACA assessment, 174
taxes: ACA revenue and expense summary, 51–54; AHCA provisions, 117; Congress suspending tax on insurance companies, 141; defeat of Clinton's health plan, 22–23; delays, 91; legal challenges to the individual mandate, 77–78; major cases seeking to invalidate the ACA, 202(table); Republican repeal proposal, 121. *See also* Cadillac tax
Tea Party, 71(table)
technical problems with implementation, 82
Tennessee: Medicaid expansion, 274; work requirement waivers, 150
Texas: anti-ACA litigation, 274–275; challenging the contraceptive mandate, 152–153; Medicaid expansion, 81, 274; veto for state exchange legislation, 78
Texas v. California, 202(table), 205–207, 279–280
Texas v. United States, 152–154
Thompson, Frank, 49
Thorpe, Kenneth, 231
Title 19, 12
Title II: 2020 ACA provisional assessment, 268–269
Truman, Harry: health policy windows of opportunity, 27(table); health reform priorities, 26; Medicare bill signing, 1–2
Trump administration: ACA sabotage, 268, 273–274; allowing short-term renewable policies, 143; *California v. Texas* litigation, 275; cases challenging Trump rules, 212; contraceptive mandate ruling, 155; Covid-19 pandemic response, 265–266; enrollment decline, 173; first moves towards repeal, 115–116; increase in ACA approval, 215; increase in uninsured numbers, 170–171; Medicaid work requirement, 212–214; repeal without replacement, 124; shutting down SHOP exchanges, 182; *Texas v. California,* 206; 2016 election, 95; upturn in ACA support after, 196–197; work-requirement waivers, 157; *Zubik v. Burwell,* 92–93, 207–209. *See also* sabotage by the Trump administration

unemployment: ACA premium costs, 173–175; Covid-19 impact, 266
unified government: the future of ACA, 289–291; Medicare for All, 283
uninsured individuals, 170(fig.); ACA assessment in 2014, 84; ACA assessment in 2016, 98; ACA backup during Covid-19 pandemic, 266; BCRA provision, 118–119; concerns over AHCA provisions, 116; drop in numbers, 91–92; economic effect of declining numbers, 246; Graham-Cassidy bill, 120; insurance companies' risk pool, 226–227; Obama's self-grade of the ACA, 97; ten-year ACA assessment, 170–171; Trump's ACA sabotage, 273–274; 2020 ACA provisional assessment, 269
universal health care: Clinton's approach, 19–21; controlling health care costs, 16–18; Holy Grail of health care coverage, 3; social insurance reformers, 232
universal social insurance, 13–16, 18–19, 21, 283
Upton, Fred, 90–91
Utah: work requirements, 149–150

value-based payments, 235–236, 245, 252–253
Van de Water, Paul, 248, 250
Verma, Seema, 213–214
Vermont: Medicaid expansion, 90; Section 1332 waivers, 131
Vietnam War: moving Medicare to universal coverage, 13
Virginia: work requirements, 149–150
voucher system, 28, 239

Waddan, Alex, 98, 185–186

Wagner, Robert, 7
Wagner-Murray-Dingell bill (1943), 8–9
Walden, Greg, 116
Walker, Scott, 81
Ward, Bruce, 186
Waxman, Henry, 17, 21
Waxman amendments, 17
website development for ACA implementation, 82–83
welfare poor: Title 19, 12
Wessel, David, 248–249
Wheaton College v. Burwell, 86
White, Joseph, 231, 245–246
Will, George, 52
window of legislative opportunity, 25–26, 27(table); ACA legislative process, 39; failure of repeal and replace efforts, 125; politics-policy intersection, 34–35, 59–61; Senator Kennedy's death, 45

Wisconsin: Medicaid expansion, 81; Medicaid waivers, 144–145; work requirements, 149
Wolf, Tom, 89
work requirement (Medicaid): AHCA provisions, 116–117; Arkansas Medicaid expansion, 145; BCRA provisions, 118; legal challenges, 212–214; litigation over, 275–276; Section 1115 waivers, 157; Trump administration's ACA sabotage, 149–150, 273–274
World War I: doctor education and training, 6
World War II, 8–9
Wyden, Ron, 129–130
Wyman, Oliver, 141

Zelizer, Julian, 200
Zubik v. Burwell, 92–93, 207–209

About the Book

In the more than a decade since the enactment of the Affordable Care Act, questions about the law continue to be vigorously debated. What political dynamics led to its passage? Why has it been subject to so many existential threats? What accounts for its survival and growth? How can its performance best be evaluated?

Addressing these questions, James Brasfield eschews partisan rhetoric to provide an in-depth discussion of the politics and policy of the ACA—from its origins to the present—assess the success of the law in achieving its goals, and project possible future scenarios.

James M. Brasfield is professor emeritus at Webster University.